THE JEWS' INDIAN

THE JEWS' INDIAN

Colonialism, Pluralism, and Belonging in America

David S. Koffman

RUTGERS UNIVERSITY PRESS
NEW BRUNSWICK, CAMDEN, AND NEWARK,
NEW JERSEY, AND LONDON

Library of Congress Cataloging-in-Publication Data

Names: Koffman, David S., author.
Title: The Jews' Indian : colonialism, pluralism, and belonging in America / David S. Koffman.
Description: New Brunswick : Rutgers University Press, [2019] | Includes bibliographical references and index.
Identifiers: LCCN 2018007353 | ISBN 9781978800878 (cloth : alk. paper) | ISBN 9781978800861 (pbk. : alk. paper)
Subjects: LCSH: Indians—Relations with Jews. | Jews—United States—History. | Jews—Identity. | United States—Ethnic relations.
Classification: LCC E184.36.I53 K64 2019 | DDC 305.892/4073—dc23
LC record available at https://lccn.loc.gov/2018007353

A British Cataloging-in-Publication record for this book is available from the British Library.

∞ The paper used in this publication meets the requirements of the American National Standard for Information Sciences—Permanence of Paper for Printed Library Materials, ANSI Z39.48-1992.

www.rutgersuniversitypress.org

Manufactured in the United States of America

CONTENTS

THE JEWS' INDIAN

INTRODUCTION

EXILE AND ABORIGINALITY, KINSHIP AND DISTANCE

In 1837, Mordecai Manuel Noah, the statesman, diplomat, newspaper editor, and one of the most influential Jewish leaders of mid-nineteenth-century America, published his *Discourse on the Evidences of the American Indians Being the Descendants of the Lost Tribes of Israel.*[1] The book rearticulated wildly popular claims that North American Indigenous Peoples had either descended from or made contact with ancient biblical Israelites.[2] The suggestion that Jews and Indians shared cultural, historical, religious, biological, or moral traits, as fantastic as they were, had found favor among a stunning variety of advocates, each with a slightly different motivation for marshaling the claim. From the middle of the seventeenth century until the early twentieth, travelers, adventurers, authors of captivity narratives, traders, ethnologists, philologists, geographers, archaeologists, civil servants, Christian missionaries, theologians, and millennial preachers argued their veracity.[3] Lost Tribes enthusiasts found a dazzling array of parallels, analogies, and sources of evidence to draw conclusions about the intermingling of Israelites and Indians.[4]

Noah himself lectured widely on the subject.[5] The idea of ancient Israelite Indians played a key role in his famous attempt to establish "Ararat," a semi-sovereign Jewish homeland he imagined could be established on Grand Island near Buffalo, New York, some thirteen years prior to the publication of his *Discourse.* Noah hoped the world's scattered and exiled Jews, including those lost tribesmen found among American Indians, would be ingathered on Grand Island in national and spiritual reunification. The themes at the heart of Noah's project—namely, the promotion of Jewish sovereignty, productivity, and belonging on American land—all found expression through this imagined sense of ancient kinship with Native Americans.[6]

Rabbi Isaac Leeser, America's preeminent Orthodox thinker, twenty-one years Noah's junior, also thought the lost-tribes theory exciting and credible. As fragments of evidence that seemed to provide "proof" to those who believed in Israelite-Indian connections circulated in the American and American Jewish popular presses in the 1840s, 1850s, and 1860s, Rabbi Leeser discussed the findings' implications for American Jewry in his newspaper *The Occident.* In 1852, he wrote that "whilst America was a forest where the red man roamed over his vast hunting-ground in pursuit of a scanty livelihood by the chase, the Israelite penetrated into the distant wilds, and left his memento in the wigwam of the savage."[7] As the first explorers and the primary bearers of culture in America, ancient Israelites, in Leeser's reading, laid a claim to America's soil that predated the Vikings' or the Pilgrims'. Jews "penetrated" America before any other "civilized race," he argued. The "son of the weary foot," a faux-Indian-sounding synonym for the Wandering Jew, he wrote, might be thought of as the original actors in America's founding drama. Leeser invited his readers to share his

> conviction that "the son of the weary foot," had been there on the plains where the buffalo's hoof makes the soil ring with his measured tread, before civilization had ventured to plant her standard by the banks of the silent Platte or the remote Arkansas, and before the fierce and silent Indian had cause to dread there the advance of the honey-bee, and the sure-following foot of the white intruder. And now behold where you find the men of Jacob! . . . Yes, we tell our readers that here in America we are destined to act our part on the theatre of life.[8]

When an Ohio farmer unearthed four stones hewn with Hebrew engravings in 1868, eight years later, Leeser proudly exclaimed that

> there are some points which are established beyond all question. First . . . that in the most remote antiquity, families came from Asia to the American Continent. If only one stone had been found we might conclude that some solitary vagrant Hebrew had become the supreme leader of a tribe of Indians, and that when he died the Indians honored his grave with a holy inscription in his own national tongue; but the fact must not be overlooked that other Hebrew inscriptions have been found in other places, several miles distant. The sons of Jacob were walking on the soil of Ohio many centuries before the birth of Columbus.[9]

Leeser and Noah had reasons to champion these claims. Connections to Indians affirmed their hope that American Jews would cease to suffer the exilic condition. If Indians and Jews shared a tie of ancient kinship, or if the Jews of antiquity had been the first to colonize America, American Jews could revel in the idea that they belonged to the New World in a cosmically significant way, unprecedented in the Jews' centuries-long entanglement with European civilizations.[10] Jews might be as aboriginal to America as the Aboriginals themselves. In arguing that their ancient ancestors had inexorable connections with pre-Columbian Native people, Jews' presence in America might be conceived of not as an extension of Exile, but as an end to it, a kind of homecoming.

But nineteenth-century American Jews did not always identify with Native Americans, nor did they consistently promote popular claims that linked Jews and Indians together. In fact, identifying Jews with Indians invited rhetorical peril for other contemporaneous American Jewish leaders. Though some found reason for electing affinities with Native Americans, many more distanced themselves from Indians, whom they understood as true outsiders to the emerging nation. Jewish critics of the lost-tribes theory, for instance, like Rabbi Isaac Meyer Wise, America's foremost Reform leader and thinker of the mid-nineteenth century, sought to distance Jews from Indians, preferring to conceive of Jews simply as fellow European white settlers, sharing the bond of European ancestry.[11] For many Jews, being identified with Indians brought dissonance by suggesting that Jews, "like Indians," were a primitive people, a survival from premodern times. Such a view implied that Jews, "like Indians," required civilizing, modernizing, or Christian enlightening. Worse for American Jews, it hinted that they, "like Indians," might be destined to vanish from history. Associations with Native Americans' reputed barbarism, crudeness, illiteracy, and violence did not serve Jewish desires for mobility and integration particularly well. Mid-nineteenth-century American Jews aimed to shed the pernicious stereotypes that dogged their departures from Europe—including the trope of being endlessly wandering seminomads, or somehow primitive. Their cultural arrival in America required promoting other more ennobling moral capacities and character qualities.

American Jewish ambivalence about the implied connections between themselves and Native Americans in lost-tribes claims reveals a fundamental tension that would cut through all the Jewish-Native American interactions over the course of the century that followed, from the mid-1800s to the mid-1900s. This ambivalence was nonetheless passionately argued. Rabbi Leeser and Rabbi Wise never resolved their debate. But it invites a host of broader questions that this book aims to explore. What did encounters between Jews and Native Americans look like? How did American Jews make use of Indians, both real and imagined, as their ambitions in America as both Americans and Jews transformed? How did American Jews understand the place of Native Americans in their own quests for integration and advancement or for helping ensure justice and equality in America? How did Jews, a newly arrived "clannish" group in a country celebrated for its diversity, openness, and meritocracy, see themselves as related to, distinct from, or refracted by those other quintessentially "tribal" Americans? More broadly, how did Jews put Indians to use in their efforts to remain Jewish or recreate Jewishness in America, as American norms for cultural, religious, and racial difference shifted across time and place?

This book is about how Jews related to Native Americans, both in the realm of their cultural imagination and in their face-to-face encounters. (It is not a book about how Native Americans related to Jews, though that is a worthwhile project that ought to be explored in depth to reveal its own set of critical insights.) Their exchanges were numerous and diverse in terms of texture, tone, and impact. At times, these interactions proved harmonious and peaceable, where Jews' and Natives people's economic interests seemed to align, when it made sense for them to overlap their respective corporate identities, their histories of suffering, persecution, exclusion, or cultural difference, and during those times they banded together or enlisted one another to enrich their rhetoric for promoting fuller democracy, richer cultural diversity, or a more equitable and just American society. Yet at other times, discord and strife dominated Jewish-Native encounters. American Jews were capable of being as exploitative of, as ignorant of, and as unsympathetic to Native cultural, social, and political issues as any other settlers. Though the Jews who left Europe in the middle and late nineteenth century fled as foreigners and outsiders, they arrived in America naturalized and eligible for immediate citizenship, and held most of the promises and rights that came with that citizenship. They enjoyed nearly all the legal, practical, and cultural benefits built on colonization writ large. This put Jews in a distinctly privileged position in relation to Native Americans, against whom the tide of settlement and a broad range of deleterious federal, state, and local policy had been aimed from the very start of the European-Indigenous encounter.

Examining Jewish encounters with Native peoples offers some unique perspectives on the racial experience in America. The meanings and messages of their interactions allow us to see more than just how two groups of American outsiders managed their differences in similar or different ways, or the diverse ways that state and society constructed differences for divergent ends (though they do this work too). An interethnic approach reveals the ways that minority identity has been constructed in a triangular manner: Jews kept Native peoples in mind as they negotiated their position vis-à-vis mainstream, white, Christian society throughout the late nineteenth and early twentieth centuries. They strategically utilized both the idea of "the Indian," an imaginary construct, as well as actual Native people in order to work through particularly modern, western, masculine, and Jewish anxieties. For Jews saw themselves as different from fellow whites but not wholly other. They understood Indigenous People, in contradistinction, as both different and other, a status that rendered them precarious outsiders.

The starting point for this study is the basic fact that American Jews told stories about American Indians. They told horror stories and stories about honor and glory, filled with longing and fantasy. They told stories about violence, redemption, belonging, exile, and progress. Of course, when Jews told tales about Native Americans, be they actual Native peoples whom they encountered or merely ones they imagined, they told tales about themselves. The messages and morals encoded in these narratives competed, overlapped, and contradicted one another. Yet they stood beside each other and, taken as a whole, show remarkable durability and consistency over time. Jews continually told stories in which they stood in a middle position, between fellow non-Jewish whites, from whom they felt distinct, and the Indians they kept in mind, those who were both different and other. As the American racial context haltingly and incompletely shifted from empire in the late nineteenth century to pluralism by the middle of the twentieth century, Jews negotiated places of belonging for themselves with reference to American Indians. Late nineteenth- and early to mid-twentieth-century American Jews engaged in a kind of ventriloquism, speaking through various puppet images of "the Indian" in order to work though puzzles and questions about how to live as Americans and who to be as American Jews. Jews' curiosity about Native Americans fueled a fanciful Jewish imagination that sometimes reproduced general white American and European stereotypes and racist misrepresentations of Native lives and at other times produced particularly Jewish iterations of these representations. Jewish stories reflected the general European and American Indian-making mythologies, wherein white Christians vacillated between their visions of America's Aboriginals as their savage foe in the early nineteenth century to noble, authentic first Americans by the early twentieth.[12] Mid-nineteenth-century Jewish stories about Indians cast them as enemies, impediments to or vehicles for their settlement and commercial aspirations.

By the middle of the twentieth century, Jews viewed Native Americans as a fellow American cultural and religious group, who, unlike themselves, were in desperate need of social, political, and economic uplift. Mid-nineteenth-century Jewish immigrants had focused their preoccupations on their own integration into American national identity as capitalism integrated the frontier, helping turn Indians into outsiders. When ideas of cultural pluralism framed the terms of ethnic identity perceptions in the mid-twentieth century, Jews would come to use Indian alterity to articulate the importance of cultural difference to America's social health, necessitating that both Jews and Indians should be considered insiders.

Jewish memoirists, journalists, and amateur historians constructed flexible images of Native Americans as a way of sorting out and making sense of tensions they found themselves struggling to resolve in America. When American Jewish immigrants, particularly along the expanding frontier, wanted to highlight their own accomplishments and promote their own utility in the settlement project to other white Americans whom they feared might exclude them from the rich resources of the West, they conceived of Indians as impediments to their immigrant aspirations, though they just as frequently recruited Native Americans and Native themes to achieve these ends. These perceptions of Indians as both barriers to and vehicles for Jewish mobility and white civility, in turn, shaped their interactions with actual Indigenous Persons. When Jews cast Indians as foils to build credibility as "pioneers," they marked their settler status, their "settledness" in America, as it were, their deservedness of privilege in the colonial process, and their whiteness. When American Jews felt preoccupied with their own aspirations to become a new kind of Jew, one who could grow out of the American context, they cast Indians as enviable (if ultimately doomed) embodiments of bravery, authenticity, and natural living and themselves as robust and natural, rooted and landed. They distanced themselves from the cultural associations they had suffered in Europe as urban, materialistic, alienated by nature, and hyperrational by Europeans debating the relative wisdom of extending full citizenship rights to Jews. The American Jews who identified with "downtrodden" Native Americans critiqued America's racism, its imperialism, and its incompleteness as a just society and tried to speak on behalf of Native American rights and plights. By the mid-twentieth century, Jews would be challenging Americans to see Native Americans in the context of ethnic difference and ethical responsibly that had been born out of a conquest thought to be completed. Making sense of these transformations and the plasticity of rhetorical and practical "uses" Jews made of Native America is the work of this book.

Its first half examines Jewish attitudes toward and behaviors vis-à-vis Native Americans during the periods of Native American history dominated by the Indian Wars (from 1828), removal policies, and allotment and assimilation policies (from 1877), wherein American authorities aimed at assimilating Native Americans by turning them into farmers or individual land owners. Late nineteenth-century Native American history was fundamentally shaped by the Dawes Severalty Act of 1887, which rationed plots of land to individual Indians, dividing communal land bases. The state maintained a number of restrictions on Indians' abilities to sell their allotted lands for twenty-five years. Indian landowners were given a limited time to learn business and farming methods. If they could transform themselves into yeoman farmers—a more or less extinct ideal from the Jacksonian era—they were given clear title to the plot. Implementing the Allotment Act resulted in the loss of more than eighty-six million acres of Native American land and created a class of one hundred thousand landless Indians.[13]

The second half of this book turns to a different group of American Jews and their engagements with Native Americans in a very different pair of Native American historical periods. Chapters 4, 5, and 6 are set during the Indian New Deal era, from the issuing of a landmark public policy study, "The Problem of Indian Administration," also known as the "Meriam Report," in 1928 through the Indian Reorganization Act (IRA) of 1934 and the subsequent period known as Termination, from the late 1940s through the 1960s. Jewish philanthropists, lawyers, journalists, civil servants, intellectuals, and rabbis from across the country played a role in defining progressive liberal ideals in their attitudes toward and dealings with other American minorities and devoted considerable effort to promote general minority rights.[14] Jewish public justice activists fought for economic improvement, political inclusion, the full range of citizenship rights, and the promotion of tolerance and pluralism for disenfranchised minorities in general. Their work for, with, and on behalf of African Americans is well known. Almost unknown is that Jewish advocates also rallied with, and on behalf of, Native Americans and eagerly promoted the acquisition of rights and protections for Native peoples as well as improved cultural understanding between whites and Indians.

The Jewish journalists, lawyers, philanthropists, anthropologists, and civic advocates who worked and argued on behalf of Native Americans and on Indian issues also—concurrently—advocated for Jewish rights. These Jews of universities, law firms, and Capitol Hill were urban, professional, well-educated elites. Like the Jews of the frontier, they too found ways of expressing and responding to Jewish anxieties about balancing ethnic identity retention and full participation in American civic life. Antiracism Jewish intellectuals and advocates serviced Jewish and Native American communities, as they hoped to change the way Americans generally thought about minority groups. But the Jewishness of these elites was hardly the same as the merchant and largely rural- and working-class new immigrant Jews of the American West during the allotment and assimilation eras. In fact, the Jews discussed in this book shared no essential and unchanging singular Jewish identity. This book, instead, assumes that Jewishness is a dynamic, situational, and contextual notion. However the actors themselves may have understood or defined their own Jewish identities—by religion, ethnicity, or race, for example—Jewishness itself formed an essential element to shape their perspectives, motivations, and outcomes. Jews are subjects in this book, irrespective of how or how much an individual Jew moved in or out of explicitly Jewish spheres.[15]

Examining Jewish encounters with Native Americans also reveals some unique perspectives on modern Jewish history more broadly. Consideration of these interchanges demands that Jewish immigration history be recast in the context into which all American ethnic immigration properly fits but within which it is rarely cast—namely, settler colonial expansion. This reframing contests the celebratory narrative that is generally inherited as received Jewish memory and cuts against the grain of much of modern Jewish history. Though Jews fled central and eastern Europe, Russia, and even the Ottoman Empire as relatively powerless victims of what could be called internal colonialism on the Continent, they arrived in America as relatively powerful agents of empire. The Jewish experience of mass migration and dislocation across continents that so fundamentally shaped the Jewish experience of modernity was, ipso facto, an experience of forging a frontier or of enjoying the benefits of a frontier already colonized. The writers of Jewish history have rarely acknowledged the complexities and ambiguities of this transformation. But the historical record is clear: Jews conceived of their own movement from Europe to America, a stunning, enormous demographic transformation with myriad social, cultural, and political implications, not as yet another displacement in their long history, but as a new beginning. Historians of Jews in the American West have reproduced this view of the Jewish immigrant experience, emphasizing individual achievement. Jews in America generally, and in the American West specifically, saw and eventually wrote their own history there as one characterized most essentially by success. New immigrant Jews in America seemed eager to leave their conceptions of themselves as victims of Europe's mistreatment back in Europe and instead focused on their roles in the making of new homes and a new nation. The interethnic encounters in which Jews played a part need to be seen within the context of the great migrations and dislocations of the long nineteenth century, for historians of western Jewish America tended to ignore the ways that Jews wrapped themselves up in structures of domination and on the side of the beneficiaries.

Anti-Jewish sentiment may not have played a significant role in the shaping of the Jewish experience of western American colonization, but that does not mean that racism itself played no part in the Jews' participation in the colonial enterprise. Encounters occurred not just in real space but also between real people; interethnic encounters have always been a ripe zone of racial construction. This study begins the work of bridging the literatures on white-Indian relations and Black-Jewish relations.[16] One key issue underlying both discussions, and indeed any analysis of Jewish-other engagements in America during the nineteenth or twentieth century, concerns race and racism. To what extent did American Jews suffer as the victims of racism, and to what extent did they reproduce or perpetrate racism against other marginalized groups in America? Laudatory and celebratory tones dominate the writing of western American Jewish history; it has been seen as a success story because racism and anti-Semitism tended not to inhibit Jews' abilities to achieve socioeconomic mobility and social inclusion.

The Jewish-Native American encounter also complicates American western history and the history of white-Indian relations by rereading it through a Jewish lens. The history of the western and mountain states in the United States, including the revisionist body of historical studies known as the "New Western History," for all its vitality and insight, tends to ignore the immigrant dimension of white settlement and almost completely elides its Jews. Jews' articulations about, and interactions with, Natives differed from those of other whites in distinct ways. Jewish immigrants' attitudes and desires for land differed from German, Irish, Italian, and Scandinavian immigrants or already American westward migrants, whose senses of belonging to a nation or people included intimate ties to land. Neither did Jewish men sexualize Native American women in their writings, as other white men did. Jews did not missionize to Indians as their Christian settler counterparts did. Nor, during the mid-twentieth century, did advocacy for Native rights by other whites have a self-serving ethnic agenda, as did Jewish work. The intersection of ethnicity, religion, economics, and politics, in other words, matters in the history of white-Indian relations.

The study of American conquest provides some direction for an examination of interactions between Jews and Native Americans. Unlike the vision of the frontier West that the founding father of American western history, Frederick Jackson Turner, offered more than a century ago—characterized as a procession of inevitable victories of whites over Indians for land and a triumph of democratic ideals that melted immigrants into a new and model American citizen stripped of ethnic particularity—New Western history has emphasized contention and friction among the populations that intersected in the West.[17] Scholars have presented a thorough and sober portrait of the West and the process of frontier incorporation as one that involved complex and contingent interactions between contesting classes, genders, and ethnicities. Following Jews as they migrated to the places they encountered Native Americans leads to a fluid geography of "the West." Geographic place plays a less significant role in helping make sense of Jewish-Native encounters than does the process that brought Jews in proximity to Natives in the first place—namely, the capitalist transformation of the American West.[18] While New Western historians have abandoned overly rigid distinctions between the West *as a place* and the frontier *as a process*, they tend to focus on the West as its own distinct region with a continuous history. Placing Jews at the center of a history of interethnic encounter demands a greater emphasis on process as a useful conceptual framework over place.

Indeed, a general consensus among historians of the Jews in the American West holds that the development of robust social life and communal institutions rose steadily there, mostly unmarred by racism or exploitation. American Jewish historian Gerald Sorin, for example, wrote that in "San Francisco and the West generally, with its Indian, Mexican, and Oriental populations, the drive to maintain white supremacy also helped dilute anti-Semitism," linking racism against Jews with racism directed at other others.[19] Jews who arrived early in towns became prominent civic and business leaders: mayors, judges, newspapermen, and the merchants who helped build their cities. Their Jewishness did not act as a barrier to their social, civic, or commercial entry into the power structure. Jeanne Abrams, Irving Howe and Kenneth Libo, Ava Kahn, Moses Richlin, and Harriet and Fred Rochlin, among innumerable amateur and professional historians writing about Jews in western states, towns, and provinces, have reinforced this orthodoxy.[20]

This consensus need not be disputed per se. The frame of reference for American western Jewish history, however, might be expanded to include the stories that Jews told about their place vis-à-vis other ethnic minorities in the West. The Jewish encounter with Native Americans has been fundamentally shaped by the much broader story of mass intercontinental human migration and conquest and the profound transformative effect it had on millions of individuals spread over a massive geographic region. A history that takes the Jewish experience of Native Americans seriously demands a reevaluation of the metanarrative of American Jewish history so that it intersects—or clashes, as the case may be—with the Indigenous narrative. The Jewish story, as conventionally told, celebrates immigrant achievement, adaptation, and success, paying no heed to the Native American experience. Given that the Native American story, on the other hand, views European immigration as a force of displacement and dispossession, a historical perspective that includes both must consider the colonial encounter as the framework for understanding the Jewish experience too. The Jewish story in America need not be "written over" the Indigenous one.[21] The two must be told, somehow, together.

Dialects of kinship and differentiation, fascination and repulsion marked the history of Jewish interactions with Native Americans. American Jews oscillated between identity and difference, using the middle ground as an arena for negotiating their own sense of place and belonging as both Jews and Americans. They imagined themselves in an ambiguous space between "red" and "white," a position that the cultural historian of modern Jewry, Sander Gilman, has theorized was common for Jews to occupy among nineteenth- and twentieth-century international frontiers. These liminal positions, according to Gilman, provided room for modern Jews to understand and define themselves in the light of their experience of the other.[22] Jews contested and accommodated popular constructions of both "the Jew" and "the Indian." Jewish interactions with Native American difference provided room for Jews to fumble, to play, and to negotiate the boundaries of their own shifting identities.[23]

Two critical questions about the ways Jews engaged American Indians and gave meaning to these encounters must be addressed from the outset. First, did anything particularly Jewish distinguish Jews' interactions with Native Americans from those of other whites? And second, did Jewish engagements with Native Americans differ from their engagements with other American minorities? Jewish engagements with Indians looked both similar to and different from the constructions of Indians by other whites. Scholars Angela Aleiss, Steven Conn, Leah Dilworth, William Lyon, and Eliza McFeely, among others, have explored the changes, meanings, and natures of whites' cultural entanglements with the Indians they kept in mind.[24] In his classic study *The White Man's Indian*, Richard Berkhofer Jr. established that images of Indians revealed more about the whites who made them than the Native Americans they supposedly represented.[25] He traced the developments and shifts in the images of Indians through science and culture, from homogenized noble savage in the theological orbit of the sixteenth century through the bloodthirsty primitive derived out of cultural conflict of the eighteenth century. "Whether evaluated as noble or ignoble, whether seen as exotic or downgraded," he wrote, "the Indian as an image was always alien to the White."[26] Whites depicted Native Americans as counterparts to their own values, as metaphors in their own struggle between savagery and civilization. The images they created tended to justify policies and actions taken for their own advantage. By the early twentieth century, social anxieties over mass migration from southern and eastern Europe shaped idealizations of the Indian as "first Americans," as cultural scholar Alan Trachtenberg has observed.[27] The influx of millions of foreigners, speaking different languages and retaining elements of their ethnic, national, and religious identities, seemed to pose a threat to white American hegemony, already daunted by fears about industrialization, urbanization, and the many changes afoot in early twentieth-century America. With Indians largely "pacified," no longer troubling white settlers with violent reprisal, and with social programs aimed at assimilating their already-small numbers into white American society, whites reconfigured Indians as primary, peaceful, and sage models for an America rushing toward a potentially dangerous future. Early twentieth-century whites imagined and used Indians, Indian lore, and their attempts at "going Indian" in order to make America itself feel more of their own, as scholar of Native American literature and ethnic studies Shari Huhndorf, among others, has argued.[28] "Going native," she claimed, offered a means for whites to express their own ambivalence about the subjugation of Indigenous Peoples, a way of founding a national mythology that placed white Americans as the natural heirs to the continent and a strategy for concealing those same claims to racial dominance.

This study follows in the footsteps of white-Indian relations scholarship, but adds specificity, for few scholarly works have been published that have dealt specifically with Irish, Chinese, or any other particular ethnic group's interactions with Native Americans.[29] Indeed, scholars have tended to assume that the "whites" who constructed whiteness in relation to the Indian other they imagined formed one more or less homogeneous group. Just as homogenizing Indians in order to construct "them" as a foil for whiteness necessarily obfuscated the important differences between different Native peoples, so too homogenizing whites obscures the complexity of racial constructions. White European Christian culture most certainly conditioned Jewish engagement with Indians. Whites both identified with and distanced themselves from Indians. While Jewish uplift efforts on behalf of Native people certainly drew these two minorities together as allies, this expenditure of Jewish energy, financial resources, and intellectual capital on social justice issues for Native peoples also consolidated Jews' distinctiveness from Native people. Ethnicity and religious difference, in other words, also mattered in the imagining of Indians.

Several critical absences mark Jewish engagements with American Indians distinct from those of white Christians, as noted. These differences, though defined and visible by what they are not more than what they are, prove critical to understanding the uniquely Jewish dimensions of Jewish-Native relations. Of course, Jews *were* like other whites in so many ways. This fact is not to be glossed over too quickly. It mattered that Jews considered themselves white vis-à-vis the Native other and that other whites took Jewish whiteness for granted.

But the differences are fascinating and revealing. Jewish men tended not to sexualize American Indian women, as did many other white men in the history of white-Indian relations.[30] The myth and trope of Pocahontas provided an enduring vehicle for whites' sexualization of Native American women and reigns as one of the dominant subthemes of white men's narrative of colonizing America.[31] This motif in the American cultural imagination involved a beautiful Indian "princess" defending her white male lover from the violent disdain her chief father feels toward the white man. Her defense of the colonizer-lover secured the white man's place in the New World. The trope cast the white male's sexual ownership over "his" Indian as a parallel or surrogate for his ownership of her land. The Indian woman, her body figured as the land itself, welcomed the white man to come onto it / into her. Hegemonic white society did not, for the most part, pass legislation or try to police or prohibit sexual relations between whites and Indians in the way that "miscegenation" between whites and Blacks became enshrined in mental and legal terms because, as historian Patrick Wolfe has argued, whites wanted Indians' land, whereas whites wanted another critical asset from Blacks—namely, their labor.[32] In order to maintain and reproduce a recognizable labor pool, whites forbade Blacks and whites from mating. Mixing white men and Indian women, by contrast, offered strategic advantages to American expansion, for if the boundary could not be marked clearly between white and Indian, neither could ownership of the land. It is particularly notable then that Jews did not reproduce this Pocahontas story in their cultural imaginary.[33] The trope of Pocahontas made almost no appearance in the Jewish western archive, either named or as an unnamed character in a story in which an Indian maiden saved a Jewish man from her tribesmen's wrath or misunderstanding. Furthermore, little evidence exists in the historical record that Jews deployed sexual violence against Indians as part of the process of conquest. Nor did Jews' discussions of western lands utilize sexual metaphors (Rabbi Isaac Leeser's metaphors, quoted above, excepted). As a community, American Jews promoted endogamy in order to preserve corporate, ethnic solidarity. Celebrating sex with the Indians ran against the grain of the larger Jewish community maintenance project in America, which provided greater marital and sexual latitude than had Europe.

The second key difference between Jews and other whites' engagements with Native Americans lies with religion. Proselytizing did not structure Jewish-Indian encounters. The lack of a conversionary thrust marks Jewish engagements with Native Americans distinct from white Christian engagements. Missionizing and converting "heathens" played no part in the Jewish engagement with Indians. Jews spent no communal or personal resources—financial, mental, or otherwise—aimed at making Native Americans more like them in terms of their religious convictions. This, of course, differs markedly from the white, Christian encounter with Native Americans, from the Spanish to the Dutch, French, and English whites, from the fifteenth through twentieth centuries.[34] The U.S. government moved the administration of its reservation Indian affairs directly into the hands of Christian denominations in the 1860s and 1870s. Indian agencies were assigned to Methodists, Orthodox Friends, Presbyterians, Episcopalians, Catholics, Hicksite Friends, Baptists, Reform Dutch Congregationalists, Unitarians, the American Board of Commissioners for Foreign Missions, and Lutherans. The federal government specifically excluded Judaism; it was neither proselytizing nor Christian.[35]

Still, Jews did take part in European and American whites' effort to "civilize" Natives. In particular, Jews acted and proudly described their own efforts to "improve" Indian lives by teaching them to be better capitalists. But unlike American Christians, Jews did not articulate this effort in spiritual, religious, or providential terms. Jews did not proselytize to Native Americans. Rather, they understood their role in Indian uplift in terms they could celebrate—namely, in service of patriotism, modernization, and the progressive march of capitalism, which appeared to benefit them all, the immigrants themselves foremost. Jews, after all, recognized that their own material success in the United States rested on the assurance of American liberalism and its nonrestrictive principle of free enterprise.

A third key difference between Jews' and other whites' engagements with Native Americans centers on the relative difference in their attitudes toward acquiring, living on, and owning large tracts of rural land. The western landscape provided a site of longing and resolution for American Jews, and they most certainly wanted to belong to it, to be *of* it if not from it, to imagine a deep connection to it that implied an end to exile, a rootedness. They wrote about land in poems, novels, diaries, letters, memoirs, newspapers, local histories, and travelogues in English, German, and Yiddish, often eloquently articulating wishes and realities of its power, its newness, its salvific potential. But Jewish immigrants did not heavily invest in acquiring large holdings for the purpose of living out future generations of Jewish life on specific plots of land. Though Jews did some farming in America, they tended to look for occupational opportunities in towns and cities. When they did pursue livelihoods in rural places, they tended to gravitate toward work with which they had experience—in commerce, peddling, and linking markets. Centuries of restrictions on land ownership for Jews in Europe, and their relative lack of experience farming, influenced Jews' general avoidance of farming and homesteading. This historical occupational legacy reduced the relative frequency with which Jews engaged in direct violent encounters with Native Americans over land as compared with other whites generally.

Did Jewish engagements with Native Americans differ from the ways in which Jews interacted with other ethnic minority groups in America? It could have hardly been otherwise. Jews and Native Americans competed for space, but only in a broad sense. Jews did not, generally, vie with Native people for local living arrangements in specific towns, cities, or neighborhoods. They did not compete with one another for jobs. Most of America's Jews, who overwhelmingly lived in cities, never met a Native person in their entire lives. Only the Jews who moved out to the rural periphery (and those intentionally engaged in scholarly or civic advocacy efforts) ever had the chance for social interaction with Native people.

Jews and Native Americans did not form an alliance that in any way resembled the Jewish-Black alliance leading to and through the civil rights era. While both Jews and African Americans largely hoped and imagined that their respective forms of corporate difference from the white Christian majority would play out—and potentially resolve within—a framework of cultural pluralism and minority rights, Native Americans often resisted the language of cultural pluralism and minority rights, advocating instead for sovereignty, freedom from efforts to integrate their communities into the mainstream, and cultural and political independence. The Jews who took interest in Native American affairs did so with the same assumption that Indigenous People ought to be conceived of and worked with, and have policy shaped, based on the assumption that they were like other minorities in American life, however their particularism be configured. But this was not, for the most part, how Native Americans themselves ever conceived of their difference. They were not a minority within a diverse nation but a distinct nation in a nation-to-nation relation with the United States.

The study of Black-Jewish encounters offers a particularly rich opportunity for comparison, although many important differences productively interfere with any effort to think about the comparison in straightforward terms. White Americans certainly perceived Jews as more like themselves than either African Americans or Native Americans.[36] Seen in a comparative light, American Jews understood themselves, were understood by others, and made practical advantages out of their whiteness.[37] At certain times and to a limited extent, Jews "identified down" with Native Americans, as they did with African Americans.[38] But the stakes of Jewish identifications with Native Americans, as opposed to African Americans, differed fundamentally, in that "identifying down" with Indians did not put Jews' own position on the socioeconomic ladder at risk. Jews' explicit aligning themselves with Natives had further limits. Unlike their views of African Americans, many Jews saw Native Americans as aliens rather than fellow citizens. Question marks hung over this basic threshold of inclusivity.

Unlike the scholarship on Jewish-African American identity dialectics, the Jewish-Native American encounter remains entirely understudied. Aside from the amateur historian Mel Marks' 1992 book *Jews Among the Indians: Tales of Adventure and Conflict in the Old West*, and a handful of focused studies on select poems, novels, and plays that Jews wrote featuring Indian characters or the Lost Tribes claim, scholars had all but neglected this pairing until recently.[39] In 2010, a small burst of academic interest surfaced in Jewish-Native encounters when three university presses published works on Jewish-Indian relations and Columbia University hosted the first academic conference on Jews and Native Americans.[40]

This study is organized both chronologically and thematically, with some overlap among themes. The book begins with an examination of the Jews who migrated west between the 1860s and 1910s and attempted to fashion "pioneer" identities for themselves in relation to the Indians they imagined. During this period, Jews expressed little concern about the impacts that white settlement would or could have on Indian life. When they expressed interest in Native Americans, it tended to be as proud colonizers, the recently released "colonized" of Europe. Chapter 1, "Inventing Pioneer Jews in the New Nation's New West," analyzes the ways that Jewish immigrants engaged with the idea of "the Indian" in order to produce a particularly western sense of belonging for themselves among their fellow white settlers. It takes a step back from the grounded details of the interethnic encounter in order to examine what the encounter meant for immigrants and American-born Jews living on the rural margins of American life. Writing both contemporaneously as new immigrants and retrospectively as they remembered the early years of Jewish settlement along the frontier, Jews saw themselves as colonial whites and their own settlements, hardships, and accomplishments as heroic contributions to the winning of the American West. With remarkably little change over time from their earliest arrivals in the trans-Mississippi West to after the end of white-Indian land wars, Jews crafted a uniquely western iteration of American immigrant success narratives. They acted as unabashed agents of colonialism as a way of combating anti-Semitic stereotypes that criticized Jewish men for lacking brawn or not pulling their weight in the nation's military operations. The complaint that Jewish men lacked sufficient masculinity to succeed in American life found particularly sharp focus in a frontier world that prized rugged individualism. Western Jews cast themselves as recapitulations of the original pilgrims, clearing the path for commerce and settlement through their efforts at both engaging Indians in productive capitalism and subduing them through acts of violence. They viewed Indians as both impediments to and vehicles of their participation in the march toward civil progress. As violent contest for lands between whites and Indians in the first half of this period gave way to postconquest decades in which whites could relate to "pacified" Indians in much different ways, frontier Jews identified with both whites and Indians.

Chapter 2, "Land and the Violent Expansion of the Immigrants' Empire," examines how Jews related to and participated in American's thirst for land and how this thirst could, at times, produce violence against Native people. It argues that immigrant Jews absorbed and fueled America's quest for imperial acquisition in the West, helping form part of its potent vision of Manifest Destiny that lead many men to embrace both an aggressive vision of expansionism and an equally martial vision of manhood.[41] America's land, both the actual, material land itself as well as the very idea of land as a symbolic placeholder of belonging, structured much of Jewish thinking about the Jewish-Native encounters in the West; it played a central role in the drama of the Jewish West and Jews' visions about and interactions with Native peoples. Nineteenth-century Jewish desire to feel existentially rooted in the new land fueled much of what Jews worked through in their imaginations of and encounters with Native Americans. Lacking land formed one of the central cruxes of the Jewish experience of European modernity and nationalism. The dissociation between Jews and land, and its unavailability to Jews in Europe, served as a critical counterpoint to the American western Jewish experience. America's western land invited and enticed Jews to reinvent themselves, distanced from European associations of Jewish alienation from the soil. Jews, like other relatively newly arrived whites, associated America's land with Native Americans, but how did Jews fit into this association? How, westward-migrating Jews wondered, might they carve out a sense of belonging to this land? Would they have to breach the Native tie to it? Or could they simply participate in the Indian-land bond, as Native peoples themselves did by imagining themselves as aboriginal to American land? Immigrant aspirations helped expand an immigrants' empire.

Chapter 3, "Jewish Middlemen Merchants, Indian Curios, and the Extensions of American Capitalism," focuses on economic encounter as a vehicle for western Jews' ambitions on the shifting frontier. The dual impulse of Jews to identify with both Indians and whites found particularly strong expression among the Jewish Indian "curio" dealers, a subset of Indian traders who positioned themselves between red and white worlds as half Indian, half ethnographer experts, representing the Indians whose "Indianness" they sold in the form of cultural objects. Commercial interaction framed the vast majority of face-to-face encounters between Jews and Native Americans since Jews went west primarily as small businessmen to pursue wealth. Commerce, however, provided more than a means to commercial ends, for Jews constructed meaning out of their roles as traders and linked this Jewish occupational profile to the nation-building process in the West. Indians provided an intimate foil for Jews keen on having petty trade recognized as beneficial for expansion.

Then the book brings the story of Jewish-Native encounters toward the middle of the twentieth century, beginning with chapter 4, "Nativist Anxieties Twinned: Jewish Rhetorical Uses of Indians in an Era of Anti-Immigration Sentiment." It shifts attention away from the business- and settlement-oriented western Jewish immigrant and first-generation American-born Jews in the rural west whose two primary concerns were social and economic mobility, to a group of much more acculturated, enfranchised Jews of the urban east who devoted considerable efforts to justice for Native Americans. Liberal and progressive Jews, despite not having shared the suffering of Native Americans, sought to undo some of the damage of nineteenth-century colonial white-Indian encounters even as they themselves, perhaps inadvertently, perpetuated colonial structures in law and social science. Chapter 4 also examines how Jewish communal anxieties overlapped with Native communal anxieties during America's nativist era, from the turn of the century, rising through the 1910s and becoming nationally visible in two pieces of legislation in 1924. Anti-immigrant sentiment tended to feed anti-Indian sentiment and vice versa. These twin forms of American exclusionism found expression in a variety of settings and sites. The National Origins Act, passed in May 1924, effectively halted Jewish immigration to the United States. Just one month later, Congress passed the Indian Citizenship Act, generally understood by historians as an effort to erase

Indian difference through assimilation, a symbolic act of inclusion that in fact stripped Indians of legal room to maneuver for political sovereignty. These two acts of legislation aimed to serve parallel ends. One was designed to repel the threat of foreign contamination by immigrants from abroad, while the other hoped to dissolve the alien within by absorption. American Jews and Native Americans fretted over their felt exclusion from the mainstream American body politic; both feared that white America's assimilatory aspiration for them would lead to their cultural obliteration. Chapter 4 thus analyzes the Jewish discussions about American Indians in their response to nativist xenophobia. It argues that Indians provided Jews with a useful and malleable rhetorical tool for confronting tensions around assimilation and disappearance, naturalization, citizenship, and the idea of "adoption" versus naturalization. Jews took advantage of the flexibility of both "the Jew" and "the Indian" in racial hierarchies in the first quarter of the twentieth century as Americans became ever more preoccupied with race thinking and its implications for national policy.

During the decades before "pacification" around the turn of the century when whites and Natives battled for land, some Jews worked as translators and Indian agents and subagents for the state, hoping to bring Natives and settlers together peaceably. Chapters 5 and 6 assess two forms of Jewish advocacy on behalf of Native Americans, which grew subsequently both in quantity and in quality in the early decades of the twentieth century. Chapter 5, "Jewish Advocacy for Native Americans on and off Capitol Hill," analyzes a related cadre of Jewish pro-Native activists. With the passage of Indian New Deal legislation in 1934, a decade after the Indian exclusionary policies of 1924, the possibilities for Indian advancement and enfranchisement took a dramatic turn. Despite the persistence of race thinking, the U.S. government initiated programs for revitalizing Indian cultural differences and attempted to make legal and legislative room for Indian political autonomy. This chapter argues that these developments would not have occurred without the labors and energies of a set of Jewish bureaucrats, lawyers, and philanthropists who worked on behalf of Indian causes both on and off Capitol Hill. Finding power and influence in the federal government for the first time in America under the Roosevelt Administration, a handful of Jews took to advancing a range of pro-Indian issues with zeal. They helped build the organizational infrastructure and intellectual foundations of the Indian civil rights movement that blossomed in Indian hands after World War II, particularly the Association on American Indian Affairs (AAIA) with the financial backing of quasi-Jewish bodies like the Robert Marshall Trust and the American Civil Liberties Union (ACLU). Within the government itself, William Zimmerman, Nathan Margold, and Felix S. Cohen played fundamental roles in drafting, passing, and implementing the 1934 IRA, consolidating federal case law on Indian affairs, and promoting Indian cultural, economic, health, education, and political interests. The Jews who worked for the Department of the Interior, particularly the Bureau of Indian Affairs (BIA), consistently linked Indian uplift with an articulation of minority rights and cultural pluralism within the United States and on international stages that went beyond Indian paternalism. Jewish activism on behalf of minority rights and cultural autonomy, in rhetoric and in policy, was, simply put, "good for the Jews." Jewish enlightened self-interest impacted the course of American Indian life in the middle of the twentieth century.

Chapter 6, "Anthropological Ventriloquism and Dovetailing Intellectual and Political Advancements," argues that Jewish social scientists (anthropologists in particular) took a significant interest in Native American life, in part as a response to certain tensions implicit in the American Jewish situation in the early middle decades of the twentieth century. Coming of age and beginning careers in a period fraught with nativism, a sizable number of Jewish intellectuals and activists followed the German Jewish "father of anthropology" Franz Boas into careers concerned with knowing, understanding, and ultimately improving the lives of Native Americans. These Jewish anthropologists played a critical role in shifting anthropology's basic framework away from its roots in race thinking, social evolutionism, and missionary work. Instead, Boasian anthropologists advanced cultural pluralism and relativism. This chapter argues that the Jewishness of so many of this first generation of professional anthropologists mattered; Jewishness shaped the profession's engagement with its principle object of study, the American Indian, just as it steered the intellectual agenda of American anthropology. It describes anthropology's antiracism agenda and considers how Jews' efforts—presented as the efforts of science itself—to salvage, collect, and preserve disappearing American Indian culture was a form of ventriloquism. Anthropologists like Edward Sapir, Paul Radin, Sol Tax, Leslie Spier, Ruth Leah Bunzel, Edgar Siskin, and many more focused on Native American families, religions, languages, and cultures. These foci dovetailed with the concerns that preoccupied American Jewry in the 1930s through the 1950s. Jewish anthropologists devoted portions of their extraprofessional energies to both Jewish and Native American causes. They promoted Native American education, political sovereignty, linguistic and cultural autonomy, economic advancement, health, and social well-being. They loaned their scholarly authority to the BIA, particularly its Ethnology Board, and the AAIA, intending to produce policy changes at the federal and state levels. These Jews' efforts on behalf of Native Americans ought to be seen through twin lenses: liberal and progressive advocacy for others and the promotion of enfranchisement for Jews. Jewish anthropologists, lawyers, philanthropists, and public activists translated various Indian cultural worlds for white American audiences and aimed to advance Native Americans' social, political, and legal lot in America. In pursuing this work, American Jewish intellectuals helped shift the terms of the discussion about race in America and acted as cultural mediators between Indians and other whites.

The book ends with a short concluding chapter that provides a framework for thinking about late twentieth-century encounters between American Jews and Native Americans. It traces the continuities between the century of encounters covered principally in this book and spells out the important discontinuities as the postwar, post-Holocaust era in which the State of Israel's existence that became fundamental to the American Jews' self-experience takes shape. It touches on the tense discussion about genocide, comparative genocide, the Americanization of genocide, various newfound bases for dialogue between Jewish and Native American groups around issues of sacred language and holy sland, cultural survival, the legacies of historical trauma and recovery, and national self-determination. During the postwar era, American Jews pursued relationships with Native American groups more frequently and more intensely than they had ever done before. Jews and Indians sat down and talked about the environment, music, youth education, parallels and explorations in religious identity and ritual, creation stories, and many other points of newly and not so newly noted overlaps.[42] The conclusion argues that the central preoccupation that Jews brought to their encounters with Native Americans in the late twentieth and early twenty-first century ought to be seen in the context of a global struggle to come to terms with the enormous legacies of colonialism. For American Jews, the struggle has two dimensions. The first concerns American Jews' willingness and ability to come to examine and relate to the Jewish role in the history of American colonialism. The second concerns the contentious debate over the degree to which the modern State of Israel is a colonial, anticolonial, or postcolonial state. What seems certain is that thinking about and interacting with American Indigenous Peoples provides some room for American Jews to think about indigeneity and the nature of Jewish claims for "aboriginality" in Israel/Palestine.

The broadest ambition of this book is its call to rethink American Jewish history, and quite possibly "new world" modern Jewish history even more broadly, as a part of the process of colonialism. The practical, epochal, and hard-to-overemphasize movement of modern Jewry away from Europe, North Africa, and the Middle East to states that barely existed in the eighteenth century is *the story* of modern Jewish life. Migration within the scope, tensions, bounds, and possibilities offered by global colonialism in all its varieties shaped modern Jewish life even more profoundly, I would venture, than emancipation itself. The conclusion highlights the tensions and ambivalences at the heart of discussions about Jews as the victims of colonialism in European modernity, as the perpetrators of colonialism in the new world, and eventually, as seekers of redress for America's colonial sins.

CHAPTER 1

INVENTING PIONEER JEWS IN THE NEW NATION'S NEW WEST

In the summer of 1877, at age eleven, Sam Aaron joined a six-horse stage en route from Cheyenne, Wyoming, to Butte, Montana. He considered himself an intrepid traveler and a rugged, Indian-taming frontiersman despite his prepubescence. "I absolutely knew no fear; nothing was too hard or too dangerous to undertake," he later wrote in his 1913 reminiscences. "I'd go into the wilds and ride for days without seeing a human being. The Apaches were on the warpath, killing and stealing."[1] However antagonistic Aaron perceived white-Apache relations to be, and however boldly he presented himself a hero, he nevertheless gave some thought to the conditions that led to settler-Indian tensions. "In those days," he reflected, "all reservations were controlled by the Indian agencies in Washington, DC. Those agencies caused the restlessness of the Indians. Instead of giving them the allotment, they would hold back some of it and the Indian was always in need and therefore, committed crimes. He felt he was being cheated of what was due to him."[2] But the sympathy and moral favor Aaron found in "the Indian, [who] had a good many principles," had its limits. Remembering one occasion, years later, after five workmen had been killed in a charcoal camp near Fort Haucha, Arizona, Aaron described how two white camp workers "killed one of the redskins, cut his head off and brought it into Charleston [Arizona]. I took the Indian skull, burned off the flesh and hair, sand papered it and made a beautiful skull. I said, 'Jim, I have something I want you to do. Climb that pole and put the Indian skull on it instead [of the flag].'"[3] In "beautifying" a murdered Indian's skull, Aaron suggested that it replace the American flag atop a flagpole, symbolically marking the frontier West as land won by the grit and independence of stateless men.

When Aaron, "a Main street clothing merchant, but a former pioneer of the frontier," reminisced about his life in Arizona, Utah, Montana, Wyoming, and California, he told the tale of his transformation from a frontiersman preoccupied with outlaws, shootouts, drinking, gambling, "wild Indians," and the general mystique of the Wild West to an upstanding citizen-businessman at the center of a western boomtown. Tales like his, he boasted, "keep alive the memories of the early history of the frontier," a history, he fretted, that might be lost. Conjoining adventure, mobility, and opportunity, Aaron cast his family history as one in which his forefathers, stripped of their Jewish pasts and rinsed of whatever linguistic, culinary, cultural, and aesthetic particularities marked them as new immigrants, followed the arc of the mythic settler West, beginning out of nowhere with the call of the wild and ending with the rugged frontiersman transformed into an upstanding main-street merchant. He did not, notably, tell the family story as one in which immigrant outsiders became part of the social fabric of new settlements on those lands America's imperial expansion enterprise captured. Aaron's elision of an immigration narrative altogether, his naturalizing of his family story, evinced a transformation already completed. But Jews had to *become* pioneers. They had to come to see themselves as embodiments of frontier settler identities and shed ideas of themselves as old-world newcomers.[4]

Like so many other Jewish memoirists from the late nineteenth-century West, Aaron glorified frontier life and the victorious outcomes of violent clashes with Native peoples, seeing his role in bringing commerce as paramount in the making of early settlement. Though he and his fellow settlers became domesticated, he conveyed the violence they perpetrated against Natives without discomfort. In telling his story, he helped create the image, the mythology, of the "earliest days" of Jews in frontier life. He wrote himself into this mythology, and he, along with dozens of western Jewish memoirists, newspaper journalists, family, and local history writers who are the subject of this chapter, turned this mythology into history, a celebratory story in which Jewish immigrants became pioneer Americans.

This process transpired in historical context. The mass movement of migrants to the United States from the 1820s to the 1920s impacted everyone and everything in its wake, including both the Jewish immigrants and the Native peoples they encountered. For millions of European immigrants, Jews among them, migration to the American West meant social mobility, relative economic security, and the creation of dozens of new communities with new textures and new timbres. For America's Native populations, most of whom had been removed to ever-shrinking parcels of land in western landscapes that became sites of intense development during those same years, the migration of settlers meant displacement and dislocation, economic turmoil, political bedlam, and radical cultural transformation. Sam Aaron's celebration of the "winning" of the frontier reveals how Jews saw their becoming settled and the role that Indians had in this process.[5]

Jewish men from Alsace, Bavaria, Posen, Prussia, and other German territories began migrating to the American West starting in the 1820s, with Jews migrating from the Russian and Austro-Hungarian empires, Lithuania, Poland, other parts of eastern Europe, the Ottoman Empire, and elsewhere from the 1850s onward through the first decades of the twentieth century. They joined many already landed first-, second-, and even third-generation American Jews migrating west concurrently and thereafter. They left a Europe in which state powers generally prohibited Jews from owning land. Many Jewish emigrants lacked robust diets and faced potentially lethal conscription and unpredictable violent persecution. Many struggled to gain or maintain citizenship rights in their counties of origin. In 1880, some 80 percent of Jewish men and women living in western American towns had been born outside the United States.[6] They had been pushed by limited employment options and pulled by the promises of social mobility, civic inclusion, and religious freedom. The West's bounty—particularly gold, silver, and fur—and the small-scale commercial opportunities generated by those looking to exploit it drew them in chain migrations through family and social contacts.[7] Between the 1840s and the 1880s, the Jewish population in America rose from 15,000 to 250,000, with new immigrants generally settling in cities—first in New York, Philadelphia, Richmond, Baltimore, and New Orleans, then in fast-growing cities like Cincinnati, St. Louis, San Francisco, Pittsburgh, Sioux City, Omaha, Milwaukee, Santa Fe, and Kansas City—and in dozens of smaller towns spread in between. In the West, the Jewish population grew to an estimated 300,000 by 1920.[8] Between 1881 and 1924, some 2.5 million Jews immigrated to America, a ten-fold increase from the six decades prior.

Once in the West, Jewish men occupied a range of vocations, including wagon drivers, freight haulers, salon keepers, lawyers, journalists, physicians, clergymen, railroad and irrigation workers, and soldiers. But the vast majority of them began their careers as peddlers and merchants. From this occupational profile, they built the institutions of Jewish social and communal life as the contested and unripe frontier zones transformed into established and settled towns and communities.[9] Immigrant newcomers headed to the margins to find and open new markets. Jewish businessmen supplied merchandise, packs, and maps to Jewish peddlers and traders who traversed underdeveloped territories. Popular historians of Jewish America Kenneth Libo and Irving Howe described these petty merchants as the "economic spearheads pointing toward a rapidly expanding frontier."[10] They traversed geographic zones with little settlement where they supplied mining camps, army forts, farms, boomtowns, and trade routes with dry goods. The pattern persisted fairly consistently in the states west of the Mississippi River. First came unmarried men who worked itinerantly for a period of time before forming basic Jewish communal institutions like burial societies and prayer quorums. Many men brought brides and wives from their hometowns in Europe or from larger cities in the American east. Once they arrived, Jewish women tended to stabilize the places where Jewish men had settled, helping build Jewish communal structures and organizations and networking dispersed homes into communities.[11] The West offered ample opportunity for speedy social mobility in the nineteenth and early twentieth centuries, more so than elsewhere in the United States.[12]

While Jews brought with them versions of their material, religious, and intellectual cultures, few brought great attachments to the European states in which they previously lived. They formed new and often intense commitments and ideological bonds, however, to the new republic and to the white citizenry that produced and embodied its values. Among whites, frontier society offered a pragmatic class structure into which Jews fit generously, although not without tensions.[13] While historians contest the rhetoric of ethnic and class openness of the West in general, relative to their experience elsewhere, particularly in their lands of origins, Jews experienced weak anti-Semitism.[14] Perceptions of Jews' biological, religious, or even moral differences operated in the West, as they did in the South and East, but Jews suffered relatively minimal victimization there. The very diversity of the West placed Jews in an advantageous position. Whites, Jews included, had others to marginalize and, at times, exploit and persecute—particularly Asians, Blacks, Mexicans, and Indians. Both immigrant and American-born Jews, in other words, enjoyed the privileges of whiteness from their immediate arrival in the American West.[15]

For Native Americans, the last two-thirds of the nineteenth century and the first third of the twentieth proved radically disruptive as a direct result of European and American migration, or conquest. In 1820, nearly every Native tribe west of the Mississippi lived on its ancestral lands, although the government had been engaged in systematic efforts to acquire land legally, semilegally, or illegally from Native Americans through treaty signings. Native American land loss was also wrought by settlers' often violent squatting or cozening, later defended by legislation, the courts, sheriffs' offices, and the military.[16] The federal government's adoption of removal policies, beginning in the 1810s and nationally sanctioned by President Andrew Jackson's Indian Removal Act in 1830, forced thousands of Native Americans from their lands in Arkansas, Georgia, Kansas, Mississippi, and Nebraska and produced a ripple effect of land relocations. These relocations disrupted subsistence patterns as well as cultural traditions and produced shifts in language patterns that adversely affected Native communities.[17] Even before the introduction of the Dawes General Allotment Act in 1887, the federal government implemented policies aimed at assimilating Indians to white ways, separating children from parents and sending them to state-run residential schools, banning a number of religious traditions, and attempting to force certain tribes to subsist through farming.[18] Between 1871 and 1934, either the American government or white settlers enabled by government policing took possession of more than two-thirds of tribally entrusted lands, some ninety million acres.

In memoirs like Sam Aaron's, Indians served as foils for both Jewish and American identity formation. Indians lay at the heart of a key slippage between *immigrant* and *pioneer* in many nineteenth- and early twentieth-century American western Jewish memoirs, and indeed, Indians served key rhetorical functions in much of western American Jewish writing in general.[19] Using *Indians* this way was but one use among many that American Jews put to the "Indians" of their writing (memoirs, history, news stories, cultural products, etc.). Immigrant Jews, like other whites in the emerging American West from the last quarter of the nineteenth century to the first quarter of the twentieth, fashioned themselves as "pioneer Americans" through their interactions with Native Americans, both imagined and real. As this chapter will show, American western Jews used both techniques of opposition (showing themselves to be different from, and even opposed to, Indians) *and* techniques of relation (showing themselves to be essentially or largely the same as Indians). Jewish men cast themselves in the role of frontiersmen, fitting themselves into the well-worn narrative form of American frontier culture when they wrote letters, diaries, and newspaper articles contemporaneously to their settlement and, retrospectively, when they wrote memoirs, family histories, and local histories. Both concurrently and retroactively, Jews mobilized frontier mythology as they envisioned themselves and their roles in the West. The uses to which Jews put Indians continued consistently over time as Jews became settled and Native Americans "pacified." Jews wrote themselves into western narratives and employed the same rhetorical techniques to affect their belonging whether they arrived in the West in the 1850s and remembered it retrospectively in the 1890s or they arrived in the 1880s and remembered it retrospectively in the 1920s. Remarkably little changed in the making of pioneer Jews over three-quarters of a century.

Jewish memoirists, letter writers, family storytellers, journalists, local history writers, and professional history writers of Jewish life in the West played with the tropes and conventions of the popular West. They aimed to craft accurate and evocative narratives of their western experience; they reproduced, perhaps less than fully consciously, the tropes, stereotypes, and conventions of settler heroes, frontier lore, and "othered" Indians on which they were fed. Several features comprised the frontier archetype into which Jewish men molded themselves as they migrated and wrote of their family's and community's "early pioneer days": rugged individualism, brawny masculinity, intimacy with the natural landscape, rigorous physical workmanship, and encounters with Indians. Archetypal American frontiersmen understood the great distance between themselves and the "wildness" that the Indian other supposedly embodied. In the American cultural imaginary, the frontiersman could be expected to tame, pacify, civilize, remove, or kill Indians to prevent their disruption of settlement's way. The frontier white could also be expected to affect Indians' assimilation into civilization by means of conversion to Christianity or through transforming the Indian from a sustenance-oriented primitive to a productive member of capitalist society, be it commercial or agricultural.

While certain aspects of this persona required a dominating and distancing stance toward the Native other, being a true frontiersman also, paradoxically, required a degree of closeness and identification across perceived differences.

The frontiersman *knew something* of Native Americans' ways, seemed comfortable among Native people, and had learned the ways of tribal life and language. He might even be accepted as an "honorary Indian," having lived among tribes for stretches of time and later reemerged into white civilization wiser, more in sync with the earth, with the soil of America itself, and with improved spirituality. The identifying impulse and the distancing impulse formed flip sides of the same coin, one that used Indians as a foil for the achievement of American national identity. As an ideology that also served to help expand America's territory and economy, this discourse both abetted and obscured the subjugation and displacement of Native Americans.[20]

Jewish immigrants had internalized Frederick Jackson Turner's influential idea of the frontier as a zone of free land that receded as westward settlement advanced, facilitating democracy, serving as a safety valve for urban discontent, and fostering the ideal of American individualistic values.[21] They developed a consciousness of their own belonging in the American West and integrated themselves into the civic and economic landscape of the new zones of the United States by plotting themselves into the role of frontiersmen in their personal, family, and communal stories. Their efforts at integration did not result in their full assimilation into a preexisting culture among whites or in their loss of a sense of themselves as Jews. For the most part, immigrant Jews of the frontier wished to remain Jewish. They pursued business opportunities generated by filial contacts and trust networks. They tended to socialize and marry among themselves. They built synagogues, schools, and fraternal societies to foster Jewish communal life as soon as they hung up their itinerant peddler's packs and settled in landed communities. They fashioned themselves according to the model the frontiersmen archetype offered, for this persona provided a vehicle for Jews' aspirations for upward mobility and social and metaphysical integration. In the memoirs, diaries, letters, newspaper articles, obituaries, and family and local history books in which Jews articulated their own senses of self as westerners, seldom did they speak of the negative dimensions of the colonial process. Jews of the nineteenth and early twentieth centuries expressed little conflict about colonialism and its imperial dimensions. Jewish history books, like white history more broadly, traditionally celebrated rather than criticized colonialism.[22]

Indeed, settler colonialism offered a range of opportunities for Jews. Immigrant Jews transformed themselves into pioneer Jews through their interactions among Natives and whites vis-à-vis Indians and by subsequently writing about these interactions, memorializing them, and eventually canonizing them in local Jewish history. In migrating and settling the West, Jews could remake themselves from outsiders among European whites to insider Americans. They transitioned from peddler to established merchant and civic builder of the nation, and they moved from migrant to naturalized American. These transformations implied that Jews went from being a landless people to landed citizens, from powerless to powerful, from colonized to colonizer, from emasculated to brawny,

Figure 1.1. "Kohlberg Brothers Cigar Factory and Store with Adolph Solomon and Siegfried Aronstein [cropped out]." This wooden Indian, located in front of the Kohlberg Brothers' Cigar Store, was said to be an "oracle" of the El Paso political campaigns during the 1890s. Leaning on the carving is Adolph Solomon, one-time mayor of El Paso, Texas. The image captures something of the confidence of immigrant Jews' economic mobility and enfranchisement on the frontier. Courtesy of the El Paso Public Library, B559.

and from unfit for expansion and the rugged work of settling new lands to exemplary models for settlement expansion. These changes empowered Jews, moving them from being full of fear of Indians to the Indians' masters, unafraid and able to pacify. Above all, these changes transformed immigrants into settlers.

Like other whites, Jews imagined the frontier and its Native inhabitants long before they migrated there. Jewish migrants set sail for America with some familiarity with the literary and historical lore about the American West, which they brought with them to their experiences of migration and settlement. Images and ideas about new-world Natives as barbaric or noble, warring or on the verge of extinction, but almost always as obstructions to settlement, reached Jews though *Haskalah* literature, in travel diaries and travel literature, in Lost Tribes discourse and other philosophical and scholarly writings from the seventeenth century onward.[23] Translations of famed works on Indian themes by James Fennimore Cooper and Henry Wadsworth Longfellow made their way into German, Polish, Russian, and eventually Yiddish and Hebrew and circulated among Jewish readers from the middle decades of the nineteenth century.[24] Jewish newspapers in English, Hebrew, German, and Yiddish ran dozens of articles about Indians focused on news, depredations, ethnographic curiosity, or translations of literary works.[25] Migrants who had made it to America also sent home letters telling tales of the Indians they heard of or encountered. Some migrants waxed poetic about the role that Indians played in their motivations for migration. Constance Mastores wrote that her grandfather's decision to leave Europe came explicitly from his interest in American Indians. He migrated to America in 1879 to "dabble in Indians," she wrote, emphasizing that "there is one point on which all accounts [about grandfather] agree. Julius Francis Behrend, at age sixteen, left his native Hamburg for America because of an overwhelming desire to have a firsthand look at the American Indian. I hold the German translations of James Fennimore Cooper largely responsible."[26]

Likewise, Eveline Brooks Auerbach wrote that her uncle gave her father, Julius Gerson Brooks, a rifle "as a going away present to fight the Indians."[27] Brooks stayed five years in California during the gold rush before returning to his hometown near Breslau, where he told stories of the new world, some seductive enough to convince the author's mother to return to the United States with her father: "Father was a wonderful exaggerator and told how money was in the streets; Indians on the warpath, fighting on the streets, carrying their bows and arrows on their backs, pistols around their waists, also the scalps of white men. Everyone believed him, and each and everyone was willing to sell their all and go back with him."[28] Auerbach's father told her stories of "his hair-breadth escape from the Indians and wild animals and of the terrible hardships and sufferings of pioneers."[29] Jewish migrants who returned to Europe or wrote letters back to their families and friends reproduced frontier lore, and the place of the Indian in it, for future migrants. Sarah Thal described her own attraction to North Dakota's Indians in terms expressly laden with Jewish overtones. "When as a child attending the religious school the story of the Sojourn of the Israelites in the Wilderness stirred my imagination," she reflected, "I too longed for a sojourn in the wilderness. I did not know that my dreams would become a reality, a reality covering long years of hardship and privation."[30] Sarah's brothers-in-law had "sent home glowing reports of conditions in America." She concluded, "We wished to try our luck in that wonderful land."

The expectations migrant Jews had of the Native Americans they would encounter shaped those encounters they actually had. Jews tended to write about Indians in ways that conformed closely to the available stereotypes they already had in mind. Jewish travelers conceived of the Indians as impediments to safe arrival at best or as hate-filled murderers, hell-bent on thwarting their immigrant ambitions, at worst. In any case, Jews considered themselves white insiders to the colonial process. Indians marred the otherwise "glowing reports of conditions in America" that family members sent back home about the West. These perceptions persisted from the 1850s through the 1910s, virtually irrespective of place. When Jews arrived in a new frontier zone, they almost invariably reproduced similar ideas about themselves and the Indian others around them, even when the threat of Indian violence had largely been removed by the late 1890s,

Figure 1.2. "Freighters on the Santa Fe Trail, Bernard Seligman, Zadoc Staab, Lehman Spiegelberg and [Hired] Kiowa Indian Scouts." The Seligmans, Staabs, and Spiegelbergs were among the powerful Jewish merchant families in New Mexico and Arizona in the 1860s, 1870s, and 1880s. Courtesy of the Palace of the Governors Photo Archives (NMHM/DCA), negative no. 007890.

owing to the state's determined policies of treaty negotiations and the removal of Native peoples to reservations.

Translating Tropes into History: Contribution, Commerce, and Community Building

In pioneer Jewish narratives, small-time Jewish entrepreneurs were transformed into upright frontier Americans. This process of becoming Jewish frontiersmen depended equally on the actual encounters between Jews and Native Americans as it did on the ways that Jewish newspaper men, memoirists, and local history writers conceived of the Jews' place in American frontier life. Becoming a frontier Jew required both historical and historiographic action—that is, the lives of Jews in the West *and* the ways these same Jews narrated their lives for themselves, for each other, for non-Jews, and for posterity. Thus amateur and professional writers of western Jewish history encoded the details of their everyday lives into one dominant narrative of the pioneer Jew. In the West, where they competed, in broad terms, with Native Americans for the land and its resources, Jews assumed a measure of their own enfranchisement when interacting with and imaging Indians.

For early Jewish pioneers, peddlers, traders, settlers, journalists from Jewish newspapers, and the local and family historians who wrote of them, becoming a "frontier Jew" sometimes involved distancing themselves from Indians and framing their Indian encounters as antagonistic, violent, and ultimately victorious. Jews told horror stories of Jews as victims of Indian depredations and stories about Jews perpetrating heroic violence against Indians.[31] These stories and these identifications expressed Jews' whiteness. They proudly described their role in the settling of the West as a process of conquering. One pioneer Jewish memoirist called Arizona a "graveyard of those heroic American and foreign-born Pioneers who boldly surrendered their valuable lives for the good and glory of the *great republic*, and the irrepressible advances of *conquering civilization*."[32] Jews sacrificed their lives for the advancing of civilization, coupled, in this memoirist's terms, with glorious imperialism. Indeed, many Jews took credit as pioneers in "subduing the Apaches, permitting [settlers] to live in peace" to feature their Americanness and to articulate to the non-Jewish world that it owed them a debt of gratitude as pathbreakers for civilization and commerce.[33] The language of contribution dominated early twentieth-century popular American Jewish history, particularly as it applied to the histories of Jews in the old West, Midwest, and Far West. Elma Ehrlich, a onetime teacher in rural Iowa and Illinois, editor of *Jewish Child Magazine*, employee of the Bureau of Jewish Education of New York, member of Hadassah, the National Council of Jewish Women, and the wife of Rabbi Lee J. Levinger, wrote thirty-five works of nonfiction and fiction bluntly aimed at fostering Jewish pride (with works on Jewish holiday stories, "great Jews" since biblical times, and great Jewish women) and manufacturing

American patriotism (with works on Jews who fought for freedom and cherished the Jewish adventure impulse in early America).[34] These latter works, like her 1920 book *The New Land: Stories of Jews Who Had a Part in the Making of Our Country*, described rapport and identification between early Jews and the Native Americans whom they encountered.[35]

Three common, overlapping tropes characterize the late nineteenth- and early twentieth-century American Jewish historical imagination about Native Americans: (1) the individual Jew as pilgrim, (2) the merchant Jew as vanguard of commercial modernity, and (3) a settled Jewish community as the rightful heir to and the future of Indigenous land. First, Jews frequently cast their own immigrant experience to the West as a recapitulation of the original pilgrim story, placing themselves at the very start of the newcomer-Native encounter and emphasizing their contribution. Popular history books about the Jewish experience in the West routinely began their stories with broad strokes, placing Jews at the earliest moments of contact, reproducing specious claims that America's land lay as a vacant and empty wilderness, waiting for cultivation by industrious settlers. When these stage-setting narratives said anything about Native inhabitants, they often linked Indians with the natural landscapes' flora and fauna. They likewise placed Jews at the center of the narrative. Just as the founding American colonists saw their encounter with the wild Indians as central to their story, so too Jews articulated their experiences of naturalization into the American landscape as a repetition of the well-known template offered by the Puritans.[36] Entries in the 1906 *Jewish Encyclopedia*, for example, reproduced this trope of settlers—Jewish ones, in this case—overcoming an Indian challenge as they triumphed in settling Colorado, Alabama, and Texas.[37] Isador Deitsch, Leopold Mayer, A. Jacobs, A. Goldsmith, F. Z. Salomon, and D. Kline made the list of "Jews who survived the hardships of the long journey, the perils from wild animals, and the attacks of savage Indians,"[38] while the entry for Texas detailed the deaths and military roles of Edward J. Johnson, Benjamin H. Mordecai, M. K. Moses, and Herman Ehrenberg in battle with Indians.[39]

Following this theme, nearly three decades later, the popular historian Anita Libman Lebeson's 1931 book *Jewish Pioneers in America, 1492–1848* described Jewish peddlers in value-laden language reflecting this wished-for transformation. "Stooping under the heavy burden of his pack, or walking erect behind an ox-team [. . . t]he Jew," she wrote, "marched into the wilderness beside the Christian pioneer. He too dreamed of the prairies awakened and the forests and rivers quickened to life by the coming of new settlers. He gave of his best energies, of his tireless labor that new communities might survive. And if he prospered—others prospered too. It was a common cause with Jew and Gentile—this building of a new land."[40] Her writing reflected a version of American Jewish frontier history that had been thoroughly absorbed into the popular Jewish imagination. It emphasized that energetic Jewish labor led to the larger economic project of expansion—namely, prosperity—as well as nation building enterprise through settlement. The Jewish contribution to this enterprise, emphasized Lebeson, ought to be celebrated, for it linked national belonging with prosperity for whites. Journalist Ruth Arnfeld put a similar rhetoric to use in her telling the story of "Some of Pittsburgh's Own Founding Fathers," Joseph Simon, David Franks, and the Gratz brothers, and their relationships with Pennsylvania's Indian fur traders.[41] Her article celebrated these Jewish Indian traders as "pioneers [of] vision and faith," the "men of good will who transformed the frontier from a dangerous place of raw wild, to the great cities of American life."[42] In

Figure 1.3. Poster for the 1930 film "Whoopee!," one of the many cultural/artistic products (films, plays, poems, novels, songs, etc.) that American Jews created in the late nineteenth and early twentieth centuries in which Native American characters and themes featured prominently. https://commons.wikimedia.org/wiki/File:Whoopee4ED6.jpg.

this hagiographic version of frontier history, Jewish men partnered harmoniously with their Christian neighbors over and against a natural world personified by the Native. Jewish immigrant men derived social capital from marching "into the wilderness," where their commercial energies and "tireless labor" brought the very land to life for the sake of the "new community" of whites. These Jewish historians echoed the perspective of Jews from the late nineteenth through the early twentieth centuries in interpreting frontier trading as more than just eking out a living at the margins. It meant building the nation. Traders cast themselves as America's commercial pioneers and pathbreakers for European settlement.

Journalists and local Jewish history writers routinely produced and reproduced this rehearsal of Jewish contribution with remarkably little geographic variation. Jews in Alaska, Minnesota, South Dakota, and Wyoming served the country by advancing capitalism in their local counties in much the same way. Likewise over time, Jews repeated this contribution to western American life with surprisingly little change. Jews in the 1860s, 1890s, and indeed throughout the first half of the twentieth century presented themselves as heroes in the same noble project of transforming new lands into economically and commercially viable civic space as they did in the early decades of the twentieth century. This process represented, according to those who hoped to write Jews into the center of American history, the most significant gift that Jews made to the development of the nation. Just as pilgrims in the colonial east framed their engagement with Native Americans in terms of the expansion of civilization and their contributions to it as a national project, so too western Jewish immigrants reproduced a narrative of their engagement with Native Americans mostly in terms of commerce and financial exchange as its necessary ingredients.

In the second thematic trope of the American western Jewish historical imagination, Jews, with the help of local Indians and yet simultaneously antagonistic and sometimes violently disruptive to Natives' lives, viewed themselves and their establishment of businesses and settled life as pathbreaking in the Southwest and far West. Turn-of-the-century historians of America's Jews like aforementioned educator, scholar, and religious leader Cyrus Adler, onetime president of the American Jewish Historical Society and author of several works an colonial Jewish history David de Sola Pool,[43] or writers Joseph Jacobs, J. Hollinger, and A. Rosenbach all noted the contributions that seventeenth- and eighteenth-century Jewish Indian traders made to establish and expand America on the ground.[44] Jewish historians interested in finding the earliest Jewish settlers of towns, states, and regions awarded eighteenth-century Indian traders like David Israel Johnson, Mordecai Moses Mordecai, Aaron and Rachel Levy, and David Franks with honorifics like the "first Jewish settlers" in their respective area.[45] Makers of Jewish history sought to write Jews into American foundation narratives, establishing Jews as founders, in some cases quite literally with places named after Jews like Solomonville, New Mexico; Ehrenberg, Arizona; Seligman,

Arizona; Garberville, California; Bieber, California; and Altman, Colorado.[46] These enfranchised and educated writers highlighted the intimate business connections Jews had among Indians.

Since most of the Jews who went west had engaged in commerce, trading with Indians in particular became a privileged status marker; Jewish pioneers applauded their own interactions with Native Americans as contributions to the commercializing of America. For them, opening up new markets and trade routes, increasing business traffic, and including new players in a larger economy seemed tantamount to bringing civilization. The Indian trader Solomon Spiegelberg, for example, earned praise from New York's Yiddish newspaper *Der Tog*, touted as the "first Jew in New Mexico" for his contributions to America as an Indian trader.[47] Pittsburgh's *Jewish Criterion* eulogized Myer Friendly for his efforts in the 1850s trading with the Indians in Texas, Oklahoma, and New Mexico.[48] Likewise in the West itself, *The Wyoming Jewish Press* praised Abe Abrahams "first as a cowboy, then as a fur trader with the Indians. His name, given by the Crow Indians is 'Deer Hide.'" Montana Jews praised Moses (or Mose) Solomon of Choteau County, Montana, as a pioneer and frontiersman still within his lifetime. "Mose figured in many Indian encounters since he located on the Marias River below Ft. Benton since 1864," the Montana newspaper wrote.[49] Born in Poland in 1825 and dead in Kendall, Montana, in 1903, Solomon could be eulogized as "one of the adventurous spirits who blazed the trail, subdued the savage, and made it possible for the less courageous to settle in safety and build up this great Commonwealth. In the upbuilding of this Nation such men have played a much more necessary part than many whose names are inscribed high in the roll of honor. Brave must he be who emerges from the frontier life with shield untarnished."[50] History makers had early settlers like Solomon emerge from frontier life untarnished—that is, still civil—despite their proximity to the "savage" forces they approached. "Such men" deserved high national honors, according to the Montana newspaper, because their bravery built the nation and paved the ground for mercantile development.

Jewish writers devoted considerable attention to constructing a narrative of their own centrality to the enterprise of pioneering and to telling themselves and their non-Jewish neighbors about their fitness for the expansion process. Pioneer stories from the second half of the nineteenth century well into the middle of the twentieth suggested that Jews played an extraordinary role not just in "upbuilding" America's commercial substructure but also in modernizing America. No longer bound by antiquated traditions and precepts in an America laudable for its religious latitude, Jews who migrated to the margins of American geographic and social life wrote stories in which their presence indicated modernization at work. The work of progressing history forward, they implied, caused Indians to disappear into the historical past, while causing Jews to emerge from the old, past-centered Europe into a new, secular, future-oriented America.

The idea of being "the first" was central to the work these sorts of immigrant narratives aimed to do. Historian Jean O'Brian has called this operation in popular and local settler history making "firsting" and has shown how its twin operation, "lasting," attempted to efface Native Americans from American history.[51] A white pioneer would be the "first" to encounter Indians. This pioneer would be assigned a privileged place in the mythological structure of a community's memory. A "last" Indian would mark the end of prehistory, the turning point in the establishment of a community of settlers. Unsurprisingly, popular Jewish history in America also recapitulates this mantle of "first." "Bogy" Johnson is touted as the first Jew in the newly opened Oklahoma territory and the "Run of 1889."[52] On the hundredth anniversary of Jewish life in Arizona, one popular history author, the editor of the *Phoenix Jewish News* described how "exactly a century ago the first Jew of record entered the wilderness which was to become their nation's youngest state." He called Herman Ehrenberg, a German Jewish immigrant, an "adventurer, traveller, soldier of Fortune and mining engineer," who arrived in Arizona in 1850 to work in a mining camp that soon had to be abandoned on account of Apache "onslaughts." This "first" soon drifted to Colorado where he was killed "by a renegade Indian."[53]

Another dimension of this pathbreaker trope involved Jews claiming to educate or civilize Native Americans, bringing them into the fold of civilization by teaching Indians commercial competence, and being the ones to provision them with state-sponsored education. The Polish-born Sol Ripinsky ran a school in Sitka, Alaska, for forty-five Native American students in 1885, whom he taught both English and Russian before serving as the principal at a government school in Chilkat, Alaska.[54] The Cincinnati-born educator Morris Friedman taught at the Phoenix Indian School at the turn of the century and served as the assistant superintendent at the Haskell Institute for Indians between 1906 and 1908, an institution that encouraged Indian arts and design, and one which eventually spit him out after students complained about his physical weakness and his inability to fit into the muscular culture of the school, evidenced by its use of corporal punishment and regular violence.[55] Friedman later replaced Richard Henry Pratt, the founder of the famous Carlisle Indian School, as its superintendent until 1914. Jewish immigrants, and those who wrote about and memorialized them in popular local Jewish history, picked up on this theme of Jews as Indian educators or civilizers and promoted those Jews who engaged in activities that appeared to be uplifting of Native Americans.

Other incarnations of this trope were found in more quotidian encounters that were nevertheless described and captured as popular memory. Arizona's Samuel and Abraham Korrick "arrange[d] to hang several pairs of denim pants from a cottonwood tree at the edge of town" in response to the "ladies [who] complained to the local merchants" about Indian men showing up without wearing pants: "When the Indians entered Phoenix to trade, they put on the Denning pants, and then left them on the same tree on their way back out.

[Korrick] family members later joked that this was their first 'branch store.'"[56] In the dozens of mentions of pioneer Jews who knew Indians, central to the historiographic claim is the Jews' trustworthiness in the eyes of the Native Americans with whom they traded or dealt. Casual, unsupported but flattering claims about Jewish upright business dealings dot Jewish popular history in Minnesota and Wisconsin of the 1840s and 1850s as much as southwestern states in the 1870s or 1880s and mountain states in the 1890s and 1900s. Julius Austrian (born Julius Oesterreicher in Wittelshofen Bay, Bavaria), a fur trader around Lake Superior in the 1840s, was apparently so trusted by the Ojibwe, according to the Reform rabbi Gunther Plaut, that they and the U.S. government agreed to have him witness their 1847 treaty.[57]

A third common trope in American western Jewish history/myth-making that used Indians was the narrative of establishing a community to account for Jews' integration into American social, civic, and political life and Jews' rapid economic mobility. Take, for example, the celebration of the founding of the first Jewish school, the Talmud Yelodim School, in Cincinnati in 1854. With prayers, rituals, and elaborate speeches, the celebration provided an opportunity for community members to articulate their own emerging community's history. One toast heaped praise upon Joseph Jonas for being "one of the earliest settlers in this region of the Union" and a man who lived to see the region "converted from the abodes of Indians and wild beasts, to well-cultivated land and beautiful cities." Another toast, widening the praise and sharing it among all Cincinnati's early Jews, added, "It is but little more than half a century since this beautiful valley was the hunting-ground of the red man. Now here stands the Queen of the West, the centre of cities, town, villages, and farms." The toastmaster marveled at the rapidity of modernization its pioneers had affected, claiming, "Thirty years since this was the far West; but where is the West now? Where is the hunting-ground of the Indians?"[58] At the school ceremony, local Jews celebrated the arrival and rooting of Jewish community and placed themselves at the center of civic life in all its midcentury forms, cities, towns, villages, and farms and the promise of a future for Jews in the place Natives once hunted. When Jews appeared, Indians disappeared; so marked advancing civilization and the erasure of Native people from local histories.

Pioneer narratives recapitulating the immigration and settlement experience shared not just one or more of the tropes just discussed, but also a common structure, themes, and overall narrative arc. The stories often started with the Jewish migrants' projections about the setting into which he would venture and moved to the fears, impediments, and curious encounters associated with traveling out West. The migrant then established roots and fought off obstacles to the founding of settlements and businesses, at which point the pioneer became a successful founder. He opened bigger commercial enterprises, established civic institutions, and played a prominent role in the building of towns, schools, and religious, political, social, and commercial organizations. At each but the last stage in these stories, Native Americans played a role both materially and rhetorically. These tropes and this narrative structure aimed to create a certain kind of Jewish masculinity that would inveigh against the myth of Jewish emasculation.[59] Gender was at work.

One New Mexico Jewish family history described the "sustenance [we drew] from the shadowed valleys that lie between the hills [and the] ruins of Indian camps."[60] The author counted his great grandfather among "Jews from the four corners of the earth" who lived a "settled merchantile [sic] life" there amid the "wild, exotic life" nearby. The West, imagined as both an empty "harsh wilderness," yet simultaneously full of "wild, exotic life," attracted some Jewish settlers brave enough to face it. David D'Ancona's *A California-Nevada Travel Diary* marked his own sense of distinction from the Native Americans he observed in Virginia City, Nevada. "The women do chores and the lazy men eat what they earn," he wrote. "The noble red man in his forest glades, painted and tattooed, brandishing his tomahawk *a la* the lamented forest may be romantic and interesting, but the noble red man, painted and tattooed, dressed in dirty overalls and linen dusters, loafing on doorsteps, and the noble red woman, in frowsy castoff finery, are simply disgusting."[61]

Jews arrived in the West not just with projections about the Indigenous People they observed but also with the desire to shed gendered biases that had been leveled against them suggesting their unfitness for life in the "Wild West." Myths of emasculated Jews, unsuited for frontier trade and life, appeared in the writings of both Jews and non-Jews and persisted for more than a century with little change over time. Emil Teichmann's *Journey to Alaska in 1868*, for example, chronicled his travels for the Alaska Commercial Company and his frequent encounters with Indians and Jewish traders. He described one Jewish trader, "whose deathly pale and distorted features still bore witness to his fright [at Indians]." This Jew "lost his head and fell down in a faint there [in Seymour's Narrows, Alaska], and was found by us later half-stunned."[62] When a "crowd of [Chinook] Indians" broke into a traders' cabin, another Jew, according to Teichmann, embodied a fear to which Teichmann himself, as well as the other whites, seemed immune. Teichmann portrayed his own attitude toward the perceived attack as calm and heroic, the Jew, by contrast, hysterically terrified. "It was amusing to see how the Jewish dealer, who had been greatly agitated by the sudden appearance of the Indians, now sought to curry favor with them. With hands still trembling with fright he prepared some coffee and distributed it among them with a lavish heaping of sugar (of which the Indians are very fond); he surpassed himself."[63] The Jew's pandering to the Indians he feared marked him, in Teichmann's narrative, as one in need of maturation. Critiques of cowardly Jewish traders led Jews themselves to question their own fitness for western expansion, the tribulations of life in the semiwilderness. Some wondered aloud if America's vision of Manifest Destiny included Jews' destiny at all. The frontier's low population densities, after all, whether in Alaska or Utah, the absence of established Jewish communities, and its reputation for lawlessness inhibited mass Jewish settlement and westward expansion. Westward migration invited caution, worry, and at times rebuke from the immigrant Jewish press suggesting that Jews ought not go too far from established Jewish communities in urban centers, as Jews might be unsuited for the trip.

Barbs were aimed at Jewish men and their apparent inadequacy for frontier life; their putative lack of masculine qualities faced both reinforcement and opposition from Jewish sources. On the one hand, like many publications, Pittsburgh's *Jewish Chronicle* offered a cautionary tale in 1880 about westward travel that fortified the myth of Jewish meekness. It reported that during their march toward White River, Colorado, General Merritt's troops "came across the naked corpse of a man, who was recognized by one of the soldiers as being that of a Jew named Isaac Goldstein, and known in these regions as 'the Jew.'"[64] Goldstein had reportedly headed toward California to rescue his fiancée from the Indians who had kidnapped her, only to be "captured by savages" himself and eventually put to death, his attempt at heroism foiled by his lack of brawn. The story displayed coded messages to its Jewish readers about the Jew's place in the sweep of frontier settlement and articulated popular Jewish attitudes about the great expanse between coastal cities and about Native Americans. Repeatedly called "savage," Indians appeared as short-tempered, easily corrupt by whimsical murderousness, and lacking justice. Natives "offered up [Goldstein's fiancée's] body as a sacrifice" as if beset by barbaric ritual requirements or unquenchable hatred for whites. They murdered even the chivalric Jew who ventured into the unknown land to rescue his love. The Jew, on the other hand, did not possess the muscle, fearlessness, or familiarity with the West's uncivilized zones to maintain his family, let alone his life. The story captured one of the central myths of the Jew in the West—namely, that Jewish men lacked both the confidence and "ruggedness" that was necessary for travel through, to make a living in, or even to assure their own survive in the West. A variation on the well-known nineteenth-century European theme of the powerless shtetl Jew and that of the medieval exile, the Jew in the raw American West suffered, according to this myth, as alienated from the land, lacking requisite masculinity, and therefore possibly unfit for citizenship.[65]

On the other hand, iterations of the myth of the ineffectual Jewish bungler faced considerable opposition. Jewish novelists, memoirists, journalists, and local history writers in the West responded to this myth of Jewish cowardice and emasculation, not coincidentally, by looking to Indians as well. Indeed Jews produced a fairly elaborate counter-myth, which they presented to one another and to a broader America showing themselves to be worthy and strong. They insisted that Jews belonged among the white men, destined to pioneer and build a new nation. The thrust of western Jewish historiography as a whole, in fact, can be read as an assertion against this myth of Jews' lack of ruggedness. Like the "New Jew" of Zionism, the frontier Jew had a transformative saga to affect. Relocated away from Europe, outside urban life in the raw space of make-it-or-be-broken individualism, Jews sought to reinvent themselves as pathbreakers for civilization and the nation. They used "the Indian" as a straw man onto which they cast their own narratives of belonging in America's central ideological myths. Jews identified with other frontier whites, with whom they shared the actual task of eking out a living, establishing communities in which to live, and building the nation. Indians real and imaginary served western Jewish communal memory in the hands of Jews struggling to articulate a particularly Jewish version of the American frontier myth.[66]

Just as western Jews told stories that transformed themselves from unfit to fit for life on the frontier, they also changed from fearful newcomer to fearless proprietor of the West. This transformation of affect represented the most important change that westward moving Jews made, a rhetorical and metaphysical change. Dozens of tales of travel expressed Jews' initial fear of Indian violence as they set out on their migrant journeys. Newspapers reported that Leo Schuster rode on a stagecoach from Santa Fe "with his eyes glued on the horizon for most of the journey for the expected appearance of attacking Indians . . . through the Indian-infested Jornado [New Mexico.]"[67] By steamer from Philadelphia to San Francisco in May 1864, and then by stagecoach from Los Angeles to Tucson, Samuel H. Drachman "intended to take passage without delay but was told that Indians all over the Territory and on the Tucson road in particular, were on the War Path, that they were killing people and stealing their stock and that several stages had been taken in and the passengers killed."[68]

From the 1860s through the 1880s, endemic violence between Native Americans and whites, particularly in the Southwest, certainly wrought warranted fear. Indeed the fears of white migrants, Jews among them, "was not without foundation," noted Eveline Brooks Auerbach in her memoirs. Describing her fear on the train she rode across the Southwest toward the frontier hamlet she would eventually call home, she recounted that "the previous train had been set upon by the Indians, and the whole train had been practically wiped out. Women and children went to sleep at nights while the men kept watch with loaded rifles, as they neared the Indian country, ready to shoot Indians or wild beasts."[69] Jewish newspaper, obituary, and memoir writers regularly associated the first weeks of Jews' first settlement in the West with depredations, the presence of potentially violent Indians who threatened their efforts to forge new lives and communities.

Becoming unafraid of Indians established the affective foundation upon which Jews could actually transform themselves from a landless people to a landed one. Perhaps Isaac Goldberg's 1894 address to the Society of Arizona Pioneers, an association devoted to inscribing pioneers' own landedness, best exemplifies the transformation of the Jew from a landless migrant to a landed American citizen, as it cast Indians as hindrances to the opening of new trade, trail, traffic, and town. His memoir showed, he claimed, "how the first pioneers of Arizona suffered from Apache Indians and desperadoes and from want of

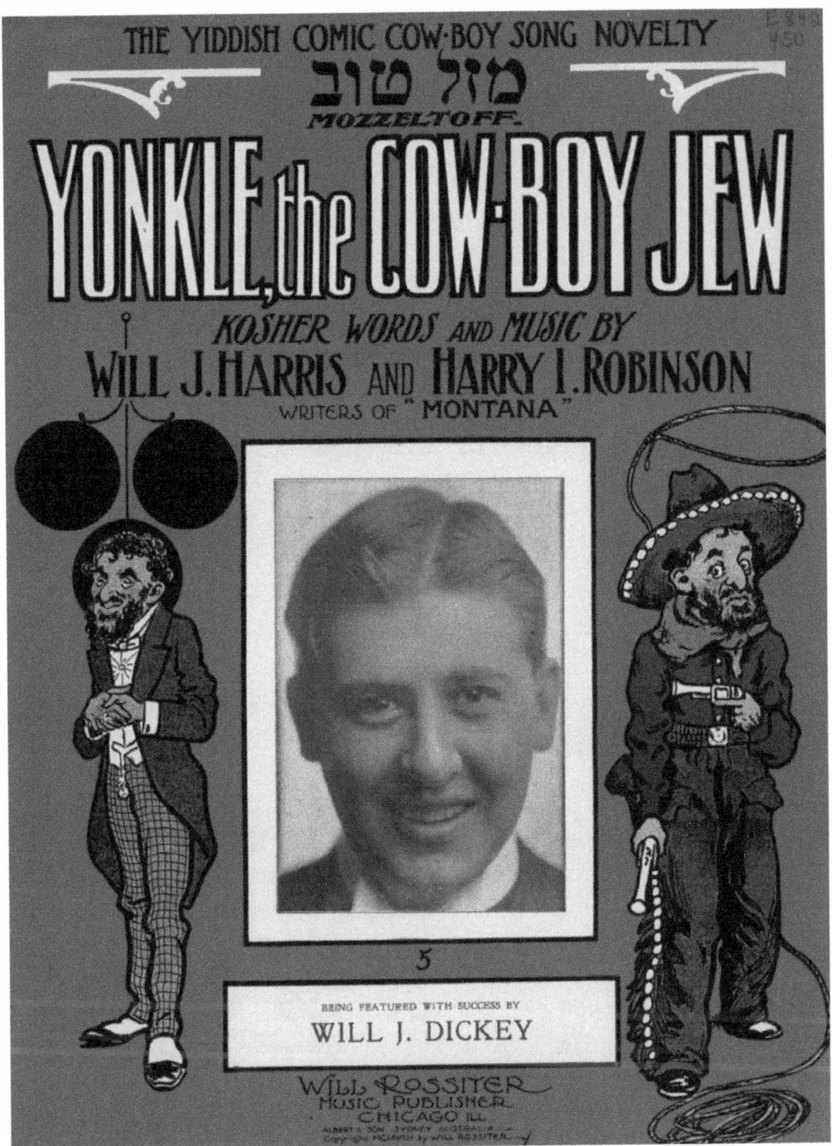

Figure 1.4. "Yonkle, the Cowboy Jew." Sheet music cover, 1907. Jews and non-Jews repeated (and mocked) stereotypes of Jewish men's supposed lack of bravery and inadequate masculinity. Baylor University Library. https://commons.wikimedia.org/wiki/File:Yonkle_the_cow_boy_Jew_1907.jpg.

water and food, also, how we opened new trails and roads," linking together Indian impediments and the expansion of settler commerce.[70] Indian violence and the absence of sustenance provided the challenges that the first pioneers would "overcome" in their own understandings of their actions as agents who opened up new land for future settlers. "When I look back upon those eventful days," wrote Goldberg, "my eyes fill with tears to think of the danger we encountered, and the hardships we experienced then, not knowing when we might lose our property, our scalps, and our lives." The dangers they faced and for which they risked their scalps, in their own retellings, paved the way for civilization to expand. Notably, they tended to omit from their stories the violence that they themselves deployed against Apache or other Indians.

Goldberg and Drachman, who "found Indian trouble of a vicious nature," all shared in the horrified and demonized view of Native Americans that formed one strand of Indian stereotypes in the white imagination in the 1860s, 1870s, and 1880s. "People were being killed, some in the most brutal manner. Instances where the poor victims were burnt at the stake were not unusual," wrote Drachman. "During the years 68–69 and 70, in my estimation, we suffered worst from the cruelties of the Apaches." Harkening back to the much-publicized "murder of Valentine, Long, Warren, Col. Stone, and party of six, and poor Price who had the flesh cut from the soles of his feet," Drachman articulated what many frontier settlers understood as the chief repercussions of the violence—namely, the disruption of business. "Many more were sent to their long home at the hands of the Apache. Business was almost at a standstill and very little, if any mining was done," never mind the disruption of Indian sustenance patterns and cultural, political, and social processes by settlers.[71]

In response to the Apaches' threat to disrupt the commercial and settlement activity of land they considered theirs, Drachman and other Jews did what many whites chose to do; they harnessed state power, or acted outside the law, taking emboldened action against Indians. Drachman applied "to the Secretary of War to supply the citizens with needed guns." In his reminiscences, Drachman reported that his "request was granted," that "each person receiv[ed] a gun," and that "for a time the people were well armed." He ended his memoir by further vaunting pioneers: "All Honor to the good and Brave Old Men. We as Pioneers, more than any other people can appreciate his great and good work in subduing the Apaches permitting us now to live in peace."[72] Through their acts of "subduing," white memoirists like himself took credit for bringing peace through violence, acting both "good" and "brave"—that is, both justly and as civilized men ought, again obscuring their own roles in actually perpetrating violence.

From Opposition to Relation: Becoming American by Imagining the Indian Within

If casting themselves as men who victoriously wrestled America away from the Indians provided one way for popular Jewish history writers to create pioneer Jews, *identifying* with Indians could likewise help confer pioneer status, particularly when Jewish writers *retrospectively* articulated what it meant to be a Jew on the frontier. Jews, in other words, used techniques of relating to Native Americans, just as they deployed techniques and tropes of distancing or opposition. At times, western American Jews, as other whites, crossed the race boundary and expressed a sense of kinship and connection to Native Americans. Feeling American, in a seemingly paradoxical twist, meant remembering the Indian within, acting like or alongside Native Americans, symbolically performing their own intimacy with American land, their aboriginality to America. Thus writers of popular western Jewish history, the diarists and newspaper writers as well as the memoir, obituary, and local history writers who later remembered western communities' first Jews, cast Jewish frontiersmen as sharing in America's indigeneity by claiming bonds of closeness with Native Americans. In memorializing Jewish colonial settlers as Indian-friend rather than Indian-foe, American Jews produced popular lore about their own essential relationships to America itself as well as helped lay out new terms for Indian life in the postconquest West. Of course, these rhetorical techniques of relation rested on the deeper given that Jews were not, in fact, Native American. Techniques of opposition undergirded techniques of relation.

They sought to root themselves as original Americans, not blemished with the sense of being a foreigner, exile, or alien from the land and its original pedigree. They did this through becoming an "honorary Indian" through acquiring or claiming fictional bonds of kinship (including Lost Tribes claims), the bonds of authentic friendship with Native Americans, through Indian language use and competency. Generations of Dittenhoeffers remembered their Uncle Sam, who arrived in New Mexico in the mid-1860s, as one who lived with the Navajos and acquired fluency in their language, becoming "a territorial celebrity," known as "Navajo Sam." Likewise, a *Jewish Criterion* journalist celebrated Edward Kanter, who "landed in America in the early [eighteen] forties without a cent in his pocket," for his ability to "converse in the Chippewa, Pottawatomic and Huron languages." The Pennsylvania newspaper proudly embellished his Indian connections, writing that "he formed many friendships among the Indians. They affectionately called him because of his restless energy the 'Fire Cracker,' . . . 'Bosh-bish-gay-bish-gon-sen.'"[73] For Jews, earning Indian honorifics implied a near-native relationship to America itself.

Jews on the margins of urban and communal Jewish life proudly doled out and received praise for their affinity and kinship with Indians. Rank-conferring nicknames marked a frontiersman's pedigree. Marking one's affinities with Indians required grooming a persona that reaped the benefits of associations whites had of Indians' wild, raw, unkempt nature, of life still tied to instinct. Throughout the American West, prominent Jewish merchants took their commercial success and their intimacy with Native Americans as proud proof of their belonging and as evidence of American cultural bona fides. One of the few details mentioned in the Jewish Museum of the American West's description of the Latvia-born, Tempe Arizona merchant Wolf Lukintsky (Lukin) was that more than two hundred Pima Indians came to his funeral at the Beth Israel Cemetery in Phoenix in 1931, thanks to the service he'd performed as the broker for Salt River (Pima) Indians to sell their wood, grain, and hay.[74]

Seattle's *Jewish Transcript: A Weekly Newspaper for the Jewish People of the Pacific Northwest* routinely featured stories like this from the turn of the twentieth century well into its middle. In 1928, it proudly described how Milwaukee's Sol Levitan, the state treasurer of Wisconsin, was "made an Indian chief for the second time," first by the Winnebago, who "adopted him into their tribe and immediately elected him as one of their chiefs," and later by the Chippewa, who prepared an elaborately described tobacco ceremony that accompanied the receipt of his new name, Bimwewegijig, Roaring Sky.[75] Twenty years later, it described "an impressive ceremony conducted by Chief Pol of the Nootka tribe," in which Hy Ginsburg was made "Chief Son of the Covenant," Mrs. Ginsburg "made a princess," and Mrs. Sam Faverman was "crowned 'Daughter of the Covenant.'" Chief Pol apparently presented a totem pole to Ginsburg and a blanket to his wife off the back of the Indian leader's wife. Ginsburg apparently asked the Nootka to "inform him by smoke signals, telegraph, or other methods of the next meeting of the tribal chieftains [so that] I will make every effort to be present."[76]

Public display of some form of identification with Indians as a way to shore up pioneer identities went considerably further among some Jews than merely acquiring an Indian name. Hagiographic stories about Jews "going native" that dot the amateur American Jewish history bookshelf further illustrate the rhetorical ambition of those sorts of identity transformation tales. Harold Sharfman's treatment of Samuel Sanders in his book *Frontier Jews* serves as a convenient case study. Reputedly together with the famed frontiersman Daniel Boone, Sanders's story of adoption began when he and Boone "[were] busily engaged in crystallizing salt at a spring just beyond the fort [Fort Boonsebor-ough on the Kentucky River], [and] Shawnee abruptly appeared and took them captive into their camp north of the Ohio River, exhibiting them proudly in different tepee villages." Sanders's abduction tale went far beyond an adventure narrative; it emphasized a full transformation in his identity, his body, his blood, his values, and his future:

> Their hair was plucked except for a scalped lock, a tuft of hair on the crown. Their "white-blood" was washed away and their bodies painted to complete the initiation ceremony. The Jewish lad and the trailblazer were then

> adopted into the tribe. Sanders . . . could have fled . . . from Shawnee captivity, [but] chose to remain. He preferred the safety and freedom among the Indians to being in Fort Boonesborough, a ready trap for any bond-servant. Moreover, he was blissfully happy with a young Shawnee beauty who shared his tepee as his wife. There was no question in Samuel's mind, Indian civilization was superior to Caucasian culture.[77]

No evidence backs the tale of Sanders's initiation into Shawnee, of his decision to remain with them, of his conjugal choices, or of his "white-blood" being "washed away." Nor should other stories that circulate in the amateur bookshelf of western Jewish history, like that of Edward Rose, who allegedly abandoned his Big Horn Basin expedition, west of Yellowstone, "to become a blood brother of the savage Crow—the Upsarodas" be uncritically accepted. In one account of Rose, "the Jew helped the braves hunt elk, deer, and antelope, the plentiful game that flew overhead as well as the mountain sheep. . . . He fought with the Crow against their deadly foe, the Blackfeet." According to further legend, Rose lead a battle against whites, killing enemies and earning his name Che-ku-ka-tes, "the man who killed five," and was "looked upon . . . from that day on as their chief."[78] Fancifully told and minimally authenticated as these tales may be, the stories of Jewish men who chose to live among Native Americans and took on Indian identities, even those explicitly and antagonistically shaped against whites, served the function in the making of local Jewish histories and lore. These stories rooted the Jewish community's early settlers into the local landscape, the bloodstream and the birthright of local Native America, in a manner that frequently mixed the biological and the cultural.

The full expression of movement from migrant to "native" occurred when Jews "went Native." For Jews, acting "red" mirrored, mimicked, and modified a long-standing cultural trope of whites claiming they had become Native.[79] When Jews wrote stories of adoption into Indian tribes, they simultaneously marked their closeness with other white Americans even as they expressed kinship and claimed profound identification with Indians. Instances of Jews living with Native communities, and then later writing about them or being written about, certainly share something in literary terms with redface performance, but they were distinct in important respects—most fundamentally, that they involved actual encounters with real Native American people. Sam Brown, for example, a supposed "Jewish boy of five years old," had begged a "band of Euchees [who] were making their way to Indian Territory" after their removal to take him along. Brown lived with the Euchees and "adopted their ways," claimed S. R. Lewis, an Oklahoma pioneer interviewed in 1937 for the Works Administration Project. "One of the Euchee leaders picked him up and put him on his horse. Thus Sam Brown became an adopted member of the Euchee tribe," he told his interviewer. Raised by Euchees, Brown apparently led a life of pan-Indian leadership, success in business, and marginally Jewish affinities.

> [Sam Brown] was a very natural leader, very shrewd and successful in business. . . . After the war he became a treasurer of the Creek Nation and a member of the House of Kings. His home was at Weelaka; near the place where Leonard is today. He had a large store there. It was while he was in business there that he was robbed of the funds belonging to the Euchees for whom he was treasurer. He also had large land holdings and fine stock. His first wife was a Creek, his second was a Yargee, one-eighth Creek, and Billy Brown is the son of this marriage. I remember him quite well; he certainly had the appearance of a Jew. He was a low, heavy set man, fair of face with a large nose. He was very resourceful and keen [in] business deals. He lived to be very old. He died in February, 1936; he claims that he was over 100 years old. I attended the tribal funeral [which] It lasted all day. . . . There were all Day services of burial ceremonies and feasting and the leading men of four tribes paid homage to him; Creeks, Euchees, Cherokees and Osages.[80]

The Jewish press ran plenty of equally possibly apocryphal stories of Jews who had been taken captive by Indians and returned to civilization years later. The Texas-born Herman Lehmann was apparently captured by Apaches near his home in 1869 at age ten, learned Apache and forgot English, and participated in Apache raids. Lehmann was caught by rangers but escaped to Comanche territory, where he lived by the name "Montecca" on a reservation in Oklahoma before he was eventually discovered as "white" and was persuaded to return to his people by Comanche chief Quanah Parker, and he eventually became part of the Loyal Valley settlement as "a good citizen . . . [who] now knows that it was wrong [to commit murder] and that no amount of provocation or under any circumstances could be induced to shed his fellow man's blood."[81] Curiously, "Montecca" was placed on the tribal roles for the convention in 1901 and granted 160 acres in Garfield, Oklahoma, which he eventually gave to a school. Lehmann appeared in county fairs and rodeos and eventually wrote a popular book, *Nine Years among the Indians, 1870–1879*. The Cincinnati newspaper *The Israelite* ran a 1869 article, "Child Stolen by Indians: Return of a White Man after Thirty Years Captivity among the Indians," for example, in order to astonish readers and encourage gratitude among them for the privileges and blessings of American life.[82] Jewish newspapers retold captivity narratives in order to bring their Jewish readers closer to strange and unfamiliar Indian worlds nearby.[83] In one, a four-year-old boy, kidnapped by Delaware Indians and adopted by the childless chief, learned about his true identity only at his adopted father's deathbed. Before the chief died, he gave his adopted son a written statement revealing his true identity.[84] In another, published in the *Boston Hebrew Observer*, a white man had become "enthralled with a squaw belonging to the tribe" and was later "induced [into] his leaving civilization to cast his fortunes with the Apaches."[85] Belle Goldstein recounted that Indians "stole" her, at age two, from her father's trading post near Juneau, Alaska, around 1890.[86] Tales of these kinds of kidnappings, near kidnappings, and chosen escapes into Indian tribal life, speckled Jewish frontier lore.[87]

By the 1880s and 1890s, captivity narratives had a long lineage as a literary genre, and readers well understood their conventions.[88] White captives forcibly went Native, or became temporarily red, eventually returning to white civilization where they often experienced difficulties reintegrating back into white society or chose to retain some aspects of their newfound Indianness. One such tale involved the abduction of the ten-year-old Adolph Korn by the Comanche in Texas on New Year's day, 1870, and Marcus Goldbaum's interventions that led to the boy's recovery.[89] Goldbaum, a Prussian-born middleman supplier of Comanche-produced beef for the U.S. Army, had close business relations with Korn's captors. (In the spring of 1886, by which time Goldbaum had become a justice of the peace in Wickenburg, Arizona, he was killed by Native Americans.[90]) As with Edward Kanter and Moses Solomon, many frontier Jews proudly chose to honor themselves or those Jews who gained inside access to Native cultural life.[91] In turn, access to Indian life lent Jewish immigrants access to America's native foundations and made them more American.

Authors of Jewish frontier life wanted to associate pioneer Jews with both the wild Indian and the civilized citizen; they both related to and opposed Native Americans. On the one hand, being associated with Indians affirmed a particularly western version of masculinity that Jews could embrace; appropriating it offered Jews a means of countering the long-standing crisis of Jewish modernity—namely, that Jews' lack of land and power meant, ipso facto, that they also lacked a home and the full benefits of citizenship owed to white men. Yet as much as Jewish writers desired that Jewish pioneers cultivate their Indian-like qualities, they also held fast to those qualities of the Jewish immigrant they considered most precious—namely, Jewish civility, the idea of Jews as harbingers of cultural modernity. The Jewish historical record celebrated those who formed bonds of kinship with Native Americans but also retained fidelity to their sense of Jewishness. The same obituaries and articles that celebrated these Jews' Indian encounters invariably lauded their contributions to general civic and specifically Jewish communal life. Though western American Jewish writers characterized their relationships with Native Americans in a host of apparently competing ways, they all, ultimately, made foils of their "Indians."

Two Distinctions in Jewish Stories about Indians

Many of the ways that Jews interacted with Natives closely matched those of other whites. Whites on the frontier moved from landless to landed, from warring with Indians to their vanquishers. In some ways, Jews took their cues about how to interact with and understand Indians from the whites with whom they shared elective affinities. However, two important differences between Jews and other whites mark this Jewish-Native encounter as distinct. First, unlike many of the white-Indian stories of frontier life, Jewish stories about Jews' closeness with Indians rarely mentioned, described, or emphasized sexual or romantic encounters or conquests, though there are exceptions. Jews did not typically write about Native women welcoming Jewish men to their land, metaphorically expressed by their sexual availability. In general, when Jewish history writers celebrated Jews' proximity to Native America, they tended to avoid language of sexual assimilation.[92]

Jewish pioneersmen could not be celebrated as Jews by Jews if they outmarried. Solomon Bibo, who has received more attention than any other frontier Jewish-Native encounter, offers an exception to this rule. A Prussian immigrant and post trader in New Mexico, Bibo married Juanna Valle, the daughter of the Acoma Pueblo governor in New Mexico. Bibo later served as the community's governor himself for at least two terms in the 1870s.[93] The political leadership role he took in the Acoma Pueblo, a position he earned though his marriage to Valle, won him accolades in a long tradition of triumphalist narratives about him as a "Jewish Indian Chief." Most of the Jewish sources on Bibo emphasized that Bibo and Valle eventually moved to San Francisco to affiliate with the Jewish community. Some even claimed that they left the reservation *in order* to live more Jewishly, though no proof exists to support such a conjecture.[94] There were, however, marriages and children born of Jewish-Native American couplings. Jacob Rader Marcus noted that "Bugsy" Johnson, an early Jewish trader in Arkansas territory after the Civil War, married a Chickasaw Indian.[95] Petty banker Joseph Sondheimer married a Cherokee woman he met while pedaling pecans.[96] Jews could remain Jews in Indian country as long as they did not cross intimate frontiers. If they did, remaining Jewish required immersion in institutions of Jewish communities.[97]

A second major difference between Jews' perceptions of and engagements with Native Americans and those of other whites, as mentioned, lay with the fact that Jews did not missionize. "Christianization" offered no vehicle for Jewish-Native engagement. Unlike Christian pioneers, Jewish migrants and settlers on the frontier mostly neglected discussing religion altogether when discussing Indians. Many white Christians spent considerable effort aimed at Christianizing Indians from the first contact between them in the sixteenth century and thereafter by the Spanish, Dutch, Portuguese, French, and English. Missionary activity formed one of the central spokes of white-Indian encounters. Late nineteenth-century missionizing was coupled so closely with the state's assimilatory ambitions for Indians that the state, under President Grant's administration, gave various portions of Indian Territory to twelve religious Christian denominations to administer instead of army officers in 1870. It assigned no portion of Indian Territory to the Jewish "church." Contemporaries even postulated that the contract of Herman Bendell, the superintendent of (otherwise all-Protestant) Indian Affairs of Arizona Territory in 1873 failed to be renewed on account of his not being a Christian.[98] Jews did not enlist religion in their discussions of civilizing Indians.

Figure 1.5. "Solomon Bibo, San Juan Garcia, Andres Ortiz, and Martin Valle, with Lincoln Canas, Acoma Pueblo, New Mexico, 1883." Solomon Bibo married Juana Valle and became for a time the governor of the Acoma Pueblo. Courtesy of the Palace of the Governors Photo Archives (NMHM/DCA), negative no. 164160.

Given what we know of Jewish endogamy practice and stance on missionary activity, it is not surprising that individual Jews would be much less likely than individual Christians to seek out (or really, to *publicize* their seeking out of) Native American women for sex or to introduce religion into their narratives of interaction with Native Americans. The fact that Jews engaged with these other popular modes of describing their interactions with Native Americans, but not these two, suggest that as radically new and different an environment the frontier was, and as much as Jews transformed themselves (and retrospectively described themselves as being transformed), Jews still undertook an emphatic project of preserving a core of Jewishness (after all, non-Christianness and endogamy are about the two most core aspects of Jewishness that get emphasized in modernity by those fighting to maintain a sense of Jewishness in the face of assimilation).

Despite these distinctions, western Jewish narratives created a set of competing mythologies about their encounters with Indian "others" in which they sometimes took on mythic Indian identities, and oftentimes radically distanced themselves from Indians. In both cases, Jews created for themselves an opportunity to play the role of the pioneer-colonizer, and be a part of the colonizing process, a reversal of power from being a minority in Europe who had suffered their own experience of persecution. Until the 1920s, Jews in the West celebrated the pleasures of power and credited their success to their thrift, industry, and courage in the face of risk. They enjoyed the West's material rewards, the sense of social inclusion it offered to them as whites, and the political enfranchisement. In their interactions with Native Americans, western Jews oscillated between identification and boundary marking. Jews distinguished themselves from the Indian other through the use of racial stereotyping, imagining Indians as irrevocably stuck in an ancient or primitive past, unable to sit at the table as civilization took root on the frontier. At times, Jews identified with Indians and "went Native," identifying simultaneously with Indians and with other whites who played Indian. Jews suggested that American whites owed them a debt of gratitude. They were to be granted an insider's sense of belonging in the American national project.

CHAPTER 2

LAND AND THE VIOLENT EXPANSION OF THE IMMIGRANTS' EMPIRE

Jews in the emerging American West told multiple and conflicting stories about the nature of their relationships to Native Americans as they sought to secure both respectable livings and a status as pioneer Americans. They came to see themselves as integral to advancing the frontier (or pushing it back) and as unquestioned members belonging to the American national expansion settlement project. The frontier, however, provided not just a metaphysical space for identity formation; it remained a physical place too. The land itself was a geography of contest. Possession of land and its resources animated the stakes of all Jewish-Native encounters, just as they underlay all the Native-newcomer encounters. In their engagements with Native Americans in the late nineteenth and early twentieth centuries in the West, Jews understood themselves as settlers, as colonists, and as whites. They were understood as such. For the most part, their actions in respect to land, their vision of the land as uninhabited, underproductive, or as a commodity, and their conceptualizations of themselves as the rightful owners of it, changed little during the years of Grant's "Peace Treaty," and the years of the allotment policy.

From the 1840s through the turn of the century, the American government invited and enabled a massive wave of European immigrants, alongside Chinese, Mexican, and African American laborers, to settle newly acquired lands. The United States had taken some of this land as spoils from its war with Mexico from 1846 to 1848.[1] It purchased the Louisiana Territory from France in 1803, Oregon from the United Kingdom in 1846, portions of New Mexico, Texas, and Arizona from Mexico in 1853, and Alaska from Russia in 1867. Most of the land, however, became available to settlers through the federal government's efforts to contain and then assimilate American Indians and to extinguish the Indian title to the land by treaty signings. "During most of the nineteenth century," states the introduction to the Records of the Bureau of Indian Affairs at the National Archives, "the chief goal of Indian policy was to clear the way for expansion on the frontier by extinguishing Indian title to the land. Until 1871 the main device used to accomplish this objective was the treaty by which the Indians gave up their claims to certain areas of land in exchange for reservations in those areas not then sought for white settlement and for compensation in money or goods often extended over a long period of time (annuity payments)."[2]

Treaty signings worked in tandem with the government's and with settlers' most powerful mechanism for acquiring Native American land—warfare. For whites, settling the West meant wrestling land away from Indians through whatever means necessary, including violence.[3] When this seizure required force, Jews' encounters with Native Americans also turned violent. Like other American whites, Jews tended to view Indians as an obstacle to civilized settlement and an unworthy opponent in broad-based struggles for ownership of territory and the use of its resources.[4]

The broad context of expansion, colonialism, and empire building thus formed the most fundamental context into which the Jewish immigrant experience in the West fit.[5] Jewish immigrants played an active part in these empire-building processes as peddlers, traders, land speculators, and entrepreneurs. Commerce served as a cutting edge for settlement expansion.[6] Furthermore, Jewish sutlers supported and enabled the military by following it around and supplying it with dry goods and foodstuffs; other Jews served in this military as soldiers and officers. Jewish settlers in the West even participated in vigilante violence against Native Americans in the protracted war over land between Native Americans and newcomers. In the most basic and material senses, settlers won this war. Nineteenth- and early twentieth-century Jews contributed to this victory and proudly described their roles in it as active agents and early movers. An immigrants' empire expanded.

Questions about land, water, control over accessing and passing over territory, and the subterranean resources under the earth's surface ("land," for short), this chapter argues, formed the context in which Jewish-Indian relations on the frontier figured. Being limited, contested, and conceptualized in distinct ways by settlers and Native Americans, land was the fundamental ground of migrant-Native relations, just as land was the cornerstone of state decisions about managing populations and managing the West more broadly. Competition over land ownership and the uses of its resources formed the central axis around which struggles for power and belonging revolved.

How did American frontier Jews understand their relationship to this contentious land? While owning land was not the driving force behind Jewish westward migrants' material ambitions, the idea of American land provided a malleable canvas upon which they could project and create the idea of home for themselves. While some Jews made considerable efforts to own land, and others to settle and work it as agriculturalists, the dominant desire for land was simply to feel part of it. Settler Jews, like all settlers, saw land as a source of valuable capital, of land as property. Unlike many other white settlers, however, they were not necessarily committed to staying on the land as permanent settlers; within single lifetimes, one or two generations, many Jews moved to larger towns in the Southwest, Far West, or further north and east to join larger Jewish communities.

Land and natural resources, of course, lay at the heart of the entire juggernaut of western American settlement, and whites generally saw Native Americans as impediments to their acquisition.[7] Land could be seen as a panacea to a range of problems, including Jewish ones—most pressingly for relatively poor immigrant Jews—like the need to gain economic traction as new settlers. Profit motives merged with other deep-seated desires in Jews' efforts to acquire land—namely, the enfranchisement and sense of home it brought in America, a counter to stereotypes of Jewish *luftmentshn*, literally, "air people," and a corrective to the myth that Jews lacked the wherewithal for the physicality of working the land. Being grounded in American soil thus offered some measure of redemptive potential.

This Jewish desire for American western land provided a partial answer to some of the most elemental anxieties of the new immigrants. Being connected to the land signified an end to exile and the long medieval and early modern history of Jewish landless wandering for those Jews who moved into new western territories. It provided an appealing vernacular, and a uniquely colonial vision of the "muscle Jew," one virtually contemporaneous with the continental version produced by European and Russian Jewry, primarily through Zionism.[8] The parallels are striking. Both emphasized industry, vigor, and a racialized Jewish body that pushed against the forces of degeneration that had been said to impact Jewish social and psychological life for generations. Unlike the European vision of Jewish muscularity, however, the American one was a form not of Jewish nationalism but of assimilation.

Thousands of Jews had cast their lots among the German, Irish, Scandinavian, and American-born migrants who rushed west to seize their opportunity for land and the chance the West offered for civic inclusion, social mobility, and religious latitude. Along with the economic opportunities promised by the West, those Jews who migrated to America's frontiers *desired* land. For them, land ownership offered three key entitlements: an avenue for social and economic mobility, a sense of belonging in the project of establishing the nation, and a reversal of the predicament of landlessness Jews faced in Europe.[9] In a more metaphysical sense, the battle for dominating land doubled as a battle for "ownership" of America itself, for advancing civilization and establishing the American national project. So for Jews, participation in this battle meant membership in one of the central dramas of the American metaphysic: taming the land and "pacifying" its "wild" inhabitants.

American Landedness: Redemption of the Jews

Migrating Jews from the American east, from central and eastern Europe, and from the Russian empire brought the internalized critique of the Jews' weakened bodies and degenerate minds, as well as Jewish memory of displacement to the American West, hoping to free themselves of these burdens. It is in this context that the harrowing tales of violent encounters Jews had with Indians ought to be understood. But in the battle for American land, Jewish stories were not all the same. In fact, their tales mixed relish and repulsion. This blending of responses to land conquest helped Jews create a sense of themselves as settlers: at times innocent and proud, at times guilty and anxious about their participation in conquest. Though Jews struggled over the ethics and necessities of violence, they saw themselves as playing a role in the drama of expansion of American imperial boundaries, the final founding of the nation. Descriptions of heroic perpetrations of frontier violence offered proof that Jews could furnish for themselves and for their non-Jewish neighbors as a rebuttal of the critique that Jews were too community oriented and not individualistic enough to succeed in the frontier world of make-it-or-be-broken Jacksonian individualism. Jews were eager to show that they too acquired strength and individuality by battling Indians off the land and that they too, therefore, ought to be appreciated as exalted model citizens.[10] Western Jews saw violence as regenerative for them in particularly Jewish ways; the anxiety of degeneracy was a prominent feature of mid-nineteenth-century Central European Jewish thought.

Jews and non-Jews had habitually fantasized about Jews acquiring vast tracts of Indian land in the United States. In 1843, nearly a decade before the settlement of Nebraska, Julius Stern, a German-born immigrant to Philadelphia, proposed that a colony of Jews be established in an area west of the Mississippi River. In the very first issue of Isaac Leeser's *The Occident*, Stern suggested that if seventy thousand Jews could settle "a large tract of land in one of the western territories, where Congress disposes of the land at $1.25 per acre," they would be eligible to apply for statehood, thereby providing one unrealized answer to the nineteenth-century European "Jewish problem."[11] It is not clear to what extent Stern's fantasizing was tongue-in-cheek. It certainly was not pursued as a matter of communal organizational policy. But his phrasing was telling. In it, the state was simply liquidating free land; with it, Jews could become their own nation. Not Americans, but a nation of Jews. Stern's aspiration echoed Mordecai Manuel Noah's famous fantasy, twenty years prior, of establishing a Jewish homeland on Grand Island, New York, to which Indians, as fellow descendants of ancient Israelites, would be welcomed.[12] A similar suggestion had been tabled a century prior by Sir Alexander Cuming in 1730. Cuming, a Scottish baronet, "concocted a plan to pay off the British national debt by placing 300,000 Jewish settlers on Cherokee lands."[13] His musings came after he had reputedly convinced Cherokee leaders to acknowledge the sovereignty of the king of England. Cuming imagined that Jews might pay for nationhood; purchasing land would help the British coffers, but his logic rested on the idea that Jews were both wealthy and stateless—sovereignty required land. Cuming did not clarify what he imagined should be done with the Cherokees whose land could be bought, though the implication of his elision was that Cherokee needed neither the land nor the sovereignty. The fantasy of Jewish settlers on Indian lands could "solve" the problem of European Jewry by solving its key problems: the Jews' landlessness, their failure to engage in "productive" labor, and their lack of national sovereignty.

Like Cuming a century prior, mid-nineteenth-century Jews assumed that American land lay empty and for the taking. Native Americans were not considered eligible for national sovereignty; they were part of the natural landscape and thereby had no claim over land. Nor could Native Americans enjoy property rights as Europeans or Americans did. Bearing these rights supposedly required subjects to have certain moral and intellectual capacities, ones that whites (and of course Jews among them) believed Jews to possess. They tended to assume that Native people did not possess such capacities and were therefore not entitled to property rights. For those immigrants who had been shut out from land ownership in Europe, coming to a "vacant" American West meant the chance to own land and experience the emancipatory process of settling it. Jews acquired land, and they proudly wrote their land acquisitions into their narrative of American integration. Describing "Georgia's Great Swamp," the *Hebrew Observer* reprinted an article from the *Atlanta Journal* for its Jewish readers, noting that "when the Indians had disappeared . . . the lands were divided up among the whites."[14] If settlers could conceive of the land as vacant, or that Indians had "disappeared" as if without cause, no form of theft, guile, or violence need have been effected to enable settlement.

Many Jews viewed the land as a key to salvation. As historian Taylor Spence has argued, "being a group long disinherited from the land in Christian society, Jews understood both the acceptance and security that having a demonstrable connection [to American land] could and did afford its possessors."[15] Philanthropic organizations aimed to assimilate eastern European Jews into mainstream American culture though farming. The would-be Jewish agrarians who did, in fact, homestead brought with them some uniquely Jewish connections to nature, seeing farming not just as an opportunity for a better life—one that might include the preservation of traditional rural ways—but perhaps as a continuation of ancient Jewish connections to nature found in the Torah.[16] From the 1880s until the 1930s, Jewish philanthropists fostered Jewish immigrants' abilities to own and farm land. The Montefiore Agricultural Aid Society, the Jewish Colonization Society, and others founded agricultural colonies hoping that the land would transform Jewish minds and bodies from rootless wanderers into civic role models. Jewish civic leaders and farming boosters saw Jewish agrarianism as a means to larger goals: the Americanization of Jews and the salvation from violence through dispersal into the countryside. Baron de Hirsch, the dominant philanthropic visionary and force behind many of the Jewish colonization farming schemes, wrote that the movement's main goal was "to reawaken in the race [the] capacity and love for agriculture" that would enable Jews to become "independent, self-respecting and reliant farm owners."[17]

Using the various U.S. Homestead Acts from 1862 to 1935, the Jewish Agricultural Society's agricultural boarding school, and the *Jewish Farmer* magazine, Hirsch put into action his plan to disperse Jews onto the land and to "teach young men [to be] true tillers of the soil." In 1900, the Jewish Agricultural and Industrial Aid Society of New York relocated nearly 900 Jews to New Jersey, Pennsylvania, and New England. By 1903, more than 10,000 Jews had been settled in forty-five states as well as in Indian Territory. By 1927, the total had jumped to 80,000, a small but significant portion of the 4,228,000 Jews in the country at the time.[18] Rabbi Henry Cohen of Galveston, Texas, one of the principle architects and advocates of the Jewish immigration program known as the Galveston Movement (1907 to 1914), offered a vision of Jewish manhood that emphasized the harmony between Jewishness and Americanization.[19] Partners of this program, the American-based Baron de Hirsch Fund and the London-based Jewish Colonization Society, established the Jewish Agricultural and Industrial Aid Society (JAIAS) with the shared vision of relocating Jews away from areas of persecution onto land as productive agriculturalists. The program shuttled about 10,000 eastern European Jews through the Port of Galveston onward to western and southwestern towns and farms; it considered itself an instrument of assimilation and regeneration.[20]

In the 1890s, Rabbi Cohen wrote about the deleterious effects that Russian restrictions and acts of violence had played on the physical body of the male Jew, hoping that homesteading in the American West would change "the very physical likeness of the Jew," transforming his "unhealthy mind" and "disturbed body."[21] Cohen, like the Jewish Immigrants' Information Bureau and the Industrial Removal Office of JAIAS and other funders and boosters of the Galveston Movement, promoted physical vigor and an ideology of self-sufficiency. Key figures in the movement, including Rabbi Cohen, Israel Zangwill, David Bressler, and Morris Waldman, envisioned their immigrants as pioneers more than farmers per se, tying their rhetoric to popular notions of the rugged and self-sufficient masters of the land. "The effect of the movement," wrote Bressler, "has been to infuse something akin to the pioneer spirit into the immigrant."[22] As Bryan Edward Stone related in his history of the Jews of Texas, periodicals written by and for Jews praised the Galveston plan for its contributions to America. Oscar Leonard, an editorial writer with the *Jewish Herald*, described America's need for "the pushful [sic] energy of the Jew" in the "great regions of the South and West [where there] are many communities, and [where] more will spring up." Leonard even hinted that Texas might be a better homeland than Palestine for worldwide Jewry given its size and the fact that "the soil [in Texas] goes a begging for cultivators."[23]

Jewish farmers, small-time traders, and more ambitious land speculators were all among those first in line when the government opened up new Indian Territories for settlers. Moses Weinberger described his efforts to rush on the first train leaving Wichita, Kansas, going to the new territory on April 22, 1889. When he reached the small tent land office in Guthrie, Oklahoma, he sold bananas, lumber, and eventually liquor to settlers and Indians alike. In an interview Weinberger gave about his pioneer days thirty-eight years later, his interviewer relayed that "when the Iowa, Sac, and Fox wins were opened in September 22, 1891, Mr. Weinberger made a run on horseback and took a claim one mile southwest of Chandler. His family lived on it 14 months, while he worked in the town of Guthrie and rode out about once a week to see how they were getting along. [But] he did not 'prove up the claim,' soon he sold his improvements, relinquished his rights to the government and moved his family back to Guthrie."[24] Weinberger himself praised settlers of his own ilk and impulse. "The people who made the run to Oklahoma," he told his interviewer, were "the most ambitious type who knowing full well that they would have to put up with all kinds of hardships, looked misfortune in the face and smiled. They had confidence in themselves that they would be able to conquer."[25] They were largely successful in Americanizing Indian Territory. Leo Meyer arrived in Syre, Oklahoma, to clerk in his uncle's store next to the Cheyenne-Arapaho Reservation in 1892; he soon after was elected to the Board of Trustees and later served on the 1906 constitutional campaign act that turned "the Indian Territory" into the state of Oklahoma.[26]

Suggestions about Jewish credit and responsibility for American land acquisitions dotted the popular Jewish press throughout the nineteenth century into the early twentieth. Western Jews celebrated their acquisition of Native American land in their writing of personal, local, and western American Jewish popular history. They "won" the land upon which to settle from Native Americans despite settlers' selective and strategic conviction that the land had been unoccupied. Ascher Silberstein and Solomon Meyer leased seventeen pastures, measuring approximately 20,000 acres of land from the Kaw Reservation Indians in 1902 and an additional 45,000 acres of grazing lands from the Kiowa and Comanche Reservations in Oklahoma for at least three years.[27] Nathan Bieber, who had immigrated to the United States in 1872, earned credit as the "first white man to claim land on which the town of Bieber [California] was founded." Bieber arrived on the frontier in 1877 to manage his uncle's store. He and the other white settlers in the area surely knew of the Pit River Indians' presence, estimated at nearly five hundred in number, for the town's residents petitioned Governor William Irwin in July 1878, requesting 180 rifles and a hundred rounds of ammunitions for each rifle so that the residents could protect themselves against the Native Americans.[28] Louis Wolf, the Alsatian immigrant to Temecula, California, knew of the presence of Pit River Indians as well. Wolf bought property, eventually enough for his substantial livestock holdings, and by the mid-1870s, he owned more than two thousand acres which he eventually subdivided and sold.[29]

Wolf, Bieber, Silberstein, and others were among the non-Natives wrapped up in profiting from the commercial transformation of California lands, supported by the capital, law, and military to dislocate Native populations to make living room for white Euro-American settlers. Jewish writers eventually celebrated Wolf as the "King of Temecula."[30] Wolf served as the model for the reformer novelist and activist Helen Hunt Jackson's trading post businessman character "Jim Hartsel" in her 1884 novel *Ramona*.[31]

Jews took credit not just as the founders of small frontier towns but also as the claimers of significantly larger swaths of the American West. In acquiring Indian land, Jews not only advanced themselves economically; according to their own accounts, they helped expand and produce America itself. Jewish ambitions for expansion were articulated as great surges of forward movement for modernity and of expansion in nation-making terms. In this sense, frontier Jews were Turnerians. This was the case even before American independence. The eighteenth-century Gratz family considered its acquisition of Native American land, and its aspirations for owning even more, along these lines: "The entire virgin Ohio Valley, including the 'Indian side' north of the river, from the Ohio River to the Mississippi River . . . [including] someday the bluegrass country of Kentucky, an Indian's no-man's-land, would sprout villages, towns, and cities; so, too, the warring Shawnee and Delaware and Miami would be subdued and their forests cleared," according to one historian of the family.[32] The Gratz family envisioned modern American agricultural and urban development where only "an Indian's no-man's-land" lay. "While attempting to found western empires on both sides of the Ohio," wrote Harold Sharfman, "the Gratzes purchased 321,000 acres on the Guyandotte, Little and Big Sandy Rivers just west of the Ohio, within a strip ceded by the Six Nations."[33]

It is worth observing the seamless blending of property acquisition and the language of empire building and service to nation. Nineteenth-century Jews also acquired large tracts of land. The Posen-born immigrant to Utah, Solomon Barth, would eventually be hailed as "the Father of Apache County" by American newspapers on account of his purchase from the Indians and one-time exclusive ownership of the Grand Canyon, a massive lot of acreage, and his later service as a representative of Apache County in the territorial legislature.[34] Most of the stories about Barth circulating between 1882 and 1928 made him out to be the progenitor of the territory, emphasizing that he had once been taken captive by Indians and nearly killed, exaggerating his heroism, and carefully describing the value of the land he acquired from Indians for the nation.[35] Others, however, cast aspersions on his character, noting that he was indicted and sentenced to ten years in prison for shady finance practices in which he speculated on "Apache County Paper," county-issued promissory notes used to pay debts in lieu of cash payment when money was short.[36] Barth also possessed a sizable portion of land, some 1,200 acres, "squatter's equities and water rights," which he won in a card game with Mexican ranchers of El Bandito.[37] Obituaries marking Barth's death held him out as an honorable pioneer, a resident "in Arizona longer than any white man living," and the "moving spirit in the organization of Apache county."[38] A typical trope of western obituary writing, Barth's obituary writer turned his captivity and victimization into a heroic act of wrestling land and control away from Indians.

The case of Alaska expands the nature of the acclaim Jews thought they deserved to even greater proportions. The *Seattle Jewish Transcript* disseminated claims made by J. E. Ballaine, a one-time secretary to the State of Washington's third governor, in a public address to Seattle's B'nai B'rith. Ballaine announced "proof" that a Jewish fur trader, Jack Goldstone, deserved America's appreciation and esteem for the United States' purchase of Alaska. Ballaine's "disclosure . . . rewrites American history," Ballaine wrote in the *Jewish Criterion*.

> I have positive proof that a Jew was responsible for the most fortunate purchase ever made in American history. . . . When Alaska was a wild land inhabited only by Indians and a few Russian trappers, Goldstone, realizing the richness of the land and fearful that the Hudson Bay traders would get Alaska as British territory, he told the Schloss family in San Francisco of his dream of America buying this land at the top of the world. The Schlosses interested Senator Cole of California . . . [who] sponsored the purchase, got Secretary of State Seward interested. Before he died the Senator told me how Goldstone was really responsible for Alaska's purchase and I have seen his letters to the same effect.[39]

Louis Schloss, a Bavarian-born immigrant, married into the Gerstle and Greenberg families. Their $7.2 million sale of "Seward's Folly" was made possible by their business dealings in Russian Alaska; these families were among the chief investors who bought out the Russian American Company, which they renamed the Alaska Commercial Company. The tale shows Jews, the frontier peddlers and the wealthy and enfranchised urbanites alike, in harmonious dialogue, from frontier to metropol, Jew to Jew to Senator; with American national interest driving their actions. Whether Goldstone deserved credit for America's ownership of Alaska hardly mattered. Jewish newspapers and fraternal societies reveled in such claims of responsibility for Americanizing land on a massive scale.

Building the American Muscle Jew through Fear and Violent Encounters with Natives

Land, and access to resources and trade routes, served as both the primary cause of and site of conflict between government agencies and Native tribes, between the military and Native Americans, and between the immigrant settlers and Native people. This contest had a long and extensively bloody and violent dimension. Jews were wrapped up in the violence as perpetrators and victims. Jewish immigrants considered settlement—their efforts to make a living, to fulfill the promises of America, and to strive for a better life for their children—to be a natural, upstanding, and innocent project. Threats of Indian violence were an endemic part of life in the American West in the last decades of the nineteenth century. Jews sometimes fell victim to Indian violence, while at other times they perpetrated violence against Native Americans "heroically."

American Jewish willingness to participate in violent contest for land is most evident in the military itself, where active service was entirely voluntary. Throughout the nineteenth century, Jews volunteered at the infantry and officer levels, serving as soldiers in Indian wars. Samuel D. Solomon fought against the "Sioux, Puants, Follavoine and Sacs" in Missouri in 1813 shortly after Louis and Clark's seminal expedition from St. Louis to the Pacific Ocean invited settlement west of the midwest.[40] L. Eichbaum soldiered the infamous Trail of Tears, which removed Cherokees west of the Mississippi River in 1835, 1836, and 1837.[41] The significance of early nineteenth-century Jewish participation in military actions must not have been lost on the soldiers themselves. This was the age of militant nationalism, and Jews in western, central, and eastern Europe, as well as in Russia, performed their military duties as a sign of their devotion to the states in which they lived and their desire to be considered notable and unquestioned citizens.[42] Such was the case in America's wars too—including those fought against Indians—for the nation was secured in winning Indian land.

The Baltimore-born German Jew Leon Dyer Myer and M. Cohen, a Charleston lawyer and eventual judge, volunteered to fight in the Second Seminole War of 1836 under the left wing of General Scott's unsuccessful summer campaign; it left one hundred American soldiers dead.[43] Cohen recorded his experiences and thoughts in a journal, which he published as *Notices of Florida*, framed as a part military strategy and part frontier adventure narrative.[44] Cohen described the Seminole, a confederation of various Native American tribes and runaway Black slaves, as politically intransigent, deceitful, and violent. He emphasized the Natives' problematic and potentially threatening distance from state control, "lying so far from the eye and control of the nation with whom they are confederate, that there had been depredations and murders committed by them."[45] His diary noted detailed military action and outlined specific strategy. It also described scenes of torture, accounted for hundreds of death and "outrages," and accounted for the causes of the war. Cohen drafted his gruesome journal entries with a surprisingly chipper tone and little trace of ambivalence about the impact of the battles against Native Americans. He found numerous justifications for violence. The "murders, depredations and outrages," he ultimately judged, "illustrate the treachery of the Indian character."[46] Cohen justified the seizure of Seminole land on twin claims, that Indian "character" was anathema to white American ideals and that their occupancy of the land, some 1,200 miles

Figure 2.1. "Carl Herberg with Jicarilla Apaches with Guns." Collection no. MS 0241, New Mexico State University Library, Archives and Special Collections, image 02410094.

of shoreline in his reckoning, rendered it underproductive. Cohen tied the measure of land's worth and people's worth to their ability to harness profit from it. The land's productivity and the inhabitants of it were twinned, suggesting that the entire imperial and expansion enterprise was deigned to advance capital growth. As for the Native peoples themselves, their "idle, vicious habits," he wrote, "presented an insuperable obstacle to the cultivation of the soil."[47] Cohen volunteered to participate in the state's application of force to win territory that might be put to commercial use, for failing to launch an imperial assault was, in Cohen's view, "too absurd to merit one moment's consideration."

Though a diary, Cohen's *Notices of Florida* was written with the intent to publish. It was composed with an audience of military and political elites in mind. It employed an authoritative tone, at times ethnographic, at times military, that presented its author in a certain light. Like all published memoirs or journals, it was self-fashioning and self-serving and ought to be understood in biographical context. *Notices* was conceived of as part of Cohen's efforts to fulfill ambitions for political office, as was his short stint as an officer with the South Carolina volunteer campaign. As an aspiring politician, his book showed him off to be an ideal patriot, volunteering to fight back the uncivil forces that threatened the expansion of the south, and as a leader with the capacities for the historical, ethnographic, and tactical. His work boosted his renown and, subsequently, his career. (Following the war, the state removed Choctaw, Yamasee, and Yuchi peoples to reservations.) Cohen served in the South Carolina state legislature as an independent Republican, a member of the admiralty court, a professor of law at Straight University in New Orleans, and eventually, as a probate judge. The book was widely read and served to deepen its readers' conceptions of the Seminole they battled as unworthy opponents undeserved of land. It also presented Cohen himself and his fellow soldiers as heroic agents of state building "martyrs in their country's cause" and justifying the capture of land.[48]

Land conquest and violent suppression of Indians occurred not only in Florida, of course, nor did it stop in the 1830s. The Indian Removal Act of 1830 relocated more Seminole Indians, as well as Cherokee, Muscogee (Creek), Chickasaw, and Choctaw nations from their homelands east of what is now Oklahoma to Indian Territory in order to secure more land for settlement. Jewish combatants in these military campaigns against Native tribes held similar attitudes toward Native people as had Myer Cohen, depicting Native Americans as uncivil and undeserved of the land upon which they lived. David Spangler Kaufman, Pennsylvania-born lawyer and later the first Jewish congressman in Texas, participated in military campaigns against the Cherokee and was wounded in an 1839 battle. His obituaries referred to him as an Indian fighter as well as a lawyer and politician.[49] Frank Dresser gave testimony to the House of Representatives on Indian Affairs about Ute "incivility" in Colorado after an "outbreak" in 1880.[50] Max Littmann, a Berlin-born immigrant, enlisted in the U.S. army within weeks after his arrival in New York in 1866 and soon helped build and garrison forts along the Bozeman Trail, a route that branched off the Oregon Trail and ran though Wyoming into Montana. The trail enabled commercial traffic to flow and mining camps to flourish after discovery of gold there in 1862; the battle clearly connected to the value of resource extraction there.[51] Littmann became known as the hero of the "Wagon Box Fight" of 1867 in which twenty-six soldiers and six civilians reputedly withstood an attack by a thousand Sioux and Cheyenne in a wagon circle. One later account of the battle described that Littmann had "dropped on one knee about 100 yards from the main corral [and had] opened a rapid fire on the advancing hordes of savages. Several fell from their ponies under his accurate fire. This man proved to be one of our sergeants, Littleman [sic] by name, who, by his courage and thoughtfulness in coming out to meet us, and the rapidity and effectiveness of his fire, saved us from being surrounded and cut off by the red devils."[52]

Narratives of individual Jewish war-gallantry fit into a larger, more political defense that Jews mounted for themselves against attacks that they failed to meet a sufficient masculinity quotient. This anxiety plagued Jews throughout European modernity.[53] After the *North American Review* printed J. M. Rogers's 1891 complaint that he could "not remember meeting one Jew in uniform or hearing of any Jewish soldier," Simon Wolf, a Bavarian-born immigrant jurist, publicist, and philanthropist, published a detailed rebuttal in the *Washington Post*. Wolf produced an annotated list of dozens of Jewish soldiers who fought throughout the Indian Wars. He included Hermann Bendell, a lieutenant colonel and one-time superintendent of Indian affairs for Arizona Territory, Edward Woog, Morris Lewis, and dozens of other "valiant and brave" Jewish "fellow-citizens."[54] Wolf also supplied a list of Jews who fought in the Revolutionary War, the Mexican War, and the Civil War. These wars, along with Indian wars, all represented

Figure 2.2. Max Littmann: Jewish soldier of the Wagon Box Fight. "Good Marksmanship and Guts DA Poster 21-45." Painting by H. Charles McBarron Jr. of the Ninth Infantry of the U.S. Army battling a band of Sioux Native Americans near Fort Philip Kearny, Wyoming, August 2, 1867. Department of the Army, U.S. Army in Action. https://commons.wikimedia.org/wiki/File:Good_Marksmanship_and_Guts._DA_Poster_21-45.jpg.

nation-making violence. Wolf's apology linked Jewish bravery and valiancy together with claims for equality among citizens. Indeed, not a few Jews felt the need to prove Jews' brawn, their sufficient masculinity, as well as their willingness to sacrifice, as other citizens would and did, for the nation's acquisition of new lands.

The writing and remembering of violent encounters between Jews and Native Americans exhibited ways that Jews, as citizens, conceived of themselves as more entitled to land than the noncitizen wards of the State. Isaac Goldberg's 1894 reminiscences included his retelling of his movement from a mining camp called Weaver's Diggings, established in 1864 near La Paz, Arizona, to Prescott, when he met Colonel Woolsey "with 50 volunteers—all brave citizens—returning from the slaughter of a band of Apaches." During "the wholesale slaughter of their dusky guests," Goldberg wrote, "each man accordingly 'took his Indian,' and made him everlastingly 'good.' . . . This terrible affair is known as 'Col. Woolsey's pinole treaty,' and resulted . . . in the slaughter of the whole of the Indians present, with the loss of but one settler's life."[55] Referencing the racist idiom, *the only good Indian is a dead Indian*, Goldberg relayed the "wholesale slaughter of their dusky guests" with pride that they lost "but one settler's life" and their subsequent plunder. The event left some sixty-three Native Americans and nine white soldiers dead. "A great deal of valuable property, consisting chiefly of buckskins, guns, lances, and mescal was secured by the victors," he added.[56]

Similarly, Henry Lesinsky, a Prussia-born copper mine speculator in Arizona and New Mexico and "a self-educated, highly intelligent, sensitive freethinker and cultivated man," according to Jacob Rader Marcus, told stories of fighting off Indians, whom he conceived to be impediments to his acquisition of the land's resources.[57] Lesinsky worked closely with the Freudenthal family. They employed some six hundred men and opened the first large-scale mining operations in Arizona Territory, which they called "Longfellow" and sold for $1.2 million in 1882.[58] Writing to his son several years later, Lesinsky recalled that he, like the other miners, "soon forgot Indians and danger, living only in the golden promise of the future."[59] Like Goldberg and many other Jewish settlers, Lesinsky looked to "living only in the golden promise of the future" from the shadows of fear that Indians might thwart their migrant dreams, the promises for which they left their homes to seize in the American West. "I could lead you back to the earlier days in New Mexico," Lesinsky wrote to his son, "to the time when the Indians prowled about the settlements, killing everything they could. I could show you the ghastly bleeding men I found killed a few hours before I reached the place where this befell. I could point out the many narrow and almost miraculous escapes I had from the unseen bloodhounds, the Apache Indians."[60] Lesinsky's vision of the good life and the Native Americans who stood in its way was typical.

Jewish newspapers from across the country published frequent stories of both horrifying and glorifying violence. Descriptions of perpetrators of violence, or mentions of them as accolades in the obituaries of Jewish pioneers, are strewn across the American Jewish archival landscape. Newsprint accounts of the Jewish western experience accentuated migrants' fears of Indian violence too. The year 1883, in the wake of the Lordsburg Road massacre of a judge and his wife in New Mexico Territory, stood out—even in the Jewish press far from the Southwest.[61] One *Boston Hebrew Observer* article condemned the Department of the Interior for the "non-suppression of the Apaches," criticizing the federal government as weak and motivated "simply and absolutely [by] fear."[62] The Indians deserved this fear, the paper implied, adding in a curious mix of race analogy—"these American Arabs are the finest fighters the world ever saw"—and describing their numerous successes against both American and Mexican forces. Another article described the "big premium [put] on dead Indians,"[63] while a third that same spring warned of "Canadian Indians on the Warpath," stoking fear that Indian violence would spread far from the "troubles" in New Mexico Territory.[64] Cleveland's *Jewish Review* reprinted articles about Indian "depredations" like its 1898 "Massacre of Cawnpore: Scene of the Indian Mutiny After that Awful Event." "The whole story was so unspeakably horrible," journalist J. W. Sherer wrote, "that it would be quite wrong in any sort of way to [exaggerate] the distressing circumstances which really existed [on the frontier]."[65] Jewish immigrants picked up on this aggressive, patriotic sensibility with particular sensitivity, given that the places from which they had come in eastern Europe and the Russian empire were experiencing anti-Jewish violence contemporaneously and reporting it consistently in the press and in letters to and fro. Whereas in Europe, citizens of modern nation states perpetrated violence against Jews, in America, the state protected its Jews and promised a great future; Native peoples were impediments to the good life.

Violence did, of course, threaten settlement; but the stories of threat and violence played a subtle but significant role in the making of frontier Jewish identity, for it encouraged Jews to identify with whites over and against Indian outsiders. Late nineteenth-century Jews told stories about contemporary Jewish victims of Indian violence as well as stories about Jews who perpetrated violence against Indians in the fight for land.[66] Furthermore, Jewish writers from the turn of the century told stories that described Jews' roles as fighters against Indians throughout American history, stretching their claims for heroism and martyrdom back to the Indian Wars of the eighteenth century. Turn-of-the-century writers retrojected Jewish militant heroism back onto a century of prior battles with Indians, aiming to ensure their own place as muscular contributors.[67] *Jewish Encyclopedia* entries from the first decade of the twentieth century, like Cyrus Adler's on "Francis Salvador," described the heroic deaths of Jewish soldiers during British-American-Indian skirmishes,[68] while subsequent Jewish popular histories periodically lauded Salvador, the South Carolinian "martyr" of the American Revolution, as they did the exploits and expeditions against Indians of other Jewish soldiers, sutlers, and victims of so-called Indian "depredations," like South Carolinian officer Joseph Levy; the decorated soldier of the French and Indians wars, Alexander Schomberg; sutlers Chapman Abraham, Gershon Levy, Ezekiel Solomon, his son William, Benjamin Lyon along the St. Lawrence River, or Isaac Levy and Sergeant Simon Magruder Levy in the Ohio Valley.[69] Simon Wolf's famous defense, *The American Jew as Patriot, Soldier and Citizen* of 1895, listed several Jews who gave their lives for the republic by battling Indians, including one Captain E. Ullman, who was "one of those in the command of General Custer on that fatal day in June [1876]; in which the entire command was surrounded by the Indians, every man being slaughtered."[70]

These descriptions of heroic Jews by Jewish writers echoed the official governmental accounts aimed at recognizing and recording the efforts of its citizens' heroism, including the heroism of Jewish soldiers, like Captain Henry A. Greene of the First Infantry, California volunteers, or Captain E. H. Bergmann of Company 1 of the First New Mexico Volunteers in the 1860s.[71] The Bavarian-born Simon Suhler received a Medal of Honor for his "bravery, in scouts and actions" for his involvement in the 1868 campaign against the Apache in Arizona, where he fought under the name Charles Gardner.[72] George Geiger also received a Medal of Honor for his role as a sergeant in Company H of the Seventh U.S. Cavalry when it fought the Lakota, Northern Cheyenne, and Arapaho tribes at the infamous Battle of the Little Bighorn in Montana in 1876.[73] Max Jacobson served with U.S. Cavalry Fourth Regiment, Troop 1, during Indian wars, involved in the 1886 surrender of Apache chief Geronimo. Oscar Pollak lost his life at the Pine Ridge Indian Reservation when Lieutenant Colonel George Custer and his detachment were killed in 1890 at the infamous Battle of the Little Bighorn.[74]

Fear of violent encounters with Native Americans, as well as actual violent episodes, featured regularly and predictably during the early years of settlement in western frontiers and towns. New settlement on the land had produced antagonism between settlers and Native Americans. Jewish memoirs and popular literature announced these fears and modeled them as reasonable ones to have. Promotional literature designed to draw immigrants to new settler territory regularly allayed these fears by describing the land as already free of potentially dangerous Indians. One German language circular distributed by the State Immigration Office of St. Pierre, South Dakota, promoting migration there called it "the richest cornchamber of the world. A country full of sunshine, healthy climate. Happy People. Its fertile fields, prospering cities and growing industry invite you and offer you a golden opportunity of existence," noting that the town site of Mitchell on the newly finished Chicago, Milwaukee, and St. Paul Railroad Line was no longer the home of the Aricara and Sioux Indians, though they had once "lived their wild life in the neighbourhood."[75] These announcements from Jewish and non-Jewish presses across the American West, those from larger cities in the east, those for exclusively Jewish readerships, those in Yiddish or German, were not just offering warnings or cautionary tales. They created a mythology of the west that repelled some and attracted others. There was a price to pay, this discourse suggested, for the risk of wealth, public service, and the emboldening frontier experience of citizen shaping. The language of spirit and risk, venture and adventure, loomed large in the broader popular imagination that captured something of turn of the century ideals of masculinity.

Local peddling and settler Jews likely heard of the killings of Jewish western settlers including Special Agent Stein in 1854, or M. Schneider, A. Schneider, and Johann Schwartz in 1862 by Minnesota Indians, or of the murdered Weisman children in the Dakota Territory.[76] They also knew of the Arizona Wickenburg Massacre of November 1873, where Yavapai Indians from the Date Creek Reservation attacked a stagecoach, killing almost all the passengers, for the signatories of the coroner's report included two Jews, Aaron Barnett and Julius A. Goldwater.[77] The incident led to the removal of the entire Yavapai tribe 180 miles to the San Carlos Reservation.[78]

Fear of Indian attack accompanied Jewish settlers, travelers, and workers alike in Arizona, New Mexico, Nebraska, Dakota, Colorado, Alaska, Texas, and most other states where settlers and Native Americans competed for land or for the control of thruways through the land. Commercial business and early settlement required state or ad hoc protection. In 1867 Omaha, Andrew Rosewater conducted surveys to determine the location for the Union Pacific tracks, "accompanied by a military escort for protection against the Indians."[79] During the Civil War years, the Prussian-born immigrant Henry Heppner saw his twenty-nine-mule pack train carrying freight from his mining operations in Idaho attacked by Indians. Rosa Katzenstein Drachman described "passing many graves of poor people who had been murdered by the Indians" when she travelled by stage from San Bernardino to Tucson in 1868.[80] After the war ended, one freed slave described being run out of Tahlequah, Oklahoma, only to be caught and taken to Old Mexico, where he was sold to a unnamed Jew, only to be "attacked by wild Indians several times, some of them were killed. . . . There were five or six different ones in the party killed by the wild Indians while they were out scouting for wood at night,"[81] according to an interview given by his son, Burl Taylor, in 1937 as part of the Indian-Pioneer Papers oral history collection.

Dozens if not hundreds of similar stories of Jewish men, mostly peddlers and small-scale entrepreneurs, who were wounded or lost their lives in attacks or counterattacks by Native Americans pepper American Jewish history texts. Harris Levi, a peddler among the homesteaders and Indians around Cedar Creek, Oklahoma, was killed by Indians in 1869.[82] The *Jewish Review* described "renegade Apaches" who "robbed the United States Troopers who were pursuing them."[83] If the Indians could mock, steal from, and endure the force meant to neutralize them, the matter warranted concern. Indian insubordination threatened to undermine Jews' efforts to feel settled on the land. Indeed, Jewish newspapers' frequent reporting of Indian violence or its potential suggested that a steady fear of Indian violence loomed over new towns, settlements, trading posts, and perhaps most especially the intermediary paths where Jews most frequently did their business.

Conflict between Indigenous People and Jewish settlers was sharper precisely because Jewish settlers were involved in an extractive economy on the periphery, transporting skins, beef, other natural resources from the land toward metropolitan markets as well as a settlement that aimed for permanent presence on the land itself. Trade between settlers and Native peoples interfered with Indigenous subsistence patterns. Economic exchange of "extractive" products went hand in hand with a broader wrestling over land ownership itself. Where settlement meant taking land, violence inevitably ensued. This kind of violence was central to the frontier experience. As historians William Cronin, George Miles, and Jay Gitlin described it, the greatest threat of violence was a subtler "but ultimately more powerful cultural invasion [that] continued the work of those who wielded the weapons. Lands taking blended imperceptibly into the . . . frontier process [of] boundary settling, the very essence of frontier life." As settlers built houses, raised children, and invested labor in their dreams on the land, the more they felt they belonged to the land and it to them; they no longer perceived themselves as "invaders." They killed and were killed in a battle to preserve their homes and livelihoods. They shed the blood that created "sacred ground" and an entitlement to belong on the land itself. The performance of violence produced what they called an "almost religious authority to their claims of ownership."[84]

The violence that Jewish soldiers committed against Native peoples was sanctioned and funded by the state. For their part, Jews publicized and celebrated the acknowledgement they received as participants in violence they committed against Natives, believing it nation-making action. But Jews also committed unsanctioned vigilante violence in order to win land or control over its resources and routes for trading from Native Americans. In frontier zones that lacked a military or police presence, Jews, along with other settlers, hoped to send stern messages to Native people that territory and access to its resources belonged to whites. With and without official state sanction, frontier Jews alongside other frontier whites deployed violence against Native Americans in efforts to put down potential "insurrections" in retributive acts of revenge and in bald displays of intimidation through violence. Louis Rose, born Louis Leffman in Neuhuas-an-der-Oste in northern Germany, a migrant to New Orleans and eventually the first Jew to settle in San Diego in 1850, volunteered in a mobilization against the "Indian insurrectionist" Antonio Garra,[85] the Mexican leader who led a band of Cupeño and Yuman raiders, killing five white American settlers in 1851. Morris Moss, a fur trader who worked the Pacific Northwest Coast, was part of a punitive expedition that brought "several Indians to justice" after the Bute Inlet road-building massacre in 1864 near Bella Coola.[86]

Settlers tended to celebrate these acts of vigilantism and considered them evidence of their ability to uphold and promote civil morality outside the courts.

In 1893, *Current Literature* ran an account of "a Hebrew Jew," Henry Abraham, who along with a group of Colfax County, New Mexican Church-goers, lynched "a half Injun an' the rest Mexican [Navajo Frank]." The journal praised Abraham and his "whole lot of public spirit" for hanging Navajo Frank "up by the neck."[87] The lynching of Indians like "Navajo Frank" appealed to whites, Jews among them, in areas where due legal process had not yet been enshrined or was thought inadequate by town and rural settlers. Acts of violence perpetrated by settlers that were not sanctioned by a chain of military command were rarely scrutinized by the military itself or by local courts. Acts of uncalibrated violence were seldom punished. The state, represented of course by local white settlers, shared the same ambition for Native pacification and land. In 1854, the *Los Angeles Star* reported news that a Jewish shopkeeper named Caspar Berhrendt chased after a "gang of Indians" who had reportedly stolen blankets from his shop. Berhrendt "started in pursuit, and finding himself unable to secure the thief, he drew a small five-shooter which he had and fired. The Indian ran a few steps and fell." With the Indian wounded, Berhrendt "delivered himself up immediately for examination to Justice Eaton, who, after a thorough investigation of the matter, discharged him, the evidence justifying the assault."[88] The theft of blankets justified gun violence.[89] Descriptions of these sorts of events betrayed something critical about frontier racial construction and the basic terms of criminality. Local courts were biased against Native Americans, whom they assumed fell outside the umbrella of the courts' protections. The private property rights of white settlers were enshrined as more valuable than Native life.

The imbalance of courts' considerations and the broader local culture that buoyed such courts' biases regarding the justification of violence against Native peoples is amply evidenced with a story from the life of the prominent businessman and developer of Arizona, William Zeckendorf. The German-born Tucson merchant had some military experience both in the Union army and against Apaches. He became a member of the Eight Territorial Legislature of Arizona Territory in 1875 and was a charter member of the Jewish Community Association.[90] The *Weekly Arizonan* likewise cast Zeckendorf "in the role of a warrior," absolving him of any criminality in his perpetration of violence against Indians.[91]

Zeckendorf came to New Mexico via New York from Hemmendorf, Germany, in 1856 to join his older brothers, who had begun building a local trade empire built on government supply contracts, mail routes, and mining and land development between Tucson, Arizona, and Albuquerque. The paper told of Zeckendorf, along with "ten Mexicans," who rode in pursuit of a band of Apache who had made off with a farmer's grazing herd. "Despite his efforts to escape into the mountains," it added, "this wild savage was quickly surrounded by Mr. Zeckendorf and three of his Mexican companions . . . the thieving red was forced to submit, and did not condescent [sic] to stretch himself at ease until after his chest had been traversed by sixteen bullets."[92] After shooting one Apache dead, Zeckendorf, "feeling somewhat exasperated by the ignoble means by which the Indian sought to take his life—by a rock—could not suffer that Apache to lie there intact so he just scalped him and returned to town on Tuesday evening with the trophy swinging at his girdle. It is needless to state that Z. does not belong to the Society of 'Friends' [Quakers]; still we admire the friendly manner in which he helped this Indian into eternity."[93]

The paper's apparent praise of Zeckendorf's violent, extrajudicial initiative reveals something of settlers' senses of justice, their justifications for violence against Indians, and a modicum of Jewish pride the newspaper authors could take in resisting the stereotype of Jews as meek and law-abiding. Scalping was, of course, conceived of as the quintessential act of "Indian savagery," of evidence of Native incivility. This violence was narrated with a measure of hard-boiled sarcasm visible in the language of "friendly help" that the Jew provided for the man's eternal afterlife. The idea that policing, justice, and good governance had to catch up to the immediacies of frontier life, which required quick resolve and unaffected confidence in the gun, certainly had popular purchase in the last quarter of the nineteenth century. Frontier whites resorted to violence then, not just in order to secure property rights but as acts conceived as establishing rule of civic society. Successful entrepreneurial Jews like Zeckendorf had substantial interest invested in insisting that the state ensure safety. Smaller-scale peddling Jews depended on the policing and security efforts of settlers, with or without the help of the state, even more than their wealthier co-religionists. They risked their lives in their itinerant efforts for sustenance and modest gain.

Western Jews knew of the broader context for the white-Indian warfare as a competition over land. When the government neglected or refused to act as an insurance firm, settlers appealed to the federal government by perpetrating violence, hoping to force its hand to intercede on their behalf, securing land and property rights. Isaac Goldberg described "mass meetings [that] were held at the courthouse, and resolutions [that] passed to the effect that the whole of the people of the nation should be made acquainted with the actual conditions of affairs in Arizona"—namely, the extent of "hostile practices" of the Indians.[94] The form of Goldberg's and his Camp Grant neighbors' publicity efforts remain unclear, but his interpretation of the etiology of and responsibility for the problem he and his fellows faced was not; it rested on the state. Goldberg continued, "nothing of consequence [has] resulted [from these efforts], chiefly owing to the apathy of the General Government, which, instead of protecting its much-harassed citizens, extended almost every possible description of assistance to their implacable enemies—the sanguinary Apaches."

Having decided that the government allied itself with the settlers' enemies over themselves, Goldberg and his fellows took it upon themselves to enact justice without state approval. He described the events that followed: "Another mass meeting was held at the same place—five or six of the bravest citizens calling and conducting it—and, as the result, a very large body of loyal Papago Indians, accompanied by about fifty Mexicans, were led by their white commanders to Arequipa Canyon, where nearly five hundred Apaches were found encamped, and mercilessly slain."[95] "Then and not until then," wrote Goldberg, likely exaggerating the number of Apaches murdered (144 Apache Indians were killed at Camp Grant in April 1871), "did 'Uncle Sam' realize that it was his bounden duty to prefer the claims of his suffering children to those of their savage tormentors, and hasten to make amends for his reprehensible neglect in the much-troubled past." Goldberg concluded his memoir by congratulating himself and his fellow migrant settlers for their bravery, their sacrifice, and their agency in the "irrepressible advances of conquering civilization."[96] Like Goldberg, Tucson whites promoted their own skill and bravery in helping civilize the frontier and remembered the violence they perpetrated only as a reminder of the privations they endured.[97]

Western Jews saw acts of vigilantism as promoting justice and restoring fairness to the lawless West rather than as acts of aggression or even as perpetuations in a war of attrition between settlers and Native Americans. Commercial losses played a significant role in motivating these frustrations since warfare threatened settlers' commercial security and violated what settlers considered their property rights. Incurring attacks by Native Americans, Jews filed depredation claims to agents, superintendents, and commissioners of Indian affairs' courts claims for revenue and resources lost to Indian attackers for at least three decades at the end of the nineteenth century. Settlers placed the responsibility for these revenue losses on the state since, as petition letters regularly read, the "United States has supervisory charge of the [given] tribe of Indians." Sara Goldbaum filed four Indian depredation claims to the federal government between 1867 and 1887 for $22,985 in Indian-theft cattle, after Apaches killed and scalped her husband, Marcus Goldbaum, in the Whetstone Mountains, southeast of Tucson, in 1886. One of her seven children, Emilio Goldbaum, a miner, was chased and shot at by four Apaches only eleven days after his father's death, an event he described in an *Arizona Star* article that also announced Goldbaum's plan to lead a search party to find and, presumably, take revenge against the attackers.[98] Lehman Spiegelman, Nathan Bibo, and Solomon Bibo all likewise filed depredation claims with the commissioner of Indian affairs from New Mexico in 1886,[99] as did Herman Levi, Jacob Levi Sr., and Jacob Levi Jr., for merchandise stolen from their company store in Graham County, Arizona, in 1891.[100] The state offered a vehicle to compensate settlers for financial losses at the hands of Indian "raiders." Native Americans were considered state wards, fundamentally different from any other persons in the West who might have engaged in commercial transaction or theft. The state would not offer recompense for the loss of goods or earnings stolen by fellow settlers. Jewish immigrants understood that the state assumed Indians interrupted fair commercial enterprise. Jewish immigrants and the state itself thus saw compensation for financial loss as a way of restoring justice to settlement interrupted by those who, by definition, were excluded from state-making action.

Frontier violence between the state, settlers, and Native Americans seemed so endemic that some Jews could go so far as to articulate a quotidian attitude that they, not alone among whites, apparently took toward incidents of Indian violence. Isadore Straussburger, for example, saw the hanging of one Native American as a "trifle" and called another series of planned lynchings of Native Americans in Colorado in 1860 a "hanging bee." In his reminiscences, Straussburger recalled an episode of an Indian man who stole gloves and an ax from his store. Settlers later lynched the man, Straussburger continued: "A few months later he went 'where good Injuns go,' to the happy hunting ground, by way of the rope. There were considerable hanging bees in early times, but as I had witnessed such trifles in '59 and '60 in Denver, it did not amuse me any more."[101] At some point in his life before they became trivial matters, presumably these lynching bees had stirred and "amused" him. Straussburger might have been referring to the work of a voluntary vigilante organization, "formed to suppress lawlessness in Virginia City," that had reputedly hanged "the bandit" some years earlier. Some settlers, in other words, clearly reckoned Native Americans as less than fully human, their lives of less worth than whites.[102]

But acts of violence were not merely dismissed as a pedestrian part of settlements' everyday life; enacting violence was part of the Jewish claim to respect and honor. In fighting Indians, Jews "proved their worth" in the national project as citizens of valor, as one *Jewish Criterion* article put it.[103] The Indianapolis *B'nai B'rith Bulletin* proudly publicized to its Jewish readers that the U.S. government recognized Sigmund Shlesinger's "heroism by a special act of Congress granting him a pension" for his services as an eighteen-year-old volunteer scout in the 1868 battle at Beecher Island, Kansas. Shlesinger and fifty other scouts defended themselves against a reputed thousand Indians' nine-day offensive. A poem about Shlesinger emphasized "the little Jew's" presence, his bravery, and his heeding the call for national duty.

When the foe charged the breast-works
  With the madness of despair.
And the bravest souls were tested,
  The little Jew was there.

When the weary dozed on duty,
  Or the wounded needed care.
When another shot was called for,
  The little Jew was there.

With the festering dead around them,
  Shedding poison in the air,
When the crippled chieftain ordered,
  The little Jew was there.[104]

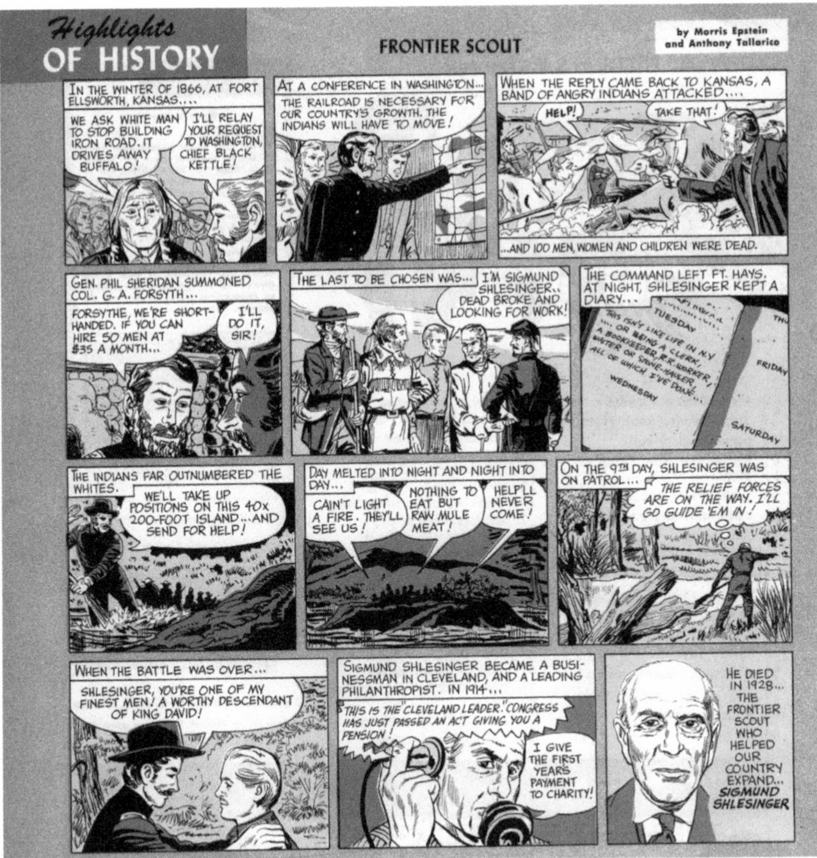

Figure 2.3. Sigmund Shlesinger, "Frontier Scout," "Highlights of History" comic strip. Board of Jewish Education of Greater New York, American Jewish Archives, MS-130, box 1, folder 3.

The Beecher Island battle became a touchstone for subsequent writers of early Kansas Jewish history, as it offered a narrative of local grounding that could unambiguously emphasize valor, triumph, and the sacrificial effort that was required to achieve communal birth. Eleanore Stearns Venter produced a poem for young Kansas Jewish readers devoted to lauding one of the cavalrymen's horses.[105] A comic-strip page from a series of "Highlights of History" pocket-sized, hardcover comic books for young readers featured Shlesinger as its central hero, the "Frontier Scout." The comic depicted Colonel G. A. Forsyth gripping the young Sigmund's shoulders, telling him, "You're one of my finest men! A worthy descendant of King David!," evoking Jewish national might and transforming him from the "little Jew" to a top soldier, a man of spiritual and imperial might.[106] In this rendition, Schlesinger helped found his own empire.

Figure 2.4. Frederic Remington, "Battle of Beecher's Island." Also known as the Battle of Arikaree Fork, the armed conflict pitted several Plains Tribes against the U.S. Army in the fall of 1868. Sigmund Shlesinger was among the dead. 1871/1909, watercolor on paper. The Museum of Fine Arts, Houston, the Hogg Brothers Collection, gift of Miss Ima Hogg. https://commons.wikimedia.org/wiki/File:Frederic_Remington_-_Battle_of_Beecher%27s_Island_-_Google_Art_Project.jpg.

Immigrant, Soldier, Speculator, State Father

Perhaps the case of Otto Mears best illustrates the ways that fear, bravery, masculinity, patriotism, and land acquisition intersected for Jewish land speculators, merchants, or entrepreneurs in the West—the Jews who were more likely to perpetrate anti-Indian violence than their sedentary farmer counterpart. Both his actions and the ways they were subsequently memorialized reveal the ways that this purposeful violence was imbued with communitarian values. Mears earned an "honored [place] within [Colorado's] borders," according to an author of early Colorado history in 1919, "because of the important part which he has played in its development . . . a most active factor in the development and up-building of the state."[107] Indians formed a fundamental part of his story as a "founding father," "civilizer," and "path-breaker" of Colorado, for in addition to his commercial successes, Mears "helped break the Navajo resistance."[108] Furthermore, he "assisted in the rescue" of captives of the Meeker Massacre, bringing several of them to Washington for their imprisonment. Most significantly, he convinced Chief Ouray and his Ute Indians to cede millions of acres of land for commercial settlement. Mears' status as a state "father"—a metaphoric progenitor of all future descendants of non-Native Coloradans—rested on his role in Colorado's founding myths, which traded on Indian resistance to land acquisition and the expansion of commerce. Mears pacified violent Indians, brought them to justice, and removed them from settlement's reach. This process freed up Indian land for white settler's commercial "up-building."

Mears' story offers one particularly well-documented case of a Jew's acquisition of Indian land and the ways the Jewish record understood this acquisition as a valuable contribution to closing the frontier and forging the nation. Mears left Kurland (Kurzeme), Russia, in 1852 at age twelve, moved through Germany to New York, and sometime after, moved to the West in search of opportunity. In 1861, he joined Company H of the First Regiment of California Volunteers. Like other Jews who enlisted, Mears saw gaining military experience as an available route to legitimation and elevated citizenship and as a mechanism to facilitate future financial growth and political enfranchisement. He served for three years under Kit Carson fighting against the Navajos in New Mexico. After his discharge, he worked as a clerk for the German Jewish merchant firms of the Staab Brothers and Elsbert & Amberg in New Mexico and Arizona. Like most other German Jewish immigrants in the frontier West, he was not a lone actor but rather a man networked by religious, linguistic, and filial connections that revolved around his German Jewishness. He opened his own trading post in Conejos, Colorado, and parlayed success upon success as a merchandiser, farmer, land speculator, road and railway builder, and eventually developer.

The state hired Mears as an interpreter in 1873 to work on failing negotiations between Ouray, the chief of the Ute, and Felix Brunot, chairman of the Board of Indians Commissioners, in its effort to secure Ute land in seven contiguous counties. Meeting Chief Ouray at the Uncompahgre Agency, Mears proposed that Ouray be offered a cash settlement as "salary" (a bribe or a payment, depending on its interpreter), but Brunot reportedly refused initially. Some debate throughout the historical record leaves several ambiguities about how, exactly, a deal came to be brokered, but Brunot eventually offered the Ute one million dollars (plus a salary for Ouray), and Ouray signed a treaty ceding the land, relinquishing Ute claims on the counties. Mears had served as an interpreter and broker; his linguistic capacities, it appears, helped him gain a modicum of Ute trust.

After the government took ownership over the land, Mears built toll roads through the Arkansas Valley and to the San Juan, established mining interests, and secured lucrative mail carrier contracts to supply settlers with tobacco, coffee, sugar, and other dry goods and foodstuffs. He gained control over the routes, charging fees for cargo, private roads, and control over the flow of resources. He also started a newspaper in 1872 at Saguache to promote the San Luis Valley for settlement.[109] With his considerable resources in the mid-1870s, Mears began planning the building of the Rio Grande Southern Railroad.[110] His ambition was to link up the resources of the mountain west with markets on both coasts. The *Saguache Chronicle*, the *Colorado Springs Gazette*, and the *El Paso County News* all printed approving editorials. The land grab was almost immediately justified in the language of productivity. Within months of the signing of the deed transfer,

Figure 2.5. Otto Mears, Chipeta, Ouray, Piah. Studio portrait (sitting and standing) of Ute Native American and white men and women in Washington, DC, for the Brunot Treaty signing. The Denver Public Library, Western History Collection X-19251. C Photo Collection 254. W. G. Chamberlain Photograph Collection.

local newspapers wrote covetously of further neighboring land still owned by Native Americans. Networking newly acquired lands was key for commercial development—the basic ambition for acquisition was to pull together regions and routes. Papers editorialized, for instance, that it "is the favorite ground of the Utes, and would, if occupied by the whites become one of the richest and most productive grain and fruit growing countries in the West, [while] now is only a broad beautiful, expanse of meadow land, over which the Utes hold unquestioned control."[111] Mears and his fellow white settlers had wrestled control away from "the painted red wards of Uncle Sam [who] guard every acre with a jealous eye." The frontier papers justified the capture of this land in terms of its utility, its ability to generate revenue for the new state of Colorado. The land could not only be made productive and profitable, they further argued; leaving the land in Ute hands would actually cost the public. Not only did "all of the [Ute] territory bring no revenue to the government," they reasoned, "on the contrary, the natives are supported at a great expense. The same land thrown open to settlement would support many rich and prosperous communities that would return to the national government."[112] Mears had begun as a mere interpreter but had become a leader in the effort to settle and commercialize Native American land.

This was not just a war of rhetoric, of course. The stakes were high. Indeed, hostilities erupted in the fall of 1879, when Utes at the White River Agency killed Nathan C. Meeker and eight Indian subagents or employees, including, incidentally, at least one Jew, Carl Goldstein. Several white settlers were taken into captivity. The local Indian agent asked Mears to intervene and serve as a negotiator to secure the release of the captives. The agency presented another treaty; Ouray died in August 1880 without signing it. The state's goal was to open land for settlement through treaty acquisitions and to legally extinguish Native titles to the land. But it also saw its role as the paternalistic protector of its "wards" and, as such, aimed to protect Natives from exploitation of private interests. During this time, Mears reputedly "privately circulated among [the Utes], giving each $2 in silver [as an inducement] to sign. They did so, and the story leaked out. G.W. Moneypenny, another member of the Indian Commission, claimed that Mears had bribed the Ute, and preferred charges against him before the Secretary of the Interior, Carl Schurz." Mears was brought up on charges and was ordered to Washington to stand trial. At his trial, Secretary of the Interior Samuel Kirkwood, under President James Garfield, asked Mears if he had paid the Indians to sign the treaty. "'Yes, Mr. Secretary,' was the reply, 'the Indians claimed $2 in cash was worth more to them than the interest on $1,800,000, which they were to receive in promises." Government officials reimbursed Mears and exonerated him of bribery charges; so far as the Ministry of the Interior was concerned, he had secured land legally. In the wake of the Meeker Massacre, popular sentiment in Colorado supported the forced removal of the remaining Utes. Mears himself was even involved in the effort to find "suitable reservation lands" for the Ute along the Green River at the present site of the Uinta Reservation in Utah and helped build the infrastructure for a new Indian Agency there. He was, in short, an active participant in almost every stage of the forced removal of the Utes, the dispossession of their lands, and their subsequent containment.

Celebrations of Mears' contributions, both as a businessman and as a pacifier of Indians, would be frequently repeated in the popular press and in local history works after his death. In particular, Jewish journalists and narrators of the Jewish western experience in the last decades of the nineteenth century through the 1930s celebrated Mears' triumph over Indians and the acquisition of their land as a means of emphasizing Jewish belonging in both the physical, geographic landscape as well as socially and affectively in the national belonging. Obituaries for Mears boiled his story down to certain essential kernels, linking the immigrant's status with empire and pacification. Boston's *Jewish Archive* ran "Otto Mears, Russian Jew Who Built Southwest Empire and Fought Indians, Dead at 91," which attributed Mears' "national fame" to his Indian fighting and laudable business skills. Aside from being one of the "outstanding builders of the Southwest and a leading figure in the pioneer days of Colorado," the paper celebrated him for his twin successes in commerce and Indian appeasement, through both violence and negotiation.[113] The paper explicitly coupled the twin forces of commerce and pacification that justified violence against Indians.[114] So too did the *Intermountain Jewish News*, with its account of the "incredible romance" of Mears' accomplishment on behalf of "his adopted country."[115] Local history, biography, and obituary writers made the Mears story into an American civics lesson that fused physical violence and commercial prowess—both commerce and aggression enabled the mobility of the Mears family and the broader settler population whose enrichment he facilitated.

Fairly consistently from the 1880s through the 1930s, stories in which the perpetration of violence against Native Americans, like those about Otto Mears, Morris Lasker, or Sigmund Shlesinger, excited the Jewish press. Local history records, news outlets, and both private and public writings on Jews in Alaska, Arizona, California, Colorado, Kansas, Missouri, Montana, Nebraska, Nevada, New Mexico, South Dakota, Texas, Oklahoma, Utah, and Wyoming situated Jews at the center of what cultural historian of the American frontier Richard Slotkin has called "regeneration through violence" narratives.[116] Stories that emphasized victimhood as well as those focused on perpetration aimed themselves at the same end. Stories about Jewish victimization from "Indian cruelties" mirrored and reversed those stories of violent perpetration, but they resulted in the same sorts of conclusions, narrative plots, and civics lessons. They both explained and justified the seizure of Indian land and the sacrifice that warranted and sanctified imperial victory. In telling stories of both varieties, Jews identified as model national subjects who took up the charge of settling, civilizing, and Americanizing the land. Family stories, obituaries, memoirs, and newspapers suggested how Jewish western settlers—German, Russian, Polish, and Yiddish-speaking, first- and second-generation, and American-born—ought to think about the meaning of frontier violence between Natives and settlers.

Late ninetieth- and early twentieth-century American Jews were inconsistent in their assessments about violence over western land. Unsurprisingly, geography played a part in these discrepancies. Frontier Jews, on the one hand, considered land a special asset, a valuable commodity, the site of Jewish futurity, and one of the key grounds for developing American belonging. Thus they were generally willing to defend the need to enact violence to secure it. On the other hand, the vast majority of American immigrant Jews lived in urban centers far from the frontier. East Coast Jews expressed far more ambivalence about warfare for land. They seemed unaware of, or not particularly animated by, the acculturation project their fellow Jews in the West were undertaking. They did not imagine Jews as pioneer "types," and having no direct encounter with actual Native American people, East Coast urban Jewish immigrants neither celebrated violence against Native Americans nor wrote about land in covetous or exalted terms.

The Jewish press in the East reported on the violent competition between settlers and Indians for western lands to its Jewish readers, predominantly easterner, urban Jews. In choosing what to report and print and with what kind of editorial language to employ to describe events of the Jewish West, newspaper editors

Figure 2.6. Otto Mears and Chief Ouray. "Sitting Studio Portrait of Native American (Tabeguache Band, Southern Ute) Chief Ouray, and Otto Mears, an Interpreter and Businessman." The Denver Public Library, Western History Collection, WHJ-10219.

made decisions about who to sympathize with—white settlers or the embattled Indians. On the one hand, a few Jewish writers and editors—particularly those with avowed left-leaning politics who lived in Atlantic seaboard cities, where they seldom if ever had face-to-face encounters with Native people—articulated a critique of American imperialism and sympathized with the Natives who suffered losses by imperialism's reach. On the other hand, plenty of eastern Jewish news items, in English, German, and Yiddish, including those from socialist and leftist newspapers, expressed no misgivings about framing Indian battle items and stories about settling Indian land in expressly colonial terms. Early twentieth-century Jews tended to express little guilt or shame about colonialism's offenses.[117] When the Jewish press celebrated acts of violence against Indians, or cheered on the capture of their lands, they affirmed the deeply held belief that history marched forward in precisely the direction they wished it would to grow vibrant Jewish communities in an enlarging and prospering American nation. Acquisition advanced immigrant Jews' ambitions for integration into America's social fabric, inclusion in its metaphysical core, and the achievement of sturdy, steady, upward economic mobility.

In general, the Jewish press sided with settlers; Jews could count fellow Jews among the whites who stood to gain from the competition over land. Occasionally, however, Jewish newspapers in the east sided with Native Americans, though seldom with a well-articulated expression of solidarity with the Native experience on its own terms. Jewish empathy was born of their perceptions of analogous experiences of marginalization and their perception of themselves as fellow dispossessed outsiders, their assumption that nonwhite groups in the United States were alike as "minorities," different from one another though they may have been. New York's Yiddish *Forverts*, with Abe Cahan's editorial agenda set to sensitizing its Yiddish-speaking immigrant Jewish readership to the affective dimensions and nuances of American life, published stories about Indian life and Indian violence from its first issue in 1897. On occasion, vigilante or legally sanctioned violence perpetrated against Indians evoked outrage by Jewish commentators. The *Forverts* wrote sympathetically of three Indians lynched by twenty-five masked whites in Bismark, South Dakota, in 1897 on the eve of the trial for the murder of a local settler family.[118] The paper cast other Indians who fought against "Mexican oppressors" as freedom fighters on a politically justified mission—these "civilized," "organized," and "self-ruling Indians . . . have a lot of sympathizers in the United States"—aiming to counteract myths its readers might have harbored about Native people as intellectually and culturally illiterate, politically unorganized, or unconcerned with sovereignty issues.[119] The *Forverts* also critiqued a Colorado warden and his deputies for firing on some two hundred Indians, five of whom died and thirty-five of whom suffered wounds in Steamboat Springs in 1897.[120] The newspaper ran items serially and relatively frequently in its first decade for its Jewish audience.[121] *Forverts* writers and readers alike differed considerably from many of the German Jewish immigrants who wrote of Native affairs in the West in the 1860s, 1870s, and 1880s. They were eastern European, more politically charged, and more urban. They were more sensitive to the failures of liberalism and to the dangers of empires, particularly the Russian empire they had fled. They did not compete with Native peoples, nor was the battle for western land particularly meaningful to them; it was far away and not particularly significant to the material circumstances of their everyday lives.

When socialist or other left-leaning Jewish writers on the East Coast defended Native Americans in their battles with white settlers, they depicted Indigenous Peoples in ways with which their readership might readily empathize. Indians' behavior, the *Forverts* language betrayed on occasion, could be seen as akin to workers organizing to make group claims to management about the conditions of their lives, threatening only when necessary. On occasion, its writers applied socialist metaphor to the conflict between the state and its wards. A 1901 article about "unsatisfied Indians" in Omaha described Sioux frustrations at the state's cutting of government support. It sympathetically described the Natives convening, organizing, and demanding a replacement of funds. Should the "White Father in Washington" decide against the replacement of funds and fail to provide these Native peoples with adequate food, the *Forverts* sympathetically wrote, an uprising would become justified, as might a labor strike closer to home.[122] Another article that same year urged its readers to bear in mind the real source of Indian unrest—namely, "what the Americans did to the Indians": giving them "poisoned blankets" and "pushing them from their homes."[123] It was a trope with which every *Forverts* reader could likely empathize, having felt pushed from his or her own home in Romania, Ukraine, or elsewhere in the Pale of Settlement and having read a constant stream of news and editorial items about fellow Jews' experience of displacement, violence, pogroms, and the tribulations of minority life in the Russian empire from which they or their parents had emigrated. Broad themes of minority persecution could never have been far from readers' minds.

But even as a socialist paper writing for a Jewish-only, Yiddish-language readership, the *Forverts* writers ultimately sided with white settlers when discussing settler-Indian warfare. It supported white settlers' and the plight of immigrants' efforts to establish new homes in this promised land of the West more than it sympathized with the downtrodden Natives who suffered at the hands of American imperialism.[124] The New York paper offered empathy to white settlers and wrote of westward-moving whites as fellow immigrants much more often than it suggested its Jewish readers could or should identify with Indians. Westward migrants were, crudely put, closer to them than were Indians. Thus the government was more frequently conceived of as a benevolent force that responded to its citizens, the Jewish public included. Native Americans, by implication, were excluded from state responsiveness and protection.[125] Reporting on a "war between the Apache and the Mormons," the paper once explained the etiology of the war as based on the Indians' attempts to "rob the locals."[126] It later gave voice to white settlers' fears of further "uprisings," claiming that the paper "received a telegram that the white community there [in Omaha] is worried about an Indian uprising by the Sioux and Cheyenne Indians" and that many had already fled their homes and began preparations for battle. The *Omaha Jewish Telegram* author identified his or her community as a community of ideal citizens and civilized settlers. Allying the Jews of the region with frontier whites, the New York Yiddish paper reinforced the telegram sender's opinion that the "government should not wait but step in with force to calm these uncivil Indians."[127] Still another article echoed settlers' call for military support to subdue Indian unrest in Oklahoma, reproducing fears that Indians might target bridges and railroad tracks and disrupt development, business, and ordinary life.[128]

Jews participated in Indian wars on the winning end of battles all across the fledgling western states in the protracted battle between settlers and Native

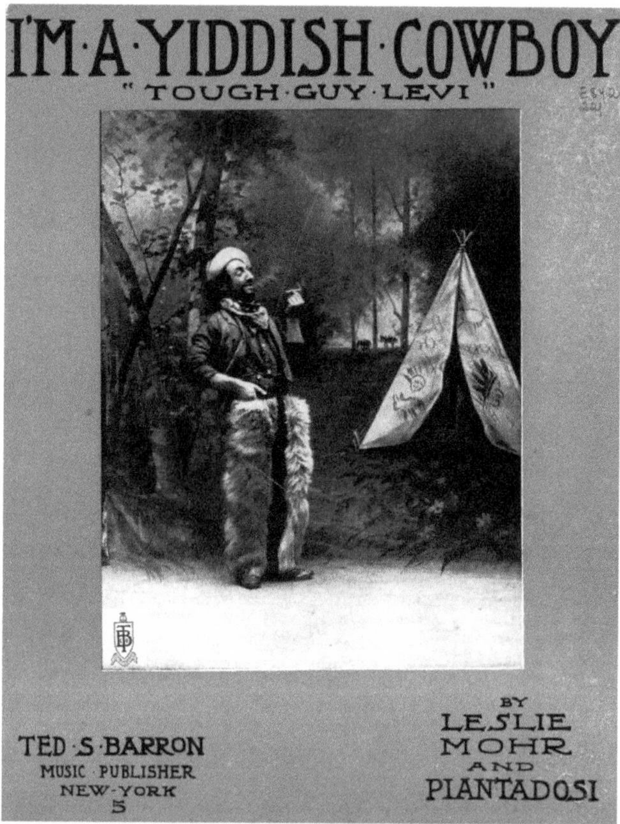

Figure 2.7. "I'm a Yiddish Cowboy, Toughguy Levi." Sheet music cover, 1908. Baylor University Library. https://commons.wikimedia.org/wiki/File:I%27m_a_yiddish_cowboy_Tough_guy_Levi_1908.jpg.

Americans. From the early nineteenth century consistently until the turn of the twentieth, Jews identified and sided with whites in the broad contest for land against Indians. Jews died in Indian reprisal battles, the so-called depredations, outbreaks, and uprisings. Jews perpetrated violence and fell victim to it, though not as Jews per se but rather as white European and American migrants. Yet Jews wrote of these participations as acts of sacrifice, as the legacy endowment they bequeathed to their progeny and to America more broadly. Participation became a matter of pride and acclaim celebrated in local, amateur, and family history and narratives of the Jewish West. In this sense, land battle stories served audiences much like other American war stories: Jews died for the sake of the nation and the advancement of American land and civilization. Killing Indians, or resisting being martyred by them, seemed a worthwhile price for admission to western America before the turn of the century and well into the twentieth. In telling stories that celebrated their own acts of land acquisition, violence against Native Americans, Jews struck against the myth that they lacked the muscular ruggedness to make them fit for the expansion enterprise. Jews benefited from the metaphysical power that came with being a colonizer, a reversal of their recent experience in Europe where Jews had suffered as the colonized.[129] Western American Jews earned for themselves a sense of home among an emerging nation of whites, the end of exile, and an almost aboriginal sense of belonging in America, its west so new. Jews battled for ownership and use of the land—desiring physical space and the upward mobility that might come from the use of it resources—and for a sense of "ownership" of America itself, for belonging among the nation. It is in such ways that the immigrant began to build his empire.

CHAPTER 3

JEWISH MIDDLEMEN MERCHANTS, INDIAN CURIOS, AND THE EXTENSIONS OF AMERICAN CAPITALISM

By the end of the nineteenth century, violent contestation for land no longer interfered to any substantial degree in the settling and building of the American West. The state-run Indian farming experiment, designed to transform Native peoples into agriculturalists, had largely failed. The U.S. government's efforts to manufacture "surplus" acreage of Indian lands for white settlement through allotting plots to Native nuclear families, however, had proved quite successful. As a result of the 1887 General Allotment Act, approximately two-thirds of the total Indian land base, some ninety million acres, had been taken out of Indigenous ownership or control. The 1906 Burke Act reduced allotments of land given to Native Americans even further, producing more land for settlers, many of them new immigrants. By the second decade of the twentieth century, Native Americans had lost another thirty million acres from sales of land titles. The Indian land question had been provisionally answered, and the vast majority of Native Americans sunk downward on America's social and economic ladder.

Jews, on the other hand, enjoyed relatively speedy upward mobility in the first decades of the twentieth century. As a whole, Jews became increasingly comfortable and enfranchised. They earned positions of power in business and politics at the local and state levels with particular speed and success in the West. They built Jewish communities with strong and multiple filial and religious ties. If social belonging and upward mobility had been the shared goal of late nineteenth-century Jews from the German territories and from further east, these goals had been resolutely accomplished.

The vast majority of face-to-face interactions between Jews and Native Americans in the second half of the nineteenth century did not directly involve antagonistic battles for the land itself, though violence did have a complicated interrelationship with commerce. Rather, commercial exchange structured most of the encounters. Jews migrated to the West in search of business opportunities; their desire to be counted among the nation's exalted subjects grew out of the ideological and cultural conditions germane to the material circumstances of the West.[1] In this regard, enterprising Jewish merchants considered the presence, not the absence, of Native Americans in the West as opportunities for productive exchange. Indeed, many Jewish peddlers traded with Native Americans for a short time in their fledgling business careers when they first migrated to the frontier. When these Jews had accumulated enough capital, they tended to move on to larger businesses, but instead of forgetting about Indian trading altogether, Jewish merchant-settlers made meaning out of their commercial engagements past. Indians were not always or only conceived of as impediments to Jewish ambitions in the frontier West; in commercial encounters, Jews saw Native

Figure 3.1. "Rose Brothers Fur Traders Company." Kenneth M. Wright. American Jewish Archives, PC-3705.

Americans as potential customers and suppliers, as boosters or vehicles for their aspirations for social and economic mobility.

Jews considered themselves the heroic protagonists in their own community's immigrant upward mobility success story. This "Horatio Alger" trope of immigrant success on the frontier was reproduced virtually without exception in popular and familial histories, newspapers, memoirs, obituaries, and local histories in the late nineteenth and early twentieth-century American West. Amateur and professional historians also reproduced it. "For Jewish men," noted historian William Toll, "the merchant role in the American West enabled them [immigrant Jews] and their families in a single generation to move from medieval artisanship and itinerant merchandising to the highest civil status."[2] While this meta-narrative of Jewish immigration achievement and ascent is virtually irrefutable, questioning its broader implications and reconsidering Jewish economic agency in the American West through a frame that is larger than one through which the immigrants themselves viewed their own experience allows us to see their experience more clearly. In their commercial interactions with Native Americans, Jewish settlers navigated ambiguous ground between Native outsiders (as they saw them) and fellow second-generation American-born Jews, acting as economic and cultural intermediaries between American whites and Native Americans.

Small scale and local business exchange offers a finer brush to consider closer encounters. While chapter 2 used a wide-angle lens to consider Jews as other whites on the frontier, suggesting that their experiences ought to be placed in the broader processes of expansion and expropriation, this chapter offers an examination of one industry, a site of economic exchange between Jews and Native Americans that was more codependent and less explicitly violent than direct contestation over land but was nonetheless experienced quite differently by each party. Jews generally celebrated their contributions to capitalism's extensions, as commerce spread to the margins of modern western and American societies. Though they rarely paid attention to the impacts of capitalism's reach on Native peoples and communities, Jews played a curious role in the advances of mercantile capitalism and the commodification of Native American cultures. They helped extend capitalism to new players, new lands, new products, and new markets as active agents of commercial development. They facilitated the flow of cash and goods between city dwellers and Native American communities.

A small portion of the Jewish businessmen who traded with Native Americans (what they dubbed "Indian trading") entered the "curio" industry, a market that involved the buying and selling of commodities that symbolized Indians themselves, objects like moccasins, totem poles, head dresses, wampum belts, baskets, and rugs. Unlike markets for furs, skins, foodstuffs, or other natural resources that Native Americans sold or traded with settlers throughout colonial history from the sixteenth century forward, curios were heritage commodities. If objects acquired from Native peoples (including land itself) derived their value by being stripped from their connections to their Native producers, hunters, or harvesters, curios' value was derived from and premised on their being somehow linked to the people who made or used them. These products were not just from Indians, they were *of* Indians; Native Peoples' culture, ideas, and identities were made into commodities with the act of buying an "Indian curio." Though curios and souvenirs had been bought and sold by whites in the Southwest, around the Great Lakes region, and in upper and lower Canada since the eighteenth century, a much larger market for these Aboriginal heritage objects boomed in the last two decades of the nineteenth century, precisely after—and perhaps because—Native Americans ceased to pose a threat to the colonial settlement project.[3] Native culture began to be considered desirable, and therefore financially valuable, in a new way, only when it was no longer seen as threatening.[4]

Scholars of modern Jewish economic history have consistently observed the Jews' position and role as middlemen, meditators, and peddlers, one made possible by the thick and wide filial networks typical of merchant minorities.[5] Modern Jews featured centrally in many emerging markets for art; some were keenly involved in the emerging markets for arts, crafts, and souvenirs in Africa, others as high-art dealers in Europe, and in particular for new, high-modern movements including abstract expressionism.[6] American Jews were intimately involved in the emergence of new art markets for Indian curios. Jewish curio dealers mediated, both financially and culturally, between Natives and settlers, selling Indian heritage to largely white consumers. This in-between space offered room for Jews to work out tensions that they lived with as they sought integration in America's West. Most centrally, Jews eagerly sought to belong among whites in this emerging nation, particularly as the question of their belonging remained thornily unanswered in the Europe from which they emigrated. This in-between space, moreover, offered them a traditional economic niche to advance themselves economically. They wanted to be included as citizens, celebrated as free enterprisers, and they wanted to establish themselves financially, socially, and politically.

Jews' occupational profile in the West during the last third of the nineteenth century served expansion's end and contributed to the particular articulation expansion would have in the United States—that is, one closely linked with and championing of capitalism and its growth, connected to major urban centers.[7] Simply doing what Jews often did to make a living—namely, peddling and engaging in small merchant exchange—gave a positive valence to economic growth and helped Jews feel a part of a bigger story of civilizing the American frontier. To the extent that fellow white Americans saw commercial intercourse as the key vehicle for settling the frontier, Jews pursuing their material betterment harmonized with the essence of the American expansion project.

Jewish-Indian Relations in Frontier Trading

The call for the extension of commercial activity enticed Jews to the West; a living could be eked out from frontier trading. As new immigrants during the era of mass migration, Jews used this commercial development to prove their utility in America. The extensions of commerce and frontier settlement were twin elements in the West's conquest. The small-scale peddling, post-trading, and merchandizing that Jews provided in the West revealed Jews' utility and productivity, for their work provided necessary goods including tools, foodstuffs, and work clothes, for virtually all the West's growth industries, particularly the business of extracting the land's natural resources. They supplied gear and goods to gold, silver, and copper to miners, tradesmen, migrant laborers, railroad builders, survey teams, and the military. In a sense, Jews provided battery power for expansion. Jews' commercial contributions to this growing system were critical in linking rural outposts together with one another and in creating a network of commercial exchange nodes, which unified scattered sites of productivity into larger commercial and, subsequently, political regions. The civic repercussions of Jews' efforts at making a living in this "wild" West therefore also helped counter the popular defamation they would have heard about themselves as underproductive saps on a more "natural" economy of primary producers such as mining or agriculture. Being a part of the commercial transformation of "empty" land, inhabited only by the "uncivil," meant participation in the expansion process as well as a means to the practical end of economic mobility.

Generally, Jewish men came to the frontier alone. They sought places in the West and found people to trade with based on their material needs. They built small businesses often apart from other Jews. Hundreds of young enterprising Jewish merchants who found their ways to the outskirts of civilization to eke out a living and build new lives with capital accumulated during the early stages of their careers in the West via Native Americans. Upon these small fortunes, through businesses including fur, clothing, dry goods, tobacco, alcohol, food provisions, and other goods, Jews built larger enterprises and, in short order, established themselves in the towns and cities that sprung up within a few decades on the western slice of the continent. There, Jews enjoyed staggering economic mobility, social integration, and a significant voice in civic and political life.[8] In larger towns, these Jews could also participate in Jewish communal life. During this segment of the male immigrant experience in the West, Indian-related commercial activity formed a seedling stage in career mobility.

These Jewish peddlers came from all the European empires that colonized the western hemisphere—Portuguese, Dutch, French, English, German, and eventually Russian. Whatever significant differences lay between the politics, religious attitudes, and cultural or civic backgrounds of these Jews, all the frontier trading Jews engaged in a similar process of economic exchange with partners who were not yet or only minimally part of the centers of economic activity.[9] Jews were agents of economic empire at the margins, making mostly marginal livings with marginal peoples. There were tens of thousands of them, fanned out over one thousand locations over thirty-one different states before the Civil War alone.[10] They were the "foot soldiers" of a far-reaching late nineteenth-century market revolution. The Jews saw themselves as part of the teleological force of American nationalism, participants in the inevitable triumph of frontier settlement, though Native people also "discovered" European settlers, assessed opportunities and threats that new encounters invited, and were likewise responsible for shaping frontier life. The market itself, which was, as Hasia Diner has shown, sometimes as simple as a door-front exchange, was one essential place of cultural mixing and mutual interpretation. Though conflict was pervasive, trades had to be arrived at through mutual understanding.[11]

Trade lent itself to frequent amicable and harmonious relations between Jews and Native Americans. According to his interview with the Works Progress Administration, the Russian-born Barney Zimmerman had entered Cherokee Nation territory immediately after they had received government relocation payments, opening a dry goods store in Antlers, Oklahoma.[12] When the Choctaws got their $103/pp buyout in 1893, Zimmerman described their commercial interactions:

> They did not get any more payments for a long while, then they got several payments I did a good business plan for they had plenty of money and bought quantities of goods. I have sold the Choctaws much good since I put up my store and until I quit business about three years ago [1937]. I used to go to the Choctaw court ground and put up a tent and sell goods at there; they would hold court for about four weeks. They did not have the money but they got scrip for their services at the court and I bought or traded goods for scrip; I would buy the scrip at a discount, hold it for a while then take it to the treasurer of the Choctaw nation and get my money out of it.[13]

In rare, granular, vernacular prose, Zimmerman's reminiscences also touched on the amicable bonds he built with his new Choctaw neighbors and his general observations and judgments about Native-newcomer relations:

> There were very few white people when I came to Antlers and the country was open . . . for there were no white people out in the country and the Indians lived so far apart that there were no houses to be seen along the road. . . . I have been in this town ever since I came here and I have raised my children here in this town; they have attended school with the Indian children. I have traded with the Indians and for years would let them have anything they wanted on credit. I never lost one penny on the Indians and they are honest and law-abiding people, just as true to their word as men can be; there are no bad Indians; I never saw about one among them. The Indians did not bother the white people. They would fight among themselves and maybe kill an Indian once

in a while but they are good people and never bothered white people at all. I have lived a long time but I never did hear of an Indian having trouble with a white man not even with the Negroes and the best friends I have are full blood Choctaws. I have been here so long that they all know me and I have treated them the best I know how they have treated me in the same way.[14]

Indian trade had certainly attracted Jewish merchants from the earliest arrival of Jews in North America. Despite significant differences in trade relationships, politics, geographies, and economies, dozens of Jewish Indian trading enterprises dotted the expanding frontier over the first two hundred years of the Jewish presence in the new world. Jacob Lumbrozo, a Portuguese Jewish planter, physician, and fur trader in the palatinate of Maryland, earned a commission to trade with the Indians as early as 1665.[15] Levy Solomons resided among and retained interests in mercantile enterprises with Indians from Michilimackinac to the Gulf of St. Lawrence and down the Hudson River in the 1770s and 1780s.[16] By supplying dry goods and foodstuffs to both Indians and the military as it roved about the frontier, Aaron Levy helped develop the commercial infrastructure of Northumberland County, Pennsylvania.[17] The English Jewish brothers Samuels ran an Indian trading post at Taylor Falls, on the Minnesota side of the St. Croix River in the early 1850s, some twelve miles from the trading post of another Jewish Indian trader, Isaac Marks.[18]

Robert Goldstein, "Alaska's first Jewish settler," arrived in Juneau from Russia in 1884. He built a trading post on the beach of Gastineau Channel, where his daughter Belle remembered "Indian traders who arrived in canoes stacked high with furs: fox, sable, beaver, mink, marten and an occasional fur seal."[19] Goldstein traded with Tlingit and Haida Indians, who canoed hundreds of miles north from British Columbia.[20] Gustav Kahn touted his involvement in wholesaling "dry goods, clothing, and notions, as well as ladies' ready-to-wear" to the Indian traders on the Navajo Reservation "for hundreds of miles around in every direction."[21] Jacob Leiser, the first Jew to settle in Missoula, Montana, in 1867 during the mining excitement, "went ahead into the strange country and struggled up to an Indian camp [where he] settled in the town, opened a store, and traded with the Indians." His daughter Esther Leiser recalled that the Salish Indians with whom he traded "were very good customers. They came to the store to be outfitted for their hunting and trapping, and if they had no money, they promised to pay later. The promises were always carried out. If the debtor died before what he owed could be paid, the family considered the debt a sacred obligation, and at all costs would see to it that the storekeeper received what was due to him."[22]

This commercial engagement had several meanings for these Jews. Selling goods on credit to Native customers helped enmesh Jews and Native Americans together in more stable, longer-term, and even multigenerational business connections. Not only did Jewish merchants assess the quality of Indian customers and the likelihood of debt repayment; they took some measure of pride in believing they had taught Indians to be better consumers, better capitalists, and therefore better Americans. Extending capitalism to new participants in the cash economy of the expanding West provided social capital on top of the actual capital gained from commercial exchange with Indians. To both Jews and non-Jews, Indian trading was sometimes seen as a kind of missionizing for capitalism. The sentiment that Jewish merchants taught, instructed, civilized, and modernized Indians found expression in the Jewish and non-Jewish popular press from the 1880s through the 1920s. The tone of these sentiments alternated between philanthropic, imperialistic, and educational. When newspaper writers reported on Indians being included in the great modern commercial system, they treated it as "good news." One *Boston Hebrew Observer* article described how Indians learned to become more savvy buyers over time, admiring their abilities to learn capitalism's logic.[23] A *Los Angeles Times* item praised Hopi traders as "Indian Jews," describing their trading acumen in detail and claiming that the Hopi "are natural traders of the keenest sort, against whom visitors from neighboring tribes have no chance whatever."[24] In this treatment, "Old Warrior Indian culture" was remade into progressive, aggressive commercial competence. These kinds of articles cast Jews as educators for capitalism or models for commercial activity, and Jews tended to embrace this mantle. Indeed, Jews hoped to show their fellow white but Christian neighbors that the patriotic pursuit of civilizing and Americanizing the American Indian did not require Christianization. Rather, the spirit of capitalism alone, to which Jews strategically laid claim, could bend outsiders into insiders in the American cauldron. Peoples could maintain their differences while building America the prosperous, a nation and its citizens praised for their material growth, the fulfilled promises of the dreams that brought the immigrants west in the first place.[25]

Merchants transformed themselves into pathbreakers for capitalism and civilization. Near Gallup, New Mexico, Jewish "Indian trader" Sam Danoff opened shop in a town that would be called Danoffville, New Mexico, where two of his brothers ran a trading post in Zuni territory near the local Indian missionary school.[26] Danoffville had the only store for miles and sold groceries, dry goods, clothes, saddles and bridles, livestock feed, and even Studebaker wagons to the Navajo and Zuni Indians who lived in the area. His son Hyman reminisced about the interactivity of commercial exchange:

> In the store we really "traded" with the Indians. They would bring their jewelry, blankets, wool and other products, and we would buy each item from them separately and pay for it. When we bought what they had to sell, we would then sell them our merchandise. We paid them top price for their goods because we anticipated making a fair profit on what we sold. On occasion we would pay the Indians a lot of money for their goods but they would only buy a few

> cents of merchandise from us. This lead to the use of "Danoff money." We used metal coins of different denominations and shapes that were good only for purchases in our store.[27]

The Danoffs helped turn their local Indian customers into manufacturers of goods for market by using their own currency, redeemable only at the Danoff store itself. This was not an uncommon practice among Indian traders, Jews and otherwise.[28] Hyman Danoff's flattering family portrait, like many family histories, memoirs, and autobiographies that remember Jewish life in the West at the turn of the century, anchors his Americana credentials in Indian relations as cash "civilizers." He boasted of his aunts and uncles Sam, Simon, and Rose as Indian traders and employers who learned to speak Zuni and Navajo "as fluently as the Indians, with all the Indian inflections" and reveled in the affection and presumed closeness with the Indians that he saw in the fact that they gave names to his family: "Big Nose," "Little Big Nose," "Fat Lady," "Fat Lady's Son," and Hyman's father Sam, "The Honest Man." Though hardly poetic, Hyman considered receiving Indian names prestigious and in his family memoirs, took this as laudatory evidence of his father's business ethics. "The Indians used to come to my father with their money, having had dealings elsewhere," he wrote, "to have him count it out for them, in order to have him tell them whether they had been cheated or not."[29] Further trumpeting the family credentials, he related that an Inter-Tribal Indian Ceremonial, established in Gallup in 1922, appointed Sam and his brothers to the original Board of Directors for this annual celebration, which drew Indians from around nation to dances, performances, and sales of handicrafts, art, jewelry, weaving, and ceramics.

American Jewish popular histories routinely figured Jewish merchants who dealt with Native Americans as role models and educators in benevolent capitalism and the nurturing role of educating Indians for commercial competency.[30] The Latvian-born Morris D. Simpson and his brother-in-law Morris Iralson arrived in Lawson, Oklahoma, on August 3, 1901, just "three days before the opening of the lottery of 3,000,000 acres of Kiowa-Comanche Indian reservation to white settlers," according to one biographical account of his life. A Jewish newspaper praised his commercializing and assimilating of Natives, claiming that "Morris Simspson's scrupulous and friendship for the Indians made him an idol for the redmen who found the Jewish trader's fair dealing and aid in time of need an extraordinary experience. Quanah Parker, the last chief of the Comanches, who lived on the fringe of Lawton for many years, named one of his sons for Simpson, 'in honor of his good white friend.'"[31] Nearly identical sentiment was expressed in Jewish western family history writing. One Creek County merchant, "unofficial headquarters for the Five Civilized Tribes," earned the ardor of his own children, who claimed that

> Indians liked him and trusted him. More than one merchant said, "Get an Indian drunk and you can sell him anything." Papa worked on another

> theory: get an Indian sober and he'll be your friend. Many Indians came to Papa's store when their money was gone and their hangovers were coming on. Indian women, in their blankets of bright, beautiful colors, spent hours in the shoe department while their men slept off their binges on cots Papa installed for that purpose in a corner of his Bargain Basement. In his store safe he kept Indians' marriage licenses, army discharges, car registrations, and often considerable sums of cash. He was proud that the Indians trusted him more than they did the bank. Papa spoke some Creek and understood a little Osage, but he had the know-how of communicating with all the tribes.[32]

Uplift practice aimed at civilizing Native Americans also took shape away from the storefront into the parlors of affluent middle-class whites like Hattie Ferrin Solomon, the first Jewish girl born, educated, and wed in Tucson, who lent out her home for local female reformers to provide "moral and financial protection for the Indian girls worked in the home of white families." Solomon was praised for her efforts to shape the behaviors and etiquette of Native women to conform with a white sense of propriety: "The ladies of Tucson . . . realized that better morals *mean better maids*," as one reformer put it, crediting Solomon in particular as a leader.[33]

Records created by non-Jews, however, occasionally tell of less-than-scrupulous Jewish commercial activity. Some described exploitative practices of Jews toward Indians, and others describe cases in which Jews and Indians work for profits together against the legal interests of white farmers. One Oklahoma pioneer, Nat Dickerson, recalled an incident soon after 1898 when "the Cherokee laws ended," opening Cherokee nation territory to white settlers. "Farmers from Tahlequah on north to Spavinaw," he said, "were complaining of this is their cattle and the charge was, that they were being taken by a bunch of young Indians and were being sold to a man by the name of John Morrison and to Sam Zeno, a Jew who had married a Cherokee girl and who had a big ranch on Lynch's Prairie."[34] Zeno and Morrison apparently named several Indians who helped them sell cattle, agreed to capture the shadily sold cattle, and then raided the Indian encampment.

The U.S. government enabled the commercializing and settling process. It established the Office of Indian Trade in 1806 as a subdivision of the War Department to facilitate the safe settlement of whites on frontier lands for trouble-free commerce.[35] As small-time merchants, gold seekers, and oil and land speculators rushed to newly available lands, Jews supplied provisions and dry goods, carving out economic niches for themselves, a pattern consistent across decades and geographies, supported by the state. With the Treaty of Guadalupe Hidalgo in 1848, Santa Fe, a centuries-old hub of commerce and intercultural activity, became American and began a significant growth spurt. Homesteaders settled in Nebraska and Kansas Territories in the late 1850s and 1860s. The Pacific Northwest boomed after the discovery of gold in British Columbia in 1858. In the early

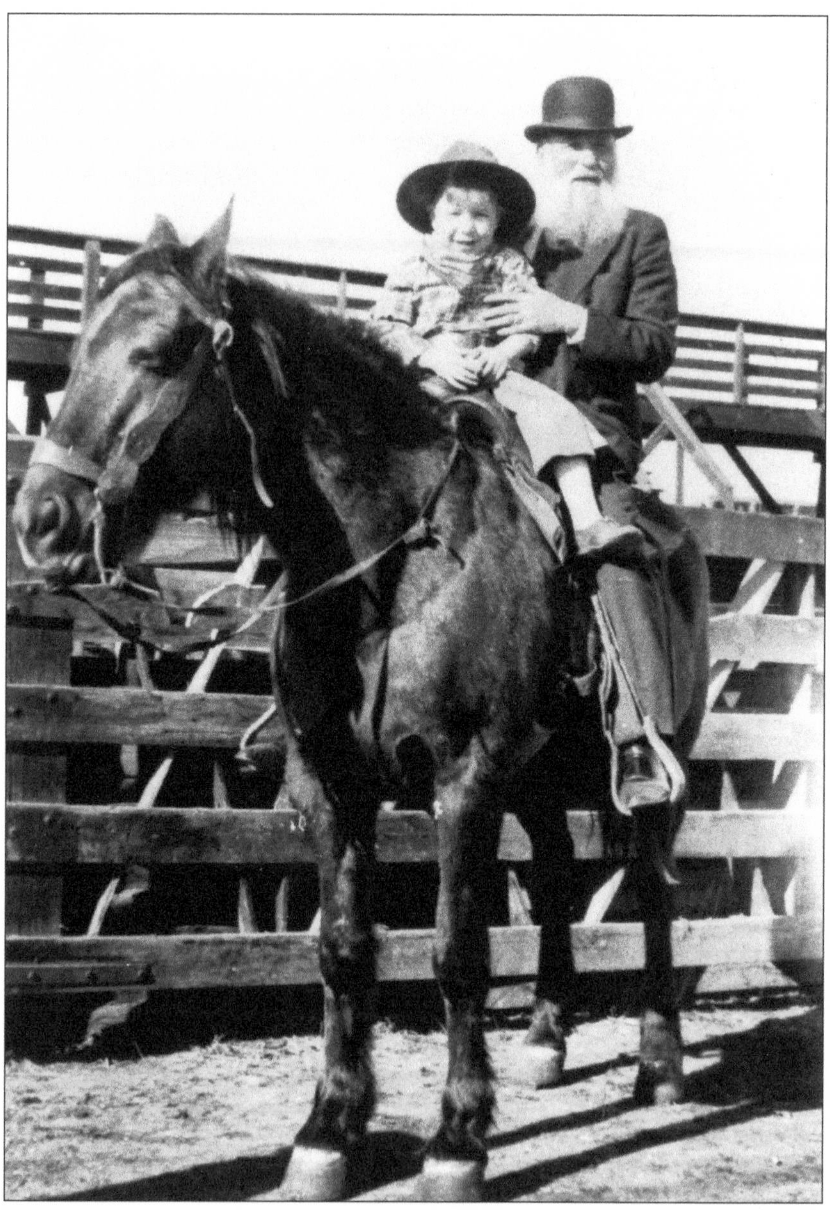

Figure 3.2. "Denver's Dean of Cattle Buyers, Lithuanian-born Robert Lazar Miller." Rocky Mountain Jewish Historical Society, Center for Judaic Studies, University of Denver.

years of inchoate frontier towns in Montana, Utah, Arizona, Colorado, New Mexico, Alaska, and elsewhere, towns that after the 1860s emerged into cities like Omaha, Santa Fe, and Victoria, Jewish men used Native Americans as a source of petty capital accumulation.

Jewish firms dominated the newly American New Mexico economy from the 1860s to the 1880s so significantly that the dean of the University of New Mexico School of Business Administration, William Parish, argued that German Jews affected nothing short of a "commercial revolution" there.[36] Historian Hal Rothman concurred, arguing that "*extranjero* [foreign] merchants, German-Jewish émigrés prominent among them, constituted the merchant class [of New Mexico in the 1880s], which played the dominant role in capital formation, intermarried with local people, and traded extensively [and] possessed the goals of an individualist mercantile culture."[37] Rothman stressed that this domination resulted from power relations between different groups on the frontier, not just Native Americans. He argued that "the colonial nature of trade in the peripheries of the Southwest gradually transferred agriculturalists' tangible assets to merchants."[38]

Jews participated in the capitalist colonial process not just as private business beneficiaries but also as allies of the state. Michael Elhart, a Dutch Jew, engaged in trade with the Creek Indians under government contract in Georgia, while the government of Alabama supported Abraham Mordecai's Indian trade along the banks of the Alabama River in the first years of the nineteenth century.[39] Jacob Marks exchanged letters with the superintendent of Indian Trade, with whom he won contracts to furnish goods to Indian traders, and with Levi Sheftall of Georgia, who served both the Office of Indian Trade and the War Department. Preoccupied with the details of payments and goods rendered, these letters revealed that Jewish traders had regular contracts with the federal government and that the state tried to exercise control over its Indian traders in its efforts to protect its wards against exploitative business interests, including some Jewish merchants.[40] Some thought Indians would buy substandard merchandise. Marks, for example, thought certain "damaged," "deficient," and "inferior" goods he had for sale would "answer tolerably well for Indian trade."[41]

Jewish frontier traders also brought Native Americans into cash economies that linked them together with merchants and connected them to larger markets as the railroads and lines of credit linked new towns and cities to greater commercial city centers.[42] Jewish merchants helped reshape the fiscal lives of many Native Americans by incorporating them into a western economy as the transcontinental railroads linked the Southwest to the seaboards by the early 1880s. In the Far West, Southwest, and mountain West, Natives participated in decades-long trading relationships with European immigrant, American, and to some extent Russian whites in the Pacific Northwest, where they exchanged furs, skins, and other natural resources in return for tools, clothes, foodstuffs, and liquor, even when such sales were banned by the government. As in the American Southwest, the British Columbia coast abounded with young Jewish men building businesses as Indian traders. At least seventeen Jews listed themselves as Indian traders in Victoria business registers, like those focused on fur and/or seals, like Leopold Boscowitz, Hyman and Fanny Cooperman, Isaac Goldsmith, W. Baranski, Jules Freidman, and Abraham Frankel, and those who explicitly call themselves Indian traders, like Morris Ellis Dobrin, Abraham and Israel Martin, Leopold Blum, Aaron Oldenburg, Samuel Harris, Nathan Solomon, and Jacob Valentine.[43] Scores of Jewish merchants like the Victoria Jewish traders also dotted the West Coast and the western territories in Oklahoma and Nebraska, Utah and Nevada, Arizona and Wyoming.[44]

Jewish-Native business connections continued well past the turn of the century as well. Historian George Colpitts' examination of Jewish merchants' interactions with First Nations trappers in Northern Canada from 1916 to 1939, as the fur trade became an industrialized business, offers one close analysis of the social and economic entanglements between Déné and Jewish trading relationships and the ways that racial understanding and economic agency (on both the Jewish and Déné parts) played out.[45] At the turn of the century, Jewish "free" fur traders, along with Roma, Arab, and Armenian merchants, began trading alongside and in competition with the Hudson's Bay Company traders.[46] With their expertise in dressing, dying, and manufacturing furs, as well as their extensive experience in the production, retail, and manufacturing of furs in connection with fur houses in Montreal, Toronto, and New York, Jewish fur traders like Sam Kirshner, Fred Shulpster, the Pinsky brothers, Jack Hurting, Alan Markis, and, most famously, "Trayder Ed" Hanson—who wrote a memoir of his fur-trading days out of Fort McMurray in Yiddish—helped open Northern territories to commercial and industrial modernism. These Jewish merchants extended more credit and offered more, better quality, and cheaper consumer goods for trade to their Déné counterparts than could the Hudson's Bay Company traders, drawing the anti-Semitic ire of both Hudson's Bay administrators and some government officials, who complained that the Jews were stealing business and corrupting Native buyers with too much economic agency. As peddlers frequently did, they supplied Natives goods based on local demand and introduced cash, and therefore greater purchasing power, as well as debt, and therefore weaker economic agency, to Native peoples. These economic encounters were lessons in the promises and perils of modern trade, as they brought their wares to an international and industrial market.

Jews and the Curios Business

Jews who bought furs from Native American trappers and Jews who sold tools, clothing, or other merchandise to Natives found themselves in an economic position between Natives at the geographic margins and their own commercial counterparts in urban centers. Jewish traders helped create new markets for new cultural commodities called "curios," either for the curious people they stood for or because they aroused the curiosity of the buyers. Jewish curio dealers provide a particularly rich subset of Jewish-Indian commercial encounters because they not only worked between Natives and whites economically, they also acted as cultural mediators, translators, and "middlemen" in white consumption of "Indianness." They sold physical proxies of their Indian clients to white buyers.

Curio traders also, quite consciously, positioned themselves in the in-between of white and Native culture and used aboriginality as currency in business. They branded themselves, alternatively, as Indians' custodians, Indians' friends, and sometimes even as near-Indians themselves. The Jewish traders who helped invent the curio market did not simply make upwardly mobile livings from the Indian heritage trade, although many did indeed do so. Through it they forged new, particularly western, solutions to their twin ambitions—integration and upward mobility. In marketing aboriginal Americana as pioneer curios, Jews participated in two simultaneous projects: the extension of capitalist enterprise, from which they benefited economically, and the commodification of Indian heritage, through which they gained social capital.[47]

A number of historical and economic forces positioned Jews to pioneer and participate in the Indian trade generally and the curio business specifically. The lure of the "pioneer spirit" that figured romance, adventure, and an exoticism unknown to Jews in the places from which they emigrated motivated some to seek business and settlement opportunities in the West.[48] More prosaically, many Jews, having migrated from the German territories and from eastern Europe for the promise of plenty that America offered, had been pushed out of seaboard cities by limited or limiting employment opportunities and found themselves on the margins of trade in the American West.[49] Merchant-class immigrant Jews on the vanguard of industrialization, as well as poorer, peddling Jewish immigrants who made their livings off the commercial opportunities that came with the expanding railroad infrastructure and the mining industries, helped shift the balance of land and power ownership away from Indians (and Hispanics) between the 1880s and the 1910s, forcing "formerly landed peoples [to sell] their chief asset . . . and [to] migrate to low-wage and lower status employment."[50] Many Jewish traders became involved in Indian trading, and in the curio business in particular, due to prior participation in complementary markets such as provisions sales, furs, hides, gold dust, land and oil speculation, small crafts, and hotels along trading routes and the new railways. Jewish merchants sold goods to and supported not just Native Americans but any and all potential client pools in the West, including the military, miners, homesteaders, and Chinese laborers. Buying and selling among Indians encouraged these Jews to familiarize themselves with various Native American languages, and cultural preferences, in order to establish business rapport, just as they had with other linguistic and cultural minorities.

Out of their involvement in complementary markets, Jews developed active roles in the Indian heritage industry, a market that linked rural outposts with national and trans-Atlantic markets for Indian things that crossed national borders. In Victoria, British Columbia, center of the Pacific northwest curio trade (including both the United States and Canada), and Santa Fe, New Mexico, the hub of the Southwest curio business, the first generations of dealers included a significant number of Jews, including Wolf Kalisher, Samuel Snow, Caspar Behrendt, Marcus Katz, Isadore Meyerowitz, Abe Cohn, Emil Strauss, Albert Rose, Elias and Henry Laupheimer, Mark Cohn, Bernard Wolf, Isaac Isaacson, Samuel Strauss, and Joseph Sondheimer. Andrew Alfred Aaronson, John J. Hart, Jacob Isaac, and Samuel Kirschenberg and his partner Fredrick Landsberg, all Jews, also owned and operated four of the five major companies active in the curio business on Johnson Street in Victoria.[51] In both places, preexisting business relationships based on contacts, linguistic capacities, trading post locations, merchandizing, and distribution channels helped establish the commercial infrastructure for the curio industry.[52] From the time of the region's initial boom, patriarchs of influential Jewish families in New Mexico like the Zeckendorfs, Ilfelds, Jaffas, Freudenthals, and Letchers established themselves via their overwhelmingly Jewish business networks as merchandisers, wholesalers, and financiers, often securing major provision contracts for the military and for government-run Indian reservations. The Spiegelbergs, one of the most powerful Jewish families in the Southwest, founded their fortune on government contracts to ship goods to and from Indian reservations in New Mexico.[53]

The curio business, in the estimation of scholar and director of the Wheelwright Museum of the American Indian Jonathan Batkin, "was the public aspect of a lopsided barter system in which dealers mined Native communities for artifacts that were later converted into cash."[54] Stimulated by widely held romantic notions of a vast, untamed wilderness and built upon the subjugation of Indigenous Peoples of the American West and their internment on reservations, the curio trade bloomed into a major industry between 1870 and 1910, as Euro-American mercantilism emerged with the completion of the transcontinental railway. To the whites who bought them, the category of Indian heritage objects included all the commodities that symbolized the Indians who may have used or made them. The Indian heritage market included all the material objects that indexed "Indianness" as an essential ingredient to their value, financial, social, and otherwise. It included ethnological specimens for the burgeoning new anthropological museums across the United States, Canada, and Europe, "relics" for the antiquities trade, sculptures and crafts for the emerging fine art market for Native works, and a huge swath of objects sold in the booming tourist market.[55] The curio market was one large element in a broader process in which Indian cultures were both commercialized and appropriated by non-Indians for profits and/or for personal or cultural gain. Scholars have mapped various forms of this appropriation and commercialization in markets, on stages, and in literary production and have described it as cultural imperialism, noting the various impacts that it has made on both Indians and non-Indians. They have teased out the connections between commercialism, appropriation, and the fashioning of modern American identity.[56]

Jews played central roles in the development of the Indian curio business. They moved Native artifacts and the meanings that could be attached to them between Native Americans and American whites and benefited both economically and metaphysically from buying and selling these objects. From the 1870s through the 1890s, Natives began trading their own heritage objects for peddler's and post traders' goods, and within a decade or two, Native Americans began producing commodities exclusively for cash sales in new markets. By the early decades of the twentieth century, Native producers began manufacturing these objects with the financial support of the U.S. Arts and Crafts Board.[57] Jewish entrepreneurs sold thousands of these objects, becoming culture brokers as well as commercial intermediaries in the buying, selling, and distribution of Indian artifacts. The curio trade grew from a small commercial interchange into an industry that had significant impacts on both Native producers and white consumers.[58]

Many Jewish traders who bought natural resources from Native Americans later pioneered and profited from the curio trade. The Polish Jewish immigrant Louis Fisher, for example, initially dealt in hides, pelts, and wool. He, along with Louis Gold and his uncle Joseph Hersch, "*El Polaco*," won grain contracts with the U.S. Army as it fought Indian wars through the 1850s. These contracts provided them with the funds and access they would later use in the 1870s and 1880s to pursue retail trade with Indians. Fisher, despite his work enabling the military to contain and pacify local Indians, began advertising, promoting, and selling Pueblo pottery and rugs from Santa Fe in 1877. In the 1870s, Louis Gold's son Jake received his own Indian trading license from Santa Fe County, enabling him to buy pottery directly from the Pueblos for the commercial market. A local newspaper reported in 1894 that Gold's "rapidly expanding business procured items from hundreds of self-employed agents with pack animals, journeying throughout remote and isolated areas of New Mexico, Arizona and Colorado, trading Germantown tools and brightly colored prints of saints for old blankets and pottery."[59] This kind of procurement of Indian blankets and pottery began as barter trade and later developed into cash commerce. John Jacob "Jack" Hart, an English Jew and former filibuster in Nicaragua, established himself as a merchant trader fifty yards from the Indian Reserve, selling liquor illegally to Haida and Tsimshian people for fur, silver, and gold work from skilled Native artisans, and eventually ran an Indian curio business in Victoria from 1880 until his death in 1900.[60]

The Northwest Coast had a network of Jewish entrepreneurs who built businesses around Indian trade. The Hudson's Bay Company, which had been granted exclusive rights for Indian trading by Great Britain, had dominated, sponsored, colonized, and policed the region. Their monopoly broke only after miners, speculators, and business-minded settlers rushed the Fraser River for gold in 1858.[61] Dozens of Jewish entrepreneurs traded with Indians for furs, fish oils, sealskins, timber, and other goods, including heritage items. Some speculated in land.[62] By the 1860s, Jewish tobacconist and fur trader Meyer Malowanski, along with his non-Jewish Croatian partner Vincent Charles Baranovich, for instance, had developed one of the largest fur trading businesses on the coast by establishing a chain of posts from Bella Bella to southern Alaska.[63] In 1867, the United States bought Alaska, orchestrated by the secretary of state William H. Seward. Money migrated to the tourist market after the fur boom busted in the 1880s. Businessmen refitted ships and shifted laborers who had once served the fur trade to the tourism industry. Companies like the Alaska Commercial Company, whose principle investors included the Gerstle, Schloss, Neibaum, Hirsch, Grunwald, Wasserman, and Barcowitz families, arranged and promoted this new form of business.[64] The Alaska Commercial Company had been purchased as the Russian American Company and renamed by Gerstle and Schloss, both Bavarian-born Jewish peddlers who worked in Kentucky and Louisiana before moving to California in the 1850s, where they opened the first Pony Express in Sacramento and eventually opened brokerage houses dealing in mining stocks out of San Francisco. The Alaska Commercial Company served as trading posts and general stores; gold, fish, and fur transfer stations; and, occasionally, as post offices and courthouses. It paid the United States some $9 million for the exclusive rights to harvest seal skin from the Pribilof and Aleutian Islands. This was an extraordinary windfall: with the 1895 discovery of gold in the Klondike River, business in the region exploded.

Jews owned and operated all three of the "Cheap John" emporium stores that catered, in part, to the first generation of West Coast tourists in Victoria. Entrepreneurs such as the brothers Levy, the brothers Shirpser, David Hart, and Mike Cohen helped grow the burgeoning industry. One claimed to do business not just in Polish, Russian, German, French, and Hebrew, but also in Mohawk, though this seems dubious, given that Mohawk was spoken in the Great Lakes region, not the Pacific Northwest Coast. When the lodes petered out, so did the Cheap John stores, though merchants like the Shirpsers and Levys continued to run Indian trading businesses.[65]

As the Indian heritage industry grew, curios reached the homes of thousands of American consumers and dozens of natural history and ethnology museums across the country and ocean, where they became objects of visual and educational consumption. Sellers created these markets through tourism and mail ordering and by supplying the art and artifacts that formed museums' exhibits. The curio dealers' marketing strategies tied direct links between American myths about Native peoples and the "Indian" items they made available for purchase. The market began to bloom in the 1870s as amateur and increasingly professional ethnology scholarship that focused on American Indians flourished and stimulated further interest among whites in owning a piece of Native America. Likewise, as American artists and intellectuals debated the Americanness of the American character, as opposed to the European past, its consciousness, and its pedigree, they searched for the roots of American authenticity among American Indian culture. Curio dealers took advantage of increased enthusiasm for things Indian and the concomitant increase in demand for tangible objects that might embody the figure of the Indian.

Jews sold Indian artifact collections to tourists and museums alike, creating new markets and creating value for heritage objects. They mediated the flow of Indian heritage objects, acquiring them from local homes and villages and distributing them into fashionable city homes in America's urban centers as decorations, tourist souvenirs, adventure memorabilia, and objects suited for playing Indian. They also moved these objects from trading posts to museums, where they formed collections as specimens of science displayed alongside exhibits of other so-called primitive peoples or exhibitions of America's natural history, geology, flora, and fauna. Victoria's J. J. Hart sold curios to middle-class tourists, mail-order consumers, and the World's Columbian Exposition in Chicago in 1893 and sold a significant collection to the German Jewish immigrant anthropologist Franz Boas.[66] Abraham A. Aaronson likewise sold hundreds of artifacts to tourists and museums, including the American Museum of Natural History, the Ottawa Field Museum, and the Royal Ontario Museum in Toronto.[67] Rose Aaronson, Abraham's wife, ran their curio shop for a time, advertising it as "the Cheapest place on the Pacific Coast to buy all kinds of Indian Baskets, Pow Wow Bags, Mats, Wood and Stone Totems, Pipes, Carved Horn and Silver Spoons, Rattles, Souvenirs, Novelties, Etc., . . . 25c and up. Postcards."[68] She sold some eighty-five carvings to collector Colonel Leigh Morgan Pearsall, whose collection eventually made it to the University of Florida. Frederick Landsberg made multiple major sales to collections, including those of the University of Pennsylvania in 1900, the Field Museum in Chicago in 1903 and 1904, the Milwaukee Public Museum, and in 1904 and 1905, the New York Museum of the American Indian. The Royal Ontario Museum in Toronto acquired Landsberg's remaining stock when his curio shop closed in 1908. Jacob Isaac arranged a shipment of Tsimshian and Nisga articles from the Nass and Skeena Rivers to the Indian commissioner Israel W. Powell in New York. The latter had earlier acted as a collector for the American Museum of Natural History and helped assemble the American centennial exhibition in Philadelphia. Isaac dealt in robes and Indian curios through his shop, called "the Indian Bazaar," for a time in the late 1880s, but by the 1890s, he had either been driven out of the market or closed shop to focus on a larger enterprise.[69]

The nineteenth-century commercial credit-reporting agency R. G. Dun & Company kept tabs on some of these Jewish "Indian dealers" and offered commentary to prospective business partners. Some were solvent and trustworthy, while others were not.[70] Dun's agents were known to harbor anti-Jewish biases; their reports on Jewish businesses frequently noted that their proprietors were Jews. About California's Louis Sloss, Dun's agents considered his wool and hides business a "very rich house and making $ rapidly."[71] They noted that New

Mexican merchant Zeckendorf family "carry a heavy stock [and] are German Jews . . . good busy men but said [to be] inclined to be tricky," while the Las Vegas' Letcher family was "of g[oo]d hab[its] . . . excellent bus[siness] capacity. Strictly honorable . . . men of good character."[72] Oklahoma and Indian Territories trader Lowenstein was noted as a "Jew, in bus[iness] 5 yrs . . . always paid promptly here, never failed . . . pushes and dabbles in everything" in 1870. Four years later, they noted he'd been in business "since 66, is a Jew . . . [and] is sharp and keen at a bargain."[73] Santa Fe Indian merchant Aaron Gold was "well known to the wholesale of their own creed" in 1871 and "a rascally thieving Jew, tried to run away but was arrested and given back . . . is not worthy of confidence or the respect of a dog" just two years later.[74] About Abe Cohn's Nevada Indian trading outfit, Dun's agents recommended doing business with him to "anyone [who] has a particular desire to get themselves well fleeced they cannot do better than sell gd. to this man of German vagabondage. Has neither means, refute nor eris [sic] not to be trusted."[75]

Curio dealers did more than just buy and sell Indian cultural objects. By creating markets for new goods, they encouraged Indian artisans to create products designed to attract white customers and exercised their economic power with artists to "evolve Indian arts and crafts designs into an art form with an appeal all its own," as historian Kathleen Howard has argued.[76] Jews helped make supplies of Indian artifacts available to a nation-sized white public. Museum curators, middle-class domestic designers, and children at play transformed these objects into symbols. Jews encouraged Indians to make particular objects—more of these, less of those—based on their value as commodities. Whether as home décor or props for childhood games of cowboys and Indians, the objects themselves fed America's appetite for the imaginary Indian.[77] Once in the hands of white consumers, curios inevitably embodied more of the imagined than the real Indian.[78] Jews thus helped shape the imaginations of the countless whites who bought curios and thereby their thinking about "Indians."

Curio dealers from the Southwest, Pacific Northwest, and the plains sold wholesale to one another in order to mix together pan-Indian collections valued by customers.[79] Dealers bundled together West Coast Haida totem poles, Southwest Navajo blankets, and plains Sioux headdresses, for example, clearly unconcerned about whether their white consumers paid attention to the cultural specifics of various Native peoples and artifacts. Jewish merchants, in search of widening mercantile opportunities, unwittingly provided the material basis on which a consuming white public absorbed ideas about Native Americans. In turn, collections spread out across the continent and around Europe into the homes and the imaginations of non-Indians, as indicated by the business registers from trader's shops like Gold's Free Museum in Santa Fe between 1892 and 1894, which recorded the names and addresses of the tourists who bought souvenirs.[80]

Like hundreds of young Jewish entrepreneurs who migrated in and through the burgeoning towns, cities, homesteads, Indian reservations, allotments, and in-between places in the shifting zone known as the western frontier, Julius Meyer forged a life and persona as an Indian trader and eventually as a curio dealer. The contours of Meyer's relationships with Indians provide an exemplary case of how Jewish settlers navigated between Natives and whites in trade and culture. Known to the Pawnees in and around Omaha, Nebraska, as "Curly-headed white chief who speaks with one tongue" and reputed to speak many tongues, including English, German, Ponca, Omaha, Winnebago, Pawnee, and Sioux, Meyer owned and operated the "Indian Wigwam," a trading post, curio shop, and somewhat of a tourist attraction on Farnam Street from the mid-1870s to the end of the century.[81]

Meyer's Omaha shop was endorsed as a credit-worthy business by agents from the R. G. Dun credit rating agency, who noted in the records they made available to potential lenders and business partners that Meyer "made some money in this bus[iness] and [is] considered safe" in 1873. With his brothers Max and Adolph, "Julius the Indian," in the cheeky words of the R. G. Dun report entry on Meyer, "is dashing into bus[iness] as hard as ever" in 1875.[82] "A master merchandiser of the Indian to white society," in the words of one journalist, Meyer began trading trinkets out of his brother Max's jewelry and cigar store for beads, moccasins, wampum pouches, tomahawks, bows and arrows, petrifications, and peace pipes as soon as he arrived in Omaha from Bromberg, Prussia, in the early 1860s.[83] He worked for a stint at the Department of the Platte, a military administrative district encompassing parts of Iowa, Nebraska, Dakota, and Utah Territories, established by the U.S. Army in 1866 to oversee the army's role along the Oregon

Figure 3.3. "Box-Ka-ne-sha-hash-ta-Ka (or Julius Meyer)." Robert N. Dennis Collection of Stereoscopic Views of Indians of North America. Stephen A. Schwarzman Building / Photography Collection, Miriam and Ira D. Wallach Division of Art, Prints and Photographs MFY Dennis Coll 92-F138. New York Public Library. https://digitalcollections.nypl.org/items/510d47e0-bb8c-a3d9-e040-e00a18064a99.

Figure 3.4. Julius Meyer and a group of Native Americans posing in front of his "Indian Curiosity" store in Omaha, Nebraska. Nebraska State Historical Society, RG2246-06.

route to Salt Lake City and the Bozman Trail through eastern Wyoming, and as an interpreter.[84] He led a delegation of Native leaders to the Paris Exposition in 1889 and boasted of his close bonds of friendship with Standing Bear, Red Cloud, Sitting Bull, and other esteemed Native American leaders whom he likely paid to pose with him in a series of portraits taken over several years.[85]

The photographs helped Meyer market his curio business, but they also provided a means for Meyer, like the dozens of other Jewish immigrant curio dealers, to capture and represent something of his own pioneer American Jewish identity—a new iteration of Diaspora Jew—constructed in dialogue with "the Indian." Curio dealers like Meyer cast themselves alternatively as authentic buckskinned frontiersmen, noble diplomats in suit-tails, scholarly minded merchants, and even as Indian chiefs themselves.[86]

Merchants like Meyer used several marketing strategies in their catalogs, shops, print advertisements, and photographs they arranged in order to sell the curio objects themselves and nurture the development of the new market. These strategies required merchants to develop alternate personae for presentation to diverse white audiences and customers, reflecting competing ideas of "the Indian" that might sell curios to white customers. The dealer dressed himself as an antique curator, an ethnologist, a scholar of natural history, a cultural rescue worker, or a salvager of ancient cultures that might soon be lost to the modern world. All these strategies relied on the sellers' differences from Indians—their whiteness. Yet at times, merchants also branded themselves as red, making themselves out to be honorary members of Indian communities or initiates into Indians' esoteric spiritual knowledge. Being in the middle of Indians and whites, overall, required a balance of identifications—some pinkness, as it were.

The marketing techniques developed by Jewish curio traders involved a certain amount of identity play on the part of the salesmen. This play served Jewish merchants' needs to Americanize themselves as well as the more immediate material goals of building the market and selling the wares. Jewish curio dealers learned a great deal about local Native life on the plains, up the Pacific Coast and in the Southwest, and touted this knowledge to bolster sales and as a way of casting themselves as men of mediation and understanding, between red and white. They dressed themselves in various roles, each distinct but all formed in opposition to "the Indian" they sold. They presented themselves as educators through their comfort and familiarity with ethnological science. As "half-way-Indian" pioneer frontiersmen, they claimed an intimacy with the exotic details of Indian daily life and ritual. They also made themselves out as leaders in diplomatic rapprochement between whites and Indians.

The protection, preservation, displays, and sale of Indian heritage objects also served local tourist industries in the West. In British Columbia, Jewish curio dealers worked with government officials to help attract tourists eager to observe and experience the exotic Natives. In his advertising campaigns, Frederick Landsberg publicized that his clients included international museums that had all sought to buy bits of Canada and its Natives through him. These businessmen promoted themselves as experts, scientists, curators, and presenters of all things Indian. Acts of self-branding helped them convey the authority they assumed would convince buyers to buy their wares. They tried to convey their mastery and control over Indians by claiming expertise and exclusive access to information about Indians. At the request of the Canadian government, Landsberg prepared a special display of artifacts and arranged a meeting with a delegation of Indian leaders for the duke and duchess of York (later King George V and Queen Mary) when they came to Victoria in 1902. The Canadian Pacific Rail's prestigious Empress Hotel bought a set of totem poles for its lobby from him, and in 1906 he obtained permission from the tourist association to open an Indian exhibition, which he titled "Landsberg's Free Museum." It doubled as an ethnological institution and gift shop. Indian culture in Victoria, as elsewhere, served as a promotional device, seductive and successful enough for the Tourist Development Agency of British Columbia to use as a principle means of attracting tourists.[87] The City of Victoria, as with Santa Fe, recognized itself as a central hub for curio distributors and provided museum collectors with guides, Jews among them, and contacts with Natives from whom such collections could be gathered.[88]

In Santa Fe, Jake Gold, who ran his own "Free Museum" sold curios to Adolph Bandelier, the early twentieth-century scholar of the Southwest, among

F. LANDSBERG
VIEW OF MR. F. LANDSBERG'S INDIAN CURIO COLLECTION, VICTORIA, B.C.
Published by T. N. Hibben & Co., Victoria, B.C. No. 53

Figure 3.5. View of Mr. Landsberg's Indian Curio Collection, Victoria, BC. Item MSC130-13430 from the Philip Francis British Columbia Postcards Collection, Simon Fraser University Library, Special Collections and Rare Books.

thousands of others. Bandelier praised Gold's "magnificent collection of Indian goods," a portion of which he acquired for the Museum fur Völkerkunde in Berlin.[89] By 1883, Gold "was the most famous curio dealer in the Southwest."[90] One of his catalogs, "Objects of Interest from the Plains and Rocky Mountains," attested to the merchant's willingness to both acquire and market himself as a purveyor of Indian heritage objects not just from the Southwest but nationwide. H. H. Tammen and W. G. Walz of El Paso, Gold's Jewish competitors, mimicked his catalogs, selling packages of goods as collections, including one, for example, of "pottery, Apache Soap Weed Basket, a Pueblo Idol, a bow, arrows, Beaded moccasins, an Indian drum, a buckskin shirt, Indian necklace, a raw hide canteen, Apache war club, mounted bird, a pair of old Spanish spurs, . . . all labeled and carefully shipped." Other catalogs organized their curios by tribe: Uncompahgre, White River Ute, Sioux, Piute, Crow, San Carlos, Apache, Zuni, Navajo, Cochita, and others.[91] Merchants sold Indian curios to whites by cloaking themselves as scientists and, in contrast to the Indians themselves, as whites.

Marketing curios as "relics" or antiques provided an additional sales strategy that pulled both purse strings and cultural strings; the ability to tie an object to a bygone era of human or Indian history increased a curio's sale price and endowed it with an aura of that certain *something* that modern civilization had lost.[92] Prior to 1910, H. H. Tammen published at least thirteen full-length catalogs and at least four supplements in color for mail-order sales from "The H.H. Tammen Curio Co." established in 1881 in Denver, Colorado. One, called "Western Echoes," from 1882, turned Indian objects into stand-ins for the ancient aboriginal American past, somehow both lost to the West and still located there.[93] These "echoes," in the form of Indian "relics," could be purchased, owned, and kept. Likewise, "Gold's Free Museum and Old Curiosity Shop," not unlike Landsberg's "Free Museum" in Victoria, boasted in an advertisement of the "Oldest Indian Cart and Plow in America, to be seen at Gold's Free Museum." The Golds sold "old stone vessels and pottery from the Cliff Dwellers of New Mexico," and Jake promoted not just his wares but New Mexico itself as the "richest field in the world of antiquities and historical curiosities."

Jake Gold's marketing strategy associated his curios with his global competitors' exotica and relics, elevated them above all, and then excoriated his customers' ignorance, hoping to convince them to buy a piece of that past:

> Americans—always comparatively ignorant of their own great nation—travel the earth over in search of novelties less marvelous than abound in New Mexico. . . . The undersigned has known and been known by the people of New Mexico for 27 years. He is familiar with their country, their customs and their languages. His collectors are all the time gathering curios from the remotest parts of the Territory where the stranger could not penetrate. There is no archeological treasure which does not come to his hands, from relics of the Stone Age to the implements used by the aborigines of to-day. All articles are genuine, and it is well known by New Mexican travelers that each article can be bought more cheaply from him than from the Indians themselves.[94]

Boasting of his own credentials as a master of Indian country, customs, and languages and his collectors' furtive and eroticized access to zones otherwise forbidden to white men, Gold claimed to have been the middleman for all local artifacts, hoping to convince buyers to bypass even Native sellers themselves. Jewish merchants not only competed with Indians for the profits of Indian heritage; they appropriated Native "identities" to expand the market and to corner sales.

If the remote past, "relics from the Stone Age," offered a certain appeal, so too could contemporary ethnological accuracy, "the implements used by the aborigines of to-day," provide another marketing strategy merchants designed for institutional collectors.[95] Gold's catalog of "Curios from the Ancient Mounds and Ruins in the Salt River Valley, Arizona [Gila]," for example, contained "many curious Articles used by the Modern Indians of Arizona and New Mexico." The 1893 advertisement pitched an "extremely low price asked for this collection [which] places it in the power of any college, public institution and many private collectors to become the owner of it."[96] A related strategy leveraged the idea of the West's natural landscape as a point of sale. Calling himself a "Purveyor of Natural History," Tammen, known in Denver as an amateur mineralogist, eventually built one of the largest curio businesses in the country, growing out of a business enterprise in which he and a partner sold inks, stereoviews, and photographs of western landscapes.[97]

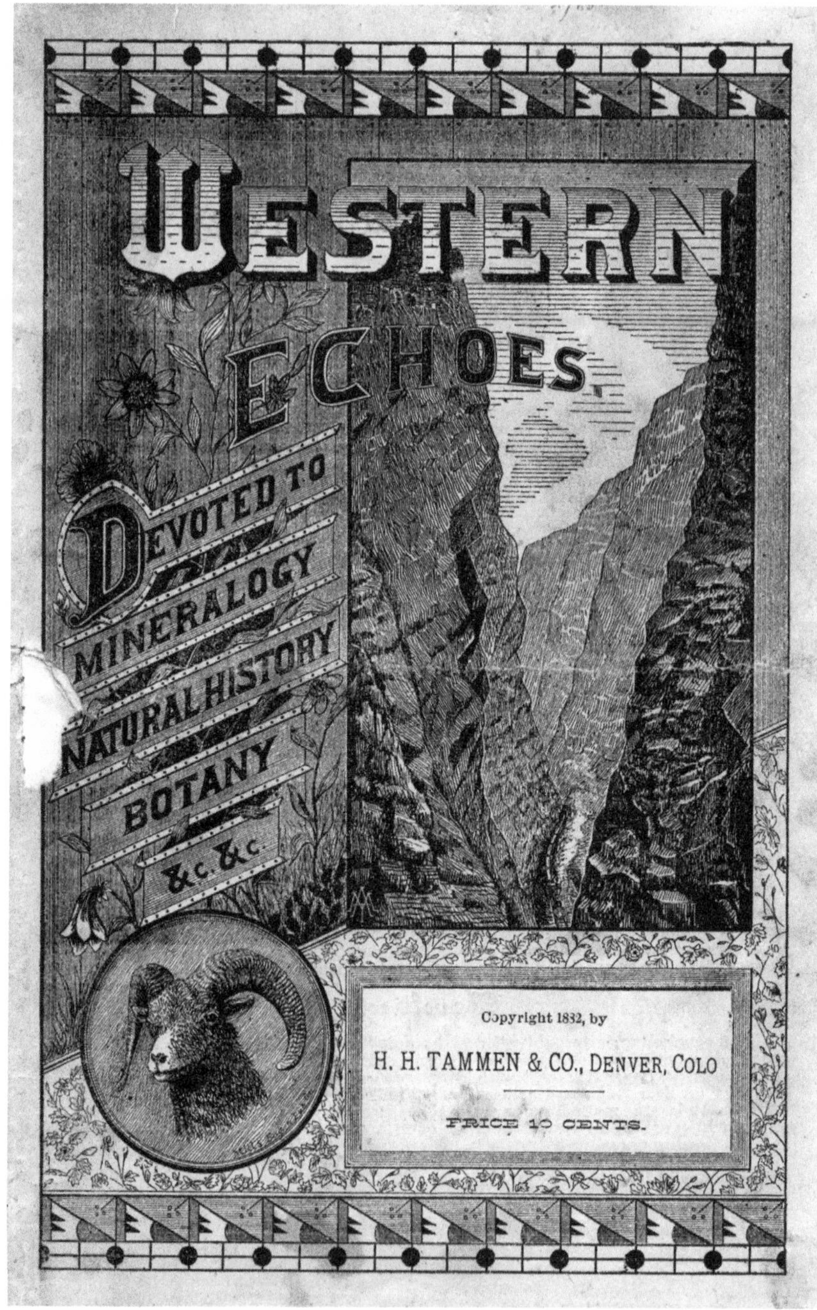

Figure 3.6. H. H. Tammen & Co., *Western Echoes: Devoted to Mineralogy, Natural History, Botany, Denver, Colo.* (1882). Special Collections, University of Delaware Library, Newark, Delaware.

Figure 3.7. "Jake Gold, dealer in Indian and Mexican curiosities, 1880(?)." Courtesy of the Palace of the Governors Photo Archives (NMHM/DCA), negative no. 009894.

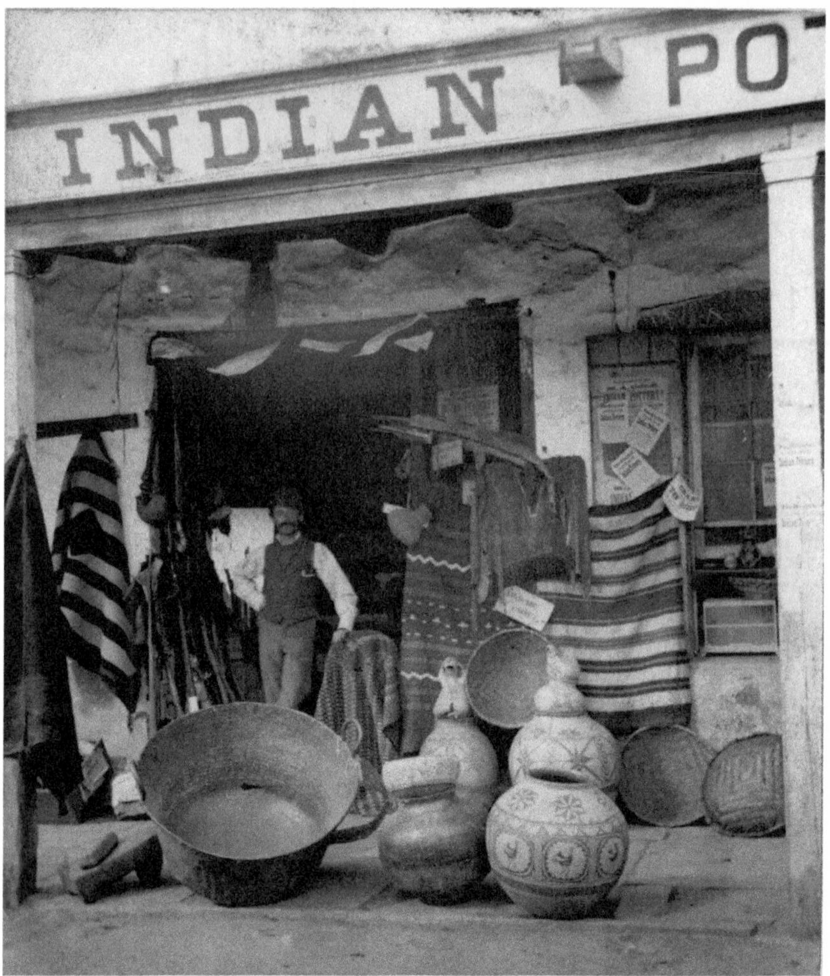

Figure 3.8. "Jake Gold's, Santa Fe, New Mexico." Ben Wittick, 1885. Courtesy of the Palace of the Governors Photo Archives (NMHM/DCA), negative no. 086877.

Other dealers emphasized the ritual power still attached to "Indian Idols" to enhance their desirability. "The Idols are made by the Cochita Indians in New Mexico," ran one advertisement, "and until recently have been worshiped by them as gods. Nothing surpasses them as an ornament for mantle pieces or brackets, and their extreme oddity makes them a valuable curiosity. . . . Should you desire any . . . write, as they are hard to obtain and not always in stock."[98] This marketing approach appealed to a dimension of *Indianthusiasm* that would develop only after the threat of violence in the West had disappeared: Indian wisdom or spirituality.[99]

The role of educator, ethnographer, and natural historian provided one further opportunity for improved sales and for Jews to carve out a comfortable

American persona. One curio catalog listed a collection of "wood, slate, stone carving, basket woven articles, wearing apparel, and miscellaneous section including doctors' aprons, Wampooms, used by the Indians as money, carved spoons, recreation games, paint, shells, bracelets, sperm-whale, bear, beaver, seal and other animals' teeth, tom toms of different sizes." As this wares list shows, curio dealers bundled together all kinds of commodities—medical, domestic, music, and play objects—and linked them seamlessly with objects of nature like shells, animal teeth, and carvings of various elemental materials. Linking Indians with nature and presenting the dealer as natural historian provided displayable objects for urban consumers eager to bring natural exotica into their homes.[100] It also allowed Jewish merchants to present themselves as knowledgeable of and connected to the land, countering the persistent stereotype that they suffered from estrangement from the land. Like "red Indians," their ties to the land felt intimate. Or like "white men," they exercised mastery over Indians. Either way, Jews connected themselves to land via their (sometimes ambivalent) connections to Native Americans. Morris Moss, an English Jewish trader on the Northwest Coast, fashioned himself an "expert" on the Natives around Bella Coola.[101] Landsberg published a pamphlet that advertised what he called "The Largest Stock of Curios on the Pacific North West," which included pseudoethnographic discussions of Indian mythology, the history of the totem pole, legends and traditions of Alaskan Indians, and a terse study of *Ne-kil-stlass*, "The Creator-The-Raven God." J. J. Hart sold shaman rattles, totem poles, canoes, baskets, masks, cedar bar rings, and bowls from his "Indian Bazaar" and fancied himself an Indian ethnographer. He published a booklet, part legend, part mythology, and wholly advertisement, promoting his shop's collection, which he claimed had the "largest and Finest Assortment of Curios on the Pacific Coast."[102]

By portraying mastery over Indian artifacts, lore, ritual objects, culture, or the ancient Indian past, Jews marked their distance and their connection with Indians as a way to exhibit their own inextricable ties to civilization. This kind of mastery invited one more role curio dealers took on for themselves, that of the Indian pacifier. Listed as a pawnbroker at the British Columbia and Alaska Colonial and Indian Exhibition in 1886, "Wild Dick" Aaronson told the British press he was "in charge of B.C. Indian curios," clearly modeling himself on the Wild West show character "Wild Bill" Hickok. Dressed in buckskin, he fibbed that he was "employed to hunt the recalcitrant Indian to his forest retreat," pushing back Indians, killing them, and selling the curious booty to white consumers of white bravado and Indian-hating.[103] The idea of conquered Indians presented an opportunity for Jewish curio dealers to play two roles: that of the Indian's conqueror and that of custodian of ancient America, now embodied in the leftover artifacts of a "disappeared," or in any event inevitably disappearing, Indian race. Dealers included dubious but enchanting historical claims in their promotional materials that equated, for example, Northwest Coast tribes with ancient civilizations like the Phoenicians, with whom one trader claimed the Haida shared linguistic traits and had made contact in ancient times.[104] Another advertising booklet contained descriptions of the artifacts at the Indian Bazaar, including a forty-foot totem pole from Skidegate on Queen Charlotte Islands, which, it claimed, "will probably be sent to London, and set up next to Cleopatra's needle; so that a specimen of ancient Egyptian and Haidah work can be seen side by side."[105]

Presenting oneself as a trusted friend of Native Americans offered one last role that curio dealers designed for themselves to improve sales and affect the kind of identity transformation that helped Jews feel at home in the West. Uncostumed Jewish merchants like Bernard Seligman, Zadoc Staab, Carl Harberg, Lehman Spiegelberg, and Julius Meyer regularly posed for photographs with costumed Indians, documenting their connections and suggesting a certain kind of closeness.[106] In Apache Oklahoma Territory, Kishinev-born Peter M. Levite arrived in 1901 at age thirty and opened a shop that served the Indian and non-Indian residents of the area for several decades and became a tourist destination and well-known geographical landmark.[107] Peter Levite's son George reported that his father's business "might not have survived had it not been for our faithful Indian customers," many of whom could neither read nor write. As a result, these customers depended on the honesty of proprietors like Levite for provisions and foodstuffs, while their traditional modes of sustenance shifted due to government removal and assimilation policies. Though Levite's reminiscences included an awareness of the Natives' growing dependence on merchants for tools, clothing, and foodstuffs, as well as details about the economics of the relationships, he emphasized the affective dimensions of the "instant rapport between the Indians and the Levites."[108] Levite preferred to leave the fundamental asymmetries in power between immigrant Jews and Native Americans that determined their relationships unacknowledged.

Curio salesmen thus "sold" more than Indian objects. They sold the idea of the Indian, flexible enough to include a range of meanings. They also sold the idea of the Plains, the Pacific Northwest, and the Southwest—the place to which many Americans, artists and intellectuals among them, would look for the inspiration of a uniquely American character.[109] These intellectuals would also come to shape federal Indian policy in the coming years.[110] The historian Kathleen Howard emphasized the change the Santa Fe Railway brought to the tourist industry as it bloomed and described the ways that retail urban curio entrepreneurs sold souvenirs along the line to a traveling public and thereby helped "invent" the Southwest.[111] The Fred Harvey Indian Department, whose key buyer and marketing strategist was a Jew named Herman Schweitzer, ramped up nationwide interest in Indian objects, both prehistoric and contemporary, an interest already piqued by World's Fairs, expositions, and Wild West shows that brought Indian life to the public.[112]

The curio trade grew out of the smallest commercial interchange to emerge as an industry that had significant impacts on both Native producers and white consumers. Jews entered the curio business for a short window of time, just long enough to accumulate sufficient capital to move on to bigger cities, bigger businesses, and frequently, bigger Jewish communities. Through this business, Jews helped invent a new heritage industry and bring some Native Americans into the capitalist system itself, thus participating in the long project of assimilating and "civilizing" Native Americans. Jews' involvement in various Indian trades, including curios, had several significant impacts. First and foremost, it made many Jews wealthier. By dint of geography, commerce with Indians provided opportunities for economic mobility. Whether short of work in larger city centers or enchanted by the "spirit of adventure," young Jewish entrepreneurs from German territories and eastern Europe emigrated in order to labor at the social and commercial margins of America, at the bottom of the economic ladder. These merchants acquired language facility; forged relationships of relative trust with Native groups; and obtained government contracts to supply reservations in virtually all the western states, including Alaska; and in the western provinces of Canada, traded furs, Indian arts and crafts, and provisions. But the effects of the Indian trade grew larger than their impacts on migrant settler Jews.

CHAPTER 4

JEWISH RHETORICAL USES OF INDIANS IN AN ERA OF NATIVIST ANXIETIES

In establishing themselves economically as commercially valuable suppliers and builders in America's West, Jews enjoyed significant upward mobility in the last decades of the nineteenth century. Part of American Jews' civic and fiscal arrival in the West owed itself to the economic opportunities generated by Jewish encounters with Native Americans. Western Jews positioned themselves as commercial traders of foodstuffs, dry goods, and inexpensive merchandise between whites and Native Americans. They served as economic middlemen between Native producers of curios and those non-Indian consumers of "Indianness" too.[1] Through their economic, social, and imagined encounters with Native Americans, Jews advanced their twin goals in the West in the late nineteenth and early twentieth centuries—namely, economic mobility and cultural integration. But the Jewish position vis-à-vis Native people in the United States was not entirely middling. Jews were not "between" settlers and Indigenous People; they were clearly part of the settler colonial population. Jews acted as colonial agents and frequently relished the privileges of being figured as white, enjoying its benefits in the frontier West. They suffered virtually none of the barriers to enfranchisement or social or economic mobility of Indians, Blacks, Asians, or Mexicans. Jews proudly identified as harbingers of civilization and active agents in the advancement of American national interests through Indian pacification and the expansion of settlement and capitalism. The crude fact is that Jews stood on the "winning" side of the frontier process that had ultimately and profoundly deleterious effects on Native American life.

In the early years of the twentieth century, with the Indian Wars largely over, the West "won," the frontier considered by most whites closed, and the explosion of new immigrant populations, Americans debated just what, exactly, constituted the heart of American identity. They wove a thorny knot of ideas about race, nation, and religion, into which Jews and Indians—alongside many other American "minority" groups—were tied. New to the ongoing discussion about corporate group identity in the early twentieth century was a befuddled mix of social, scientific, polity oriented, popular, and high cultural discourses concentrated around the notion of "race." Those who offered a vision to "protect" the white, Christian, "original" inhabitants of the United States from new off-white and non-Protestant immigrants or other racial outsiders were known as nativists; their anti-immigrant and often anti-Indian movement was generally referred to as nativism.[2]

Who were the Jews and who were Indians in these discussions? What was a race? Were Jews or Indians examples of a "pure race"? Was being a "mixed race" a justification for exclusion or evidence of assimilability and virtue? How were Jewish and Indian "racial" identities linked to or detached from those other categories that were also used to define peoplehood—namely, nation, and religion? Where were Jews and Indians respectively located in the social imagination? How did Jews intervene in this rhetoric, and how did they use Indians in those interventions?

American nativist sentiment in the early decades of the twentieth century targeted Jews and Native Americans and forced both groups to develop strategies of resistance. Anti-Semitism and anti-Indian sentiment paralleled one another and spurred Jewish and Indian fiction writers and journalists to contest ideas about them that were underpinned by the same ideological "structure of domination."[3] This chapter describes where and how Jews and Native Americans were figured in American nativist discourse. It shows that Jews responded to nativism and that part of this response involved evoking rhetorical uses of Indians in support of their aims. American Jews deployed ideas about American Indians in their engagements with, responses to, and creation of racial discourse. In defending themselves against an array of defamations, and in waging a discursive and ultimately failed war with the forces that aimed to halt new Jewish immigration from eastern Europe to the United States, American Jews made rhetorical uses of Indians that were far from consistent. On the one hand, they recapitulated hierarchical visions of racial belonging that put Native Americans beneath Jews, thereby agreeing to the terms of nativist sentiment and arguing, as selective nativists themselves, for their own rightful place in the emerging landscape of belonging. On the other hand, American Jews also inveighed against race thinking altogether and developed a new antirace ideology that they hoped would end acrimony directed at Jews, Native Americans, and all other American minorities.

American Jews pursued both these strategies despite the fact that the two were at odds with one another. While one strategy aimed to leverage exclusionist understandings of corporate difference to elevate Jewish standing to those with the most privilege, the other tried to level the playing field, placing Jews as a minority among other minorities. The contradiction seemed not to have mattered. American Jews were poised between champions of the broader colonial settler population in the late nineteenth-century West (discussed in chapters 1, 2, and 3) and the liberal, progressive attitude many Jews would take up by the middle of the twentieth century (discussed in chapters 5 and 6). Jewish efforts to intervene against anti-immigration policy in particular—the most potent manifestation of early twentieth-century American nativism as far as Jews were concerned—led to a newfound antirace impulse among a portion of American Jews, an essential part of which inspired many midcentury Jews to social justice and civil and human rights work for and with Native Americans.

Jews and Indians in the Rise of American Racial Thinking

Though race thinking had a century-long history by the turn of the twentieth century, its scope and popularity skyrocketed after 1900. Race science and eugenics impacted virtually all fields of social life, from churches to the military, from sports and entertainment to higher education, and in health, banking, food, vice, sex, marriage, and childhood. Many of the most influential race science operatives, executives, and chief advocates received funding from the same sources. They were affiliated with a set of interconnected bodies founded in the first two decades of the twentieth century, including the Immigration Restriction League, the American Breeders Association, the Race Betterment Foundation, the International Federation of Eugenics Organizations, the Galton Society, the American Eugenics Society, the Pioneer Fund, and its main driving force, Wickliffe Preston Draper.[4] Mainstream social scientists and other civic activists funded popular dissemination of books, pamphlets, and journals like *Western Destiny*, *Mankind Quarterly*, and the *Liberty Lobby*. Racial theory dealt not just with the scientific explorations about group identity but also with rights: who could or should be educated, enjoy citizenship and the franchise, and even have children. For race thinkers, race provided the key to social progress, public education, social harmony, national welfare, and the future of humanity.[5]

American nativists linked together the fear that true Americans might, for the first time in its history, run out of usable land with the longstanding conviction that Indians would inevitably disappear from modernity or be fully assimilated to white ways. This toxic blend of anxiety and misunderstanding shifted many American discussions about race, land, and citizenship away from Native Americans and toward Blacks and, to a growing extent, the ethnic urban immigrant poor. The early decades of the twentieth century saw a hardening of race thinking into two categories—Black and white—and a growing disquiet about the possibilities of crossing the divide. Yet in virtually all the hierarchies of race that eugenicists, racial thinkers, social commentators, and scholars created, Indians were ranked at or near the bottom. Those peoples who remained stubbornly neither "white" nor "black" were frequently slated into one of the two categories; Indians became problematically Black, while Jews became problematically white. While Jews, unlike Indians, Mexicans, and Asians, for the most part benefited from this hardening of peoplehood into a racial binary, the questions that were brought to bear on one minority were also brought to bear on the others: were these "others" assimilable? Could they make good citizens? What would mixing with them do to the nation's body politic, its religious character, or the mental and moral health of its future generations? Their existence and persistence raised challenges and fears about the singularity and superiority of the white race.[6]

By the turn of the twentieth century, Jews were receiving considerable attention and worry in nativist racial schemas. As historian Eric Goldstein has shown, by the 1890s, Jewish racial stereotypes had become popular on the vaudeville stage; in humor magazines, weekly magazines, and journals; and social commentaries.[7] Their putative nervousness, intellectuality, and lack of physical development—all Indian opposites—exemplified effects of life confined to cities, a metropolis, alienated from nature, where American identity was ideally forged (frontier or farm).[8] As Jewish immigration from eastern Europe swelled to unprecedented numbers, Jews became objects in popular media representations like plays, jokes, political cartoons, and songs as well as in social and political discourse preoccupied with American ideals, its future character, and the nature of Americanism. Jews served as a convenient symbol for a host of social problems and issues that were of mounting concern, linked as they were in the popular mind to commerce, the city, and modernity itself.

The case was the reverse for American Indians. Before the twentieth century, Indians took up a great deal of space in the social imaginary of corporate difference, while in the twentieth they began to recede from the nation's discussion. Blacks and immigrants, by contrast, took stage at the center of the drama of American belonging. With a few noteworthy exceptions, Indians appeared surprisingly few times, and often merely in passing, from the canonical texts of race scientists and eugenics writers. Elided from the discourse on race, according to a logic that assumed social evolution and accorded tremendous virtue in longevity, the idea of Indian disappearance became central to notions of race longevity and crucial to the debate about assimilability of various nonwhite races.

Native Americans invariably ranked at or close to the bottom of the racial hierarchies that American scholars, commentators, and nativists imagined, while Jews were classed more ambiguously, though in all cases higher than Indians. American assessments about race occasionally discussed both Jews and Native Americans in the same text. Newspapers, journals, lawyers, and activists, for example, repeatedly compared the trial of Spotted Hawk and Little Whirlwind, wrongly accused for the murder of a white herder in Miles City, Montana, in the late 1890s to the Dreyfus Affair.[9] The Philadelphia physician Samuel George Morton, whose book *Crania Americana*, supplied data on the cranial capacities of some eight hundred skulls, found Indians "averse to cultivation," "altogether repulsive . . . slow & stupid," with vacant expressions on their faces.[10] An esteemed scientists and protoethnographer in his day, Morton viewed the differences between humans as a matter of species difference (rather than of variety among humans).[11] He described the Delaware Tribe with reference to Jews, concluding that "their bodies were strong, but of a strength rather fitted to endure hardship than to sustain much bodily labor; their features were regular; their countenances sometimes fierce, in common rather resembling a Jew than a Christian."[12] Morton's conclusions about "Hebrews" echoed qualities he had ascribed to Indians: "[The Hebrew's] zealous attachment to their religion, and their patient endurance of adversity," he wrote, "are among the most striking traits of their character."[13] For Morton, Jews and Indians were similar in their zeal, their attachment to old religion, their being stiff-necked and past-oriented people. Jews, however, succeeded at survival, whereas Indians, he assumed, were failing.

Other scholars suggested parallels between the Jewish and the Indian "character." Writers throughout the late nineteenth and early twentieth centuries frequently fashioned both Jews and Indians as ancient peoples. In some writers' hands, the ancient Jewish past was intimately interwoven into the Jews' character, culture, or even blood, while in others' readings, modernity had severed the Jews' ancient moral and religious underpinning. Jews were imagined as simultaneously the most ancient of peoples and the most modern, as a people able to preserve their ancient ways and employ them as a moral guide as they faced the complexities of modernity.[14] According to this line of thinking, Jews might serve as a model of how Americans might survive the degradation of the modern world with their religious and value systems intact, unlike Indians, who could not serve as any useful model, given their inevitable disappearance. American Indians' "ancientness," by contrast, apparently inured them to the benefits of modernity and made them the subjects of Christian missionary and government efforts, which had ultimately failed to domesticate or assimilate Indians.[15]

Jews and Native Americans symbolized many different things to the non-Jews and non-Indians who wrote about them after the turn of the century. Jews symbolized the capitalist ethos, for which they were alternately praised or condemned, while Indians, by contrast, were perennially accused of dismal and woefully inadequate business acumen, as the symbolic figure for whom modernity—its capitalism and its urbanism—would inevitably leave behind. The matter of the "pure" or "mixed" status of so-called racial groups in America at times placed Jews and Indians into relation with one another. The place of Jews in racialist thinking was sometimes honored and celebrated for Jews' apparent purity of race, often contrasted with Indians, the quintessentially "mongrelized," as one leading historian, journalist, eugenicist, political theorist, anti-immigration advocate, and champion of scientific racism, Theodore Lothrop Stoddard, put it.[16] Another nativist, Alfred Schultz, claimed to account for the rises and falls of the ancient races on earth and the implications of these patterns on American immigration policy in his book *Race or Mongrel?* Schultz referenced "Indians" from dozens of countries, each time as "interbred," "mongrelized," "crossed," and "compounded." Schultz argued, by contrast, that "the Jews' knowledge of the physiological law that promiscuous crossing degrades, deteriorates, mongrelizes the participants, enabled them to develop from a small Eastern tribe into one of the great nations of the earth. . . . The Jews have brought forth poets, writers, artists, scientists, financiers, and philanthropists."[17] Indians ceased to be a pure race and, in so far as they blended with others, deteriorated their purity. Jews succeeded, he claimed,

> because . . . they belong to a great race, and they kept and do keep that race pure. The greatest mongrelizing machine of antiquity, the empire called the Roman did not succeed in mongrelizing them. America will not be able to destroy them. The Jews have overcome well-nigh insurmountable obstacles; they are succeeding everywhere, because they have been and do remain true to themselves, that is, true to their race instincts. They demonstrate to the world that the blood that courses in the veins of the individual is more sacred than gold, silver, territory flag, and country. . . . Race purity is the secret of the success of the Jews.[18]

For Schultz, the inevitable future success of the Jews in America rested on Jews' supposed racial purity, while by contrast, Indians' inevitable decline rested on Indians' inability to remain racially pure. Jews and Indians, in his schema, were object lessons for white America, case studies that ought to inspire intense racial boundary enforcement.

In some popular, scholarly, and policy-oriented projections that grappled with ideas of racial purity or with totems of modernity, Jews and Indians were presented as opposite "types." But in other discussions, writers cut Jews and Indians from precisely the same cloth. The essential preoccupation that would bring any commentator to consider both Jews and Indians concerned the extent to which either was assimilable. Nonwhite groups were routinely compared and pitted against one another as better or worse candidates for successful assimilation. Nathaniel Shaler's 1904 work, *The Neighbor*, argued that both Jews and Indians could be assimilated into white America, though the differences and comparisons between them were instructive. Shaler, the dean of Harvard's Lawrence Scientific School, observed that Jews, "like blacks and Indians," inspired repugnance on account of their racial features. He nonetheless argued that Jews were "nearer to ourselves than the people of any other stock" and that the "inter-tribal repugnance" experienced with them "should certainly be much less than that which we experience in meeting Africans or American Indians."[19]

Shaler suggested that both peoples held the promise of being full humans, on par in some ways and perhaps even superior to whites in others. While "people of [American Indian] stock are, as regards their general intelligence, little, if at all, below the average of Europeans," he claimed, "their physical development is probably rather above the plane of the so-called Aryan folk."[20] Indians' innate qualities, however, had limitations that rendered them easily subjected to external rule. For Shaler, Indians lacked "energetic power," and therefore they suffered as incompetent laborers. "This lack of capacity to apply energy in a continuous manner," he wrote, "appears to be due to some peculiarity of the nervous system. . . . The fate of the Indian in contact with the peoples of northern Europe appears to have been in large measure determined by his inability to labor."[21] Similarly, Shaler concluded that the Jews, despite their good quality "stock" of innate qualities, were out of step with the kind of labor that modernity required of races to succeed. "The Semite is, on the whole, the ablest type of man the world has known," he wrote, "but a type which is somewhat archaic for the reason that its powers are not those most intimately related to the life of the genus in its present stage or in its foreseeable future."[22] As a racial type, Shaler's Jews were of the highest order but stuck in the past and held back by tradition, which curtailed Jews' ability to assimilate or progress.

Amid all his traffic in racial stereotyping, Shaler concluded his best-selling book with a surprisingly liberal plea for his white readers to transcend these misconstrued stereotypes. Arguing against the stereotypes that shape "our" Aryan impressions of others, he beseeched his readers to consider how intensely social categories and "habits of mind" misshape real people and therefore distort and curb their abilities to live decent American lives. Reflecting on his own unchecked assumptions as a rhetorical device, as a way of modeling his own thinking for his readers, he wrote that "the dominating power of the categorizing habit that the Indian . . . appears to me as he does to the frontiersman as that kind of man who is good when he is dead. So it is in all our contacts with our fellow-men; we have inherited from the lower life, that of the brutes and brutal man, a habit which leads to a classification of our kind, embodying hatreds as animal in their nature as those which exist between dogs and foxes—such categories as are labeled 'Vile Jew' and the like."[23] Shaler protested against all these "classification" prejudices and aimed his readers at overcoming them, concluding that

> whoever will essay this task [of reexamining biases] will be surprised to find how differently the fellow-man appears in the new light; how changed indeed is the whole world with the old scales fallen from our eyes. There are no more common people, "dogs of Jews," or "Indians good when they are dead," but each stands before us in the dignity of his manhood as a presentation of the hundred million years of life of this world summed in that marvelous personality of man. Whoever sees this in his fellow has seen into the promised land; he has in a true sense gained religion.[24]

Shaler stood out as one who argued on behalf of Indian and Jewish assimilability, going so far as to suggest that those Americans who could recognize the humanity in these and other outsiders would receive divine favor. Others, however, suggested that Jews but not Indians, or neither Jews nor Indians, could assimilate on account of their supposed racial status. The most popular anti-Jewish integration stance of the early twentieth century emphasized the Jews' supposed fixed racial nature, making any change nary impossible, a view most bluntly articulated by Madison Grant. Unlike Shaler, Grant argued that no amount of racial intermixing would change the core racial makeup of groups that he perceived as nonwhite like Jews or Native Americans. "A cross between a white man and an Indian is an Indian, white man and a Hindu is a Hindu, white and negro is a negro and the cross between any of the three European races and a Jew is a Jew," he wrote in his highly influential book, *The Passing of the Great Race*, in 1913. "Whether we like to admit it or not, the result of the mixture of two races in the long run, gives us a race reverting to the most ancient, generalized and lower type," he concluded, leading to his judgment of intermarriage as a "social and racial crime."[25] Grant loathed the Jews' supposed "dwarf stature, peculiar mentality, and ruthless concentration of self-interest," which, he argued, "are being engrafted upon the stock of the nation."[26] In a letter he wrote to the House Committee on Immigration and Naturalization more than a decade later, Grant emphasized the principle argument of immigration restrictionism and encouraged the committee to establish quotas from the nations that "furnish very undesirable immigrants [like . . .] the Mexicans who come into the United States [who are] overwhelmingly of Indian blood."[27] Grant was far from alone in his conviction that Jews were racially fixed and, as such, could neither assimilate nor become naturalized Americans, nor that Indians were racially mixed and therefore unable to assimilate. Dozens of commentators were preoccupied with questions about whether the apparent fixedness of the Jewish, Indian, Black, and Chinese races rendered them incapable of assimilation.

If the degree to which Jews and Indians could be assimilated, their capacities for labor, or the extent to which they were essentially ancient people (for better or for worse) were three versions of the same question about Jews' and Indians' respective differences from white America, commentators, policy makers, and scholars also analyzed other dimensions of their differences. Jews and Indians were likewise assessed and compared in relation to their agrarian capacities, their tendencies to segregate, their location on imagined evolutionary ladders of human civilization and with respect to the likelihood of their respective collective disappearance. Anti-Jewish and anti-Indian sentiment that stressed how both groups were fundamentally incompatible with agrarian life cast Jews as quintessential urbanites, unable to handle farm life, and Indians as unable to learn to farm or sustain a living from it. William Z. Ripley, an economist who had written a 624-page tome *The Races of Europe* in 1899, delivered a lecture at MIT in 1908 called "The Migration of Races," which described the "unfavorable influence of city life" and the "physically degenerate" impact it made on the Jew, who congregated in commercial centers with his "inherent dislike of labor and physical exercise."[28] With "narrow chests," "defective stature," and "deficient lung capacity," he claimed, Jews remained "one of the most stunted peoples in Europe."[29] Indians, by contrast, were simply incapable of achieving agrarian success.

A distinct strain of exclusionary animus suggested that Jews and Indians were races who self-segregated and were thereby incompatible with others on the land, the inevitable instigators of violent group conflict. "Groups that cannot mix segregate," wrote William Christie Macleod, "thus we get the Jewish Ghetto, the negro quarters in American cities, and reservations of the Indians."[30]

Scholars also observed/imagined symmetries between Jewish and Indian religious life—their rites, lore, or cosmology—which suggested that ancient Jews and more-or-less contemporary Indians were located on the same evolutionary rung.[31] In one remarkable series of pages in a volume on biblical anthropology from 1929, H. J. D. Astley switched between Israelite and Indian rites and categories without pause, making it, on occasion, difficult to tell whose rites he was discussing at a given point (perhaps by design).[32] He concluded, "There is no race of men that has not passed through a period of totemism in the course of its upward progress from savagery through barbarism to civilization: it was certainly the case among the Semites, of whom the Hebrews were a younger and comparatively modern branch; we may see it surviving among the American Indians."[33]

Finally, non-Jewish American writers, even ones with no particular affection for the Jews, thought that Indians would inevitably disappear but generally speaking did not think the same for the Jews. In most cases, available evidence was tied to emerging theories about genetics. Mendel's discovery of genetic laws of heredity inspired the search for various "unit characters" attached to various peoples, units that might include, in the case of Jews, "nomadism, habitual wandering, and 'thalasophilia' [leaving home for sea]."[34] Edward East's *Heredity and Human Affairs* claimed that the longevity of the Jews and their perpetual interbreeding insulated them from the tides of changing historical circumstance because and only because Jews engaged in stringently selective breeding. "The degenerate product of a bad genetic combination," on the other hand, wrote East, "is not saved by the record made by others of his race." "Historically the Jews are great," he argued. "[T]hey have wandered over the earth and have mingled their blood with the blood of other peoples . . . starting as a mixed race, they have become more mixed."[35] On the other hand, "the American Indian as a group have little of genetic value to contribute to the higher white or yellow subraces"; their interbreeding led only to degeneration. "One may assume," he concluded, "that the Indian will gradually disappear. He will be absorbed by the dominant white, without affecting the white race materially."[36]

So one essential claim in American racial schemata was the notion that history would leave Indians behind; they were the disappearing, the disappeared. While Jews appeared as the focal point of so many awkward assessments of modernity's impact on America, Indians stood—with ever decreasing visibility—on the margins of consciousness as a kind of object lesson for those wishing to fully refuse modernity. As Goldstein, again, has shown, by the late nineteenth century, Americans expressed misgivings about modernity and the challenges it afforded to American identity. Ideas about racial outsiders—Jews, Indians, or others—reflected both broader reservations about the deleterious effects that modernization had on American life and the confident and forward-looking prowess of the wealth, growth, and power that Americans expected America would soon achieve.[37] It is perhaps not surprising then that the key associations that dominated American racial thinking about the Jews all found counterparts in Indians. The "Jewish qualities" of nervousness, intellectuality, and lack of physical developments were mirrored by "Indian qualities" of calm, corporeal competence, physical prowess, and connection to nature. These qualities were not just opposed to one another; they were characterizations of modernity itself and the kinds of human beings that modernity, and particularly urban American modernity, created.

Denying the Pioneer Jew

Perhaps the most popular motif in early twentieth-century discussions by non-Jewish writers that linked Jews and Native Americans centered on the retrospective accounting of late nineteenth-century pioneering and the extent to which "immigrants" could or should be excluded from the category "pioneer." By the 1910s, just a handful of years after Frederick Jackson Turner famously declared the frontier "closed," a new conceptual cleavage had opened up that distinguished between the European immigrant and American-born settler "pioneers" of the West and the post-1880 immigrants and Americans who arrived in that same West after the so-called closing. Looking back retrospectively from the early twentieth century, at a moment of enormous growth in new immigrant populations, many American commentators and scholars delineated what they argued to be a fundamental distinction between the older "pioneers/colonists" and the newer "immigrants." Concerned about competition for jobs; the fast pace of urbanization, industrial growth, and factory conditions in American cities; and the seismic shifts in economic production, a slew of authors published best-selling works, written in panicked diction, about the immigrant "invasion."

In his 1907 book, *Races and Immigrants in America*, University of Wisconsin scholar John Commons argued that Americanization happened in "the earlier days, [when] the most powerful agency of assimilation was frontier life [where pioneers] developed a spirit of self-reliance, a capacity for self-government, which are the most prominent characteristics of the American people."[38] Jews, according to Commons, lacked this sort of industry and thrift. They had no time to be forged into Americans, for they "passed over" the critical pioneer stage, arriving straight from Europe to the "parasitic motives . . . conditions of poverty and pauperism in the metropolis."[39] Commons emphasized that pioneers' actions and virtues, by contrast, were at root racial and that their dispossession of Native Americans took place because it conformed to a simple if brute truth about racial superiority. "The long series of crimes against the Indians," he wrote, "must be looked upon as the mob spirit of a superior race bent on despoiling a despised and inferior race."[40] The grounds for justifying dispossession, argued Commons, was that "the Indian has not accepted the white man's standard of civilisation [sic][. . . but] has remained true to his primitive tastes. In spite of a fair degree of opportunity to obtain training in the arts and sciences, an opportunity accepted by several thousand individuals, he has produced no man of real note. . . . One may assume, I believe, that the Indian will gradually disappear. He will be absorbed by the dominant white, without affecting the white race materially."[41] For Commons, as for many of those scholars who commented on race and immigration, Jews did not and could not participate in the pioneering process. *Races and Immigrants in America* offered the notion that "the Jewish immigrant, particularly, is unfitted for the life of a pioneer. Remarkably individualistic in character, his field of enterprise is society, and not the land."[42] For Commons, Jews seemed to be too civilized and too modern; they could not have *modernized* or *civilized* the frontier. Since Native Americans, on the other hand of this logic, could not be civilized, they would not participate in modernity. Arguing against more orthodox race thinkers, Commons claimed that even if the white race "absorbed" Indians, Indian race blood would not affect the white race "materially." Commons' critique of new immigrants typically featured American Indians as those who disappeared, defeated. Their defeat produced pioneers; *pioneers became Americans* by defeating Indian enemies. Once defeated, Indians were assumed to disappear altogether. Immigrants, in this circular logic, could therefore become neither pioneers nor Americans since they lacked Indians to defeat.

Similar sentiments were echoed the following year in Prescott Farnsworth Hall's best-selling book, *Immigration and Its Effects upon the United States*, which repeated the distinction between "colonist" and "immigrant," the former having battled Indians, while the latter had not. "In popular discussions of the immigration question it is often said that all who have come to this continent since its discovery should be considered equally as immigrants, and that only the aboriginal inhabitants can be properly called natives," wrote Hall. This logic, however, he found "entirely misleading; for one cannot speak of immigration to a country until that country has entered upon a career of national existence. . . . Those who took part in building the political framework of the thirteen colonies" were colonists proper, different from "those who have arrived to find the United States Government and its social and political institutions in working operation. The former class have [sic] been called colonists, the latter are immigrants proper. In discussing the immigration question, this distinction is important; for it does not follow that because, as against the native Indians, all comers might be considered as intruders and equally without claim of right."[43]

Hall distinguished "between the migration of tribes by means of conquest, and peaceful emigration which is the movement of individual units." Peaceful emigrants were, essentially, the already conquered, as exemplified by the "Huguenots banished from France, the Jews driven from Spain, and, later, from Russia by the May Laws, and the Italians from the slums of Naples, [all] are instances of individuals conquered at home."[44] His book mentioned Jews more than fifty times, generally distinguishing Jews from those "Pilgrims and Puritans [who sought] liberty and a chance to develop a new and lofty type of civil and religious commonwealth produced a civilization which, in spite of obvious defects, has excited the admiration of mankind." These original colonists were to be contrasted with recent immigrants, who were "not led by the hope of bursting its bonds, but by the allurements of promised wealth and material comfort": "The Jews we have received hitherto have . . . a keen personal ambition, and such lawbreaking as they do is usually in the breach of sanitary regulations or in trying to gain some monetary advantage by craft and deceit. Although the history of many of these immigrants in Europe is something for which they are not responsible, it does not augur well for their future as American citizens. . . . The physical degeneration of the Jew in New York and Philadelphia has been accompanied to some extent by a moral and political degeneration."[45] Hall's chapter on "The Importance of Race Stock" argued that Jews constituted a menacing danger to American institutions and organic life, more far-reaching and potent than other threats. "The government, the state, society, industry, the political party, social and political ideals—all are concepts and conventions created by individual men; and when individuals change these change with them," he wrote.[46]

For Hall, religion was just as central as race: "Difference in religious belief may be one of the chief causes of heterogeneity, and one of the greatest of hindrances to assimilation. Members of the same religious sect, especially if surrounded by others of a different faith, tend to become clannish and separatist, and to affiliate only with newcomers of like faith, or, as sometimes is the case in New York City and elsewhere, with those of like faith and the same race. Difference in religion is a powerful bar to intermarriage, as in the case of the Jews."[47] Hall's constant juxtaposition of pilgrims versus new immigrants also reflected his conviction that Jews' (and others') lack of practice with democracy rendered them dangerous for the American project: "The early colonists of this country . . . were on the whole reverent of law and disposed to uphold the authorities constituted by the people. The later immigration was mostly from States and races long familiar with representative government. With the more recent immigration the case is quite otherwise. The more ignorant Italians, the Slavic races, the Syrians and other Asiatics, the Russian Hebrews,—all have come from lands where democracy is unknown, and where law is represented to the people by soldiers, tax collectors, and gendarmerie."[48] Jews' lack of exposure to democracy, Hall believed, weakened their suitability for immigration.[49]

The Jews' potential to corrupt the ballot box, undermine democratic practice through law bending and subterfuge, or become a draining force on urban economies as wards of the state were not the only reasons that Jews could not be seen in and among those idealized frontier colonial types according to nativists thinkers of the early twentieth century. Frank Julian Warne's 1913 book, *The Immigrant Invasion*, added concern about Jews as threats to the displacement of already American workers, the rising of consumer goods prices, and the driving down of wages, the building of shanty living arrangements, the rise of disability, and the decrease of patriotism. Warne, a journalist and economist who had served as the secretary of the immigration department of the National Civic Federation of New York, the New York State Immigration Commission, and the U.S. Census Bureau, even suggested that new immigrants were to blame in the persistence of "the negro problem," since, he reasoned, new immigrants were replacing the low-paying service jobs that Blacks often had, increasing Black poverty and disenfranchisement. Constantly deploying words like "threat," "invasion," "foreign," and "impact," Warne celebrated "the Older immigration" as hearty, muscular, rugged, homesteading, Indian clearing pioneers, industrious, and those who were able to invent a vision of democracy.[50] The common task of American-born and new immigrants from the 1810s to 1840s had been one that seamlessly blended the economic, racial, political, and social to provide a national boon in defeating and removing Indians. Post-1860s immigrants, by contrast, lived in cities and were overly preoccupied with competition. Claimed Warne,

> The remarkable story of this westward march prior to the eighties of our older foreign-born population, and its consequences to us as a nation, . . . the interior West was taken from the Indian, cleared of its forests, and only now is being subjected to supplying the wants and needs of modern civilization. There the native American and the European immigrant had a common task, and they became neighbors and friends, intermarriage was made easy, and the Teutonic and Celtic races, which in Europe had for centuries been developing separate and apart, were welded or fused racially as one people. Not only was the environment such as to amalgamate them physically but also to assimilate them politically and socially.[51]

The "old newcomers" were colonists; the crucible of the old West fused the English, Irish, Welsh, Scotch, Norwegian, Dane, Swede, Swiss, Hollander, and Canadian, a "great movement of population out of Europe . . . toward the setting sun . . . [whose] longings and struggles of the race of mankind in their peopling of the New World with a new race, and in their travail to give birth and perpetuate a government of, by and for the people . . . those anxious and stirring days when the path of the pioneer crossed the path of the Indian, and the axe and the plough of the white settler replaced the tomahawk and bow of the red man. . . . For they too concern themselves with fundamental human forces out of which alone a new epoch grows." New newcomers—the Jews chief among them—were merely immigrants.

For nativists, then, Jews were excluded from identification in the frontier "type." The fact that so many commentators and scholars who discussed Jews, Indians, and the nature of the frontier experience failed to recognize that there were many actual encounters between Jews and Native Americans—that Jews were indeed colonial settlers on the frontier (described at length in the first half of this book)—further served to smear immigrants by disqualifying them from participation in the model, exalted citizen of America's national imagination. The setup of implied oppositions—those between frontiersmen and Indians and between frontiersmen and Jews—also says something about perceptions of both Indians and Jews—namely, that Jews and Indians were in relation with one another as mutual, twinned foils to colonist pioneers, albeit on opposing ends of exclusion. Both forms of differentiation echo the 1924 Acts, twin gestures of white primacy.

1924: Interweaving Nativist Acts of Congress

Jewish and Native American experiences overlapped, intersected, and contradicted one another in discussions about the nature of American national identity by non-Jews and non-Indians about who truly belonged in the American people, who threatened it, and about just how Christian America was or ought to have been. These overlaps, intersections, and contradictions played out in both academic discussions and policy venues. They came to a head in 1924, as two congressional acts of thematically interrelated legislation emerged, each of them aiming to shape the American character by crafting boundaries about who belonged and who did not.

Congress passed the Immigration Act, also known as the Johnson-Reed Act, in May 1924. The Immigration Act included the National Origins Act, which effectively halted southern and eastern European immigration, including Jewish immigration, to the United States. The act also included the Asia Exclusion Act, which entirely banned Asian immigration. In the congressional record, restrictionists explicitly denounced theories of Nordic superiority. Nevertheless, the quota system enacted in the act itself drew from deep-rooted assumptions about the racial, moral, physical, and intellectual qualities of potential immigrants. The National Origins Act spoke to a widely shared nativist xenophobia that President Coolidge, in his inaugural address, captured when he supported immigration restriction, declaring that "America must be kept American. For this purpose it is necessary to continue a policy of restricted immigration."[52]

Just one month later, Congress passed the Indian Citizenship Act, following an earlier act of 1919, which had given citizenship to those Indians who had served in armed forces during the Great War. The Indian Citizenship Act granted citizenship to those remaining Native American men who had not been previously naturalized by treaty, though full suffrage was not completed for many, and several states refused to recognize Indians as citizens altogether. The Indian Citizenship Act is widely understood by historians and Native intellectuals to have been an effort to erase Indian difference through assimilation, a symbolic act of inclusion that in fact stripped Indians of legal room to fight for political sovereignty.[53]

These two acts of legislation reveal an America preoccupied with threats about membership and anxieties about identity and difference.[54] Both acts served one end—namely, to further root American identity in its Anglo-cultural, religiously Christian, and racially white heritage. One aimed to repel the threat of foreign contamination by immigrants from without, while the other aimed to dissolve the alien within by absorption.

Of course, major differences separated the two discussions. The fraught debate about immigration restriction occupied a central place in American social, legal, historical, and even scientific discussion and had been percolating from the 1880s, if not earlier. On the other hand, the debate about Indian citizenship preoccupied only a small public.[55] The discussion grew out of civil servants' efforts to assimilate American Indians, drawing from a long tradition entangled in missionary activity and piecemeal actions and protocols by local, state, and BIA initiatives. (These efforts were supported, in part, by some Native American leaders and by the Indian Rights Association, an influential group of policy activists whose express goal was to "bring about the complete civilization of the Indians and their admission to citizenship."[56]) The federal government had sponsored compulsory assimilation programs for Native Americans as a matter of national policy going back to Ulysses Grant's "Peace Policy" of the 1870s and the Dawes Act of 1887 (and its amendments in 1891 and 1906), which offered Native peoples land allotments and promoted individual ownership and freed up millions of acres of land for further settlement. Assimilationist policies continued through the turn of the century with residential boarding schools, several key legal decisions, and the suppression of certain Native religious practices until the Indian New Deal under John Collier at the BIA and the Roosevelt Administration.

The assimilation campaign that Jews faced, on the other hand, was ad hoc; it was subtler and relatively more benign than the one faced by Native Americans. Most importantly, the campaign that targeted Jews for assimilation was only in the realm of culture; it was not waged against Jews through legislative or judicial mechanisms. Though American Jews felt pressures to adjust or transform their bodies, speech patterns, styles of dress, tastes in food, and the ways they practiced religious rites or prayer, chose occupations, or even shaped their unwritten values, these pressures were never mounted as official state or federal policy. This point is worth emphasizing: whereas the state sponsored assimilationist policies directed at Native Americans, it pursued no such campaigns aimed at Jews.

Yet despite the clear differences, civil servants and lawmakers entangled Jews and Indians in the debates on the bills that lead up to the passage of the 1924 Acts and in the acts themselves. The chairman of the House Immigration Committee, Albert Johnson, read from consular cables provided by the State Department during one of Congress's debates on an immigration restriction bill, attesting to Jews as "subnormal," "twisted," "deteriorated," and "full of perverted ideas," who—in contrast to the normal, straight, invigorated immigrant pioneers—"are not those [immigrants] who hewed the forests, . . . conquered the wastes, and built America. These are beaten folk."[57] Jews' apparent inability to conquer Indians rendered them unappealing candidates for naturalization.

Even the language of these two acts tangled immigrants and Indians together. The Indian Citizenship Act alluded to immigrants, and the National Origins Act referred to Native Americans. The one-sentence-long Indian Citizenship Act specified that it proclaimed citizens of "all non citizen Indians *born within the territorial limits of the United States*"—that is, Indians who did not migrate to U.S. territory after birth.[58] The language of the act went out of its way to define Indians as nonimmigrants. And for its part, the National Origins Act, despite its express focus on immigrants, went out of its way to reference Native Americans in order to define its most basic terms; it used Indians as the foil through which to define nonnaturalized non-Americans. In its language, immigrants were "aliens," a term the act clarified as including "any individual not a native-born or naturalized citizen of the U.S.," adding, critically, express terms to exclude Indians (and the populations of America's colonial holdings) from the category of *alien*. The act stated, "This definition [of aliens] shall not be held to include Indians of the U.S. not taxed, nor citizens of the islands under the jurisdiction of the U.S."[59] Both of these 1924 race-based laws struggled with awkward caveats, granting and withholding, in order to exclude racialized minorities.

These two acts also evoked (or re-evoked) long-standing fears shared by Jews and Indians alike. The acts inflamed Jewish and Indian responses to predictions about the inevitable disappearance both of Jews as such and of Indians as such. American Jews and Native Americans both fretted over their felt exclusion from the mainstream American body politic, and both feared that their corporate identities might be lost. Jews and Native Americans both articulated and worked through these parallel anxieties. Both mobilized, both organized, and both publicized counter-polemics.[60] The enactments of these two policies make evident the consequences of racial discourse on mass populations of both Indians and immigrants in the United States.

Rhetorical Uses of Immigrant vs. Indian

Jewish journalists, politicians, scholars, and writers countered nativist racist, anti-Jewish, and anti-immigrant sentiment. In a wide host of forums and settings, Jews offered several complementary arguments. While some argued that the Jewish race or people had made adequate contributions to American life, others insisted that there was no such thing as race. Still other Jewish commentators asserted that restrictionist policies were logically inconsistent or incompatible with fundamental values of America or its constitution; they mounted legal challenges. American Jews also proffered moral suasion based on their history or suffering and their brethren's contemporary afflictions in Europe and Russia. Immigration constituted a prime object of concern for practically every major Jewish defense and community-relations organization. American Jews helped establish and finance nonsectarian groups like the National Liberal Immigration League and the Citizens Committee for Displaced Persons. They were perhaps "the single most persistent pressure group favoring a liberal immigration policy in the United States in the entire immigration debate beginning in 1881," as historian Kevin MacDonald has argued.[61] In undertaking to sway immigration policy in a liberal direction, Jewish spokesmen and organizations demonstrated a degree of energy "unsurpassed by any other interested pressure group."[62]

Jews were among many religious, business, and legal voices that protested nativist currents and the bills that eventually became the National Origins Act.[63] Young urban Jews argued against restriction on the floor of Congress. Only two of the seventeen members of Congress's committee voted against the lead bill, both of whom were Jews: Adolph Sabath and Samuel Dickstein, who notably later chaired the House of Representatives Subcommittee on Indian Affairs in the late 1930s. Meyer Jacobstein, Nathan Perlman, and Emanuel Celler (who, notably, later introduced both the Immigration and Nationality Act of 1965, which abolished the quota system based on national origins in place since the 1920s, and the Indian Civil Rights Act of 1968) all challenged the race-implied assumptions in the proposal. They argued against the explicit racism of the anti-immigrant lobby, spearheaded by Madison Grant, the previously discussed lifelong eugenics campaigner. Grant belonged to, founded, or sat on the executive board of some thirty-five different organizations that represented a wide net of American race preservation fights for white supremacy, including the American Eugenics Society, the Eugenics Research Association, the International Congress of Eugenics, and the Galton Society.[64] Grant also served as the chair of Congress' Committee on Selective Immigration. His book, *The Passing of the Great Race*, served as one of the core texts in the immigration restriction debate. Grant and his fellow nativists—what historian Jonathan Spiro has called an "interlocking directorate" of eugenicists and anti-immigration activists—flooded journals and newspapers in support of the 2 percent 1890 immigrant ratio quota that was suggested and eventually adopted in the 1924 Act, arguing that such restriction would save America from parasitical races. This formula allowed for the entry of 2 percent of the total number of immigrants by homeland of origin that were admitted in the year 1890. The *Saturday Evening Post*, *American Magazine*, the *North American Review*, and even the *New York Times* used words like *poison*, *infection*, and *parasite* in reference to immigration and showed an obsession with digestion metaphors.[65]

In concert with these metaphors of disease and indigestion, non-Jewish, non-Indian writers served up a steady stream of commentary that stressed that both groups would inevitably disappear. Anxiety about group erasure frequently gnawed at the periphery of American Jewish consciousness and found articulation among a diverse group of Jewish journalists, novelists, rabbis, and scholars.[66] As a general response to nativist anti-immigrant sentiment, Jews themselves wrote of a sense of kinship and identification with American Indians. On occasion, Jewish writers supported Indian land claims against federal governments at home (and abroad) with the explicit recognition that having a land of one's own would preserve Indian tribes and keep them from the dustbin of history. One journalist writing in the *Jewish Criterion* evoked the Hebrew Bible (Leviticus 23) in support of the "Mexican Indians" and their rising up to possess land.[67]

Jewish intellectuals had long feared Jewish corporate disappearance and had a history of using Indians in their rhetorical appeals when they gave voice to it. In his 1899 *History of Yiddish Literature in the Nineteenth Century*, Leo Wiener wrote of his concern for the loss of Jewish literature, language, and cultural forms, all of which he believed were threatened by the assimilative forces of an America unconcerned with cloistering Jews in a separate sphere.[68] Wiener, a Russian-born Polish Jew, historian, linguist, translator of Tolstoy, and professor of Slavic languages at Harvard University, bemoaned the assimilatory prospects of Jews in America, suggesting that the literatures and languages of "the Gypsies, the Malay, and the American Indian" had greater chances for linguistic survival given their continued seclusion. Wiener's fear of the disappearance of Yiddish bespoke a greater fear that many Jews shared about their cultural and biological disappearance altogether. Scholars and writers worried that linguistic assimilation could lead to more insidious forms of assimilation.[69]

In a radio talk during his much-feted tour of the United States to study American Indians, the German Jewish art historian Aby Warburg feared aloud that the Jews' fate in America might follow that of the Indian, that the pressures on American peoples to assimilate lead to the homogenization of cultures and "mental habits." One Jewish newspaper concurred with Warburg's expressed fears of "the standardization of minds and emotions of Red Indians."[70] Warburg fretted that the loss of this more soulful aspect of group cultural life would have even more deleterious effects on Jewish life—as it had on Indian life—than even the loss of traditional linguistic vernacular, the impact of materialism, or the loss of Jewish folkways. The consequences of artistic "standardization," a proxy for a culture's very soul, Warburg worried, could be catastrophic. The standardization of mind, and "not the adoption by American Jews of the English language for the use in their daily intercourse and in the home, or the material comforts of America, or certain traditional folkways of the land [is what] makes Mr. Warburg fearful for the future of Jewry in this country."[71]

Of particular interest are the ways that Jewish antirestrictionist agents regularly used tropes of "the Indian" in their proimmigration polemics. While they promoted Jewish immigration and integration with consistent appeals to Indians, the nature of this rhetorical Indian with whom Jews alternatively allied themselves or contrasted themselves with changed dramatically, depending on the utility of a given argument. The figure of the Indian proved malleable and flexible in the hands of Jewish rhetoricians. The Hebrew Immigrant Aid Society, dedicated to encouraging the free flow of Jews from eastern Europe into a safe America willing to absorb them, used its newspaper arm, the *Jewish Immigrant*, for example, as a platform on "the immigration question" by constructing various rhetorical Indians in its arguments. It published New York congressman William Sulzer's proimmigration, proassimilation polemic, an "eloquent plea for justice to the immigrants," in which he argued that Jews belonged in America because as white immigrants, they wished to blend into America's white body and could labor on the otherwise useless "millions and millions of acres of rich, fertile land waiting to be cultivated."[72] His counterarguments to anti-immigration proponents rested on the expansionist idea that America needed quality laborers who might easily adapt to American social norms and make the vast tracts of lands productive. As if empty of persons and empty of productive utility, Indian lands lay "waiting to be cultivated," since, he implied, government efforts to make Indians into productive agricultural laborers had amounted to little. Immigrants' adaptability, in counter-distinction, rested in their racial characteristics and their closeness to other white Americans, Hungarians, Italians, and Germans. For Sulzer, the value of immigrants' labor capacities and racial flexibility trumped even the idea, as he reasoned it, that being white did not, ipso facto, make one into a "real" part of the nation. "Many of the people opposed to immigration," he insisted, "never stop to consider that none of us are real Americans—Americans in the fullest sense of the word. THE INDIAN IS THE ONLY REAL AMERICAN."[73]

The trope of Indians as the immigrant's opposite recurred again and again in Jewish public discourse in the early decades of the twentieth century and was linked to themes of productivity, disease, capacity for assimilation, contribution to civilization, prospects for leadership, and the generation of local or national wealth. Jews regularly located the essence of citizenship and national belonging in productivity and in harnessing the land and its resources for prosperity. To the extent that Jews assumed that Indians failed to structure their communal lives with this goal in mind, they also excluded Indians from the nation itself. This discourse did not consider Native Americans in their own right, but only as a mute foil. One prong of proimmigration rhetoric sought to decenter the idea of American natural authenticity by linking it with Indians—if the only "natural" Americans were Native Americans, no immigrant could be considered an authentic American. Though this rhetorical strategy devalued the actual places and circumstances of Native Americans in American life and implied that Native Americans lacked the capacity to be productive, civic, or just American, the implication was easily expendable. Few advocates for American Indians ever weighed in to discussions about immigration and naturalization; advocacy work for Indians in health, education, or any other sector simply was not on the radar in way that it was for Blacks or poor whites.

Jews mobilized the idea of Indian aboriginality against the forces that aimed to exclude eastern and southern European immigrant groups. Pittsburgh's *Jewish Criterion* steadily ran editorials and articles from the 1910s through the 1940s espousing this view. Its editor, Charles H. Joseph, argued for the rights of immigrant citizens as co-equals to American-born whites, writing that immigrants adopted America just as America adopted its immigrants "in the same way that all other people of the earth have adopted it."[74] Only Indians stood outside this principle of adoption. "The Indians alone are the real Americans," he wrote. "All the remainder of the population consists of foreigners. But under our Constitution when a foreigner becomes naturalized and secures his citizen papers, he has the same rights, without respect to his religious beliefs, as the gentlemen who ran over in the Mayflower."[75] In Joseph's proimmigration rhetoric, all foreigners, even the founding fathers, had to become "real Americans" like the Indians through naturalizing.

The rhetoric was manifestly confused. Indians were the only real Americans; they made Americans but somehow could never be real Americans. The essence of American identity, so ran the argument, was focused instead on rights and citizens' abilities or capacities to act them out. Joseph's newspaper ran editorials over the next three decades to similar effects, shifting rhetorical uses of Indians. "It is singular," wrote one of its editorialists, "nay it is unpardonable, to hear the chauvinistic cry, to see the intolerant wave of anti-foreign sentiments emanate from people themselves of foreign parentage, of a nationality which is a composite of many foreign nationalities, transferred to these shores, earlier or later, and here mixed and modified in the American crucible.... The only 'original' Americans are the aboriginal tribes of Indians, fast perishing and never suggested to the thought of the civilized world by that name, but rather by the name of 'the Red man of North America.'"[76]

Jewish proimmigration rhetoric utilized the idea of the Indian in competing, complementary, and even contradictory ways. In some polemics, Jews could be counted as nationals among a nation of non-Indians. Simply being an immigrant or having descended from one offered sufficient reason for a people's welcome in America. In other polemics, however, all forms of intolerance were deemed inimical to American values. Racism aiming to exclude Jews, other immigrant groups, or Indians was said to sting with equal perniciousness. An editorial by Rabbi Beryl D. Cohon argued "that there is no such thing as an American by race. Americanism cannot be based on race, for the American is a combination of every race of Europe."[77] He claimed that "the American holds within his veins the blood of the American Indians, plus the blood of the Negroes, and plus the blood of some Asiatic folk," mixing natives and newcomers into an amalgamated ideal citizen.[78] Welcoming immigrants and loving America's Indian and Negro "blood" went hand in hand. Any form of exclusionary racism, the rabbi suggested, offended Americans as a nation without race. In this argument, American nationality trumped racial distinctions between minorities in America.

Some Jewish proimmigration rhetoric made use of the idea that only Indians enjoyed the status of nonimmigrants in America. Other strategies aimed to undermine both anti-immigrant and anti-Indian sentiment. In both rhetorics of advocacy, Jews sought to undermine racist sentiment while preserving ethnic corporate solidarity. But not every strategy Jews took to keep America's doors open to future Jewish immigration explicitly criticized racialist thinking. On occasion, Jewish voices for liberal immigration policy deployed racist sentiment too, though they pointed it at non-Jews. Joshua Kantrowitz of the B'nai B'rith and Judge B. A. Rosenblatt of the American Jewish Congress argued for the restriction of Asians but entitlements for Jews. William Edlin, the editor of *Der Yiddishe Tog*, likewise suggested that Jews, on account of their relative racial closeness to the founding races of America, should be accepted, while the exclusions should only apply to nonwhites. "I am speaking here on behalf of the Caucasian race," he wrote, "to which we all belong. I do not want to take in those races which [sic] do not assimilate readily. . . . After all . . . the Chinese, Hindus and other races do not have those things that we call civilization, and I look upon those people as too far from us for assimilation purposes."[79] Jewish proimmigrant rhetoric was far from consistent in anything other than its ultimate objective.

Such proimmigration and assimilation polemics by Jewish writers certainly faced rebuttals by non-Jewish nativists. The most successful and dominant metaphor for racial integration in America was by far the idea of the "melting pot," a term that was catapulted into the American public imagination after the Washington debut of a play of the same name by British Jewish author Israel Zangwill in 1909 (at which President Teddy Roosevelt was in attendance). The play told a story about a Russian Jewish immigrant and his effort to wed a Christian woman. Victorious in the end, the play celebrated America as "the great melting pot where all the races of Europe are melting and re-forming!"[80] As a phrase that would come to capture the Turnerian idea of race amalgamation in the West and expanded it to a broader American public, including later periods of immigration, restrictionist writers took aim at the "melting pot" trope.

Henry Pratt Fairchild's 1926 best-selling book, *The Melting Pot Mistake*, for instance, aimed to account for the ultimate effects upon the "vitality and solidarity of this stupendous injection of foreign elements" and argued that the melting pot was a false ideal because racial outsiders could not assimilate.[81] True citizens, the book argued (even after the restrictionist victory of the National Origins Act of 1924), could not be made out of aliens, but the efforts to try to square a round peg by allowing unchecked immigration necessarily impacted "the vigor and permanence of our life as a nation."[82] The metaphor of the melting pot, wrote Fairchild, was invented "to convince the American that immigration did not threaten its unity, but tended to produce an even finer type of unity. It failed because it did not take into account the true nature of group unity, of the conditions of its preservation, or of the actual consequences of such in-roads upon unity as are involved in an immigration movement."[83] Concerned with race mixing and degeneration, Fairchild marshaled racialist arguments from biology and evolution and concluded that "*the primary basis of group unity is therefore racial*," and suggested that "one of the chief courses of fallacy in the figure of the melting pot lay in the failure to make this crucial distinction . . . race traits are due solely to inheritance," which he considered transmitted hereditarily and fixed from birth to death.[84] The traits of nationality, he argued, on the other hand, were distinctly group or social realities (rather than biological ones) since they "impress themselves on the individual but by no means ineradicably. Race is inherited, nationality is acquired."[85]

Fairchild considered new immigration "a New Menace." Of "the great bulk of Hebrew immigration in recent years," he wrote, "the immigration problem in the US has become increasingly a racial problem in two distinct ways, first by altering profoundly the Nordic predominance in the American population, and second by introducing new elements which, while of uncertain volume, are so radically different from any of the old ingredients that even small quantities are deeply significant."[86] Fairchild argued that there could be no "give-and-take" in assimilation, that race mixing could only have deleterious effects, and that immigrants must lose all traces of foreign origin, including language, religion, political ideas, moral standards, economic abilities, dress, recreation, food, ornamentation, family customs, habits, traditions, beliefs and loyalties.[87] "In all of these particulars," he advised, "the immigrant must be transformed into the type of the receiving nationality."[88]

Fairchild also tried to rebut those of his opponents who lumped together all non-Native Americans as fellow immigrants in their championing of immigration and assimilation. "Speakers who pose as champions of a 'liberal' policy may frequently be heard to declare, The only true Americans are the Red Indians. All the rest of us are immigrants, or the descendants of immigrants," he wrote. Following this logic, he argued, one would have to conclude that the only thing that "constitutes an American is ancient residence upon a certain territory, which was not even called America until after the white men discovered it." But Fairchild insisted that Indians had no "better claim to the honored title [of native] than the later arrivals, for they themselves are the descendants of wanderers who came from somewhere else," that they were, in effect, immigrants too.[89]

He took specific umbrage with leaders of the "Hebrew population" who wished to preserve and maintain Jewish cultural and religious heritage as the "dangerous . . . type of foreigner who lacks the will to assimilate includ[ing] those who, on high intellectual and cultural grounds, oppose assimilation because of the in-roads it makes into the strength of their own original nationalities"; he criticized the "considerable propaganda in existence in the US at this present time designed to encourage immigrants to oppose and resist assimilation . . . [by] Rabbis and other prominent Jewish leaders." He pointed out that these exact sentiments were admirable "when displayed by Americans in foreign lands" as proud patriotism. Such persons, however, "constitute an undeniable menace to American national stability," since the antiassimilation impulse leads to a kind of split loyalty. "The wholesome place for the display of patriotism is at home," under normal circumstances, he wrote. However, "the difficulty in the case of the Jews is that they have no home. They have no nation to the upbuilding of which they can devote their restless activities, and about the future of which they can entwine their ardent aspirations. . . . This is wholly defensible from the point of view of the Jews. It is intolerable from the point of view of other nationalities."[90]

The puzzle of identifying the nature of Jewish difference and then evaluating the possibility of Jewish belonging was made into a matter of race science,

Figure 4.1. "History of the USA." The comic strip presents a narrative western U.S. history in which the American pioneer and patriot removed the Indian from the land, only to be ousted by the Jewish immigrant. Courtesy of National Museum of American Jewish History, Philadelphia, Peter H. Schweitzer Collection of Jewish Americana, print 2006.1.6258

geography, connections to an ancient past, character, biology, and heredity. It was also made, finally, a matter of religion since Anglo-Saxon supremacist thinking shared a common link with Protestants who considered America as a fulfillment of a Christian vision of society and modernity. The Jews' difference from Christians in respect to religion and Indian difference varied greatly. Avowedly Christian writers also took an active interest in immigration debates, offering both pro- and anti-immigration perspectives. In their 1913 study, *The New America: A Study in Immigration*, for example, Mary Clark Barnes and Lemuel Barnes advocated for keeping the immigration doors open to Jews with arguments drawn from religious grounds.[91] The book was issued under the direction of the Council of Women for Home Missions, as part of its Interdenominational Home Mission Study Course set of books, which also included titles like *Under Our Flag*, *God's Melting Pot*, *Comrades from Other Lands*, and *Some Immigrant Neighbors.* The book aimed to Christianize "the strangers within our gates" and promoted immigration among the illiterate for cheap labor, the growth of national wealth, and the expansion of Christianity. Christianity provided a route to economic success. The authors advocated for Jewish immigration on the grounds that Jews would fare well and that they were important targets of conversion efforts. The racial characterization of Jews in works like these served to affirm a preexisting religious conviction that America offered a space for the flourishing and future of Christianity. Jews' supposed tenacity in life and their innate "tenacity of purpose" rendered them ideal immigrants and objects for missionizing.[92]

High rates of literacy, the eagerness of children to learn, and the ability to blend civics and religion were all virtues that Jews supposedly helped import to North America. Even the Jews' idea of God was an import. "And, behold, the glory of the God of Israel came from the way of the East," they quoted from scripture, as a proof text for the notion of God as a force for amalgamation and Christian consolidation in America.[93] "It must not be forgotten that the fundamental literature of America is not American, nor African, nor even European, but Asiatic. . . . 'The father of the faithful' was a wandering Asiatic sheik. The God of Abraham, Isaac and Jacob is our God. . . . Most of all, the supreme center of the divine revelation to us is in One who was primarily not American, or European but Asiatic."[94]

Turning toward Activism

A wide manner of American writings about immigration, race, and nation made use of Indians to produce competing ideas about home and belonging, which sometimes included Jews and sometimes excluded them. Anti-Jewish and anti-Indian sentiments were all nourished from the same well. These twin forms of American exclusionism found multiple and competing expressions in a variety of settings and sites throughout the early decades of the twentieth century. They shaped the Immigration Act and the Indian Citizenship Act of 1924. These strands of exclusionism were continuously braided in the writings of racial theorists, eugenicists, immigration commentators, and assessors of the recent American past who eagerly sought to define exalted citizens by focusing on peoples excluded from its making: Jews, Blacks and Indians.

Jews themselves intervened in these discussions; they responded with their own rhetorical uses of Indians. Fearing that white America's assimilatory aspiration for them would lead to their cultural obliteration, Jews looked to Indians as a bellwether, a cautionary tale, and a foil in situating themselves in recent American history. Their "Indians" were mostly imagined. Their supposed distance from mainstream newcomer, Christian, white Americans made Indians, in the social unconscious of early twentieth-century American Jews, convenient oppositional figures that Jews used to define their own relative closeness to the Americans they hoped would include and embrace them. Indian difference was both different and other; Jewish difference, Jews hoped, would merely be different. Yet in using Indians rhetorically in arguments promoting belonging and continued liberal immigration policy, Jews began schooling themselves in the language of a broader, more inclusive antirace rhetoric, which, as chapter 5 will show, they deployed in an intensely activist manner on behalf of Native Americans.

American Jewish responses to nativist xenophobia took recourse in American Indians; the idea of "Indians" provided Jews with a useful and malleable rhetorical tool for confronting tensions around themes that unsettled Jewish consciousness: assimilation and disappearance, naturalization, citizenship, the idea of adoption, and the nature and impact of Jewish religious difference. Jews took advantage of the flexibility that both "the Jew" and "the Indian" had in racial hierarchies in the first quarter of the twentieth century, as Americans became ever more preoccupied with race thinking and its implications for national policy. Though nativists consistently cast Jews in hierarchically superior standing to Indians, they often put Jews and Indians into relation with one another in their discussions of racial character types and their debates about who could be assimilated to the national ideal type. Over the same years, nativists cut Jews from the conceptual category of "pioneers" as part of a broader anti-immigration polemic and, in so doing, denied the complicated relationships that actual Jews had with actual Native Americans. Anti-Jewish and anti-Indian sentiments intertwined, coming to a head at the highest echelons of American life in 1924, with the passing of both the National Origins Act and the Indian Citizenship Act.

CHAPTER 5

JEWISH ADVOCACY FOR NATIVE AMERICANS ON AND OFF CAPITOL HILL

In 1953, Felix S. Cohen, likely the most influential American Jew in the history of Jewish-Native American relations, was invited to deliver an address at City College of New York, one of the three universities at which he was teaching law at the time alongside his private practice. His talk, entitled "The Meaning of Americanism," aimed to elucidate the qualities and sources at the heart of America's noblest virtues.[1] Cohen argued that the roots of "Americanism" lay in twin influences: Judaism and Native American culture. On the one hand, he judged America's "foundational ideal," its core moral imperative, to be the Hebrew Bible's injunction to "care for the stranger." This beaconing, according to Cohen, undergirded the best of the nation's attitude toward immigration, its social welfare innovations, and its domestic public policy. It animated America's purpose. In order to make this foundational ideal American and to operationalize this ethic in political terms, however, it had to be combined with a second influence, which for Cohen was the nations' "spirit of tolerance." The biblical injunction could not remain in the realm of the national alone. Cohen located the second key force of Americanism in the Iroquois Confederacy, the Indigenous political pact that had long enshrined the cooperation of the five nations—Mohawk, Oneida, Onondaga, Cayuga, and Seneca (and later a sixth, the Tuscarora Nation), the so-called People of the Longhouse. Admiring the skills that Native American leaders had at forming political confederations, he said, underwrote the expedience and wisdom necessary for America's very system of government, its libertarian yet communalistic tolerance. Cohen, in other words, traced the two most fundamental ingredients for his vision of America's highest ideals to Jews on the one hand and to Native Americans on the other.

We know a great deal about the nature and character of midcentury American Jewish efforts on behalf of African Americans. The story of Jewish advocacy work on Native American issues and causes, by contrast, has not yet been told. This chapter illustrates and examines how and why a significant number of Jews devoted money, time, energy, political capital, and expertise to various efforts aimed at improving the lives of American Indians during the middle decades of the twentieth century using the arc of Felix Cohen's professional contributions to midcentury American Indian and Jewish affairs as a reference point and a point of departure. Cohen's work offers a crystallization of an entire cadre of midcentury Jewish liberals', socialists', and progressives' work and sensibilities as they helped fashion the Roosevelt Administration's "Indian New Deal" under the leadership of John Collier (who was not Jewish), commissioner of Indian Affairs and the Department of the Interior beginning in the 1930s. These Jews worked at the highest echelons of leadership, drafting and shaping pro-Indian policy and federal law. They helped launch, fund, and staff some of the most important not-for-profit efforts at advancing Native Americans of the day; they shared and were shaped by a common sociology of community organizing, faith in the law as a vehicle for social change, and a Jewish sensibility inculcated by their socialization and communal attachments. They worked assiduously on Indian affairs after the demise of the New Deal too, well into the conservative, post–World War II era of Indian history known as "Termination." They were instrumental in establishing the institutional basis of what we may call "enfranchised resistance" that some Native American activists and leaders would begin championing in the 1960s. Non-Indians, chiefly among them Jews, initiated some of the strategies—legal challenges, legislative leverage, and policy lobbying—that the American Indian Movement pursued aimed at self-determination.

Midcentury American Jews were engaged in a rich and complex critique of United States imperialism and its past governments' mistreatment of Native Americans. Many devoted their professional lives to grappling with the legacies and impacts of settler society in North America. The large number of Jews engaged in progressive and reformist uplift or activist initiatives on behalf of Native Americans at various levels of politics and society is significant, though the matter of exactly how the Jewishness of these intellectuals and pragmatic citizens shaped or distorted, constrained or freed them to craft interventions in law, public consciousness, or the actual lives of Native Americans themselves was uneven. How did the Jewish backgrounds or attachments, anxieties or motivations, shape their critiques of the U.S. government, its Indian policies, or American civil discourse about Native America? These American Jewish leaders fought the state both from within as civil servants and from without as nongovernmental advocates for Indian rights; yet these Jews were profoundly devoted to America, its ideals, and its future. Their work for stronger Native American communities grew out of their interests in ensuring a Jewish future in the United States to bolster the state's liberalism in order to protect the communities and cultures of their own origin from racism and maltreatment.[2]

President Franklin D. Roosevelt took office in 1933 after the Great Depression and, in response to it, ushered in the New Deal era—which lasted until World War II. Progressives at the BIA advanced an ambitious program and vision for Native American cultural and economic recuperation, known as the Indian New Deal; Jews had much to do with its conceptualization and realization. This chapter focuses on the roles that Jewish civil servants played in the conception, formulation, and execution of the Indian New Deal in the 1930s and early 1940s and their continued social justice efforts on behalf of Native Americans in the late 1940s, 1950s, and early 1960s after the Indian New Deal was replaced by a set of conservative, assimilationist Indian affairs policies. In advancing Indian New Deal policy, particularly the IRA and the Indian Claims Commission (ICC), American Jews helped build the institutional structure for postwar Indian activism.[3]

The chapter describes these Jews' efforts both inside and outside government and shows that Jews played an instrumental role in establishing some of the key institutions, techniques, and organizations that Native American leaders would themselves use to expand their power and capacity later in the twentieth century. It also argues that these Jews' advocacy efforts were circumscribed; as Jews, their professional activities were shaped by the particular values, subject positions, and limitations that their Jewish backgrounds and investments had over them. They lacked both intimate knowledge of and deep existential ties to Native Americans' experiences and visions for their own futures. The intellectual and political perspectives that midcentury Jews assumed to be good for all American "minorities"—including an almost sacrosanct view of statist liberalism and an idealistic confidence in the tools of lobbying, policy making, and the law to affect change—limited these Jewish contributions to reshaping Native Americans' well-being and their communities' futures as they themselves might have wished it.

The Indian New Deal and its policies, programs, attitudes toward Native Americans, and legacies all betrayed some of the assumptions that mid-twentieth-century American Jews like Felix Cohen made about Native Americans based on their own vision of cultural pluralism, minority rights, and the promises of American liberalism in which they were deeply invested and, indeed, helped foster.[4] Jews' efforts on behalf of Native Americans were shaped by a core assumption of liberalism—namely, that other minority groups would behave like the Jews themselves had done in America; others would value liberalism enough to adjust their own communities' differences to mainstream norms in order to achieve enfranchisement. Enfranchised Jews working in law firms, at the nation's capital, at not-for-profit organizations, and in academic institutions were steadfast and utterly sincere in their wishes to improve the lives and communities of Native Americans around the country, just as they had for the rights and enrichment of many American minority groups, Blacks chief among them. For these Jewish liberal actors, advancing Native America was but one prong of the higher goal of advancing all groups whose rights and cultural self-determination needed securing and ensuring that individuals from any group would receive the protection of the law to shape their own cultural, economic, and religious destinies. America's liberalism was its core virtue.

But their work also betrayed some of the assimilationist impulses that American Jews accepted as a fundamental given of the American Jewish experience. On a basic level, they assumed that all "minorities" shared a vision for a more inclusive nation. When these Jewish professionals grappled with the deleterious impacts of colonialism on Indigenous communities, they assumed that Native Americans were, in this sense, like other immigrant groups who saw themselves as minorities. They did not put forth a vision for "decolonizing" America and were less vociferous about ensuring the full expression of Native Americans' *political* self-determination. Rather, they pursued a politics of redress and justice through incorporation into the benefits and virtues of America. They grappled with the legacies of the colonization of Native Americans in ways that made sense to them as Jews and in ways that fit their commitments to accommodation to liberalism and to the framework of national pluralism. They thereby inadvertently perpetuated some of the core colonialist structures that continued to shape American Indian life, even as they helped produce a more liberal and fair playing field for them. Self-directed Indian self-determination work grew out of both the successes of this progressive liberal moment and criticisms of it.

Pre–New Deal Era Precedents

Although the main thrust of advocacy efforts by Jews—often not as explicitly in service of their Jewishness but rather as liberals, progressives, or socialists—was most intense in the second quarter of the twentieth century, precedents abounded. A handful of individual Jews during the second half of the nineteenth and early twentieth-century in Oregon, Nebraska, and elsewhere in the West had criticized allotment and assimilation policies well before the Indian New Deal. A letter received by the Office of Indian Affairs by a field agent from the Alcea Indian Subagency of Oregon in 1860, for example, reported of "one Hebrew, a perfectly worthless Cur who lived with the Indians above Scottsburg," who was "constantly annoying me by talking to the Indians and telling them not to go, that the President had not given them orders to move them."[5] Though the Jew reportedly provided safety and support for Native Americans resisting removal, the agent nevertheless reported his success in removing the tribe. This Jewish Indian trader was cognizant of the settler-Indian battles in which he lived and acted as a small thorn in the side of local Indian agents. The unnamed "Cur" was similar to the upwardly mobile Jewish editor of the *Omaha Bee*, Edward Rosewater, who likewise resisted the state. Rosewater worked with Omaha and Winnebago Indians to remove a corrupt Indian agent at the Omaha and Winnebago Agency in Nebraska in 1903. He and his allies helped bring the agent to justice for colluding in selling off Indian lands illegally while enjoying the governmental position of power. Rosewater drafted memoranda and sent letters to the commissioner of Indian Affairs, notating exhibits of affidavits and documentation showing the Indian agent's complicity in securing large tracts of Winnebago Reservation land for vastly undermarket prices. He even traveled to Washington to present documentary proof of fraud operations to the commissioner in 1903 and continued his work "in the interest of the public service in justice to the defenseless Indians, who are being cheated and robbed and demoralized through the connivance of the agent with the Indian trader and an organized band of land speculators" for several years.[6]

These examples point to a trend that grew as Jews gained power and resolved some of the preoccupations they faced as immigrants, even—as chapter 4 showed—as immigration itself was hotly debated and Jews evoked Native America in these debates. By the late 1920s and early 1930s, by which point Jewish immigration had slowed to a trickle, Jews actively involved themselves in a range of not-for-profit agencies that championed Native American causes. The New York lawyer Joseph W. Latimer argued in "The American Indian: Captive or Citizen" in 1932 that the Indian Bureau was an affront to democracy and a stain on America's justice system that it should be dismantled.[7] His sentiments were reflected in the work of Max L. Rosenberg and Fred M. Stein, who served as regional treasurers of the American Indian Defense Association, founded in 1923 to protect religious freedom and tribal property, and Leo J. Rabinowitz, who directed the American Indian Defense Organization of Central and Northern California.[8] As a leading advocate of civil liberties in twentieth-century America and the general counsel to the ACLU from 1929 to 1955, Morris Ernst, an Alabama-born son of German Jewish immigrants, worked with the Association on American Indian Affairs (AAIA), the Indian Rights Association, the Department of the Interior, and the Office of Indian Affairs and also championed many Jewish causes.[9] In the 1930s, the ACLU organized a Committee on Indian Civil Rights to lobby for restoring tribal autonomy and control over land, trying to establish criminal penalties for kidnapping Native American children and taking them to federal boarding schools, and to lobby for repeal of an old espionage act that allowed reservation superintendents to restrict communications by Native Americans with one another or with outside sympathizers. In 1933, the ACLU committee sponsored an all-day conference on Native American rights in Washington and lobbied for the 1934 IRA.[10]

Jews and the Indian New Deal

But it was under the Roosevelt Administration's Indian New Deal that Jews' advocacy for Native Americans actually gained enormous traction. Roosevelt and his senior advisors were more meritocratic than previous federal administrations, and many Jews (and individuals from many other ethnic minorities) found work in its expanse. These children and grandchildren of urban immigrants placed their faith in education and the liberal promise that America held out for them. The system would reward hard work, creativity, and talent.[11] Finding civil service work in an administration more willing than previous administrations to hire staff irrespective of their "race" was an achievement in and of itself for Jews and a reinforcement of the commitment Jews tended to make to the state and its liberal values.

Jews found a particularly robust role in the Department of the Interior.[12] As Jews took their place at the tables of legislative power and enjoyed the privileges of hitherto unheard of levels of enfranchisement, the Depression had left most Indian communities—and many American Jews—in bad shape.[13] Assimilationist and allotment policies had adversely affected Native Americans despite their resistance to adopting the habits, culture, and lifestyles of settlers. The Brookings Institute, based on visits to ninety-five Indian reservations, issued the influential Meriam Report in 1928, which chronicled the severe conditions faced by Indians, including extreme poverty, devastating epidemics, inadequate food, and inadequate formal education. Mounting public criticism of the federal government policies led to sentiment in favor of restoring tribal independence. Roosevelt named John Collier, then director of the American Indian Defense Association and the Interior Department's most persistent and energetic critic of Indian Affairs as the Indian commissioner. The Department of the Interior also tapped a group of young lawyers, including Nathan Margold and Felix Cohen, and authorized them to begin working on major legislation to try to solve Indian problems at the broadest possible level of legislative initiative. Their brainchild, the IRA, was the first federal Indian policy in more than a hundred years that did not have the explicit purpose of undermining the status of Indian nations.[14]

American Jews had been influential in shaping American legal realism, the dominant view of the law in the 1930s—a legal philosophy that would have tremendous impact on Native American policy and legal affairs.[15] Lawyers like Louis Brandeis, Benjamin Cardozo, Nathan Isaacs, Harold Laski, Felix Frankfurter, Jerome Frank, Morris Raphael Cohen, and his son, Felix Cohen, hoped that the law would be able to help answer questions of society's values instead of remaining aloofly agnostic about them. Legal realism was derived, in part, from legal scholars' (both Jewish and non-Jewish) progressive politics. They linked the law of books to law in action, convinced that the social dislocations of industrialization and corporate concentration had severed the connection between law and social justice. They aimed to remake that connection.[16] Leadership roles in the Department of the Interior provided Jews with the opportunity to mobilize these moral commitments and legal principles as the spearheads of progressive efforts at reshaping American Indian policy. Many Jews were central in the drafting and conceptualizing of the Indian New Deal. These Jewish lawyers, intellectuals, and civil servants worked for the benefit of Native Americans (as they themselves conceived of it), even as their work was inextricably connected to their Jewish backgrounds, sensibilities, and the historical and cultural conditions of contemporaneous American Jewish life. These Jews are perhaps best understood as belonging to what historian David Hollinger referred to as "dispersionist" Jewish history, those persons with Jewish ancestry whose work is fruitfully understood within the context of diaspora Jewish life, irrespective of the degree of their ascribed or declared Jewishness.[17]

A handful of young Jewish attorneys in the Department of the Interior played instrumental roles in the drafting of the IRA despite the fact that few of them had experience with Native American life before their appointments in government. In 1926, Nathan Margold, an NAACP lawyer and activist who would later work for the Department of the Interior, had published "The Plight of the Pueblos" in the *Nation*, describing their "eleventh hour resort to litigation" to retain irrigation rights.[18] In 1933, Margold hired Melvin Siegel from his clerkship with Justice Benjamin Cordozo. He also hired Felix Cohen, the son of the Minsk-born philosopher Morris Raphael Cohen, as the assistant solicitor in that same year. Cohen would serve in that capacity until 1947. Melvin Siegel, Walter Woeklke, and Allan Harper all had a hand in drafting the IRA. Assistant Commissioner of Indian Affairs William Zimmerman, Nathan Margold, and Robert Marshall served as principle advisers on IRA.[19]

From his coming of age until his death at age forty-six, Felix Cohen's intellectual and political pursuits centered on Indian rights.[20] He campaigned for American Indian legal rights and recognition more intensely than any other American Jew.[21] Felix and his wife, Lucy Kramer Cohen, were card-carrying members of the Socialist Party for a time. They belonged to the League for Industrial Democracy, the ACLU Intercollegiate Socialist Society, and the Jews' Industrial Research Group. Critics of the Indian New Deal who accused Cohen of trying to "make Reds of the red men" were partially correct.[22] The staff of the two congressmen who sponsored the bill (and after whom the IRA was named), Wheeler and Howard, pruned details and removed the revolutionary jargon that Cohen had used in his draft, fearing that the drafting of the bill might lead Congress to reject it for being communist.[23] Cohen felt the final version of the IRA (the Wheeler-Howard Act) had "emasculated" his original legislation.[24] His vision for Indian renaissance was emblematic of the most progressive strand of non-Native ideas for Native Americans at the time. His work was crucial in its actualization.

Cohen's Indian New Deal work fell into three parts: (1) the IRA, which restored land to Native tribes and created limited self-government through tribal constitutions; (2) the *Handbook of Federal Indian Law*, which Cohen created for all matters of Indian law; and (3) the ICC, which would adjudicate claims against federal government. The centerpiece of these civic reformist efforts was the passage of federal legislation, the four-pronged 1934 IRA, also known as the Wheeler-Howard Act, which aimed to fundamentally reformulate national Indian policy to set the government's goal as the establishment of Indian self-governance and provide Native American communities with sufficient authority and powers to represent reservation populations. The creators of the IRA designed it to solve problems associated with the previous policies in effect since the Dawes General

Allotment Act of 1877. The IRA aimed to promote, instead, cultural pluralism, tribal sovereignty, and some measure of self-government. The IRA had many provisions; it ended future land allotment (dividing up reservation lands into small parcels and giving them to individual Indians to farm or sell) and allowed Native Americans to voluntarily exchange allotments so that Native groups could consolidate land instead of living on checkerboarded reservations. It restored to tribal ownership the remaining surplus lands created by the implementation of the allotment system. The IRA provided Indians with economic aid and appropriated annual funds for the acquisition of additional land for landless Indians. Tribes had the right to exclude themselves from the provisions of the IRA altogether. It was law only for those tribes who opted in. Tribes that accepted the IRA could draft constitutions defining their powers of self-government and establish business charters that permitted them to borrow money from a revolving credit fund. More than two-thirds of eligible tribes voted to accept the IRA; more than one-third wrote constitutions.[25]

The IRA was a remarkably progressive set of policies and one of the most influential and radical bills of American Indian history. Aiming to minimize the discretionary powers that the Department of the Interior, the Office of Indian Affairs, and Indian agents in the field had long had over Native peoples, the IRA provided provisions to help tribes organize for their own welfare, adopt constitutions and bylaws, and employ legal counsel. It encouraged Indian employment in government service by offering preferential hiring of Indians and waiving civil service requirements. It created an educational loan program for vocational high school and college. "Whereas prior administrations had offered Indians citizenship to lure them [Native Americans] away from their cultural and religious traditions," wrote historian Alison Bernstein, "the Indian New Deal used the constitutional guarantees under citizenship to reinforce the bonds between Indians and their customs."[26] The IRA, perhaps most radically, authorized tribal councils established under the act itself to negotiate with—and litigate against—the federal, state, and local governments. It recognized inherent powers available to tribes and resurrected them in a form in which they could be used at the discretion of the tribe, so long as enrolled members voted within a two-year period to accept the terms of the IRA itself; it was an unusually liberal gesture of Congress in that legislators attempted to draft law that rescinded governmental powers (not as an attempt to shrink government agencies for right-leaning ideological reasons but in order to provide redress to its own failings, aware of the impacts that centuries of law, policy, and war had made on Native Americans). The intention of New Deal administrators was to return as much power and land as possible to communal status. All land purchased by IRA funds thus came under tribal control. The drafters of the IRA hoped to move power away from the Indian bureaucracy in Washington to the reservation governments. The opportunities made available to tribes under this act were, in the assessment of Native American legal historians Vine Deloria Jr. and Clifford Lytle, immense.[27]

The Department of Justice's Indian Law Survey appointed Cohen as its head in 1939. The survey resulted in a forty-six-volume compendium of treaties, statutes, and decisions, which Cohen edited and summarized, spending "enormous efforts to unequivocally state the primacy of treaties in Indian law, and their basis in consent of the governed," according to his biographer.[28] It opened with the observation that the right of first discovery of American land lay with Indian nations, not with the United States or its colonial predecessors. The *Handbook* became the single most important resource in state and federal legal proceedings on matters of Indian law and became known as the "bible" for American Indian law.[29] It was a reference work, though it came to be viewed by many who used it as the ultimate expression of Indian law despite its intent as a concise manual for the practicing attorney or judge might need to reference or review various cases and statutes that established law on matters of treaties, water rights, taxation, civil and criminal jurisdiction, or property.[30] The *Handbook* reflected Cohen's vision, one that was not necessarily shared in America beyond the circle of Interior Department reformers and their allies out of office.

Cohen also drafted the ICC Act, which gave Native Americans the elemental right to sue for damages suffered at the hands of the United States without first having to get the permission of Congress.[31] After he left government service, he also interpreted the IRA as an attorney hired by tribes to represent them in their legal battles against the government. He assisted several Native American tribes in writing their own constitutions. He wrote briefs on behalf of the Council of Karluk Native Village in Alaska for the founding of a Chippewa, Mohawk, and Oneida confederated lobbying organization and dozens of articles, editorials, and letters to editors of major American newspapers concerning contemporary legislative issues of import to Native Americans, ceaselessly observing misconceptions about Indians and calling out the state's unfair treatment of Native American communities.[32] He argued against relocation policies that violated laws of property rights, for example, and critiqued national consciousness outside the courts, suggesting that state and citizen alike adopt and apply the "Golden Rule to Indian affairs: Whatsoever is hateful to thee do not do unto any Indian," playing with the biblical moral idiom.[33] He wrote that "we [Americans] have often disposed them [Indians], spiritually by denying their existence as a people, or by taking refuge in the Myth of the Vanishing Indian, or by blaming our grandfathers for the wrongs we commit. In this way, we have often assured ourselves that our national sins are of purely antiquarian significance."[34]

Cohen's Jewish Investments

Cohen can be credited for making a greater overall impact on Native Americans in the federal courts, in Congress, and in the daily lives of the greatest number of Native Americans than any other American Jew, and he did so with some measure of Jewish self-consciousness. His identification with Native American issues illustrated in a concentrated manner how mid-twentieth-century liberal Jews tried to mediate between political insiders and minority outsiders, between power and powerlessness in American civil life. Occupying this middle zone served several simultaneous functions. It allowed enfranchised Jews like Cohen and the lawyers, boosters, and board members of a panoply of Indian rights organizations, still absorbed with the memory and recent historic experience of Jewish disempowerment, to feel both settled in America and Jewish by identifying "down" with Americans whose collective corporate fate had fared worse than had the Jews' fate in America. It also allowed Jews to enact their devotion to liberalism and foster the American institutions and values they, as Jewish liberals, cared for—namely, tolerance, equality, the rule of law, and the protection and preservation of minority rights and cultures. These outcomes, they believed, would secure the brightest future for America and for all its minorities, Jews and Native Americans among them, because they had seen the ways that these principles of American liberalism had served their immigrant families and communities. They helped fashion American Indian law so that its adversarial and truth-seeking methods could be used to ensure greater possibilities for the liberal order.

Cohen saw Indian advocacy work as inextricably linked with the work of defending all minorities, Jews very much on his radar. In fact, he coupled nearly all his appeals for antidiscrimination law and public opinion *about Jews* with appeals on behalf of other American minorities. He consistently featured Native Americans as his exemplary American "minority." Cohen saw his advocacy on behalf of Jews, Native Americans, and other American minorities as important buttressing of America's national institutions. He argued that Jewish and Native American traditions developed these foundational ideals, underscoring his efforts to have the state remain accountable to its own ideals through the workings of the law.

Cohen's convictions spilled out beyond abstractions and rhetoric to active civil work. He paired his investments in Jewish and Indian issues throughout his career. His Indian advocacy began in the shadow of the Nazi rise to power in the mid-1930s. His "Powers of Indian Tribes," published in 1934 soon after he joined the Department of the Interior legal staff, was his earliest attempt to bring together a statement on the residual powers still attached to original tribal sovereignty and the legal basis underpinning the IRA.[35] The essay foregrounded the principle of inherent sovereignty and showed the enduring significance of treaties. It also broke down racist legitimation of Anglo paternal governance by its presumption that Indian nations had "duly constituted organs of government."[36] In the early 1940s, Cohen emphasized the importance of protecting diverse groups and stressed that the government's failure to fulfill its obligations to Native Americans was not a problem of contract law; it was, for him, an act of oppression, banned by the Constitution. In a particularly sharp criticism of the state that presciently foreshadowed early twenty-first-century Indigenous critique, Cohen argued that the law was part of a system of violence "concealed or justified by a social ritual and ideology, a set of forms or phrases, a system of constantly reiterated ideals, which portrays the law as a moral force."[37]

Yet like many second- and third-generation American Jews who had assimilated enough to take on elite leadership roles but who nonetheless cared deeply about Jewish life, Cohen did not wish to destroy the apparatus of the state. On the contrary, for him, fighting the state's imperial sins offered a path to rescuing its soul. The state, for Cohen, was not an enemy to be weakened, but a virtuous if compromised system that longed for expiation. "Racial oppression seldom destroyed the people that was oppressed," he wrote, though "it [racial oppression] has always in the end destroyed the oppressor."[38] Cultural pluralism, he believed, was critical to America's democratic traditions and institutions. Cohen's 1951 article, "Colonialism: U.S. Style," published in the *Progressive*, described the U.S. government's actions in respect to Native Americans as "divide and conquer colonialism," a strategy he believed was "still fully utilized in justifying the expansion of Indian Bureau power over Indian life."[39]

Cohen railed against corruption at the BIA and likened it to "the corruption of prisons, insane asylums, concentration camps, fascist and communist states and other societies in which men cannot 'talk back' to officials."[40] Instead, Cohen advocated for extending democratic powers to Indians to make their own mistakes. In other words, "to let Indians spend their own money, run their own schools, use or lease their own lands, and hire their own lawyers to defend their rights, just as neighboring white communities do. . . . If to this simple measure of justice were added a full and prompt settlement of all Federal debts to our Indian fellow-citizens, we would have no need to worry about how they would fare under the self-determination we have so long promised and so long withheld."[41] He also saw the Indian's role in America as analogous to the Jewish experience in Europe. His 1948 pamphlet, "Combating Totalitarian Propaganda," examined anti-Semitism and other racist propaganda and various techniques available for fighting it.[42] In 1953, reflecting back on two decades of Jewish and Indian advocacy, he gave voice to the motivations that drove his work, writing, "We have a vital concern with Indian self-government because the Native American is to America what the Jew was to the Russian Czars and Hitler's Germany. For us the Indian tribe is the miner's canary, and when it flutters and droops we know that the poison gasses of intolerance threaten all other minorities in our land."[43]

Cohen did not just make rhetorical use of Jewish themes and Jewish historical suffering when advancing his points in support of justice for American Indians. Emblematic of a larger pattern of American Jewish intellectual and political work, Cohen like many other Jews, worked on Jewish immigration and minority recognition issues and twinned professional commitments to Native Americans with Jewish defense work.[44] In addition to the energy that Cohen devoted to Indian affairs, he also spent material intellectual resources on Jewish causes. On behalf of the Consultative Council of Jewish Organizations, comprised of the

American Jewish Committee (AJC), the Alliance Israélite Universelle, and British Jewry's Anglo-Jewish Association, he penned a memorandum on the prevention of discrimination and protection of minorities submitted to the United Nations Commission on Human Rights.[45] He took on a role as a legal advisor, director, and member of the Institute of Ethnic Affairs and founded the Institute of Living Law in 1940, which worked with government agencies to combat propaganda warfare, among other things. The aims of both organizations fit liberal Jewish interests.[46]

Cohen worked for the AJC on several projects too, underscoring his commitment to fighting anti-Jewish discrimination in the United States and abroad and the clear presence of his motivation as a Jew. He wrote the economic section of a statement the AJC submitted to the Senate Immigration Subcommittee calling for the total elimination of racial discrimination from the National Origins quota system legislation, which had stunted Jewish immigration throughout the years of Nazi terror.[47] Cohen's enthusiasm for the Jewish causes, and the AJC in particular, grew after World War II ended. In a letter he wrote hoping to recruit Harry Rosenfield (the Commissioner of the Displaced Persons Commission and the Executive Director of President Truman's Commission on Immigration and Naturalization in the late 1940s and early 1950s) to the AJC, Cohen celebrated its "fight against prejudice and discrimination, in developing greater understanding between Jews and other Americans, and in defending the civil and religious rights of Jews and other minority groups everywhere."[48] Jews, he insisted, ought to fight to defend the civil and religious rights of others, alongside themselves. His essays and editorials also suggest that his work on behalf of minorities in general all aimed to serve Jewish ends as well. "The need is greater than ever for a Jewish organization," ran his letter to Rosenfield, "that claims for Jews only those rights which it is willing to help other minorities to achieve."[49]

Traces from his archive suggest that he maintained continued commitments to Jewish matters. One telling scrap of ephemera is a copy of a Yiddish poem that he wrote on his own letterhead:

I live in fear
And great danger,
My suffering knows no bounds.
I must flee
By the light of the moon
Because I am oppressed,
I am not allowed
To raise my head.
They inflict every evil upon us
They yell "Jews,
You live by swindling,

You prey on the Christians."
Jerusalem—My dear holy land.[50]

Cohen clearly knew Yiddish, and the sentiments of the poem itself about an oppressed Jew, mournful and frustrated at his lack of power amid a generally hostile Gentile/Christian world, somehow resonated. Cohen, in short, worked on some of the most anxious issues that American Jews faced in the late 1930s and 1940s—namely, immigration restriction, minority rights both domestically and internationally, and countering racial fascist propaganda.[51]

Cohen reserved a special place in his imagination for Alaska and its potential for revitalization, curiously, for both Jews and Indians. He would return to the theme of Alaska's prospects several times between the late 1930s and his death in 1951. Perhaps Alaska—at the edge of the continent, still somewhat of a frontier society, generally underpopulated, rich in natural resources, and home to a large population of Native Americans—could stand in as a placeholder for the America he wished to create. In 1939, the secretary of the Interior, Harold Ickes, put Cohen to work on a proposal to settle Jews in Alaska. Ickes pushed the idea as a means to develop that "vast underdeveloped" territory. Congress rejected the proposal.[52] By the time World War II ended, Cohen was seeing Indigenous issues play out in Alaska too.[53]

In 1948, Cohen wrote to a Jewish audience about "Alaska's Nuremberg Laws," calling the Tongass Timber Act of 1947 "the first racial expropriation law to be passed by Congress."[54] He urged his Jewish readership to be concerned with the problems of race discrimination in general and with the dilemmas of Native Americans in particular. The Tongass Timber Act required Jewish action. All Americans, he wrote, "have paid much attention to the manifestations of prejudice against Negroes, Jews, Orientals, Catholics, and the foreign-born." Few Americans, however, he chided, "have recognized that it is the Indian who typically serves as the guinea pig for new forms of race-discrimination in our land. Slavery, racial disenfranchisement, and other indicia of 'second-class citizenship' have generally been tried out first on the Indians."[55] Cohen aimed to correct that lack of attention, both because of his convictions that Native Americans deserved a concerted effort by liberals and because he believed Jews, as a relatively secure minority, ought to devote efforts to protect minority rights for all: "Techniques of oppression that proved successful have then been applied to other minorities.... What is done to Indians or Eskimos in Alaska today, can be done to Negroes in the South tomorrow, and to Jews, Catholics or descendants of non-Anglo-Saxon strains the day after tomorrow."[56] Cohen was constantly concerned and motivated to speak about Jewish suffering in Europe under the Nazis and was cognizant of the struggles that all minorities faced under totalitarian regimes, though he was clearly preoccupied with the Jewish situation. He regularly voiced these concerns in Jewish and legal publications.[57] In a speech shortly after the Japanese attack on Pearl Harbor, Cohen criticized American Jews who downplayed the anti-Semitic nature of totalitarian regimes in Europe as well as those who chose not to call attention to discussions about authoritarianism. "No nation crushes the Jews in its midst until it has come to despise reason and morality and the dignity of the human soul," he wrote. "We have a special responsibility to safeguard our country against the forces that would destroy our Republic by undermining the moral principles of liberty and tolerance on which the Republic is based."[58]

Felix Cohen's twinned work on Jewish and Indian causes highlights not just his own personal proclivities but a broader trend among a cadre of Jewish activists who focused on groups and associations and fought for pluralism. As individuals, these lawyers and civil servants sought and found power in a federal administration that was open to hardworking professionals, quite aware of the general background of racism that Jews—and Native Americans—faced. Though Indian affairs had not been a priority or a motivation to seek work in Washington, this group of aspiring, progressive Jews took the opportunity to advance certain interests once in a position to do so. They spoke from a place of Jewish concern for American society; serving both Jewish and Native constituencies that fostered the ideals and institutions they cherished most about America. The political pluralism they promoted provided them, as Jews, a means of reconciling their liberal (or socialist) backgrounds and their own desires for partial assimilation into liberal American society.[59]

From the Indian New Deal to the Era of Termination

Jews' impact on Indian Affairs waned at the level of official government policy as Roosevelt's administration was passed to that of Harry S. Truman in 1945. World War II brought an end to federal government policy initiatives aimed at building Native American tribal sovereignty. Collier resigned in 1945, after twelve years as the commissioner of Indian Affairs; the transition between the Indian New Deal and the era of Termination was sharp and harsh. The progressive policy direction for Indian affairs that Jews had helped institutionalize for more than a decade ended abruptly. Critics charged Collier with attempting to institute socialism on the reservations. A new coalition of forces called for unilateral termination to federal assistance to Indians. Conservatives interested in federal budget cuts genuinely believed that Indians, once removed from government restrictions, would experience a more profound awakening. These conservatives allied with liberals who seemed to have learned that some of America's laws were reminiscent of the racial restrictions imposed on minorities by the Axis powers that they had recently defeated. Together they sought the immediate release of racial minorities from legislation altogether, conceiving of it as the "burden of legislation."[60] Truman appointed Dillon Myer, the non-Jewish former director of the War Relocation Authority, as the new Indian commissioner in 1950. With his experience between 1942 and 1946 supervising the detention camp program for Japanese

Americans during World War II, Truman's appointment leveraged Myer's experience in operationalizing and managing race-based, large-scale population transfers and their politics of containment. Progressive reformers were out. Cold War conservatives were in.

Looking for ways to reduce federal expenditures, the Senate Civil Service Committee of the conservative Republican Congress of 1947 dismantled New Deal programs. Congress asked the acting commissioner of Indian Affairs, William Zimmerman Jr., himself Jewish, to testify about the BIA's programs that same year. To evaluate tribal conditions, Congress demanded that Zimmerman provide lists of those tribes that could immediately succeed without further federal help, tribes that could be ready to live on their own within a short period of time, and tribes that would need continued federal assistance before the federal government could terminate its special relationship with it. Zimmerman produced the lists but cautioned that "significant and substantial changes and protections must be instituted before a tribe could successfully stand on its own feet."[61] Despite his objections to the Termination policy, Zimmerman played an important role in the move toward Termination. Following his testimony, the federal government began unilaterally withdrawing relationships with individual tribes. Termination meant that states, rather than the federal government, would provide tribes with such services as education, social welfare, law enforcement, and economic assistance.[62] The basic elements of Termination included fundamental changes in land ownership, the ending of the trust relationship, the imposition of state legislative jurisdiction and judicial authority, ending exemptions from state taxing authority, discontinuing federal programs to tribes, discontinuing federal programs to individuals, and effectively ending tribal sovereignty.[63] Legislative changes were made without consultation with Indians.[64] Termination meant the cessation of the federal tribal relationship, established through treaty or otherwise. Between 1953 and 1964, Congress passed twelve Termination bills, eliminating the government's relationship with 109 tribes and removing approximately 2.5 million acres of trust land from protected status. Approximately 12,000 Native Americans lost tribal affiliation.[65] Termination was an extension of the impulse to assimilate Indians, an impulse that dominated Congress during the 1950s and most of the 1960s.

The new Indian commissioner, Dillon Myer, also required the resignation of the two remaining progressive Jews in the bureau, Zimmerman and Theodore Haas, the bureau's chief counsel.[66] Felix Cohen mourned President Truman's decision to appoint Myer rather than the acting commissioner, Zimmerman. About the dismissals of Zimmerman and Haas, Cohen wrote,

> For 17 years, Bill Zimmerman gave his best energies to defending Indians and employees of the Indian Service against all attacks. . . . It is a great tragedy for the Indians, and especially for the Natives of Alaska, that Assistant Commissioner Zimmerman should now be replaced by a man who has no knowledge

> of past promises, and no prior experience in Indian Affairs except for a slight connection with the infamous Tongass Bill depriving Alaskan Indians of their timber. . . . In losing Ted Haas, the Indian has lost its conscience, and in losing Bill Zimmerman it loses its memory. It is now free to disregard past promises and to repeat past mistakes without awareness of either. . . . The road ahead for all of us who seek to protect Indian rights looks harder and more dangerous than it has been since 1928.[67]

Zimmerman and Haas were the last of the Jewish Indian New Dealers to work for the BIA. Out of office, this cadre of Jews persisted in their efforts. While the Jews who had been working for Indian social justice under the Roosevelt Administration had lost their positions of power by the late 1940s, Jewish advocates persisted in their justice work through a variety of other institutional efforts, lobbying initiatives, public relations campaigns, and funding support. Yet despite the diminishment of their access to influence state power, Jewish activists did not cease their work for Indian justice as they construed it. They worked with and for a variety of nongovernmental organizations (NGOs) that promoted Indian enfranchisement—most significantly, the AAIA. They involved themselves in litigation cases against the federal government that had recently been their employer.

One important vehicle for Indian empowerment during the era of Termination was the ICC, a creation of Felix Cohen and other New Deal liberals that was nevertheless implemented by conservatives in the Truman Administration. Indeed, the ICC was a crucial element of the IRA since it provided a dramatic venue wherein Indian tribes represented by lawyers could litigate against the federal government for damages.[68] Felix Cohen and Ernest Wilkinson, a devout Mormon who had successfully litigated on behalf of Ute claims in Utah and eventually a president of Brigham Young University, wrote legislation for the ICC in 1935, 1940, and 1943.[69] The two—a Jew and a Mormon—fashioned a bill as favorable to the Indians as possible without alienating congressional support. They then shepherded the bill through Congress.[70] Together they drafted the amendments. Truman signed the bill into law in August 1946 and articulated its logic. The statement read, "I am glad to sign my name to a measure which . . . removes a lingering discrimination against our First Americans and gives them the same opportunities that our laws extend to all other American citizens to vindicate their property rights and contracts in the courts against violations by the Federal Government itself . . . with this final settlement of our outstanding claims which this measure ensures, Indians can take their place without special handicap or special advantage in the economic life of our nation and share fully in its progress."[71]

Congress authorized the commission to hear two separate categories of cases. The first were for claims in which the United States was accused of making treaties or agreements with tribes fraudulently or coercing tribes into treaties, ones that offered tribes only "unconscionable consideration" and ones made by mutual or unilateral mistake. The second were for "claims based upon fair and honorable dealings that are not recognized by any rule of law or equity."[72] The ICC Act waived any statute of limitations defense by the government so that Indian groups could sue for wrongs that had been committed by the United States since the creation of the country.[73] Cohen and others conceived of (and had approved) a commission that was meant to enjoy broad, extrajudicial powers to fashion solutions for legitimate tribal claims.

This was quite novel. Congress empowered the commission "to look at the history of American expansion not only as it had actually occurred but also as it *ought* to have occurred," according to historian, lawyer, and son of Jewish Indian advocate Arthur Lazarus, Edward Lazarus. "[T]he commission could reach back in history and rewrite treaties as a 'fair and honorable' nation would have written them originally—and then pay in coin for the moral and legal failings of America's Indian policy. In theory, no forum had ever provided a better opportunity to recover for government wrongs."[74] The commission was to understand that abandonment of land under duress should not end a tribes' right to its land. During the treaty-making period, distinct Indian nations negotiated away some two billion acres of North America in 370 treaties, leaving about 140 million acres in 1868, when the last treaty was ratified.[75]

The ICC was an attempt to use the law as a tool of recompense. Cohen hoped it would settle historical acts of inequitable treaties and play a part in creating a just basis for a pluralistic future grappling as American legal activists with the legacies of colonialism. The federal government's obligation toward Native Americans, anchored within treaties, was also an obligation toward all minority groups and society at large.[76] Cohen hoped the ICC might rectify some of the perfidy that American Indians had suffered by at the hands of Indian agents; the U.S. Congress passed the act to clear the decks of Indians' claims during the same ten years it expected to terminate Indian status.[77]

If the IRA of the late 1940s set out to refute the antiquated policy of assimilation and allotment, Cohen wanted the ICC to rewrite the *future* by providing a forum for tribes to voice their versions of American history, according to legal scholar Dalia Tsuk Mitchell. He wanted the commission's proceedings to become exercises in hearing and learning from the testimony of the Indians by investigating what he called "the entire field of Indian claims, even for the tribes which may be too poor to hire their own lawyers, and bring in within a reasonable period of time a report which will conclude once and for all this chapter of . . . National history."[78] The commission was to provide some recompense for what Cohen called "the backwash of a great national experiment in dictatorship and racial extermination."[79]

The 1946 Act allowed for "identifiable" groups of Native descendants to bring a cause of action without regard to their federal recognition status. As stated in the signing statement that Felix Cohen himself had apparently drafted for President Truman to read,

> this bill makes perfectly clear what many men and women, here and abroad, have failed to recognize, that in our transactions with the Indian tribes we have at least since the Northwest Ordinance of 1787 set for ourselves the standard of fair and honorable dealings, pledging respect for all Indian property rights . . . it would be a miracle if in the course of these dealings—the largest real estate transaction history—we had not made some mistakes and occasionally fail to live up to the precise terms of our treaties and agreements with some 200 tribes. But we stand ready to submit all such controversies to the judgment impartial tribunals. We stand ready to correct any mistakes we have made.[80]

The commission was meant to be the tool the state would use against itself to redress its own wrongs. More than 850 claims inundated the commission. In its first decade, the commission decided only one-eighth of the claims on the docket. Of the 102 cases that reached the commission in those first ten years, Indians won only 21. Of the nearly $1 billion claimed by the tribes, it awarded judgments totaling only $13 million, less than 2 percent. Tribes were aware of the need for proper representation but faced constant struggles to secure and hold legal help, some of which were born of state resistance. Myer refused approval of tribal contracts for a number of attorneys trusted and requested by the tribes; more than forty different tribes complained of bureau interference.[81] The ICC had to be renewed in 1957, 1961, 1972, and 1976 so that the commission could consider all the claims that had been filed.[82] It would outlive the Indian New Deal itself by decades.

Implementing the ICC

The ICC provides a window into the mid-twentieth-century Termination climate, for its actual workings had a much more circumscribed impact on Native American life than Cohen had envisioned for it. The ICC did not provide the ultimate vehicle for Indian redress. As one part of the broader history of Jewish-Native American relations, the Jewish role in the ICC shows how Jewish assumptions and motivations impacted Indian affairs and thus actual Native American lives. The ICC opened career opportunities for hundreds of lawyers, historians, and anthropologists.[83] Jewish attorneys worked a disproportionate volume of the ICC's caseload.

In many instances, attorneys working for wronged tribes had been the only voice of support and avenue of protest in the judicial arena.[84] Lawyers actively perused the scraps of legal doctrines, according to Deloria Jr. and Lytle's assessment, "to ensure the maximum benefits accrue to Indians from the multitude of legal documents that chart the development of the relationship between particular tribes and the U.S."[85]

Cohen, Wilkinson, Margold, and others had designed and envisioned the commission as an avenue of recourse and conceived of it as a grand expression of America's legal conscience, hopeful that it would provide meaningful expiation for the sins of conquest. But in practice, the ICC was operated so as to apply the Termination policy. The commission adopted court-like rules of procedure. The practical result was far from what the liberals had envisioned; it became a stingy tribunal that fought Indian claimants tooth and nail, agonistically—even antagonistically.[86] Instead of hearing moral claims based on fair and honorable dealings that were not recognized by any existing rules of law (in addition to strictly legal claims), the commissioners converted the ICC into a traditional adjudicatory body, something like a substitute court of claims for Indians.[87] Cohen had worked not only in the drafting of the ICC Act itself but also later in private practice on many matters related to the ICC. He took a leadership role in managing and thinking about the entire claims process and the value and virtue of having good quality representation for tribes.

He was not the only Jew to take an active role in the claims process. At least eighteen of the plaintiff attorneys during the first handful of years in the late 1950s of the commission were Jews. Lone attorneys, legal teams of Jews and non-Jews, and all-Jewish legal teams represented 48 of the 319 cases that the Claims Commission heard.[88] If the Indian bar had been a relatively low-status legal venue before the ICC, the opportunities to litigate against the federal government, potentially earn lucrative winnings, and fight principled liberal battles for embattled Native American clients made it, almost overnight, prestigious. It was also a field of law that had few barriers to entry, as few or no established firms monopolized representing tribes. As a start-up field, Indian claims law was prime ground for competitive, industrious, and liberal minded attorneys. It is not surprising that many Jewish lawyers and firms were attracted to it. Indian law was underdetermined; the number and diversity of treaties, statutes, and regulations promulgated over centuries were not written in contract language that lawyers were trained to interpret and utilize. But litigating against the federal government for justice and minority rights was both high profile and morally upstanding. Attorneys in private practice, those employed by federal agencies, and those working for public interest nonprofit firms all had to deal in murky legal territories on matters such as the "trust relationship," the protection of tribes against state incursions into tribal sovereignty, and the scope of the state's discretionary powers in respect to natural resources.[89] These legal questions had profound impacts on Native American life; lawyers, not policy makers, generally worked out their solutions.[90]

Some lawyers worked for decades on exceedingly complex cases. The Jewish attorneys who worked on the Sioux's claim for the Black Hills in South Dakota in the 1950s and 1960s stand out. (The Sioux had been in and out of courts for decades already; the Standing Rock, Rosebud, Crow Creek, and Lower Brûlé Sioux tribes were involved in these rounds of litigation both together and independently.) Jewish lawyers like Marvin Sonosky and Richard Schifter had already accrued some experience in Indian claims. Sonosky had worked for the Justice Department and was handling claims work for a number of tribes. His Washington firm, Sonosky, Chambers, Sachse & Endreson, had helped draft national legislation protecting Indian rights, including one statute that allowed tribes to sue in federal courts without regard to jurisdictional limitations. Sonosky served as general counsel for Assiniboine, Santee, Sioux, and Shoshone clients in Montana, Wyoming, and the Dakotas, for whom he successfully litigated several land claims. He directly lobbied the Department of the Interior from the mid-1950s through the 1960s. He was particularly active in opposing the 1958 Lakota Referenda and Public Law 280 of 1953, which established that states would assume jurisdiction over reservation Indians (as opposed to the federal government), including law enforcement authority.[91] Sonosky's private law practice included four Sioux clients, Shoshone and Chippewa clients, and several small tribes for which he acted as the general counsel. He handled land claims, including that of the Mississippi River Sioux bands' claim for land in Minnesota, for which he obtained a $12.2 million settlement, one of the largest on record.

The Sioux's other main attorney was Richard Schifter, born in Vienna in 1923 to Polish immigrants, the only member of his Jewish family who was able to obtain a U.S. visa in 1938. Schifter served in the U.S. Army as one of the so-called Ritchie Boys, young Jewish German refugees whom the U.S. Army trained in psychological warfare. He worked for twenty-four years to get the Black Hills returned to the Sioux.[92] The settlement that Sonosky, Schifter, and their teams representing the Black Hills Sioux reached with the state was the largest financial settlement of the ICC. The Sioux themselves ultimately rejected it.[93]

While most of the claims that tribes and their lawyers brought to the commission were land claims or claims regarding the mismanagement of tribal funds, some asserted claims based on moral grounds with no basis in law. Some Jewish lawyers exploited these opportunities, influenced by their left-leaning backgrounds. One was made on behalf of the Chiricahua Apache, who had been imprisoned for more than a quarter century on army bases in Florida, Alabama, and Oklahoma.[94] The Jewish attorney brothers Israel "Lefty" Weissbrodt and Abraham W. Weissbrodt, born to illiterate Jewish immigrants from Galicia and reared in the Bronx, brought the case.[95] Together with David Cobb, a Gentile descendant of the Mayflower, the Weissbrodt brothers also represented the Tlingit and Haida Indians in 1945 and 1948. Through effective advocacy and sheer perseverance over a thirty-year claims process, they succeeded in winning for their clients a settlement from the federal government of roughly $22 million, the seventh largest tribal recovery at the time, forty times what the tribe had asked for. Using documents from the National Archives, Cobb and the brothers Weissbrodt established that Apache territory had been stolen and detailed the government's dishonorable dealings. By 1961, the firm had also won judgments from the commission totaling nearly $7 million from the Confederated Tribes of the Colville Reservation in Washington, the Nez Perce Indians in Washington and Idaho, and the Omaha tribe in Nebraska.[96]

Despite some successes at the commission, many cases did not get put on the docket, and many lost. And as critics of the ICC process have pointed out, few of the tribes' lawyers were willing to risk breaking uncharted legal ground and thus failed to take advantage of the most flexible recourses available to them. Few brought cases in which Indians had been refused to practice their religion or speak their own languages, were denied adequate education, or were deprived of the means of economic self-sufficiency. Attorneys seemed unwilling or unable to bear the risk of lawsuits even if they recognized the possibility of asserting novel claims based on the "fair and honorable dealings" clause. Some of this lawyerly work, in other words, was merely instrumental rather than ideologically driven.

And not all of the ICC's Jewish attorneys worked to mitigate the damages that colonial settlement or unfair dealings with the American federal government had wrought on Native American groups. Nor did those who acted on behalf of Native clients use the full set of tools that were made available by the ICC to right such wrongs. A handful of Jewish attorneys worked as defense council to the United States in claims cases too.[97] These defense council lawyers, Deloria and Lytle went out of their way to point out, "established a proud and just record in their representation of the US and did not become emotionally 'anti-Indian' although the pressures to adopt personally the postures they were expected to carry in the courtroom must have been tremendous."[98] The government attorney for the Black Hills Sioux case, for example, was Maurice Cooperman, who did all the things defense council for the federal government ought to have done: rejecting his opposing counsel's charges of government fraud, duress, and misappropriation, countering with the defense that the government acted in good faith and in compliance with the 1868 treaty that shaped the Sioux claim, arguing that the government had expended tens of millions of dollars for the benefit of the tribe rendering the land compensated for, rather than confiscated, and supporting the government's case with well-researched exhibits.[99]

Indian Advocacy off Capitol Hill

The ICC was a major venue of Jewish efforts for Native American justice. But it was by no means the only one. Beyond the legal and quasi-legal work, Jewish pro-Indian advocacy work took shape in public relations and education, lobbying, and Native American community capacity building. Walter Hart Blumenthal, the Jewish encyclopedist, literary critic, and editor (and onetime chronicler of "Lost Tribes" claims), published a volume in 1955 entitled *American Indians Dispossessed: Fraud in Land Cessions Forced upon the Tribes*, which aimed to educate a broad reading public about injustices.[100] After leaving the federal government work, Felix Cohen worked as an associate at his cousin Henry Cohen's firm Curry, Bingham & Cohen alongside James Curry, an active member of the ACLU and other left groups or socialists and the legal counsel to the National Congress of American Indians (NCAI).[101] Later working out of the private general law practice Riegelman, Strasser, Schwartz & Spiegelberg, Cohen opened a Washington office and handled pro bono cases including land claims cases, matters of tribal sovereignty and self-governance, cases that helped secure social security and other government-promised benefits, and one case to ensure Native Americans the right to vote in New Mexico and Arizona. He served as general counsel for numerous tribes and for the AAIA and established a Joint Efforts Group, comprised of more than a dozen law firms interested in Indian claims that was meant to facilitate research, reduce duplication efforts, and pool resources to explore legal questions of mutual concern.[102] (Arthur Lazarus took up some of Cohen's workload in 1952.[103])

Perhaps the strongest illustration of Jewish involvement with Indian causes lies in the thorough and deep connections between individual Jews, Jewish community organizations, and the AAIA.[104] What is most significant about this relationship is not the mere fact that Jews supported Indian advocacy work, but that this service simultaneously supported outcomes that these Jews considered good for their own (and for America's) liberalism and antiracist solidarity. Originally the Eastern Association of Indian Affairs, the AAIA formed in 1922 principally by non-Indians interested in Pueblo arts and crafts. Soon thereafter, the AAIA shifted its focus to the defense of rights and the promotion of the welfare of Native Americans. Jews were at its forefront. Its early meetings were hosted by Jews: Mrs. Victor Morawetz and later Dr. Frederick Hoffman.[105] Jesse L. Nusbaum served on its board from 1932 until 1936, taking up fights against the bill that attempted to restrict the inheritance rights of so-called Civilized Tribes. The AAIA initiated several humanitarian projects, including emergency relief efforts in respect to tuberculosis among numerous tribes.[106]

In 1946, the AAIA began to reappraise its organizational needs and methods under the leadership of the non-Jewish (and non-Native) writer, anthropologist, and activist Oliver La Farge. The AAIA built new programs and hired the (Jewish) anthropologist Alexander Lesser as its first full-time executive director. A year later, it created the position of legal counsel and hired Felix Cohen after his departure from the Department of the Interior to fight legal battles, produce scholarship, and promote public education.[107] It launched the *American Indian* quarterly, with a circulation of about eight thousand, and its newsletter, *Indian Affairs*, with an even larger circulation. It helped repeal a Massachusetts scalping reward law that had lingered on the books.[108]

The records of the AAIA seldom explicitly reflect on the extent to which Jewish people staffed or funded its work, but the record is replete with the names of Jewish women and men, lay leaders and professionals, educators and businessmen. In the late 1930s, Mrs. A. E. Grossman, Howard S. Gans, Eustace Seligman, Rose Goldman, and Fred and Mable Stein took up active leadership roles in the association, and much of its early funding came from more than two dozen mostly New York Jewish donors.[109] Ethel Cutler Freeman ran its Coordinating Committee National Arts Club.[110] Contribution lists from 1948 to 1952 include Hollywood Jews Darryl Zanuck of Twentieth Century Fox, Walter Lantz Productions, Leo Spitz of Universal-International Studios, as well as Louis Stulberg of the ILGWU Fund and David Dubinsky, its president.[111] In an internal memo from La Verne Madigan to La Farge in the spring of 1955, Simon Gross, the director of Marshall Civil Liberties Trust, referred to his fundraising efforts directed at "a special appeal to selected alrightniks," referring to the "American-Yiddish word which Miss Hermelin and Mrs. Pollack use to describe some of our contributors. It means people whose bank account is in very good shape indeed."[112] The AAIA's 1965 contributors list included sixty-five individual Jewish donors, including those from synagogues like Temple Judea of Tarzana, California, and Temple Sharey Shalom in Springfield, New Jersey.[113]

There is something notable about a situation in which the Jewish general counsel of an organization (Felix Cohen) writes to the Jewish executive director of that same organization (Alexander Lesser) about the organization's statement of purpose and its program for American Indians that will be funded largely by Jewish patrons. The same liberal, antiassimilationist, cultural pluralistic impulse that led Jews to preserve and celebrate what was unique in their culture fueled the long hours of advocacy work for Native American justice. "To many of us," wrote Felix Cohen about the AAIA's mission, "the 'assimilation of the Indians into our general population' means the wiping out of all distinctive Indian traits of character or culture, in line with the 'melting-pot' idea of wiping out all non-Anglo-Saxon traits in immigrant groups. This is a widely prevalent attitude toward Indians, Jews, and all other minorities. But to many of us the attitude appears to be narrow and un-American."[114] As Cohen articulated it, these Jews active in the AAIA, and perhaps in the broader pattern of Jewish civil activists and intellectuals working for Native American causes, fought against what they deemed "un-American" behavior inimical to their values.

Yet for all this advocacy work done on behalf of Native Americans by Jews, Cohen maintained a troubled sense of the paternalism potentially involved in work done by enfranchised Jews on behalf of Native Americans, and he warned his fellow advocates that Indians themselves might look upon the work of the AAIA in "the same light as those who like the bottle might look upon the W.C.T.U. [Woman's Christian Temperance Union]." He also recognized that at some level, the broadest goal of reformers like his own cadre of people involved in the AAIA was for degrees of assimilation. "There is no question about the sincerity or high-mindedness of the would-be reformer," he wrote, "but there is a natural resentment [that Indians might have] at being treated as something to be reformed by persons with a 'holier-than-thou' attitude. If anybody should tell me, a Jew of Russian descent, that I ought to be beneficially assimilated into the Anglo-Saxon protestant [sic] main stream of American life, my first impulse would be to punch my would-be reformer in the nose."[115]

Felix Cohen and Alexander Lesser were well aware of the extent to which the AAIA was a "Jewish" organization and were keenly attuned to the inherent parochialism or "holier-than-thou" dimension of such uplift practices. Still, the AAIA (and all of its Jewish employees and boosters) rarely dwelled on this awareness or anxiety. They tirelessly worked on specific issues in the courts, the public, the world of scholarship, and on Capitol Hill, sometimes in conjunction with Jewish community organizations. There was some measure of back and forth between the AAIA and the AJC in the early 1950s. The AJC's Commission on Law and Social Action Reports, which focused on cases involving religious liberty, segregation, discrimination, and civil rights, referred to two Indian land cases.[116] Cohen helped the AJC gather useful information on the American Indian social, legal, and economic situation so as to be included in the AJC's pamphlet, which they issued jointly with NAACP's "Civil Rights in the US—A Balance Sheet of Group Relations."

As general counsel to the AAIA, Arthur Lazarus filed amicus curiae briefs in almost every Indian litigation case heard by the Supreme Court during the 1960s. Many of these cases involved questions of tribal sovereignty, such as the extent of tribal civil and criminal jurisdiction, tribal taxing power, and water or treaty rights. Lazarus also engaged in substantial lobbying on behalf of Indian causes. He and Sonosky worked closely with North Carolina Senator Sam Ervin's staff to ensure that the Indian Civil Rights Act adequately safeguarded tribal autonomy and provided for the suspension of Public Law 280. Lazarus drafted the "native version" of what became the landmark Alaska Native Claims Settlement Act of 1971, perhaps the most generous settlement ever achieved between the conquering sovereign and its Aboriginal Peoples.[117]

Indeed, Jews advocated in a variety of settings beyond the law and the ICC. Jewish Indian advocates channeled their efforts in both government and nonprofit sectors, working on behalf of a range of Indian issues, including defense, economic advancement, and health. Jewish advocates for Indians likely educated a fair portion of the non-Native American social workers and civil justice and economic uplift activists who might have been interested in learning more about Native issues in New York or Washington. The AAIA's speaker's bureau included nearly a dozen Jewish speakers by the mid-1950s, including active Jewish attorneys, leading advocates, former civil servants, and prominent social scientists. William Zimmerman, Richard Schifter, and Arthur Lazarus Jr. made themselves available to lecture public audiences on current Indian legislation, citizenship, and the history of removal. Lucy Kramer Cohen spoke on citizenship and judicial anthropology. Dr. Harry L. Shapiro of the American Museum of Natural History and Mrs. Abraham Eisenberg, state chairman of American Indian Committee in Collingswood, New Jersey, spoke on Indian education.

Jews who were interested in learning more about Native American justice issues often found Jewish experts from whom to learn (from among the mostly non-Native experts). Jewish organizations, and organizations with Jews in key leadership roles, actively sought out opportunities to learn more and become involved in Native rights too. Rabbi Marius Ranson of Temple Sharey Tefilo in Orange, New Jersey, a member of the National Advisory Council of the Clergy League of America, invited representatives from the AAIA to teach rabbis, ministers, and priests in 1938 about Indian justice affairs. Secretary Max Bernstein and President Louis Joshua Hurwitz of "the Yo-Men," a community welfare and cultural group of the Grand Street Boys Association of New York, likewise solicited a speaker from the AAIA, noting that "our members consist of young business and professional men in NYC who are honestly looking for causes which they can assist actively. . . . I am quite confident," they wrote, "that it would be to our mutual advantage [to hear a speaker on Indian affairs]."[118]

Explicitly Jewish institutions struck strategic liaisons with organizations that touched on Indian affairs, couching Indian advocacy under the broader tent of civic activism and social justice. Many partnered with the explicitly Indian-centered groups; Indian affairs advocacy work served left-wing Jewish activities and organizations' broader priorities of minority protections and civil rights. In the early 1950s, Maurice Moss, the chairman of the National Urban League for Equal Economic Opportunity, and Arnold Aronson, secretary of the Leadership Conference on Civil Rights, cooperated with the AAIA, the National Association of Intergroup Relations (Chicago) Officials, and the American Council on Race Relations, on whose board of directors Aronson sat, along with Maurice Fagan of the Jewish community relations council of Philadelphia and Louis Wirth, sociologist and author of the seminal book *The Ghetto*, representing the American Council on Race Relations. At the 1953 National Conference of Social Work in Cleveland, these organizations strategized about Indian affairs issues and promoted their progressive thinking in their publication arm, the *Nairo Reporter*, under the editorship of Samuel Spiegler.[119] It is not a stretch to imagine just how "Jewish" the feeling in the room must have been witnessing Arthur Lazarus, Felix Cohen, or any of the other speakers on the AAIA's speakers bureau discussing Indian affairs with David A. Brody of the Anti-Defamation League of the B'nai B'rith, Rabbi Richard G. Hirsch of Union of American Hebrew Congregations, Roy H. Millenson of the AJC, Denise Tourover of Hadassah, Philip Schiff and Olya Margolin of the National Council of Jewish Women, Bernard Weitzer of the Jewish War Veterans, and Paul Sifton and Samuel Jacobs of the UAW-CIO. Connections to the prominent and powerful Jewish organizations of American life helped facilitate cross-pollinated minority rights advocacy and linked Indian affairs to the people and institutions that promoted Jewish concerns.

Philanthropic Engagement

American Jews, and their donations, were also at the forefront of philanthropic efforts to support progressive Indian causes during the New Deal and Termination eras from the 1920s, as noted, well into the 1960s. Their money, and their willingness to give it to Native causes, mattered. The Louis M. Rabinowitz

Foundation supported D'Arcy McNickle, perhaps the most prominent Native American activist of the 1950s and 1960s, and the Sidney Hillman Foundation and the Charles and Lily H. Weinberg Foundation financed nongovernmental Indian affairs activism.[120] Indian educational and civil rights funding also came from Jewish charitable, educational, and religious institutions, including the Federation of Jewish Philanthropies, the National Conference of Christians and Jews, the Jewish Federation of Chicago, the Congregation Emanu-El of New York, the AJC, and the Jewish Community Centers of Chicago.[121] The Emil Schwarzhaupt Foundation bequeathed a substantial share of its founder's estate to Jewish and Indian causes mostly in Chicago.[122]

Financial support for small civic advocacy groups was, of course, vital to their very existence.[123] The extent to which Jewish supporters dominated the funding of midcentury Indian rights activism was even noted by the son of John Collier, John Collier Jr., who recalled that his father drew his financing to support his family and political activities on Capitol Hill largely from Jews. "Financing a full-time lobbyist is costly, especially when the lobbyist's family must be supported too," wrote the son. "My father was remarkably adroit in gathering donations, and he approached his own upper class with a demanding confidence. His most loyal patrons included a circle of wealthy Jewish lawyers and civic leaders in San Francisco and elsewhere. Jewish intellectuals were among the most responsive to the plight of Indian ethnicity. . . . Through the years of private lobbying our family was completely supported by this group, who also volunteered their legal skills in fighting the early legal battles."[124] These patrons supported Collier and made common cause for the benefit of Indian rights and recognition. Collier Jr. suggested that Jews responded "to the plight of Indian[s]," because of their "empathy, based on their own minority survival." As an "ancient people with thousands of years of unbroken lineage," he wrote, "the Jewish people in turn responded to the ancient life and heritage of the Southwest Indians."[125]

One funding organization, the Robert Marshall Civil Liberties Trust, warrants focused attention as a central hub of Jewish-supported Indian philanthropy. The trust was named after Robert Marshall, the conservationist, environmentalist, explorer, ecologist, part-time anthropologist, and son of American Jewish scion Louis Marshall. Robert served as the director of forestry for the Office of Indian Affairs from 1933 to 1937. After his sudden death at age thirty-eight, virtually all of his $1.5 million estate was left to three causes dear to him: socialism, wilderness preservation, and civil liberties, under whose banner the AAIA and the NCAI's expenses were supported from 1940 until the funds ran out in 1962.[126] The trust spent its resources supporting Native land claims, water title battles, public information campaigns, lobbying efforts, studies and statements in the public press criticizing state and federal government handling of Indian affairs, and policy papers with recommendations for its improvement.

A sizable number of Jewish activists worked for and with the Marshall Trust on matters critical to Native American groups across the nation as it built decades-long relationships supporting the work of four of the first Native-run activist organizations: the AAIA, the Council on Indian Affairs, the Indian Rights Association, and the NCAI.[127] One of the trust's key funding recipients was the American Indian Fund. The trust paid Felix Cohen and Arthur Lazarus to argue for full citizen rights on behalf of Apache and Hualapai tribes of Arizona, and its funds helped win a federal court decision on Arizona Indians civil rights in 1953.[128] The philanthropists' goal of allowing Native Americans to enjoy the full enjoyment of American citizenship was progressive and genuine, but it also betrayed the liberal bias that fit hand-in-glove with the activists' and philanthropists' own vision for addressing Jewish difference in the postwar era. Jews had successfully been incorporated into American civil, economic, and cultural life without relinquishing their unique cultural and religious identities.

Liberal and Pluralistic Biases

The American Jewish expenditure of effort, intellect, and money on American Indian affairs was doubtlessly significant and sincere. Criticism about Indian New Deal practices and the ideology that birthed these practices, however, tempers the impulse to laud these Jewish advocates and end the analysis there. Rather, criticisms of the Indian New Deal in general offer an important hint at the Jewish dimension to this story: these Jewish advocates perpetuated some fundamental colonialist impulses that they themselves seemed not to notice. Nearly all the major policy initiatives, including the ICC, while profoundly liberal in some respects, were also flawed. The IRA certainly signaled the state's change in attitude toward Indians and tribal governments. The Indian New Deal offered an opportunity for tribes to organize for their common welfare, to write constitutions that would be formally approved by the secretary of the Interior, and to be granted status as federally chartered corporations. But liberal advocacy efforts were premised on a vision of inclusion, liberalism, and pluralism that ultimately lauded the United States and its ideals. The Jews among these policy makers were devoted to the state, just as they were devoted to a comfortable future within it for themselves as descendants of settlers and for Native Americans. They were agents of the state, not antagonists of it. They did not advocate for full sovereignty for Native Americans, nor did they argue for anything close to what decolonization scholars would in the twenty-first century. They spoke from a perspective of statist liberalism and its limitations, having enjoyed the benefits of the state's embrace of Jews and their enfranchised place within it. They accepted the state liberalism's values of sacrosanct individual rights and property ownership despite the fact that these values were, in many respects, inimical to Indigenous worldviews.

Practical failures of implementing the Indian New Deal vision also reveal that some of these Jewish reformers were ill-equipped to operationalize policy in real, complex, and diverse Native American communities, each with its own internal disagreements about best paths forward. They lacked deep and long-standing relationships with Native American leaders and did not foresee many of the problems, having inadequately consulted with Native communities at the local level. Problems permeated Indian New Deal policies and their successful implementation. According to one historian of Indian Termination, IRA funds sometimes went to individuals who had no right of heirship over land instead of being used to purchase lands to be put under tribal control (a system known as the communal land tenure system). Council members and tribal chairmen occasionally selected the best land for themselves. Without a clear title to the land, individual Indians were reluctant to build homes or make permanent improvements. The well-intentioned policy threatened perpetual government supervision over many competent individuals, made it difficult to secure loans from private sources, and discouraged Indians from developing their land resources.[129] The Department of the Interior also insisted that only tribes who voted to be under the provisions of the IRA could access the Revolving Loan Fund.[130] Left-leaning Jewish lawyers and philanthropists were entirely sincere and well-meaning in their fight for Native rights, but their lack of knowledge or connections with Native American communities, and their self-interested attachment to the state, meant that their policies were often flawed.

The Native American tribal constitutions that Cohen (and others) drafted and whose implementation they supported provide a fitting example of this problematic paternalism. Cohen and his colleagues believed that tribal organization via written tribal constitutions, charters, and bylaws provided Native nations adequate means to protect and exercise their basic right of political and economic self-determination. The constitutions were influenced by the regulations of municipal governments, an influence that was likely inappropriate. In Cohen's view, tribal constitutional governments were to be like town governments (with certain federal protections and special rights). The bibliography Cohen used for drafting tribal constitutions contained dozens of references to books, articles, and government documents that dealt with administration, city planning, health and sanitation, housing, and other matters associated with establishing and running municipal governments.[131] The model was hardly a perfect fit for Indian reservations or tribal self-government based on the unique histories and political organization of specific peoples. Critics have maintained that the administration forced western-style constitutions on reluctant tribes, which eclipsed the traditional systems that had survived the previous century of coercive assimilation. "Traditional Indians of almost every tribe," according to Vine Deloria Jr., "strongly objected to this method of organizing and criticized the IRA as simply another means of imposing white institutions on the tribes. In some constitutions the traditional Indians were able to protect themselves by insisting that the tribal government derive from the more ancient form of government and be subjected in its operation to the powers of the people had allocated to it. Other tribes rejected the idea of a formal, and small, tribal council governing them and demanded that the tribal council consist of the whole tribe meeting in concert."[132] As the Osage anthropologist Jean Dennison has demonstrated, midcentury reform efforts could make lasting and knotty impacts on tribes' political operations and their ideas about nationhood and sovereignty far into the future.[133]

Felix Cohen's *Handbook* faced the criticism that it reduced the complex and diverse set of legal and policy outputs to an oversimplified and largely mythical set of principles and doctrines, unwittingly doing a profound disservice to tribal nations and their legal relationship to the federal and state governments. Cohen and Margold were criticized for shunting aside much of the actual historical record. Although Cohen was an advocate of Native peoples, "the court's use of his [Cohen's] functional approach has to some extent facilitated the weakening of Native American rights."[134] Deloria observed that Cohen's *Handbook* was written not from a pro-Indian or even neutral perspective but had a clear "federal bias in that no question is ever raised as to whether federal actions were proper or whether or not the federal government violated previously agreed upon principles of the federal-Indian relationship"[135]

The ICC Act's foundational premise assumed that Native American communities would both desire and accept money as compensation for losses. From Nathan Margold's initial 1929 proposal to the 1946 act, legislative drafters, commissioners, and even the attorneys who engaged the claims process all seem to have assumed that American Indians would accept that land could be valued (and compensated) in dollars. The non-Natives who influenced the ICC—Jews central among them—misjudged the depth of attachments most Native American groups had to their specific ancestral lands. In this sense, the act was assimilationist; to engage in the claims commission was, perforce, to accept that the Anglo-American legal system provided the venue to resolve "nation-to-nation" conflict.[136]

Other problems lay in the implementation of the ICC, more pragmatic in nature than problems marred by ideological assumptions. According to critics of the ICC, the *commission* was turned into a *court*, stripping it of all the flexibility that it had been established to consider, as previously mentioned. Native American tribes had been wronged by the state in so many ways. By mandate, Cohen and others had designed the ICC to consider fundamental moral claims, not just strictly legal ones with their high and technical burden of proof. But the attorneys involved in the process, according to Deloria Jr., stripped the commission of its capacity to engage in moral reckoning and instead transformed it into a court. "High moral purpose aside," he wrote, "the Act provided a long and lucrative future for a select group of attorneys in Indian law and career employees of the US."[137]

John EchoHawk, a Pawnee attorney and the founder of the Native American Rights Fund, leveled this criticism of the role of lawyers in the ICC even more sharply, when he wrote that "we [self-determinationist Native Americans] discovered that [non-Indian] lawyers working through the ICC were less interested in seeking the justice inherent in that system than they were in the money. . . . They came along and grabbed these claims; they didn't cost us anything, but after they took their 10 percent, they were gone . . . our people talked about sovereignty but our lawyers wouldn't."[138] Myer, the commissioner of Indian affairs during the Termination era, leveled a distinct criticism at these Jewish lawyers, accusing Felix Cohen of misleading "well meaning organizations and the general public for their own personal gain," particularly in respect to his efforts to coordinate law firms in their respective cases against the state. Cohen and other attorneys, he wrote, had "learned [that Indian affairs is complex] long before we [Termination era bureaucrats] did and have very effectively capitalized on the fact by getting themselves placed in positions where they could use certain organizations as their front. By use of propaganda, either directly or indirectly, the organizations have misled and confused both the public and the Indians involved."[139]

Acknowledging Cohen's intensive involvements in Indian law during and after his work in the Department of the Interior, Myer accused Cohen of extortion, fraud, immoral dealings, and corruption, arguing that he "used this organization [AAIA] as his front. He has either directly or indirectly put out falsehoods, distorted information and misrepresentation of the worst type while posing as an idealistic lawyer whose main interest lies in helping the Indian people."[140] He furthered his attack on Cohen: "Actually Mr. Cohen has a very substantial personal financial stake in the Indian law business both in terms of direct representation of the Indian tribes for a fee and through his consultant fees from the joint efforts groups. . . . It has been evident that Mr. Cohen is very successful in aiding and abetting a group of alleged tribal leaders with a modicum of Indian blood, some of whom have exploited other tribal members who are less competent then they are, through shady real estate deals or utilization of tribal funds to maintain themselves in power."[141] These accusations leveled at Cohen and his associates rightly point out that the lawyers involved in the ICC process had financial stakes in it, but the suggestion that they were solely motivated by monetary incentives were both unfounded and traded on anti-Semitic tropes. Most of these litigators had some measure of ideological or moral commitment wrapped up in their work, even if they made assumptions that their Native clients would accept monetary compensation. After all, they were hired by Native communities to litigate for dollar earnings.

The ICC Act was extraordinarily broad, as Felix Cohen wrote it, insofar as it would allow claims "not recognized by any existing rule of law or equity." This language was meant to open up space for new sorts of legal challenges in order to provide maximum room for Native people to seek redress, though as previously mentioned, few tribal attorneys brought claims outside the scope of familiar legal concepts, and few brought claims other than ones for land loss or administrative spending redress. The commission was unable to transform legal theories based on the rights of individuals in order to recognize the fundamental injury that tribal groups had suffered, like the destruction of their identity and culture. The few tribes that sought compensation for this injury—notably, the Pima and Maricopa, the Joseph Band, and the Chiricahua—were rebuffed without a trial. The attorneys and judges lacked the intellectual tools for resolving such claims, even though the language of the act seemed to give the commission the authority to hear them under the fair and honorable dealings clause.[142] Further still, the creation of an entity that used Anglo-American dispute resolution techniques to mete out justice, instead of one that mediated claims as the Indians had done for disputes among tribal members, was a prime example of the state continuing to impose its own methods, enshrined in its own legal system. It was, from one perspective, colonialism continued. It asked the appointed commissioners to deal with claims alleging that the government had acted dishonorably without requiring that they have any experience with Indian affairs and without providing written standards to guide their decision-making. It appointed no Indians to the commission for its first twenty years (after which point President Richard Nixon appointed the first and only Indian to serve).[143]

The commission's achievements and shortcomings were central to the broader history of Native Americans' fates and struggles in the hands of the state, even when those agents acting for and against the state aimed to counter the deleterious effects of the colonial legacy it created. What is important for our argument is that the Jews who were wrapped up in these struggles to provide Native Americans some relief from the impacts of colonial settlement used the tools they had acquired and trusted in order to hold the state to task for bearing responsibility. They used law and government policy to try to forge an America that was more equitable and inclusive. While the work of Jewish Indian advocates like Felix Cohen made important contributions to Indian rights and fostered mechanisms that would later be used by the Native activist renaissance, Jewish involvement in Indian affairs was shaped by their relative lack of appreciation for the depth of many Native American communities' commitments to sovereignty. These American Jewish advocates' trust in the efficacy of these tools, and their sense that these tools were the ones best suited to undertake such advocacy work, was derived from their experience as members of a newly enfranchised and accepted minority group in America. They doubled down on their commitments to liberalism, even as their efforts to improve the liberal state's treatment of Native Americans reinforced the very same tools of statism—law and policy—that perpetuated colonial institutions and methods, relationships, and worldviews.

On occasion, critics of the Indian New Deal articulated their objections to policy with reference to Jews. These criticisms reveal a measure of anti-Jewish sentiment that had crept into assessments of the policy makers. Jews played a prominent enough role in crafting Indian policy that non-Jews noticed and made something of the fact. The American Indian Federation (AIF), an entirely Native American organization and likely the fiercest critic of federal Indian policies during the New Deal, for example, offered a series of programmatic criticisms and forged solidarities with far-right groups, including avowed anti-Semites. It held a rugged individualistic ideology and found the Indian New Deal's paternalism intolerable and un-American. Indians, reasoned the AIF, must be permitted to work out their own problems. AIF leaders considered Indians who worked for or with the BIA to be traitors and were suspicious of anthropologists.[144] Some of these Native American leaders—Christians—also objected to the BIA's restriction of missionary work in Indian country. The AIF president, Joseph Bruner, a Creek and eastern Oklahoma leader, urged complete integration into the white mainstream, and despite his traditionalist background, he was a leading proponent of "emancipating" Indians by urging a final cash settlement of all claims that Indians had against the government through congressional legislation.[145] The anti-Indian New Deal message of the AIF drew attention from conservative members of Congress as well as anti-Semitic, anti-Black, and even fascist protesters. Right-wing groups including the Daughters of the American Revolution, William Dudley Pelley's Silver Shirts of America, and James True, a leading American fascist, helped the AIF in its attack against the New Deal programs. In the 1930s, the AIF engaged in a smear campaign using the rhetoric of the far right to discredit the Interior Department. It accused the commissioner of being anti-Christian, atheistic, and communist and having the support of the ACLU; certain members of the AIF, according to historian Laurence Hauptman, "reflected the intolerance of the age, especially in attitudes toward Jewish and black Americans."[146] Since a significant number of key personnel in the Interior Department were Jewish, "hatred of Collier's social engineering project spilled over into outright or veiled anti-Semitic statements at AIF meetings or their propaganda sheets."[147] The AIF developed friendly ties with the German American Bund and anti-Semitic groups. According to a memo written for the AAIA by a spy who infiltrated a meeting of the German American Bund in San Francisco in the spring of 1939, Robert Towner boasted of the close relationship of Indians to Germany, an affinity based on the twin claims "that they had the same form of government and that they were both anti-Semitic."[148] He referred to President Franklin Delano Roosevelt as "Roosenfelt," a slur meant to Judaize the President, and claimed that the administration, the Supreme Court, and the press were all controlled by Jews, whom he referred to as "Chuck-na-gin, an Indian name designating them [Jews] as Children of Satan and Goldworshippers."[149] Towner also claimed that some 75,000 gold-shirted Indians were organized and ready to cooperate with Germany in its drive against the Jews. He stated that the aim of all Gentile people now should be to encircle the globe and exterminate the Jew.[150]

It was these sorts of sentiments that Theodore Haas must have had in mind when he wrote to Lucy Kramer Cohen in the summer of 1936, sarcastically noting, "I was thinking about Felix to-day when I read in the New Masses that an anti-Semite had charged Nathan R. Margold with communizing the American Indians. I supposed that the Redmen are so indoctrinated with fine American principals of freedom as to be inoculated against alien red ideas . . . with best regards to you and Big Chief Red Pants [Felix Cohen]."[151] The anti-Jewish sentiment that he, Kramer, Margold, Cohen, and others faced and sloughed off likely reinforced their commitments to liberal-socialism, their faith in law and good governance, and their convictions that their work on behalf of Native Americans was a benefit for all minorities in the American polity and, therefore, for America itself.

Limits of Liberalism and the Perpetuation of Colonial Structures

Cohen died in 1953 at age forty-six from lung cancer. Indians lost their "Double Runner," as the Blackfeet called him. As Supreme Court justice William Douglas later observed, "No mind that ever delved into Indian affairs was keener, more discerning, more enlightened."[152] Theodore Haas called Cohen "no cloistered philosopher, no impractical idealist, but an effective defender of disadvantaged people against powerful opponents."[153] According to legal scholar David Wilkins, most commentators agree that Cohen deserves great credit for his Indian related work, asserting that his efforts during the Indian New Deal paved the way for the revitalization of tribal sovereignty in cultural and economic self-determination, the reaffirmation of treaty rights, and the extension of civil liberties to tribal citizens.[154] Cohen's *Handbook* and his work to develop systems of local governance were, arguably, two of the most critical contributions that helped fuel the Native Renaissance that burst forth in the 1960s. They provided the legal, political, and economic framework and the institutional mechanisms necessary to enable many tribal nations to challenge Termination and other nefarious policies. They enabled many Indigenous nations to develop the institutional machinery and use the legal authority necessary to continue their march toward self-determination. (Cohen's concept of inherent sovereignty for America's "domestic dependent nations" even became part of the foundation of international movement for Indigenous rights, culminating in the 2007 U.N. Declaration on the Rights of Indigenous People.[155])

While a number of opportunities for Indian revitalization were initiated under the IRA, the redemptive possibilities that the Indian New Dealers envisioned did not come to fruition.[156] Allotment-era policies had taken a heavy toll on Native American communities. Customs had eroded or vanished. The IRA tried to protect Indian culture, but tragically and ironically, according to historian Alison Bernstein, "superimposing white political organization on tribal structures appealed primarily to younger, more educated mixed-blood Indians and white intellectuals who shared [Collier's] vision of cultural pluralism. They did not question whether these newly-formed tribal governments would disrupt traditional decision making patterns. In this sense, the Act was not as pure an attempt to preserve the Indian way of life as its defenders insisted . . . the Act drew opposition from both traditionalist and assimilated Indians alike."[157] Indian New

Deal liberals, Jews chief among them, were stuck in the bind they helped create, the "conundrum . . . of preserving Indian societies with foreign instruments."[158] Cohen may very well have been naïve in assuming that federal law could be used "as a tool for remediating collective traumas, particularly Indian trauma of colonization," or that the law was sufficient to rectify the problems that federal law itself had created, even if his—and others'—efforts laid some of the groundwork for the renaissance that would later unfold in the hands of Native American activists.[159] Perhaps Felix Cohen failed to grasp that his plans for Indian land consolidation and tribal governance were rooted in western ideologies and cultural paradigms that were products of his own socialist-liberal pluralism and were "not necessarily suitable for the customs and traditions of Indian tribes."[160]

American Jews' legal activism aimed to advance American Indians, all the while remaining consonant with Jewish progressive logic about what would benefit American Jewry as well. Cohen and the cadre of midcentury Jewish liberals and progressives of whom he was a part, had been reared with the values and perspectives of their enfranchisement. These lawyers, legislators, philanthropists, and activists created some of the tools and institutions that Native American leaders themselves would wield soon after the New Deal types had passed from the scene. Indian-led initiatives grew under a generation of Indian leaders, many of whom returned from serving in World War II, not content to let non-Indians determine their destiny. They rallied under the national slogan of the NCAI, "Let Indians speak for themselves," a phrase that reflected the emerging political philosophy of self-determination for individuals and tribal groups, one that can be traced to Indian New Deal efforts to give tribes political and economic legitimacy.[161] Urban Indians joined in the cultural and social upheaval that was transforming the nation's campuses and major cities. Having witnessed the Black civil rights movement and the fishing rights protests of reservation Indians, hearing the powerful rhetoric of Stokely Carmichael and Malcolm X, and watching the tide against the Vietnam War, many city Indians embraced the politics of militancy under the banner of Red Power. Native American leaders offered a powerful critique of the non-Indian advocates who had appropriated their cause. The fact that non-Indians spoke about and for Native people rendered Native Americans themselves passive and voiceless. And yet despite these valid criticisms, it is hard to imagine some of the self-determination strategies Native Americans deployed in the 1960s and 1970s without the influence of their non-Native predecessors.

The Indian-run organizations sprang from the federal government BIA during the New Deal era and the people who helped design, support, and execute it. John Collier and William Zimmerman encouraged national Indian mobilization in the spring of 1944 and encouraged communication among Indian employees of the BIA to discuss common interests. It was largely bureau employees who founded the NCAI. According to historian Thomas Cowger, McNickle, Archie Phinny (Nez Perce, superintendent of the Idaho Indian Agency), and other

Native American civil servants at the BIA played a large role in formation of the NCAI.[162] McNickle invited the AAIA to establish the NCAI since they deemed it "truly sympathetic to the needs of Indians," with substantial funding coming from the Robert Marshall Civil Liberties Trust. As the new center of lobbying efforts, the NCAI solicited and received support from organizations interested in minority civil rights, Jewish and others, including the Indian Committee of the ACLU, the Institute of Ethnic Affairs, the AAIA, the National Council of Negro Women, the Japanese-American Citizens League, the National Jewish Welfare Board, the Congregational Christian Churches, the NAACP, the American Jewish Congress, and the B'nai B'rith.[163] The seeds for the founding of the organization, in other words, were laid in the government and not-for-profit offices.[164]

By the mid-1950s, more and more Native Americans began taking leadership roles in the public fight for rights in courts and venues of public opinion that greater American white public consumed and in matters of policy making. Progressive and earnest, if parochial, whites had intervened in this one crucial period in the long history of Indian activism. By the late 1950s, Indians themselves began spearheading their own efforts at lobbying to a degree to which they had never done before.[165]

No better example of midcentury Native American enfranchised activism generated by and for Native people themselves can be found than the NCAI, which first arose in 1944 as a national pan-Indian organization that "campaigned fervently and, on the whole, successfully against the termination policy."[166] It was "an innovative vehicle of resistance to changes in federal Indian policy in that it served as an important instrument for the preservation of Indian culture and identity."[167] By the first half of the twentieth century, Indian groups such as the Society of American Indians, the AIF, and the NCAI, different as they were from one another, had learned to set their own agendas and pursue their interests in larger regional and national political arenas.[168]

These pan-Native- and Native-run groups engaged with Jewish organizations and individuals. The NAACP and the ACLU issued amicus curiae to the courts on innumerable Indian affairs cases. The NCAI met with Jack Greenberg of the NAACP Legal Defense and Educational Fund to discuss establishing an independent nonprofit. Rarely, it seems, did leaders of these organizations explicitly point out affiliations or connections between the Jews who sought to advance Native American civil liberties and the Jewishness of those advocates. But self-consciousness did arise here and there. Speaking at the NCAI National Convention in Denver in 1948, James E. Curry, the NCAI's general counsel, commended delegates for their efforts to protect Indian rights. Work on behalf of Alaskan Natives reminded him of "Sinn Feiners who had fought for freedom in Ireland . . . the farmers who protested in the US to defend their livelihood, . . . [and] the Jews, who had preserved their homeland in Israel."[169] The NCAI partnered with a host of organizations that either involved Jews, were dominated by them, or were explicitly construed as Jewish organizations, including the Indian Committee of the ACLU, the Institute of Ethnic Affairs, the National Jewish Welfare Board, the American Jewish Congress, and the B'nai B'rith, among other, non-Jewish sectarian and nonsectarian organizations (Christian, Japanese, and Black organizations) in 1950. These friendly institutional moments of cooperation were not just related to funding, or to public relations campaigns, but were in service of improving operational capacities of the Native-led groups. They consulted on a range of technical, administrative, and legal issues to improve their capacities for effective advocacy work.[170]

Jewish Indian advocates were a sort of midwife of the American Indian Movement. Despite the valid criticisms of Jewish advocacy on behalf of Native Americans through the twentieth century, it nevertheless remains true that their work in government, law, and community organizing from the 1940s into the 1960s and beyond helped create and foster some of the most important spaces and tools that Native activists would come to use in their own initiatives.

Yet it is equally true that, in retrospect, the liberals and progressives of the Indian New Deal, despite their pro-Indian achievements, offered notable continuities in the history and application of colonialism. Only Indians could make a radical break from it. One Cohen biographer called the Indian New Deal "the turning point in colonialism," arguing that "Margold and Cohen . . . counteracted the long-standing European position that military conquest overrides diplomatic treaties" and that Cohen "saw his mitzvah . . . to find a lawful foundation to free Indian citizens from Anglo domination."[171] But these are overstatements. What the criticisms rightly note is that the colonial structures and its tools persisted despite being used as essential weapons in the battle for Indian social justice. Jewish lawyers like Cohen, as well as philanthropists and anthropologists, all advocated for Native Americans, positioning themselves between white and Native American worlds, hoping to bring the white public closer to the realities of Indigenous life, and thereby help enfranchise them, and helping bring American Indians closer to enfranchisement by providing some of the tools of the colonizers in the fight to seek justice and recompense.

Unlike frontier Jews who competed with Native Americans for land, sometimes violently, liberal activists came from the urban, enfranchised east and had less concern with distinguishing themselves from Indian outsiders. Instead, they utilized their chosen kinship with Native peoples in an effort to establish general racial and ethnic rapprochement and promote pluralism in America during the time of its greatest anti-Jewish sentiment. Intellectual engagement with Native Americans served both Jewish and Native ends, for through advocacy work, Jews supported political changes that aimed to ensure Jewish social and political security and futurity in America. There were profound differences between the two groups of Jews and profoundly different attitudes toward colonialism and toward Native American people. The former were settlers, preoccupied with establishing themselves and fitting in among settler whites. They were, in simple terms, colonists who used their interactions with Indigenous People to advance their own ambitions, unperturbed by the politics of colonialism and generally (though not exclusively) proud to engage in the white man's burden of the so-called civilizing mission.

Two or three decades later, and from the vantage point of New York, San Francisco, and Washington, Jews who had achieved their immigrant parents' and grandparents' aspirations engaged in a serious battle with the state and aimed to reverse the harm wrought on Indians by colonialism itself. Despite these profound differences, the settler, immigrant Jews discussed in chapters 1, 2, and 3 had something in common with the enfranchised Jewish lawyers, philanthropists, civil servants, and activists of this chapter (and the next): all were devoted to the United States and the Jewish future in it. And despite the distinctions between these two populations of American Jews—western and East Coast Jews, late nineteenth-century settlers and early twentieth-century progressives—Jewish engagements with Native America consistently doubled as acts of devotion to America and on behalf of a Jewish future in America. All these distinct subgroups of American Jews, shaped by the distinct needs of their moments and the changing conditions of the social worlds surrounding them, used their engagements with Native American people, ideas, and issues in order to help them think through questions about their own belonging as Jews in America.

CHAPTER 6

ANTHROPOLOGICAL VENTRILOQUISM AND DOVETAILING INTELLECTUAL AND POLITICAL ADVANCEMENTS

In the middle decades of the twentieth-century, American Jews assiduously deployed a range of advocacy efforts aimed at promoting equal legal and social footing for themselves. Concurrent and parallel to the work of lawyers, civil servants, and philanthropists on behalf of Native Americans (the subjects of chapter 5) was the work of Jewish social scientists (the subjects of this chapter). Midcentury American Jewish social scientists, particularly anthropologists and linguists, took to the study of Native American culture and language with fervor. As part of the first cadre of scholars professionally trained under the German Jewish immigrant pioneer of cultural relativism, Franz Boas, and his linguistic-anthropology counterpart Edward Sapir, a sizable number of Jewish men and women lived with Native American tribes, learned their languages, made personal connections with people on reservations, and wrote hundreds of thousands of pages of scholarly and public-political writings about Indian life, history, sociology, and the status and fate of hundreds of tribes. Jewish anthropologists and linguists concerned themselves with understanding Native American cultures and with communicating this knowledge in a politically liberal voice to non-Indians. They helped refashion non-Native people's understandings of Native American cultures according to the dictates of their own progressive Jewish liberalism, using the tools and perspectives of the social sciences they helped develop.

As individuals, many of these anthropologists and linguists aimed to improve Native lives too. Between the 1920s and the 1960s, from immigration restriction to the American Indian Movement—more or less the same years the cohort of lawyers and civil servants fought for Native justice on and off Capitol Hill—Boas and his students shifted anthropology's basic framework from one that assumed successive developmental stages of human societies to one rooted in cultural pluralism and relativism, by and large using American Indians as their objects of study. The profundity of this intellectual transformation can hardly be overestimated. While Native Americans supplied the vast majority of the evidentiary basis for American anthropology's claims about human societies and cultures, mythology and language, religion, and social organization, the impacts of American anthropology went far beyond Native American communities. Social scientific ideas about culture shifted American thinking about corporate existence. Anthropology developed the idea of "culture" to replace the concept of "race" and, in part, to promote cultural pluralism as an exalted aspect of the American democratic spirit.

This chapter explores the ways that the intellectual work of anthropology, its moral underpinning, and its reliance on Native American "data" was shaped in part by the Jewishness of the anthropologists and linguists who made it. Flattening hierarchies between people, and conceiving of cultural wholes, each as legitimate, interesting, and worthwhile as the next, was an attempt to level the moral and intellectual playing field of American cultural difference. Anthropologists tried to articulate a vision, based on careful studies of myriad and local cultural differences, of how America could tolerate or even embrace diversity. Through the promotion of understanding cultural differences, their scholarship was meant to achieve greater levels of pluralism and relativism. The success of both of these concepts would offer tremendous room for the ongoing vibrancy and even existence of peoples as different from the American white norm as the Indian tribes they studied as well as the peoples not so distant from those American whites from which many of these anthropologists sprung.

These Jewish social scientists shared much with the Jewish philanthropists, lawyers, and employees of the federal government and the NGOs discussed in chapter 5: the development of scholarly knowledge about Native American life indirectly served contemporary Jewish political needs while speaking directly to the perceived political needs of Indians. Jewish anthropologists sought to dig under the imaginary Indian of American culture; to learn about Native American social organization, lore, language, worldview, family, religion, and many other aspects of Indian life; to see realities specific to Native American traditional tribal perspectives; and to shift America's overall conception of "the Indian" from the mythical, misunderstood, or misused toward the real, the human, the equal.

As antiracism specialists and advocates, anthropologists engaged, then, in a kind of ventriloquism. They spoke by and large *to* white, middle-class, scholarly, and public audiences, but they spoke *about* Indian culture and life. They also spoke *through* Native Americans—that is, they championed moral and political messages of respect for cultural diversity, the promotion of tolerance, and its necessity for a healthy American (and global) liberal order using American Indians as the basis of their evidence. Like the Jewish Indian-curio dealers of the late nineteenth and early twentieth centuries (discussed in chapter 3), Jewish social scientists played a significant role in shaping non-Indigenous American's perceptions of Native American cultures and peoples of their time, even as they assumed that their own Jewishness would remain an invisible and insignificant force in shaping the ideas they would use to shape ideas about others.

Indeed, much of the criticism of twentieth-century anthropology (by anthropology's critics, by Native Americans, and by many anthropologists themselves) centers on the essential fact that anthropologists spoke *for* their subjects. What is often missing from these legitimate criticisms of anthropology is that at least some of the motivations of anthropology as a field dovetailed with concerns about belonging and pluralism that midcentury Jews faced and surely animated some of the field's pioneering and influential practitioners. The habits, practices, methodologies, and basic articulation of the principles of nonjudgmental relativism that professional anthropology cultivated all served contemporaneous Jewish life, for they promoted a broad cultural ideology that supported ethnic solidarity and cultural continuity among American minorities.

The central claim of this chapter, then, is that American Jewish social scientists found American Indian difference useful to think with and used talking about Native American culture and life to work through Jewish community identity conundrums and articulate them in universalized scientific and moral language.[1] These scholarly and political engagements with Native Americans can and should be understood as social encounters that created social and political realities of their own. These encounters were shaped by midcentury American Jewish concerns, and the ideas and behaviors of scholars from Jewish backgrounds reflect midcentury American Jewish sensibilities. They were, in yet another way, a Jewish "use" of Native America; their engagements fit into the context of American Jewish life and reflect changes in the preoccupations of Jews' perceptions of their place in the American landscape of belonging. This argument shares something in common with the literary scholar Jennifer Glaser, whose book *Borrowed Voices: Writing and Racial Ventriloquism in the Jewish American Imagination* examines the "racial ventriloquism" of American Jewish literary creators from the late 1960s onward and argues that these authors appropriated the voices of African American and Native American characters as a way of disavowing the privileges of whiteness that Jews had accrued by the late 1960s. While Glaser argues that "American Jewish authors used racialized others to articulate their own anxieties about hot button issues in American life such as Israel, race, postwar acculturation and the Holocaust," in order to reclaim their own Jewish "otherness," my study shows that Jewish anthropologists of the 1920s through 1950s—in contrast to the Jewish fiction creators of the 1960s and beyond of Glaser's study—engaged in a kind of ventriloquism (talking about American

Indians while also speaking about Jewish concerns) not in order to *accentuate* Jewish ethnic difference but rather to claim the ground of science and truth in order to undermine the stigma of all cultural variation from mainstream, white, Christian America.[2]

This may be a somewhat controversial claim. For the most part, mid-twentieth-century professional anthropologists who were born Jewish—whether they identified with Jewish communities or organizations or practiced religious Judaism throughout their lives—rarely linked their professional intellectual work with their Jewishness. It is tempting to see these anthropologists as they, for the most part, cast themselves as men and women *scientists* who devoted themselves to advancing scholarship on Native North America and who wrote about culture, cosmology, ritual, kinship, and language, perfectly unencumbered by their particular ethnic pasts. Indeed, part of their articulation of the culture concept relied on their seeming ability to transcend precisely those narrow, parochial, and "tribal" perspectives and concerns. But these scholars, at least to a significant extent in their strictly professional contributions, effaced their own Jewish backgrounds, possible biases, and investments in the Jewish predicaments of contemporaneous American life. They rarely talked about Jewish matters in their professional print lives. For the most part, they sought to elaborate upon and argue for the need to respect *American Indian* difference, to maintain, preserve, and foster it. At the same time, they minimized their Jewish difference, irrespective of the degree to which they publicly identified as Jews. These Jews found their ways to American Indian subjects based on contingent historical conditions (as opposed to some essential Jewishness that necessitated and drove their attraction to Native American subjects): anthropology's and linguistics' openness as new fields of scholarship and the fields' potential for advancing antiracist messages. Anthropology and linguistics were well suited to these immigrants' (or children of immigrants') capacities to pay attention to the dynamics and predicaments of "other" cultures and their abilities to make these differences legible to the mainstream via their literary and scholastic skills.[3]

The "Jewishness" of these social scientists and the "Indianness" they represented and discussed to non-Indian audiences intersected. The writings and the actions of these anthropologists reveal both a commonality and a difference between the experience of American Jews and American Indians more generally; Jews and Indians shared the need to navigate the tension between assimilation and self-determination. Indians and Jews wrestled to improve their lots in American life in part by adopting the values and norms of the mainstream, while at the same time protecting their respective culture projects and values. Yet despite this key commonality, a profound difference divided Jews and Native Americans. While Americans developed national policy about uncountable aspects of Indians' lives, no such policies were directed at Jews qua *Jews*. Furthermore, Jewish difference slowly diminished from the overriding political and social framework of group relations, in which Americans fashioned Black and Indian difference as paramount. By the 1950s, Jews were configured, more or less, as white. Anthropologists created and participated in this distillation too, aiming to aid Native peoples but in many respects perpetuating Native people's outsider status. They provided no radical disjuncture in the ongoing American colonial enterprise. Even as they championed Indian culture and fought for justice for Indians, they also helped create new ideas, policy perspectives, and institutions of influence that perpetuated hierarchy, parochialism, and the maintenance of certain versions of Indian difference that Native people themselves had not construed. As creators of these ideas and realities, they were very much in a position of power, a position that rendered their own Jewish difference nearly invisible, as many of them wished it to be.

The Jewish Entrance into Anthropology

Jews seeking admission to academia had faced considerable obstacles in the first third of the twentieth century. Gatekeepers of the humanities fields used the "social refinements" and "gentlemanly qualities" that the profession valued as spurns for Jewish admissions, as the unofficial but widely recognized quotas limited Jewish students in Ivy League universities.[4] While the established disciplines of history, philosophy, and English placed quotas on Jewish enrollment and inhibited hiring and promoting Jews to tenure throughout the 1920s, 1930s, and 1940s, Jews sought a place for themselves and found intellectual homes in the newer fields like sociology, linguistics, psychology, and economics.[5] They engaged in a negotiation of their own identities as aspiring scholars and their Jewish difference, a process historian Susanne Klingenstein described as the "dynamic of intellectual assimilation."[6] Anthropology in particular attracted Jewish students because as a field, it responded to two social anxieties that American Jews faced—namely, the fear of corporate disappearance and pervasive racism. Early twentieth-century anthropology concerned itself with salvage ethnography, the collecting and preserving of cultures perceived to be on the brink of disappearance, as well as fighting against racist explanations for human and social behavior. While the main intellectual focus for anthropology concerned examining what scholars supposed were the fundamental institutions of human life and their evolution or diffusion from what they conceived of as early human or "primitive" bases, the field's dominant political motivation and the ideological thrust that propelled it as an intellectual enterprise aimed to reduce "race" to a blurry, contingent, and effectively useless category and replace it with a flexible, malleable force called "culture." If the category of race disappeared from Americans' conceptual lexicons, so too would racism and, by extension, anti-Semitism. The new field attracted young Jewish intellectuals in part because its concerns resonated with contemporary Jewish experiences.

The political contexts that shaped anthropological ideas about Native Americans, American anthropology's primary objects of study, of course, changed over time. Few Jews practiced anthropology during the Victorian era, when the discipline was dominated by evolutionary perspectives and when the discipline was practiced in museums and state-sponsored institutions. It emerged as a discipline, with journals and professional societies, housed in secular universities as opposed to sectarian ones, with graduate study and a strong research tradition, in the years between 1865 and 1890, but the discipline's arrival at the university system would not occur for another two decades.[7] A committee of highly placed anthropologists including Boas, P. E. Goddard, E. A. Hooton, A. L. Kroeber, George Grant MacCurdy, Frank Speck, and A. M. Tozzer, all of whom had museum backgrounds, established the first Department of Anthropology at an American university in 1916, at Columbia University. The study of American Indians dominated each of anthropology's four subfields—cultural, archaeology, physical, and linguistic—though some of the early anthropology dissertations were written and defended in departments of zoology, sociology, philology, and social science.[8] A great majority of the dissertations written in anthropology between 1911 and 1930 examined Indian topics. Doctorates grew exponentially over the next two decades. In the teens and 1920s, when Jews helped pioneer the discipline, anthropological work tended to lack overt political charge, though its assumption that Native Americans' cultures and languages would inevitably disappear was, in a manner, political. The best anthropology could do was capture aspects of Indian civilizations before their inevitable vanishing. Beginning in the New Deal era, however, anthropology's pursuits became more overtly political. Anthropologists began emphasizing cultural relativism with a conviction that Native American cultures and languages could and should survive. By the 1950s and early 1960s, in the context of Termination policies and the Cold War, anthropologists actively defended and promoted Indian self-determination.

Political Action among Jewish Anthropologists

In addition to the fieldwork, ethnographies, and public and scholarly writings that they produced about American Indians, many American Jewish anthropologists also devoted considerable time and attention to Jewish causes both in their professional print life and in private. Political action formed a part of many anthropologists' sense of the intellectual mission of the field. Their findings, and the framings of distinct cultures, each worthy of careful attention in its own right, mattered to social existence in the United States. Their scholarship on Native American cultures and languages developed alongside their personal and political work on behalf of Jewish causes, though Jewish anthropologists neither conceived of themselves as a group per se nor interacted in intentional concert with one another. Spanning two or three scholarly generations, these social scientists came of age in different environments, differing from one another in respect to age, temperament, political disposition, research interests, and theoretical orientations. Some were more committed to their Jewishness than others. They related to their Jewishness in a range of ways too. They were hardly a unified group. Yet while those differences mattered in many respects, there were profound and significant continuities in their academic and nonacademic life and work.

One such continuity was that the Jewishness of these anthropologists shaped the engagements they had with Native people. As historian of anthropology George Stocking Jr. put it, Boas's drive to build institutions to enshrine anthropological thinking and his unceasing attacks on pseudoscientific racism were "influenced by his liberal philosophy, his strict attachment to scientific accuracy, and, perhaps most important, his Jewish identity."[9] Like the Jewish organizations of his day, Boas rarely attacked anti-Semitism explicitly in public, perhaps fearing that discussion of anti-Semitism might stimulate more of it instead. But Boas, like the Jewish institutions with whom he worked, attacked anti-Black and anti-Indian sentiment using the strategy of "fight[ing] anti-Semitism by remote control," to use David L. Lewis's phrase.[10] In a 1934 speech noting that much important research on race was "the product of Jewish students and scholars," Boas himself acknowledged that many scholars who joined the antiracism cause were Jewish.[11] His writing aimed to combat American narcissism, innocence, and provincialism, and he put his science in service of the public. His "moral science . . . promote[d] rational inquiry free of economic indebtedness, political dependence or cultural myopia" and intimately connected to his lifelong crusade against racial intolerance.[12]

If Boas was among the first to enshrine anthropology in the academy, the field's institutional footing grew rapidly in its first three decades. Many anthropologists, like many elite and ordinary non-Indian Americans, assumed that Native people and cultures would perish in due time. They practiced salvage anthropology working under the assumption of the inevitable disappearance of organic, precontact cultures. To a certain extent, they also believed in the inevitability of assimilation of Indians into mainstream American life, another form of disappearance to be countered by building a robust scholarly record of a tribe's way of life, its systems for reckoning family relationships and governing, its rituals and cosmology, and its language.

Jews were disproportionately represented among the pioneers and professionalizers of the discipline and helped establish departments of anthropology across America's university campuses. Yet as Jews, anthropologists seldom discussed Jewish anxieties explicitly or in print. They generally did not train their professional gaze upon Jews either. Rather, they studied American Indians as they wrote about themes and issues that concerned contemporary Jewish social questions. Anthropology's scholarly and educational agenda can be seen as a form of advocacy work, for the field sought to reeducate Americans about the nature of Native America and other "exotic" peoples and change the categories that Americans would use to understand the identities and differences of all groups. Boas and his fellow Jewish immigrant students Edward Sapir, Paul Radin, and Robert Lowie, along with dozens of their students, recorded, classified, and analyzed the cultures of "disappearing" Native worlds.[13] Most of these anthropologists came of age in New York in the 1920s, and more than half of them trained at Columbia University under Boas. They either descended from eastern or central European Jewish immigrants or had immigrated themselves. These Jews tended to marry other Jews, be buried in Jewish cemeteries, and socialize with fellow Jews, all core features of Jewish ethnicity, though they conceived of themselves as agents of science and enlightenment, not Jewish activists. And while Jewish anthropologists spoke *against* the idea of race, against the broad cultural mode of thinking that explained Indigenous Peoples' positions in the world, their pasts, and their destinies in terms of immutable, fixed biological traits, American anthropology had chosen Native Americans as the main object for its research gaze, not for reasons intrinsic to American Indians and their great diversity, but first and foremost because of their availability as subjects.[14] Indians were more accessible than any of the colonial subjects they, as Americans, might have had relatively easy access to in Tahiti or Guam. These anthropologists also positioned themselves both inside and outside academia as translators, and, in offering support for American Indians, they simultaneously argued for the rights of minorities.[15] Taken together, the scholarship of Jews like George Herzog, Leonard Bloomfield, Leslie Spier, and Alexander Goldenweiser, along with Boas, Sapir, Lowie, Radin, and dozens of others on Indian life, represented a significant portion of American's scholarly knowledge of Native American life.[16]

Three Types of "Jewish" Anthropologists: Jacobs, Radin, Sapir

The lives and biographies of prominent Jewish pioneers of American anthropology bear out certain patterns. Melville Jacobs provides a telling case study of the interethnic stakes of anthropological work by Jewish scholars. The only child of Bavarian Jewish immigrant parents, Jacobs earned his doctorate from Columbia and pursued lifelong work documenting and preserving Native American languages of the Pacific Northwest.[17] His scholarly interests began with a focus on salvaging everything possible of the Oregon Indian groups that appeared to be on the verge of extinction: their folklore, music, and languages.[18] By the 1930s, he had shifted his focus to combating pernicious ideas of racial differences and improving race relations. As a political actor, Jacobs worked with field officers as a translator between government agents and tribes whose languages he had studied. He lectured on Indian affairs issues to the ACLU and worked with the American Indian Fund in the 1930s and 1940s, though it is worth noting that Jacobs refused an offer to work with the Office of Indian Affairs and criticized "anthropologists who accept employment by colonial governments or corporate enterprises for the purpose of more deftly securing or maintaining undemocratic controls over natives."[19] While he recognized that a good deal of uplift work by reformers had done serious damage to Native communities despite their good intentions, Jacobs nevertheless advocated for liberal intervention.

In a speech he delivered on "Anthropology and Social Work," Jacobs described two parallel vocations, both of which required their practitioners be able to develop acceptance and trust between clients or informants.[20] Both social work and anthropology, he claimed, required respect for cultural differences when researching minorities. Jacobs distinguished between American minority groups including Mexicans, Blacks, and Jews all on the one hand from American Indians on the other, whom he considered categorically different. "Social workers, especially those in family agencies, have reported on numbers of cases where the client was Mexican, negro or Jewish," he wrote. But the activist who develops "a relationship with a client whose background is that of some one of a hundred or more American Indian groups which are in varying degrees of cultural metamorphosis and modernization, is more often than not stymied. He is unable to peer over a kind of stone wall which separates him from his Indian client."[21] According to Jacobs, the reasons for the failures of both anthropology and social work in respect to Indian work lay in the particular history of the relationship between whites and Indians, whom he found were frequently filled with well-earned distrust of whites. "A few organizations and agencies which ostensibly work for the acceptance of minorities," he opined, "radiate influences which strengthen customs of segregation and non-acceptance: a number of Jewish and

Figure 6.1. Anthropology professor Melville Jacobs recording the voice of Annie Miner Peterson from the Coos Native American tribe with his newly built portable electric phonograph during his visit to Charleston, Oregon, July 1934. University of Washington Libraries, Special Collections. Melville Jacobs Collection, acc. no. 1693-71-13, negative no. UW 29168z.

negro leaders have taken harmful theoretical positions which lay the basis for undemocratic policies of further segregation."[22]

Jacobs also promoted a variety of liberal-democratic causes, some of them specifically Jewish ones, and helped try to undermine Americans' belief in the veracity of race thinking. As a member of the American Committee for Democracy and Intellectual Freedom, Jacobs worked alongside Boas, the committee's national chairman, on the campaign "Manifesto for Educators" in 1939. Eventually signed by approximately two-thousand teachers and professors, the manifesto aimed to "eliminate the term 'race' from school books, even when it is used 'harmlessly.'" To advance their antiracism goal, Boas, Jacobs, and others on the committee made scholarly material, popular publications, radio spots, and speakers' bureau lectures available to a broad public audience. Jacobs also sat on Abner Green's American Committee for Protection of Foreign Born and Adolph Sabath's American Council on Race Relations, which helped design and disseminate public pamphlets and popular books combatting racism.[23]

As a political actor on behalf of Jewish issues, Jacobs worked with the Academic Friends of Hebrew University, the Conference of Christians and Jews, the Hillel Foundation, the B'nai B'rith, the Anti-Defamation League (ADL), and YIVO. He scrawled marginalia on the ADL bulletins to which he subscribed on matters of Jewish concern, including Nazism and the fate of Jewish communists.[24] Dozens of items in his personal archives make clear that Jacobs keenly read about Jewish issues and felt them sharply in the 1930s and 1940s.[25]

If Jacobs provides an obvious case of that trifecta of scholarship, Jewish/liberal social action, and Native American advocacy, Paul Radin, by contrast, provides an example of a different type of Jewish anthropologist, a scholar who appeared to be intellectually detached and nonactivist, yet who nonetheless was at least partly motivated by his Jewish background and his political positions. Unlike Jacobs, Boas, and many others, Radin did not work for Jewish organizations, nor did he lend his scholarly authority to activist causes, Jewish, Native, or otherwise. He was born in Łódź in Russian Poland; his father was a Reform rabbi and scholar. Radin completed his PhD in 1911 and was the same age as two of Boas's other Jewish students, Frank Speck and Alexander Goldenweiser, both of whom worked on Native American subjects.

Yet even Radin's work was not entirely apolitical. He worked at the Bureau of American Ethnology from 1911 to 1912 and as a field ethnologist at the Geological Survey of Canada from 1914 to 1919 studying Ojibwe of southwestern Ontario, and supervised some two hundred workers who interviewed ethnic groups in the San Francisco Bay Area for the State Emergency Relief Administration of California between 1934 and 1935 (eventually published as part of a survey of San Francisco's minorities in 1935). A specialist in Winnebago legends, its peyote cult, religion, and worldview, Radin wrote more than two hundred publications about literary aspects of North American Indian mythology. Exercising some literary license, Stanley Diamond characterized Radin as a "Jew of the Enlightenment" and "a contemporary transformation of an eighteenth century Hasidic rabbi, Poet-thinker."[26] Radin was a humanist, rationalist, and skeptic, but his concern with religion and ethics "maintained a distinctively Jewish cast," which his biographer described as cosmopolitan and radical, imbued with an understanding of learning as a moral enterprise, "elements that characterize the Jewish scholar *en passage* from the traditional milieu to the modern industrial and urban world."[27] Alongside the American Zionist leader and founder of Hadassah, the Women's Zionist Organization of America, Henrietta Szold, Radin helped translate Louis Ginzberg's *The Legends of the Jews*.[28] He addressed the Jewish Historical Society of England on the topic of monotheism among primitive peoples in 1924.[29] He was, in other words, hardly devoid of or divorced from the influences of his Jewish milieu.

A sketch of Edward Sapir's twinned efforts helps flesh out another variation on the theme of Jewish investments shaping anthropologists' work. Sapir was, like Boas, his teacher, an immigrant and an active/activist scholar with investments in both Jewish and Native American lives. And like Boas, Jacobs, and Radin, Sapir was a towering figure of anthropology, a prolific scholar, humanist, and public intellectual. His father, Jacob Sapir, worked as a *schochet*, a rabbi, and a cantor and dabbled in Native Americana when he composed musical transcriptions for Frank Speck's *Ceremonial Songs of the Creek and Yuchi* in 1911.[30] The Jewish influences in Edward's early life remained with him; he was not a Jew by mere birth alone. He learned Hebrew, engaged in the study of Torah, and excluded shellfish and pork from his diet, though he did not observe Jewish holidays. His first marriage was to a Jewish woman, Florence Delson, his cousin, and his second, to Jean Victoria McClenaghan, was said to have endured rough patches on account of his Jewish background.[31]

In 1910, Sapir moved to Ottawa to head the Division of Anthropology at the Canadian National Museum. He secured a teaching position at the University of Chicago in 1926, where he moved for five years, eventually moving on to Yale, where he taught until his death at fifty-eight.[32] His scholarly work on Indian language and culture was prodigious. He studied Wasco and Wishram Chinook in Washington State as a graduate student, wrote a dissertation on the Tekelma and Chasta Costa at the Siletz Reservation in Oregon, and followed Alfred Kroeber's mandate to map the enormous cultural and linguistic diversity of American Indians. He reconstructed a protolanguage connecting Tlingit and Haida, recorded thirty-nine different Amerindian languages, and transcribed folklore texts. His major synthetic works formalized the Boasian paradigm in methodological terms.[33] Preoccupied with endangered languages, he used salvage ethnography's tools and comparative Indo-European linguistics to reconstruct unwritten languages and grammars. Nearly all the major linguists in the 1940s or 1950s were his students, and many of them, including Stanley Newman, Morris Swadesh, Morris Opler, and Leo Rosten, were Jewish.[34] These scholars consolidated and outlined fundamental historical and structural linguistic problems, laid the foundations for phonemic theory, and mapped language families across space.

The breadth and depth of Sapir's interests were legion, as was his commitment to Native Americans as a humanist and human rights activist. Less well known is that he was also occupied with Jewish problems.[35] Indeed, Sapir's Jewish background continuously influenced and intersected with his scholarship on American Indians. Sapir's biography shows a fascinating parallel preoccupation with both Native and Jewish social issues. These tracks run side by side, concerned as both were with parallel questions about ethnic survival, adaptability, dignity, cultural autonomy, and ethnicity. Using Canadian National Museum research resources, he lobbied Canada's commissioner of Indian affairs, Duncan Campbell Scott, "as a first step in trying to do what I can to see justice done the West Coast Indians."[36] He kept his division of the museum involved in details of Native life in Canada, "where scientific expertise could aid Indian causes."[37] Sapir took the initiative to have eleven wampum treaty belts that were being exhibited at the University of Pennsylvania Museum (identified by his colleague and fellow Jewish anthropologist Frank Speck) repatriated to the Six Nations Iroquois Reserve in Ontario in 1904. He placed the scientific skills of his division at the disposal of Native communities as well as the federal government. His biography reveals a steady punctuation of Jewish interests in and among his continued and substantial contributions to American Indian culture and linguistics. While working to repeal an antipotlach law in Canada, for example, he was writing his "Notes on Judeo-German Phonology."[38]

Sapir worked with Leonard Bloomfield, another dominating force of the newly professionalizing field of linguistics (and also Jewish), on a 1925 project for the American Association for the Advancement of Science. The two linguists prepared a list of American Indian languages still spoken, a catalog of published and unpublished scholarship on them, and a list of organizations that might help cooperate in studying them. While at the University of Chicago between 1926 and 1931, Sapir thrived in the social milieu of Chicago Jewish intelligentsia as a frequent guest at the homes of Louis Wirth, Henry Schultz, Jacob Viner, Morris Swadesh, Max Radin, Paul Radin, and Ralph Linton. Through ethnomusicologist George Herzog's wife Betsy, Sapir was introduced to wealthy Chicago Jewry with whom he socialized.[39] In 1931, Sapir moved to Yale, where, according to his biographer Regna Darnell, he became "more and more engrossed in and concerned with the problems of being a Jew and with the turmoil of modern events."[40] His personal experience with anti-Semitism at Yale, combined with the growth of anti-Semitism worldwide, seems to have profoundly impacted his Jewish identification. Jews, he concluded, were stuck in a conflict between cultures that was "perpetually insoluble," a predicament with which he himself must have certainly identified. In New Haven, he also befriended Maurice Zigmond, a nonpracticing orthodox rabbi and Yale Semitics PhD, with whom he discussed Talmud. He also struck up a friendship and talked at length about Jewish matters with Edgar Siskin, another rabbi cum graduate student at Yale (in anthropology). Sapir sat on YIVO's honorary committee with some of the most prominent Jewish intellectuals of the twentieth century: Salo Baron, Horrace Kallen, Simon Dubnow, Albert Einstein, Sigmund Freud, Moses Gaster, Berhard Wachsein, and Chaim Zhitlovsky.[41] Sapir wrote to colleagues on behalf of YIVO in 1933 about a project that he, Boas, Wirth, and Weinreich hoped to undertake for an "extensive study of personality of the eastern European Jew under conditions of rapid social change."[42] He established the American Intra-University Committee on Jewish Social Science with Leonard Bloomfield, Melville Herskovits, Max Radin, Henry Schultz, and Louis Wirth. "I cannot imagine a more exalted and a more practical way for bringing the Jewish masses of Eastern Europe and America into strong contact with the world culture," he wrote, "than forging a language [Yiddish] held in scorn into an instrument of a magnificent, clear, creative expression."[43] Sapir was one of the founders of the Conference on Jewish Social Studies, which launched the journal *Jewish Social Studies* in 1939, served as its vice president until his death, and helped organize the Conference on Jewish Relations, a national committee of eminent Jewish scholars interested in the scientific evaluation of social trends effecting Jews. "In conversation," recalled one of his Jewish students, Sapir "would occasionally tell how profoundly Judaism had affected his life." He wrote of "the necessity of having a cultural background if one is to be oneself."[44] He grew a sizable library of Judaica, read the Bible in Hebrew, and acquired several sets of the Talmud.[45] He agonized over Hitler's rise to power. As president of the American Anthropological Association, Sapir wrote to Boas about drafting a protest statement against the Nazi government and its treatment of the Jews; Boas, along with 13,000 distinguished signatories, published a letter in *Nature* magazine denouncing Nazism.

Sapir used the tools of social science, motivated by the spirit of relativism and liberalism, to promote ethnic Jewish identity as well as the social and economic health of Jewish communal, urban, cultural, and even religious life. Yet of twenty-six biographical sketches and appraisals of his life and contributions composed between 1939 and 1980, only two mentioned his Jewishness (those by Morris Swadesh and David Mandelbaum, both Jews themselves). Almost none described his relationships with Native people, issues, politics, involvements, or investments. Few mentioned his activist political engagements or work worth contributing to anything but scholarship. But Sapir was very much engaged in social and political activities that impacted both Jews' and Indians' lives throughout his extraordinarily productive career.

Despite their differences in scholarship, approach, and theory, the Jewishness of the Jewish anthropologists like Boas, Jacobs, Radin, and Sapir mattered. The projects of understanding Indian cultures they shared, and the realities of the contemporaneous American Jewish life they lived, were intricately intertwined. They brought an activist agenda to an academic pursuit. They crossed over into the political sphere, and whether they saw themselves as progressives, liberals, or socialists, they appropriated Native American lives and cultures to transmit intellectual and political agendas that neither began nor ended with Native Americans. They used Native American subjects as convenient examples to base claims about humanity writ large. They spoke for and about Indian customs, language, family structures, and cosmologies, ironically helping render Indian persons themselves silent. They made Indians the objects of serious academic concern, and they wrote to a crossover audience, hoping to make Indians more legible to white outsiders. They aimed to debunk myths about Indians but also represented them (making it appear that Indians themselves—"informants"—were representing themselves through them) in a way that domineered.

But these and still other Jewish anthropologists took to the study of American Indian life with an explicit, progressive, antirace agenda. As scholars and as Jews, they provided a dual service: to a liberalism that promoted ethically grounded, limited intellectual relativism on the one hand and to these scholars' sense of how liberalism would best serve different peoples' needs on the other.[46] They studied Native American cultures and understood this effort as a contribution to building a more multiethnic America. Their work was simultaneously ethnographic and social-justice oriented. Ruth Leah Bunzel, once a student, secretary, and editorial assistant of Boas, made contributions to Pueblo studies and to the Blood Indians of Alberta; she also studied alcoholism as a barrier to economic and political advances.[47] As a public advocate and anthropologist, the Brooklyn-born Erna Gunther studied the Salish and Makah peoples, built anthropology departments in Washington State and Alaska, and devoted "untiring efforts to develop public appreciation for Northwest Coast Native culture."[48] A supporter of Native American civil rights, she also participated in the founding of the Congress of American Indians.[49] Gunther saw herself as a cultural mediator, participating in and therefore able to speak across white and Indian cultures. She fundraised and recruited legal pro bono help from Jesse Epstein and Robert Schulman of Seattle for tribal governmental issues in the late 1950s and 1960s. She also worked with the AAIA, helping establish its Seattle and Alaska chapters, organizing or promoting legal workshops and conferences and examining court issues, voting rights, and tribal rolls, all activist interventions in the face of financial and political loss of West Coast tribes in the wake of Termination.[50]

Thinking about the Jewish influences of the central European immigrants who pioneered American anthropology—without reducing their lives' works to this single influence—allows us to see one way that American Jews took advantage of the opportunities they fought for to enter the mainstream and take up positions of influence, using Indians to help themselves think through Jewish differences.

By the time of the Indian New Deal, anthropology departments had been established in universities across the country. The discipline was fast becoming a major professional branch of the social sciences. For twenty years prior, as Boas, Sapir, and their respective cadres of students promoted their view of humanity and culture, anthropologists had few footholds in the apparatus of state power in respect to Indian life. To a limited extent, they critiqued the state. They showed only mild interest in reservation social problems and the ways that Indian life was changing as it faced new historical circumstances. But by the 1930s, not only had anthropologists become insiders within the university, they also drew much closer to the sites of political power in both the government and the nongovernment agencies that influenced, designed, and implemented policy concerning American Indians. Here, the influence of their Jewish immigrant (or children of immigrant) experiences became more salient. Indeed, academic interest among Boasian anthropologists in Native Americans in the 1930s and 1940s regularly bled into political action not just on behalf of both Native Americans but also in aiming to tackle a variety of issues that American Jews themselves faced.

Anthropologists and Their Investments in Jewish Issues

Jewish anthropologist students of Native American life of the mid-twentieth century can be broken into three groups, roughly paralleling the differences previously noted between Jacobs, Radin, and Sapir, though the classification is heuristic. The first are those with no Jewish investments in either their scholarship or their private lives. The second includes those who did not write about Jewish matters but nonetheless maintained interests in Jewish issues outside their professional persona. And the third includes those who engaged in Jewish matters both professionally and privately. These Jewish anthropologists, however, were not all of one piece in respect to their individual commitments to Jewish life or the attention they brought to bear on Jewish social or political issues in America. They can be plotted along a spectrum, from those who happened to be Jewish but spent little or no time considering or reflecting upon Jewish subjects or their own Jewish identities in print or devoted to Jewish issues in their private lives on one end to those fully engaged with Jewish matters on the other.[51] The sheer number of mid-twentieth-century Jewish anthropologists who devoted a significant portion of their professional lives to understanding, explaining, and in some cases advocating for Native American cultures evinces a pattern that is telling precisely because it can be observed in the aggregate.

This observation is significant beyond the mere fact that American Jews participated in this scholarly tradition; inventing and promoting the field anthropology offered a channel through which American Jewish intellectuals implemented a political ideology and set of liberal and libertarian values that supported Jewish religious and cultural continuity and respect for diversity. These Jewish scholars, leading acculturated lives, aimed to push against the disastrous effects of settlement on Indian life. Yet it would be too blunt to reduce their scholarly and advocacy work to Jewish activism by remote control. The Jewish and the Native American threads of their work ran parallel, sometimes intertwined, sometimes not. What is important to observe is not just the pattern itself, but that the Jewishness of these social scientists was underdetermined. Individual scholars were interested in Native Americans for a range of reasons. They could take on or cast off their Jewish investments freely and chose to engage in diverse ways.

It is certainly true that there were a significant number of Jewish anthropologists and linguists who distanced themselves in their professional and private lives from Jewish matters as they made significant scholarly contributions to Native American studies. Edwin Meyer Loeb, born into the highly assimilated Guggenheim Loeb German-Jewish family, taught anthropology at Berkeley for nearly a decade, wrote more than eighty publications on Pomo and Apache Indian religion, folklore and ethnography and Indonesia and Africa.[52] Leonard Bloomfield, born to Austrian Jewish parents in Chicago, led the development of structural linguistics during the 1930s and the 1940s and published grammars, lexicons, and text collections on Fox, Cree, Menominee, and Ojibwe, among many other contributions to linguistics.[53] Morris Swadesh, master linguist whose own mother tongue was Yiddish, was born to Jewish parents from Bessarabia. He conducted extensive fieldwork on more than twenty Indigenous languages of the Americas, including Chitimacha of Louisiana, Wisconsin Menominee, and New York Mahican.[54] All of them made significant contributions to the study of Native American cultures and languages; none of them wrote a word about Jews, neither did they engage in any sort of civic activism.[55]

Being politically active did not, of course, require a Jewish-born scholar to be interested or motivated by Jewish interests. Many were active in applied politics but nevertheless distanced themselves from Jewish matters. The Buffalo-born Jewish anthropologist Opler brothers, for example, had no involvement with the Jewish world, though both made significant contributions to scholarship and applied politics.[56] Morris Edward Opler, an expert on Jicarilla, Lipan, and Chiricahua Apache ethnology, folklore, myths, and tales, was involved in implementing parts of the IRA, including the ICC.[57] His scholarship had a strong political charge, and he used the language of imperialism explicitly. He worked on land claims filed in 1950s and 1960s.[58] A report he prepared for the ICC on "The Territories of the Apache Groups of the American Southwest" framed territorial boundaries before, during, and immediately after the "American Occupation."[59] He made no bones about criticizing the Federal Indian Administration in his teaching at the Sequoyah Indian School or in penning scathing condemnations of the conditions on the Mescalero and Jicarilla Apache reservations during Collier's tenure as commissioner, having worked at the BIA in the late 1930s.[60] Likewise, his brother, Marvin Kauffman Opler, wrote on acculturation of the Ute and Paiute Indians in Colorado and Utah, the Mescalero Apache in New Mexico, and the Inuit and Northwest Coast Indians in Oregon.[61] Opler's work was concerned with the relationship between societies, cultures, and mental health issues, and he helped develop social psychiatry, a synthesis of psychiatry, the social sciences, and epidemiology.[62]

Scholars like the brothers Opler, Loeb, Bloomfield, and Stern are absent from literature on American Jewish intellectual life, not surprisingly because they were scholars of Native American life who happened to be Jewish but seem to have made no contributions to Jewish life. While it is a stretch to argue that making significant contributions to other American minority groups is tantamount to contributing to the American Jewish life, witnessing a pattern of scholarly interest in American Native peoples of Jewish anthropologists indicates one way that American Jews chose to work through questions about identity, race, and belonging in a time of quiet angst about the nature of Jewishness and its capacities to limit prospects for success and integration in America. Studying Native America and representing it to a broader non-Indigenous public became a Jewish concern, at least in part because it allowed Jews—both those who were committed to Jews or Judaism in some way and those who were not—to engage with the crucial questions that impinged upon their communities of birth.

Scholars have grappled with the observation that many twentieth-century Jewish intellectuals—whether they were of privileged or modest social origins, immigrants or belonging to the second or third generation, children of rabbis or assimilated parents—regularly turned away from their Jewish backgrounds and avoided referencing their own Jewish backgrounds in public and in their writings, mostly for careerist reasons, as a way of "escaping Jewishness" or transcending the particularistic by merging with the universalistic.[63] Giants of twentieth-century letters like Abraham Kardiner, Karl Deutsch, and Paul Lazarsfeld devoted not a single moment of their long professional lives to Jewish questions.[64] Karl Popper experienced Jewishness as an object of race hatred but made no mention of race pride, instead explicitly rejecting Jewishness.[65] Harold Laski, the son of Polish orthodox Jews, declared, "I am English, not Polish; agnostic, not a Jew."[66] Central European Jewish intellectuals, refugees, immigrants, and exiles in psychology and psychoanalysis, sociology and social thought, economics, political science and theory, humanities, philosophy, and theology adopted the code of civility and entered into modernity in the United States via universities, breaking with their distinctive Jewish identity. The occupations would not tolerate particularistic affiliation that could be considered anachronistic or alienating.[67] To out oneself as a Jew would be to hinder one's professional standing or chances of achieving continued success in one's respective field, in one's respective university environment. Overt public identification with Jewish issues may also have undermined or diminished one's scholarly reputation. This practical constraint goes some distance in explaining why Native American subjects appealed to Jews who chose to research and write about some of the very same social and political questions that impacted Jewish life without saying a word about their own Jewish backgrounds.

Frank Speck is a useful example. As a social scientist disassociated from his Jewish identity, Speck invested in his elective affinities with Native Americans. One of Boas's first students and a lifetime career anthropologist who wrote more than four hundred books, monographs, and articles on the Eastern Woodland tribes, the Algonquian and Iroquois, and later, Cherokee linguistics, kinship, and culture, Speck, a salvage ethnographer for those tribes, built the anthropology department at the University of Pennsylvania. Speck embodied the ventriloquist wholeheartedly and aimed to speak for Native Americans and render their cultures accessible to American whites, effacing his Jewish origins altogether.[68] Speck was adopted into the turtle clan of the Seneca Nation, given the name Gahehdagowa, the Great Porcupine. He told colleague and eventual biographer Horace Beck that "he was part Indian and that as a child he had had an Indian woman as a nurse."[69] Speck conducted fieldwork among the Yuchi Indians of Oklahoma in 1904. An integral part of Speck's fieldwork was collecting material culture centered on Iroquois ceremonialism. He helped New England tribes gain federal tribal recognition by intervening with BIA agents and helped demonstrate that Algonkian hunters of the North American forests had developed sophisticated and legitimate property rights in hunting grounds (evidence that was used by Felix Cohen, among others, in an Indian claims case before the ICC).[70]

In the hands of his biographer, the ethnic arc of Speck's life moved from Jewish origins to Indian identification, albeit precariously balanced between Jewish-outsider and Indian-outsider, much like the model of the ethnographer itself, the participant-observer. "Indians became his life," wrote Beck.

> His office and his home literally became museums filled with the material cultures of these people. . . . But he wasn't satisfied with the study of a few Indian groups . . . his greatest service was, perhaps, that of salvage. From the ashes of destruction he moved about in the northeast salvaging scraps of cultures that everyone else believed to be long dead. . . . *He was more Indian than the Indians.* He was beloved by them—in many cases almost revered by them. They were his friends, and he was one of them . . . the reason that Frank had such a fondness for Indians was deeper than any mere childhood or blood ties.[71]

The case of Speck's biographer claiming that the salvage anthropologist "was more Indian than the Indians" themselves harkens back to Jewish frontiersmen and their "moves to innocence." Though a bona fide scholar, Speck bore a certain similarity to the frontier Jews discussed in chapter 1, leveraging knowledge of and intimacy with Native Americans in order to heighten his professional bona fides.

Some Jewish anthropologists avoided referencing Jewishness in their professional writing. Some even avoided using Jewish examples to illustrate more general points in their scholarly publications and in their writings for public audiences in newspapers, popular journals, pamphlets writing on race, or in other public forums. This absence is certainly remarkable, but to focus on scholars' scholarly writing alone misses an important point—namely, that many Jewish anthropologists and other social scientists maintained some measure of existential filiation with their Jewishness, irrespective of how they construed this

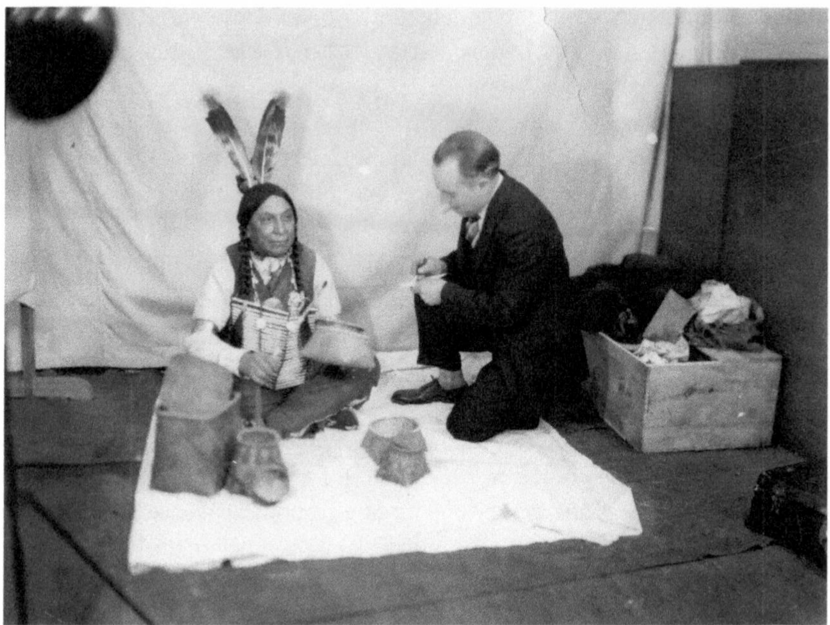

Figure 6.2. Anthropologist Frank Speck and Delaware Lenape chief Witapanoxwe, circa 1923–1928, graphic 4173. Courtesy of the American Philosophical Society.

Jewishness. They kept abreast of American and international Jewish news and issues, subscribed to Jewish papers, sat on the boards of Jewish organizations, and maintained correspondences with Jewish communal agencies, even if they avoided Jewish matters in print. May Mandelbaum Edel, for example, who conducted her initial fieldwork among the Tillamook and Salish Indians of Northwestern Oregon, was active among Jewish communists in the 1930s and 1940s.[72]

They often socialized in Jewish circles and ritually marked their own lives with Jewish rite of passage rituals (like weddings and funerals). Some Jewish anthropologists married one another: Erna Gunther and Leslie Spier, and Gene Weltfish and Alexander Lesser.[73] David Mandelbaum's classmate and fellow rabbi, Edgar Siskin, found him a job and introduced him to his future wife, Ruth Weiss. Maurice Zigmond, their Yale classmate and fellow rabbi, married the two.[74] These Jewish scholars were engaged with Jewish questions, in other words, if inconsistently and unevenly, even as they avoided writing about Jews or Jewish subjects.

Many of this second category of anthropologists saw their Jewishness as paraprofessional. It was, for them, a private matter, a matter of religion or the largely irrelevant familial past. In contrast, Indians were public; the anthropologist's professional commitment was to understanding Indians on their own terms and to communicate these understandings to public audiences. Native objects were the canvas upon which anthropologists promoted the culture concept, aimed at decentering race as an organizing principle and shaper of policy choices large and small. It is not altogether surprising that many anthropologists took active roles in social welfare, policy, and public intellectual discussion in defense of American Indians nor that they served as boosters of Native American well-being, even if their specific actions had competing visions of what the "best interests" of Native American communities or individuals might be. Just as it made little sense for Jews in the social sciences to study Jewish communities or frame their scholarly contributions in terms that would appear to cast doubt on their objectivity or credibility, so too it made little sense for the Jewish social scientists who studied Native Americans to make explicit parallels between Natives and Jews. Drawing such parallels would not be helpful or useful to either of their mandates. Discussing Jews in the midst of their professional writing on Indians might taint the ways others evaluated their professional judgment. They wanted to be seen as motivated only by science and liberalism, not ethnic investment. Evoking Indians in their Jewish advocacy work provided no obvious leverage; rather, it would have only increased the degree of difference between them and their Gentile whites, when the aim was to reduce this sense of difference to a negligent matter of confessional choice—almost an aesthetic matter, not one of existential import.

This is not to say, however, that no anthropologist of Jewish persuasion focused their professional attention on Jewish subjects during the 1930s and 1940s. Among those Jews who trained under Boas or Sapir but never landed jobs in the academy, a few pursued careers in Jewish research and Jewish communal service using the tools and training of Boasian and Sapirian anthropology. Many trained with Indian subjects but did not devote their careers to research and political engagement around American Indian affairs and life, like Radin, Jacobs, Sapir, Boas, and many others. The archival records of Jewish anthropologists who chose to study Jews show a parallelism in which preoccupations with both Native and Jewish social issues run concurrently.

From the vantage point of the history of ethnic construction in America, the stakes of these twin preoccupations were concerned with the analogous questions about ethnic survival and the adaptability, dignity, and cultural autonomy of "ethnic groups" in America. This smaller subset of Jewish anthropologists used the tools of social science to promote ethnic Jewish identity and bolster the social, economic, cultural, and even religious health of the American Jewish community. Motivated by the spirits of relativism and liberalism, and some measure of filial duty, they saw America's Jews as a constituent part of the American, white mainstream and likely viewed themselves in terms that minimized any prospective differences between themselves and their fellow white liberals from other religious heritages, alienated or otherwise. Their lives' works are replete with efforts to combat the race idea and promote Jewish difference. They cut their teeth on basic theory when they earned anthropology PhDs and continued to read and write on Indian subjects. They lectured to Jewish audiences on Indian life, sometimes as case studies for or examples of their larger arguments about cultural relativism and the bankruptcy of the idea of race and sometimes in the context of communal education of the young, sermons, holidays, life cycles, and other Jewish events.

Ruth Schlossberg Landes, Anita Brenner, and George Herzog paired but did not partner their intellectual interests in Jews and Indians, pursuing scholarship and activism as distinct but parallel interests without integration; they took no interest in the history of encounters between Jews and Native Americans, nor did they attempt to build bridges or connections between living actors. Herzog spent some time engaging in government programs aimed at Indian uplift and cultural creativity, consulting with John Collier to establish an Indian Music program; his "extracurricular" passion was Jewish music.[75] Anita Brenner, born in Mexico to Latvian Jewish immigrants, a student of Boas and an expert on Mexican art and Mexican revolutionary history, was also a lifelong Jewish political activist. She contributed to and kept clips from the Yiddish-language *Jewish Morning Journal*, the *Menorah Journal*, and the *Jewish Telegraphic Agency*.[76] Her records reveal a steady shuttling between Indigenous affairs and Jewish ones. Brenner's files on Nahuas Indians sat next to ones on anti-Semitism, "mi primer Judio" transcripts, folders concerned with "What is Being Jewish," Jewish immigration, and the Jews in Mexico.[77] Files on Indian rural education and Mexican indigenous art were squeezed between files on Israeli fruit and vegetables, prayer books, and notes on "the Jewish question."[78] She corresponded with Rabbi Martin Zielonka, a Reform rabbi of El Paso Texas, about the B'nai B'rith's resettlement of eight thousand Jewish refugees from Europe.[79]

In the first two decades of Ruth Schlossberg Landes' work, she too shuttled between Jewish and Native American subjects and would maintain an interest in race relations throughout the rest of her distinguished career in anthropology. The daughter of New York Yiddish labor socialist activist and a founder of the Amalgamated Clothing Workers of America, Joseph Schlossberg, Landes completed a PhD in the social organization of the Ojibwe in Manitou Rapids, Ontario, in 1936.[80] By that time, she had already conducted a study of the Black Jews of Harlem for her master's thesis.[81] In the 1940s, she conducted fieldwork on the Chippewa of Red Lake, Minnesota, the Santee Dakota in Minnesota, and the Potawatomi in Kansas. She also did research for the American Jewish Congress, wherein she studied Jewish families as part of a team of six anthropologists for Columbia's Research in Contemporary Cultures project during those same years under contract with the Office of Naval Research under Mead's direction, understanding and predicting the political behavior, problems of culture change, assimilation, acculturation, and new values of Czechs, Russians, Chinese, French, and eastern European, Syrian, and German Jews and how they adapted and contributed to American culture. She was also a part of the team that studied Jewish life in eastern European small towns, which became the influential and oft-reprinted volume *Life Is with People* by her colleague Mark Zborowski, with whom she co-authored a study of the eastern European Jewish family. In

1945, she directed an interdenominational clergy to analyze antidiscrimination legislation in New York.[82] While she is known for her work on Sioux, Ojibwe, Santee Dakota, and Potawatomi religion and culture (and later Brazilian subjects), she also kept files with scholarly notes on "Jews and Judaism," "the Jewish soldier," and dozens of clippings on Jewish subjects.[83]

These anthropologists shared the same twinned concerns, as much politically oriented as academically. The proximity of association of these preoccupations implies a dynamic relevance between them. The fascinating absence of explicit talk by this category of Jewish anthropologist about the connections and relationships between their respective Jewish and Indian work perhaps rests in the fact that for these scholars, Jewish matters tended to be existential, personal, and for many, ambivalent. Indian interests, on the other hand, were highly significant for research purposes, for the extension of anthropological theory, and were compelling with respect to social justice. They did not, however, embroil the scholars' own selves. The *foreignness* of Native American tribes, their vast diversity, and the popular understanding of Native American cultures as somehow more connected to earlier, more essential, and natural humanness raised their utility for anthropological ambitions in the public realm. Indians also provided Jewish anthropologists a cloak (and a kind of foil) for working through uncomfortable questions about Jewish difference. Indian difference, unlike Jewish difference, was thought of as considerably more foreign vis-à-vis the broader world of white, affluent, enfranchised elites (anthropology's audience). Service to both Jewish and Indian subjects, however, served many of the same ideological ends: the promotion of multiculturalism, diversity, tolerance, and pluralism.

Anthropologist-Rabbis

Anthropologists who remained quiet about their own connections to the Jewish experience were not the only ones to pair investments in Jewish and Native American causes and studies. Several ordained rabbis' lives and work show this kind of parallelism. Working through issues about settler society and their place in it was both an American struggle and a Jewish one. These are cases in which Jewish existential commitments might be expected to be stronger, though in some cases they were just as ambivalent as the anthropologists who remained quiet about Jewish interests altogether.

The towering figure in American anthropology, Melville J. Herskovits, born in Ohio to Austro-Hungarian Jewish immigrants, attended Reform Judaism's seminary, the Hebrew Union College, for eight years but left in the year of his would-be ordination to begin a PhD under Boas. While he is mostly known for his work on Africa and African Americans, Herskovits also devoted some time to American Indians, consulting with the Department of the Interior about tribal constitutions, tribal organizations, and economic and social rehabilitation, especially in respect to land acquisition and natural resources.[84] He advocated for better anthropological training for Indian service employees. According to one of his biographers, growing up in his assimilated Jewish family fed his "sensitivity to [questions about his identity and his place in American society, which] foreshadowed his interest in cultural change as a student, teacher, and practitioner of anthropology."[85]

Perhaps speaking from his experiences of anti-Semitism (one at the University of Chicago in 1927, where a student social club tried to hold separate Jewish-Gentile dances, and another when Margaret Mead's landlord refused to sublet her apartment to him on account of his being Jewish), Herskovits wrote that "the Jew has ever taken on the color of the culture in which he lives, and far from identifying himself with his own typical culture (whatever there may be of it) he usually tries to become as completely acculturated as is possible to the culture in which he finds himself."[86] The common cultural heritage of Jews, he wrote, was "the feeling which is ground into every Jew from the time he is old enough to realize that he is somebody different from the people about him" . . . "All Jews have much the same . . . feeling that they are different from their neighbors," though he also confessed that "neither in training, in tradition, in religious beliefs, nor in culture am I what might be termed a person any more Jewish than any other American born and reared in a typical Middle Western milieu."[87] Herskovits also wrote polemics in public, nonscholarly venues, defending immigrants, Blacks from miscegenation laws, and Native American self-governance.[88] All of this work was part of his lifelong attack on scientific racism.

Though he occupies a slim place on the American Jewish history bookshelf, Herskovits maintained a steady interest in Jewish affairs from the 1920s until his death, actively engaging with the B'nai B'rith of Cincinnati, its Hillel Foundation, magazine, and orphanage, the Conference on Jewish Relations, the National Conference of Jews and Christians, the Jewish Bibliographic Bureau, Chicago's Jewish People's Institute, the Jewish Charities of Chicago, the Council of Jewish Federations, and the Welfare Funds of the Bureau of Jewish Social Research.[89] He helped Jewish scholars flee from German occupied territory in the 1930s and early 1940s, arranged assistance, coordinated with foreign diplomats, raised money, and located American jobs. He distributed anti-Nazi pamphlets to refute Nazi propaganda and wrote and lectured widely on the scientific distortions of racial difference, on racism as the spearhead of fascism, and on racism as an infection of American life. The effects of racism, Herskovits noted, impacted "the Negro, the Oriental, the Mexican, the Indian" as a matter of physical characteristics and as a matter of cultural and linguistic peculiarity, as is the case of various immigrant groups, including Jews, about whom he wrote, "As in the case of the Jew, it may be a combination of all these factors."[90] He delivered antiracism lectures to Jewish audiences too. He spoke at a Temple Men's Club and a Chicago Roundtable National Conference of Christians and Jews for Chicago teachers and maintained relationships throughout the 1930s and 1940s with YIVO, Louis Finkelstein of the Jewish Theological Seminary, the Hebrew Union College, and Rabbi Bertram W. Korn, the Reform rabbi in Philadelphia and historian of American Jewry.[91]

Herskovits applauded anthropologists who worked as Indian New Deal civil servants and defended those who cooperated with the Roosevelt Administration, which he felt was "unequivocally on the side of the native."[92] His "Native Self-Government" article in *Foreign Affairs* appealed to public and civic leaders around the world during World War II to seriously consider the status of aboriginal groups once the war would come to an end. He made an appeal to usher in an era of sovereignty and autonomy worldwide, hoping that the war's end could be taken as opportunity to end colonialism, reconfigure imperial administration, and make room for the full participation of aboriginal groups in shaping global economics, politics, and culture. The postwar plans of European and American leaders toward colonized peoples, he beseeched, "shall preserve the interests of the native populations during some undetermined transitional period and instruct them in the art of governing themselves." The then-current approach to Indigenous self-governance did not, he argued, adequately consult Natives, though such an approach appeared "acceptable to us because it feeds a congeal belief in our own superiority [. . .] for among Europeans and Americans ethnocentrism has been raised almost to an article of faith." Wrote Herskovits,

> Only such peoples as have been transplanted to reserves, or whose aboriginal habitat has been invaded by foreigners in large numbers, or who have been compelled to live under conditions that prevented key elements in their culture from functioning, would find it impossible to exercise even local cultural control over their own societies . . . they would be the exception in the colonial world rather than the rule—they would present the sort of situation which has arisen in North America . . . the difficulty lies in our unwillingness to admit the worth of native ways of life, to refrain from passing judgment upon their values and traditions merely because they differ from our own.[93]

As this defense of Native peoples' ways of life and their deserving of both respect and sovereignty aptly attests, Herskovits "unquestioningly approved of using the insights gained from anthropology to educate Americans as to proper values," to quote from one of his biographers.[94]

Herskovits was not the only Jewish scholar of Indian life or language to have worked toward a rabbinic degree, earned one, or actually practiced from the pulpit. Bernard Stern, Melford Spiro, Maurice Zigmond, and David Mandelbaum all trained as both anthropologists and rabbis. Stern, a Marxist social anthropologist and a specialist on the Lummi Indians, earned a rabbinical degree from the Hebrew Union College before his PhD under Boas and worked as a pulpit rabbi for several years.[95] He wrote extensively about socialized medicine, freedom of speech, rights of the foreign-born, and Indians as one among many American minorities. He wrote a "Treatise on Anti-Semitism" for the AJC in 1945, wrote but did not publish an "Outline of Negroes and Jews in the White Protestant Culture: An American Pattern" in 1940, and considered co-authoring an introductory textbook on the sociology of the Jews in the United States in 1946.[96] He maintained a sustained interest in Jewish matters including Zionism, evidenced by his library, his teaching and lecturing career, and archival holdings.[97]

Melford E. Spiro received his rabbinic ordination from Conservative Judaism's Jewish Theological Seminary then later a PhD in anthropology, after which he conducted fieldwork in many points around the globe, including among North America's Ojibwe Indians, on Ifaluk Atoll in the South Pacific, and on Israeli kibbutzim.[98] These two rabbi-anthropologists clearly shared political and intellectual interests in both Native Americans and Jews.

We find a similar story in Maurice Zigmond, the Reform-ordained Yale PhD who combined rabbinate and anthropological research during these same years. Born in Denver to Hungarian immigrants, Zigmond began his career as a counselor for Jewish college students in 1935. He taught anthropology at Yale from 1948 to 1961, established Hillel foundations at both Yale and the University of Connecticut, and directed Hillel centers at Harvard and Radcliffe. As a member of the Central Conference of American Rabbis and its editorial board, he had extensive involvements in Jewish life.[99] He also wrote on the Kawaiisu tribe of southeast California with data he collected from 1936 to 1940, and Kawaiisu mythology.[100] While he focused on Kawaiisu "disruption of traditional family life," intermarriage, material culture losses, and other aspects of the "disintegrating process [that] began as soon as the non-Indians made an appearance," in particular, as exemplification of Jewish adaptability. in particular, as exemplification of Jewish adaptability. Albert Isaac Gordon too was both ordained (by the Jewish Theological Seminary in 1929) and a PhD (in sociology from the University of Minnesota in 1948) and authored three monographs on Jewish subjects (among dozens of other articles, lectures, and sermons), each of which focused on some aspect of Jewish acculturation: immigrant adjustment, intermarriage, and suburbia.[101] While working as a pulpit rabbi and executive director of the United Synagogue of America later in the 1940s, Gordon also wrote on the Sioux, though never on Jewish-Sioux relations despite his interest in interfaith, interracial, and interethnic relationships.[102] While the Jewish and Native American aspects in the work of anthropologist-rabbis like Gordon, Zigmond, and Spiro ran parallel but did not intertwine, other midcentury Jewish scholars brought these two strands of their intellectual interests to bear on one another.

Though some used the tools of anthropology—conducting ethnographic fieldwork in Jewish communities and viewing local Jewish communities from within in order to translate their cultures into the scholarly idiom for outside audiences—the reverse did not occur. The intellectual perspectives, tools, and techniques from the rabbinate or from traditional Jewish religious hermeneutics did not impact the anthropology of Jewish rabbi-anthropologists. David

Goodman Mandelbaum, for example, studied the Jewish community in Ansonia, Connecticut, applying ethnographic principles and methodologies developed for the study of Native Americans to Jews. He began his career conducting fieldwork on the Saskatchewan Plains Cree in 1940, and though he trained in classic American Indian–focused anthropology at Yale under Sapir and Leslie Spier, Mandelbaum devoted scholarly consideration to and deployed the tools of anthropology on both Jewish and Native American objects throughout the 1930s.[103] Throughout his career, Mandelbaum maintained a steady concern with social justice matters, the defense of American Indians, and the deepening of American liberal democratic values. One anti-imperialist essay, a revision of the Apache war in which the Apache were victims of imperial menacing state aggression, entitled "All American All-Americans: Geronimo," describes how Apache Indians were "beguiled into captivity by the broken word of the American commander" as part of a "tide of domination" that diminished Apache cultural ways, land, dignity.[104] His writing on Geronimo during World War II urged American readers not to "be fooled by propaganda that Indians are menacing," perhaps paraphrasing the Nazi slogan "Jews are a menace to Germany." Instead, he insisted, "America needs Indians!" in order to "re-America: restore America!"[105]

Figure 6.3. "American Anthropologist David Mandelbaum (Center) Was Allowed to Observe Aspects of the Cree Sun Dance in the 1930s. Photographed at the Sweetgrass Reserve in Saskatchewan, 1934." From Katherine Pettipas, *Severing the Ties That Bind.* Saskatchewan Archives Board, Provincial Archives of Saskatchewan, photo R-A2577.

Mandelbaum conducted fieldwork on the San Carlos Apache (1933), the Plains Cree (1934–1935), and the Jews of Urbana (1936), the same year as his essay on "Friendship in North America" about the Chippewa.[106] He eventually became most well-known for his anthropological studies on the Kola and the Cochin Jews of India.[107] His work was informed by a vision of anthropological research as a means to combat racism and an educational prerogative. His work on the Jews of Urbana aimed to combat anti-Semitism with information, construing Jews as "social whole," a culture to be understood on its own terms and translated for broad audiences, just he had framed the Cree Indians whom he had previously studied. The Jewish objects of his study read as a small-town middle-class "genontrocracy," a social group governed by old men, social organization, class, kinship, and dietary and dress habits, in which they mostly abandoned religious commitments but maintained a strong group identification and feeling of defense of Jews, a solidarity "that welds the Jewish community into a compact group."[108] Mandelbaum did, however, perceive differences between the Cree and Jews as objects of ethnographic practice since, "of course," he remarked in a reflection on his own life work, "one cannot hire an old Jew by the day to impart information, as is possible with an old Indian."[109] Methodologically, he concluded, "it takes little subtlety of technique to secure many notes from an *Urbana* informant on himself and his culture." The distance between Jew and the readers of his anthropology, was, in his perception, smaller than the distance between Cree and the readers of his anthropology. Yet despite the relative closeness or distance he assumed to exist between his Jewish objects and his Apache or Cree objects, the objective of the scholarly presentation was remarkably similar; the scholarship was designed to undermine racial or essentialist constructions of the cultural groups, Jews or otherwise.

This would prove to be a theme that Mandelbaum would return to explicitly in respect to the Cochin Jews of India he would later study. "If any further proof be needed that Judaism is a social and not a physical heritage, that it is a matter of cultural conditioning and not of congenital acquisition," he wrote, "the black Jews are a prime case in point. Although anthropometric measurements and blood tests equate them physically with the other autochthonous inhabitants of Malabar, culturally they are vastly different from their Hindu neighbors. The Judaism of the black Jews is a wholehearted faith and a strictly observed code of conduct."[110] Mandelbaum even went so far as to undermine Jews' supposed cultural characteristics in Europe and America, using the Jews of India as counterpoint, asserting that "the characteristics which are supposed to go hand in hand with Judaism [scholasticism, commercially competitive, taking on a large role in public life, neurotic, and experienced in anti-Semitism] are markedly lacking among the Jews of Cochin."[111] His reading of the Jews of India was antiessentialist. His broader goal was to use social science to explain and understand American Jews, to "present an objective and scientifically analytic picture of what contemporary Jewish life in America is like" because while a student of culture could easily "turn to adequate sources if he would know the societal organization of a Mexican village or an Eskimo band," he had difficulty when trying to "find a scientific delineation of the life of a modern Jewish community."[112]

In one project that Mandelbaum worked on, sponsored by the Conference for Jewish Relations and conducted under direction of Morris Raphael Cohen (the father of Felix Cohen) and Edward Sapir, he aimed to "furnish methodological specifications for conducting such studies."[113] "Since Jewish anthropologists and sociologists tend to sheer away from Jewish matters, it is the professional schools for social work which must furnish the necessary impetus for this research. . . . The criteria for the study of Urbana can be applied to a study of the Don Cossack settlement or of the Omaha tribe. Every social group has its unique history and distinctive functioning. A Jewish group is no more and no less unique than any other."[114]

The strategies and techniques that he deployed in studying Urbana Jews in 1936 were later applied to broader trends in American Jewish life that he would return to reflect upon nearly twenty years later. His 1954 study of the Jews of Glencoe, Illinois, charted change over the course of a single generation.[115] Notable is what changed between the late 1930s context of Jewish uncertainty in Urbana with the sense of rootedness in 1950s Glencoe. Mandelbaum's position ambiguously straddles the ethnographic, observational viewpoint of the anthropologist and the engaged, steward-like voice of the communal rabbi.[116] Mandelbaum emphasized that individual Jews held the responsibility to promote Jewish values and uphold Jewish social cohesion, "that Jews stand steadfast as Jews," just as he bemoaned that "the outer edges . . . of Judaism have indeed been changed under the impact of American culture."[117] The work was no longer about cultural wholes but about individuals making decisions.

One final example of the anthropologist-rabbi who fused interest in the methods of anthropology for the purpose of Jewish communal advancement was Edgar Siskin. Siskin published works on American Indians and American Jews and continuously returned to the themes and dynamics of assimilation and acculturation among both Native Americans and American Jews. Siskin, an Edinburgh, Scotland-born son of a rabbi and cantor, who trained both under Sapir at Yale and at the Hebrew Union College, served for forty-four years as a pulpit rabbi at the prestigious Reform congregations—at Mishkan Israel in New Haven and at the North Shore Congregational Israel in Glencoe, Illinois, where Mandelbaum had conducted his research. He was a civic leader in Chicago and its Jewish suburbs.[118]

What is significant about Siskin beyond the fact that he researched both Jews and Native Americans was the fact that he, uniquely, explicitly reflected on their intersection.[119] He took his summers off from the pulpit to do fieldwork, first among the Washo Indians from 1937 to 1939 and then several times thereafter, focusing on shamanism, peyote, conflict in religious models, and questions of authority. "I would leave [to do fieldwork] the day after confirmation and return the week before Rosh Hashanah," struggling with a broader "dilemma as to which vocational path I would follow" in the longer term.[120] "Anthropology and the rabbinate would seem to make an odd couple," opened his later-in-life autobiographical reflection, *A Rabbi-Anthropologist in Israel.* But describing the "affinity between them," Siskin wrote that the "rabbinate and anthropology were closely, sometimes frustratingly, juxtaposed in my life."[121] Anthropological thinking, and in particular Edward Sapir, transformed his life and thinking as he became "familiar with a new world of information and ideas. Beyond this, I discovered a new way of looking at life. Anthropology now became a principle preoccupation."[122]

Siskin's preoccupations with Reform Jews and Sapirian anthropology stand out in a 1952 lecture he delivered to the Central Conference of American Rabbis, "The Impact of American Culture Upon the Jew," which concerned religious practice and themes of adaptation, assimilation, and extraneous influence on religion.[123] Speaking to an audience of rabbis as a fellow rabbi and as an anthropologist, Siskin deployed anthropological evidence and perspective about well-rehearsed criticisms of American Jewish life: its religious apathy, decline in the learning ideal, and the replacement of clergy and scholars as leaders by "the captains of business and industry, together with the managers and public relations counsels."[124] These were all problems that led to Jews divesting from their own Jewish identities and communities, leaving many with "emotional distress, moral disorientation," "divided, rootless, alienated, partially accepted, partially assimilated . . . at home neither in nor outside the ghetto." Speaking as a rabbi to fellow rabbis, Siskin drew "hope from the anthropological maxim that culture is restless, that its progress is ever on the move." He deployed anthropology's concern with group cohesion in order to meet the needs of communal leaders who feared that Jewishness would be lost to the ruptures of suburban life and the lowering of barriers for Jewish participation in society, politics, and culture for enfranchised Jews no longer struggling as immigrants in the 1950s. "For us in the rabbinate—there is this to nerve us in our task: there will be those who will never yield up their group identity or their faith . . . survival depends on *sh'ar yashuv*, a stubborn remnant that will stand, an island in an alien ocean. When did Israel's strength lie in numbers? The remnant has always saved us. The swirling tide of acculturation will carry off the weak, the indifferent, the divided. The strong will cling to the rock." He emphasized the role of activist leaders in preserving community rather than describing social change from a detached perspective.

Beyond this emphasis on leadership, Siskin's own faith came through in his religious language, a radical departure from the ethnographic voice: "And that rock? *Habilu el tzur chatsaviem.* The rock whence we were hewn. The peoplehood of the Jew. And to yet another rock. *Hatsur tomim po'olo, ki chol d'rochov mishpot.* The faith of the Jew. The Rock, His work is perfect, for all His ways are just."[125] Siskin's question about how Jews would survive America was much more rabbinic than anthropological, driven by his shared existential commitment to the other rabbis in the room more than his dispassionate if sympathetic view of Native American cultural dilution. Would Jewish culture die like the Washo culture he had studied as an anthropologist? Siskin's study of the Washo had concerned itself with the historical diffusion of Washo customs throughout the Great Basin cultural area. Though his study claimed to describe the "totality" of Washo religious culture, it made no mention of contemporary influences. In other words, Siskin understood the tenuous nature of both American Jewish and American Indian cultures in different ways. Jews were "the Hapax Legomenon among the peoples of the world," as he put it, unique among peoples like a phrase in the Bible that only appears once. Writing as a man of faith, a believer in God, and a believer of the uniqueness of Jewish peoplehood, Siskin suggested that Jews might be the "stubborn exception to the tidy operation of culture process," that culture as a process perhaps excluded the Jews on account of the surviving stubborn remnant of the truly faithful.[126] If his American Indian subjects seemed bound to pass away with the fading last memories of the elderly and the Washo struggles with American acculturation he observed led to cultural disintegration, anxieties about the failures of cultural continuity among his own community of American Jews could find relief in the notion of theological election ("chosenness").

Siskin's writings also betray a key ambiguity. "I saw native Indian culture with all its spirit—world sanctities crumble under the impact of Euro-American Culture, its religious universe evanesce, its language abandoned," he wrote. "*It was no different with American Jews.* I have been a profound personal witness to cultural assimilation among both native and American Jews."[127] Siskin's respective professional personae—rabbi and anthropologist—blurred in a fundamental but uni-directional way. He was deeply affected in witnessing Washo "world sanctities crumble" under the weight of Euro-American culture and found motivation to battle those same Euro-American forces insofar as they threatened American Jewish spiritual life. What he witnessed as an anthropologist seemed to motivate him to double down on his commitments to distinctly nonscientific, rabbinical interventions in Jewish life. He deployed Jewish mystical and theological claims as a bulwark to protect Jewish religious culture. The reverse did not happen: nowhere did Rabbi Siskin's perspective about spiritual life ever bleed into his work as an anthropologist on or for Washo Indians.

Shifting Periods, Continued Advocacy

Siskin's reflections on the parallels and divergences between American Jews and American Indians were written during the height of Termination, an era in which activist anthropologists had increasingly less political leverage. The change had occurred quite suddenly. In the Indian New Deal era, NGOs, government workers, and academics worked together, and the Boasian view of the cultural determination of human behavior had a strong influence on both social science and public policy. The AAIA had cultivated relationships with anthropologists, utilized their scholarly work in promoting its Indian rights and uplift agenda, and recruited anthropologists to do its intellectual scholarly, ethnographic, historical, and moral work. Its executive director, Alexander Lesser, was a trained anthropologist, and its field research initiatives, government relations efforts, and leadership all the way up to the executive level deployed and employed anthropologists, including a large number of fellow Jewish anthropologists including Frank Speck, Otto Kleinberg, Gene Weltfish, and many others.[128] Lawyer Theodore Haas and anthropologist Walter Goldschmidt had worked in the field with Tlingit teachers to document occupation in their villages.[129] William Zimmerman, named the director of a new Washington office of AAIA after his resignation as the acting commissioner of Indian affairs, worked with Erna Gunther on Washington Indian issues as the field director of the AAIA.[130]

Though their recourse to institutional mechanisms of power had diminished with the end of the New Deal and the advent of Termination, Jewish anthropologists remained engaged in advocacy on behalf of Native Americans during Termination. And if the late 1940s and early 1950s represented a major change in terms of eras for Native Americans, the handful of years also saw profound shifts in American Jewish periods. The Nazi war against the Jews was slowly being parsed out and understood, and the State of Israel was established in 1948. At the same time, early 1950s American Jewry was more enfranchised than ever before in American history. Jews proudly took their place alongside Protestants and Catholics as exalted subjects, accepted ideal types of Americans, in what Will Herberg famously called the triple melting pot.[131] Jewish difference was less visible than ever; Jewish communities were quickly suburbanizing, and overt forms of anti-Semitism were at an unprecedented low. But with respect to Jewish anthropological engagement with Indians, continuities were simply more important than the changes hastened by world historical events or major policy changes. If the postwar climate and the changes in modern Jewish affairs had any impact on those Jews who were interested in anthropology, it was that it made it easier for them to take up Jewish subjects in their professional lives and not just treat Jews and Jewish interests extracurricularly, as many of the anthropologists we have touched on did.

Examples from the late 1940s and 1950s abound.[132] Irene Rozeney, who wrote *Ojibwa Sociology* and *The Ojibwa Woman*, turned to study the Black Jews of Harlem and researched work on Jewish soldiers and the stereotype of Jewish quarreling.[133] Natalie Joffe, a fellow *Life Is with People* researcher, wrote on themes of acculturation and governance among Shoshone, Ute, and Fox Indians, as well as socioeconomic patterns among eastern European Jews.[134] Zellig Sabbetai Harris, born in Balta, Russia, founded the linguistics department at the University of Pennsylvania and worked on the Kota, Hidatsa, Cherokee, and Hebrew languages. The major issues that dominated his *political* work, on the other hand, were Jewish: Arab-Jewish relations, the kibbutz movement in Palestine, and the problems of American Jewry. Harris became a staunch kibbutznik, eventually splitting his time between research in American academia and a life of communal labor at Kibbutz Hazorea in the Jezreel Valley. Neither Joffe, Rozeney, or Harris felt the need to quietly exclude their interest in Jewish subjects from their professional pursuits.

The ICC and the Chicago Conference on American Indians

Two additional arenas in which Jewish anthropologists mobilized critical progressive-political contributions for what they conceived of as beneficial for Native Americans during Termination lay in the implementation of the ICC (discussed in chapter 5) and in the highly influential and generative Chicago Conference on American Indians (CCAI). Anthropological ideas and actors operated in spheres beyond classrooms, scholarly meetings, and the publication arms of the academic profession in the quasi-legal sphere of the ICC and in the grassroots political organizing forum of the CCAI.

The role of the anthropologist as expert witness at the ICC was tremendous. Lawyers trying cases between tribes and the federal government had used anthropologists as expert witnesses in cases well before the establishment of the ICC. The commissioners seemed to think that Native Americans involved in litigation against the federal government could not be seen as impartial bearers of historical, geographic, or ethnographic facts that had some bearing on their own claims. Oral history on the stand was not admissible. The suspicion of conflict of interest in these cases rendered Native American witnesses or elders unauthoritative. Believed to be the commission's most reliable, objective, and knowledgeable carriers of the legacy of Native American experience, at least as far as the commissioners themselves and the lawyers who aimed to persuade them were concerned, anthropologists dominated the expert witness role during the ICC's tenure.

Of course, defense attorneys at the ICC engaged anthropologists as experts too since state lawyers also needed expert witnesses in their fights against tribal claims. According to one historian of the ICC, competing arguments based on anthropologists' testimony confused the commissioners vested with the authority to resolve claims. The confusion also led to smears upon the integrity of both anthropologist and lawyers.[135] The ICC process and the expert witnesses who participated in it were riddled with challenges. The claims had to consider tricky extralegal matters about the nature and precise validity of treaties, about property boundaries in situations where no western-style ownership was ever practiced, about what constituted informed consent, and about who had the rightful authority to sign treaties on behalf of Indian groups. As detailed in chapter 5, some of the lawyers involved lacked the full breadth of experience and perspective to effectively engage the cases. Though anthropologists had sounder knowledge bases of the communities involved in claims cases than their attorneys, they were unaccustomed to the role and constraints of doing anthropology in a court-like setting. Experts were asked to establish property ownership from before contact with settlers even though the concept of ownership, in the European sense, did not exist for many Indigenous communities before contact. The lawyers and expert witnesses were likewise compelled to determine territorial exclusivity despite the vast variety among Native American systems and cultures of natural resource use. Even the basic terminology that was necessary to win claims in this Anglo-American legal sphere was unstable when it came to Native Americans: the word *tribe*, for example, was an artificial creation by whites. According to the anthropologist (and Jew) Milton Fried, experts were asked to "prove a lie": the idea that "claims for indemnification should require acceptance of a myth to satisfy the legal preconceptions of an infringing state"—including the acknowledgement of permanent land tenure and the idea of sale and alienation of land.[136]

The fact that scholars examining the same evidence often came to contrary conclusions, depending on which side of the case the particular anthropologist was hired to support, did not, however, undermine anthropologists' key roles in providing actionable facts to the commission. In the Chiricahua Apache Indians' claim, for example, the case pivoted around the testimony of Morris Opler, who at the time was the president of the American Anthropological Association, based on his research from the 1930s. The commission quoted extensively from Opler's testimony in its unanimous victory issued by the ICC in a land claim, which eventuated in a $16.5 million plus another $7 million in trespassory damages award.[137] The commission was convinced that 15.6 million acres had been taken illegally from the Apaches and should be valued based on the date when Geronimo surrendered in Skeleton Canyon in 1868.[138]

In addition to the ICC, the final key area of practical contribution that anthropologists made to Native American political-action organization in the pre–American Indian Movement era was in helping establish the American Indian Chicago Conference, which came into being largely because of Sol Tax and the Action Anthropology movement. There is perhaps no sharper example of the kind of political scholarship than the Action Anthropology, created in the early 1960s by Sol Tax and his students. Though Action Anthropology clearly grew out of the politically charged scholarship of the day, it was also clearly influenced by Tax's own Jewish milieu. Born in 1907 in Chicago to "mildly Zionist" Russian immigrant parents whose ancestors included a "line of rabbis," Tax was raised in Milwaukee's labor organization for youth socialists.[139] He conducted fieldwork among Mesquakie (Fox) and Sauk Indians in 1930s, and while his research focused on issues of kinship and social organization, he also served in more overtly political roles. He acted as the president of the NCAI and the Carnegie Corporation Cross-Cultural Education Project among Cherokee Indians in eastern Oklahoma, which was almost run aground by charges from the Cherokee establishment that the project was an attempt by Tax, a "Zionist Communist," to turn Cherokees into communists or Zionists.[140] Tax had worked together with Zimmerman and Lesser and the AAIA on issues of discrimination in Nebraska and on land ownership and social disintegration in Utah. He had written lectures, pamphlets, letters for funding, and progress reports as editor of *American Anthropologist* in the 1950s, deeply engaged in promoting a public education campaign for Native rights and recognition.[141] His scholarly work too was considerably more focused on practical, present-day, policy-oriented work than most of anthropological history prior, with essays that announced the kind of engaged scholarship he would come to symbolize for a generation of anthropologists. They bore titles like "Termination vs. The Needs of a Positive Policy for American Indians" and "Can Social Science Help to Set Values or Offer a Choice between Alternative Value Systems?"[142]

In the late 1940s, Tax developed Action Anthropology and concluded from his research experience, "It would be impossible for [anthropologists] to remain detached, aloof observers of the culture under investigation."[143] The alternative methodology he framed insisted, instead, that anthropologists "help a group of people solve a problem, and . . . learn something in the process."[144] Action Anthropology provided a method of community action that put community members rather than experts in charge of identifying their issues and creating solutions to remedy those issues, aiming to counteract some of the destructive consequences of terminating federal responsibilities to American Indian tribes whenever and wherever possible, by helping Indians themselves have a say in the matter. Action Anthropology found expression in the Fox Project from 1948 to 1962 at the Fort Berthold Reservation in North Dakota and many other sites.

This kind of grassroots, community-organizing perspective that Tax and others brought to anthropology was supported by the most influential of Native American advocacy groups of the 1960s, the National Conference of American Indians (NCAI).[145] Tax delivered the keynote address at its 1960 annual convention in Denver. Tax helped launch the American Indian Chicago Conference the next year. The Chicago Conference aimed to bring representatives of American Indian groups together to prepare statements about the conditions and needs of their people. It was a "major watershed in the history of contemporary native peoples" and politics.[146] Tax, together with Nancy Lurie and D'Arcy McNickle (Blackfoot), helped ensure that the conference was run for Indians by Indians. Tax found advisers and publicized results to the public and to those who formulated Indian policy.[147] Representatives at the conference presented a cross section of the American Indian community and included urban Indians, traditional Indians, modern Indians, and Indians from both recognized and nonrecognized tribes with several hundred people attending. The 439 registered attendees represented seventy-nine tribes, who together drafted "the Declaration of Indian Purpose," a document that dealt with problems and proposed approaches to solutions, which asked for a redirection of "the responsibility of the United States toward the Indian people in terms of a positive national obligation to modify or remove the conditions which produce the poverty and lack of social justice, as these prevail as the outstanding attributes of Indian life today."[148] Representatives of American Indian tribes presented the declaration to President John F. Kennedy in September 1962. The document—and the American Indian Chicago Conference—can, without exaggeration, be said to mark the emergence of self-determination as a policy objective for Native Americans.[149] Self-determination ideology became salient in the legal battles and lobbying efforts of the 1960s and the Red Power Movement in the 1970s and would continue to dominate the lion's share of Native American ideology for decades.[150]

While there is some debate about the extent to which Tax himself saw his Jewish identity as having any particular influence on his anthropological work or his politics, there can be little doubt that it had at least some influence. He kept his own "Jewish-ness File" in his records and toward the end of his life recalled that he had "always identified as Jewish," and had all his life "at least nominally kept Jewish dietary habits and restrictions and the major holidays," though he explicitly cautioned that he "never thought of [his Jewishness] as important in my life" and certainly it less influential than had been his socialist leanings.[151] But he himself suggested a link between his Jewish experience and his anthropological orientation, and unpublished materials from his early career suggest that his Jewishness was a more significant factor in the formation of his intellectual identity than later published autobiographical reflections suggest. His parents spoke Yiddish. His early education was in a *chaider*. He had a bar mitzvah.[152] As an undergraduate at the University of Wisconsin, where he dealt with the outbreak of "gentlemanly anti-Semitism" in 1928, most of his friends were Jewish communists. He wrote an editorial for the *Hillel Review* arguing that this anti-Semitism was "so deep in the social fabric" that there was "little hope" of eradicating it. At the time, Tax recommended that Jews "adjust" and "adapt" to "conditions as they exist."[153] He was involved in Hillel extracurricular activities to such an extent that his grades at the University of Chicago suffered; he was asked to leave the university.[154] Later in his life, Tax spoke of the profound influence that attending a Passover seder in Algeria with Arab Jews had on him in 1930.

And aside from these explicit elements of his Jewish biography, Tax—like so many of the Jewish anthropologists treated here before him—also put his Jewish existential investment into action. He involved himself with Jewish organizational life around Hyde Park and beyond; he was active at YIVO, the AJC, the ADL, the American Zionist Council, the B'nai B'rith, the Council of Hyde Park and Kenwood Churches and Synagogues, and the Hillel Foundation of the University of Chicago. In the early 1950s, Tax served on the national advisory board of the American Friends of ICHUD, Martin Buber's and Judah Magnes's Israel/Palestine unity movement.[155]

For Tax, as for many of the anthropologists described in this chapter, the Native and the Jewish investments never appeared to overlap or intersect. In an interview later in life, Tax recalled, "There was no occasion that I remember when the question arose" while conducting fieldwork among Native American groups, nor did he recall ever having "talked about it" with non-Indians with whom he worked. Despite this, later in life Tax came to feel that "[my] basic point of view in anthropology [was] influenced by my Jewish background."[156] For a colloquium on Jewish life in the United States in 1979, Tax used his own life experience as a "native participant" to offer "perspectives from anthropology." He made an analogy between the "miracle of Jewish survival" on the one hand and the fact of North American Indian societies "surviving against impossible odds with their basic religion and worldview intact" on the other.[157]

A Legacy of Influencers

Intersections between Jewish anthropologists and Native Americans continued among a number of Sol Tax's students and their students' students in turn as they had with Boas, his students, and his students' students and with Sapir, his students, and his students' students. There is a certain intergenerational transfer among anthropologists who "happened to be Jews" in evidence (though, of course, the profession was by no means an exclusively or explicitly Jewish one). Robert Rietz was a PhD under Sol Tax and one of the original six members of the Fox Project, which hoped to assist the members of the Three Affiliated Tribes (Hidatsa, Mandan, Arikara) in relocating from their lands following the construction of the Garrison Dam, approved in the late 1940s and concluded in 1953. In the early 1950s, Rietz worked as a community analyst and relocation officer for the BIA at the Fort Berthold Indian Reservation, North Dakota, and engaged in a number of other educational and health care projects meant to provide for Native American populations, including an arts and crafts cooperative called "Tamacraft" and the Summer Workshops for Native American Indian College Students, of which he was a founder, later working for the Native American Educational Services.[158] Rietz became the director of the American Indian Center in Chicago in 1958.[159]

One of Rietz's students, Alfred Wahrhaftig, described a fascinating experience in 1965 in which his Jewishness helped secure for him the trust of the Cherokee Indians with whom he hoped to work as an action anthropologist at the Briggs School house in rural Cherokee County, Oklahoma. He described "a confrontation [that had erupted] between armed and bellicose Cherokees and armed and hostile sheriffs [which] was likely to result in a disastrous shootout" after Delaware County law enforcement officials had arrested Cherokee members for hunting out of season and without hunting licenses. In an effort to forestall violence, someone suggested that the Cherokee men wait for someone "from Washington" who could brief them on their treaty rights. According to Wahrhaftig's account, one Cherokee man "objected [to Wahrhaftig serving in that roll], pointing out that I was a white man." Another speaker, however, "opined that I was not a white man; I was a Jew," after which there followed "a long discussion [which] had to do with whether Jews are white men or not." The discussion is one of the rare instances on record of Native Americans assessing the racial status of American Jews. Wahrhaftig reported that "the consensus was that Jews are not white men. They are like a tribe of Indians from the other side of the water and, as they have a language of their own, a home land, and a sacred history attested in the Bible, they are unlike white men who have none of these."[160]

These Cherokee men concluded that Jews were Indigenous Peoples, evidenced by their having a language, a homeland presumably in the State of Israel, and sacred history, enshrined in scripture attesting to its historicity. "On these grounds, I continued to serve as the English language secretary of what came to be known as the Five County Northeastern Cherokee Organization and later as the Original Cherokee Community Organization."[161]

The episode was a rare case in which the anthropologist's Jewishness played a decisive and explicit role in allowing him to take on a role as an anthropologist and activist among Native people in the era of aggressive, sometimes militant self-determination that dominated the landscape of mid-1960s American Indian life. Wahrhaftig's story is perhaps the fullest extension of the subject position and its influence that we have seen, even if Wahrhaftig himself did not make a big deal out of the Jewish background that may have helped shape his anthropology. Rare though this explicit intersection was, important continuities characterize the work and experience of several generations of American Jewish anthropologists. While some twinned their interests in Jews and Native Americans, and still others distanced themselves from all matters Jewish as they pursued Indian work, they were consistently committed to a similar set of social concerns. This consistency was maintained *irrespective* of the major Jewish events of the mid-twentieth century: immigration restriction, the Holocaust, and the founding of the State of Israel. It was maintained *irrespective* of the place of birth of the anthropologist in question. The German, Hungarian, Austrian, Russian, Latvian, Hungarian, Lithuanian, Polish, and Mexican-born anthropologists shared far more in common with their American-born counterparts than they differed from their non-Jewish immigrant counterparts.

While this legacy has not been fully assessed, there can be little doubt that dozens of Jewish anthropologists taught at dozens of universities, for dozens of years each, and would have made some meaningful impact on countless numbers of university students, some portion of which would do further work in or for Native American communities. Over the course of at least five decades, Jewish scholars reached and influenced thousands of students regarding all sorts of matters of Indian life, in rural and urban settings, in all regions of the United States. They trained countless individuals who, after obtaining their college degrees, found work in Indian policy, law, business, and the arts at the federal, state, and county levels, offering them most likely the first sustained intellectual exposure to untold numbers of future educators who taught non-Indians about Indian life in high schools and grade school classrooms. Three decades of anthropological writing about American Indians *essentially replaced* America's bookshelves' books about Indians. Where once there had been missionary writing, armchair ethnology, and half fiction, anthropology went some distance in revamping America's knowledge about Native Americans with what it conceived of as unbiased social science description, classification, and analysis.

Treating the "Jewish element" of any single anthropologist would yield a certain kind of debate about the extent to which he or she acknowledged or appreciated how his or her Jewish background influenced his work, whether or not it mattered or should be debated. While these debates are legitimate, attention to the individual trees blinds us to a larger forest fact—namely, that publicly engaged Jewish scholars made material impacts on Native Americans, on policies affecting them, and on countless non-Indians whose ideas and actions contributed to the shaping of Native American life in the second half of the twentieth century. American anthropology and its engagement with Native Americans is, in part, an American Jewish story. The point is not to celebrate Jewish contributions to social justice history or the American left. Rather, aggregating the work of these anthropologists, and seeing their lives' works in the broader context of American Jewish encounters with Native Americans, reveals how American Jews as a whole grappled with the predicaments of the broader context in which they and their communities and families belonged—namely, colonial settlement modernity. In this sense too, Jews were implicated in empire; they gained social capital and benefitted financially by producing knowledge about Indians.

These anthropologists certainly expended effort to maintain Indian difference in the spirit of pluralism and liberalism; they promoted Indian cultural autonomy, Indian arts, and even to some extent political autonomy. Most did not argue on behalf of the same for Jews. For them, Jewishness was more frequently a subset of American liberalism. They insisted on the absence of race, yet were often silent on the distinctiveness of Jews. Fascinating is that they actively promoted Indian difference in empathic, nonjudgmental, respectful language, seeing themselves as those who could speak to a broader American public about American Indian life and identity. In their popular writing for larger nonacademic audiences, these scholars critiqued America, western imperialism (in the cultural and pop cultural spheres as much as in the political-historical one), and the impacts of European domination over Indian life. If scholars paired but did not partner their intellectual interests, perused them in parallel but without connection or integration, they did so because Jewish matters touched deeply personal and sometimes tremendously ambivalent nerves. Indian interests, on the other hand, offered fascinating and sometimes pressing moral, intellectual, and theoretical cases to work with. The basis for their utility lay in their foreignness. Where writing too much about Jewishness would have compromised their scholarly pursuit, credentials, and the antirace agenda that animated them, Indians provided a kind of foil that boosted these scholars' Americanness by separating them from their foreign subjects. Indian difference, unlike Jewish difference, was of another order to the white, affluent, enfranchised elites among whom these Jewish scholars lived and identified. They rarely recognized that Jews might have played a role in this process or had something to gain from it. For them, western American colonists, whenever and wherever they came from, were never ethnic; they were white, unambiguously powerful, and Christian. That is, Jewish liberals did not see themselves as settler colonial Jews or descendants of them (despite the substantial history of Jews as settler colonists outlined in the first half of this book).

CONCLUSION

PATHS OF PERSECUTION, STAKES OF COLONIAL MODERNITY

The emergence of Jewish activists and scholars who advocated for Native Americans in the early and middle decades of the twentieth century signaled a seismic change from the ways that American Jews had, for the most part, imagined and interacted with Native Americans in the preceding half century. A general arc of Jewish representations of Native peoples spanned the course of this hundred years, from vehicles or impediments for mobility and integration on the expanding frontier to communities in need of uplift and empowerment in an America whose geography had been secured but for whom the issue of racial belonging had not. If Jewish immigrants saw Indians as tools or adversaries in finding a settled place in the frontier West, by the time Jews reaped the rewards of their political enfranchisement and economic mobility, many came to identify with Native Americans' experience of historical persecution and marginalization and see Native American communities, their lives, and their corporate historical experience as apt subjects for their (Jewish) advocacy efforts.

Of course, these engagements between Jews and Native Americans and the ways they fit into the larger dynamics of colonization, migration, persecution, and privilege did not end in the late 1960s. In fact, Jewish-Native encounters became even more robust during the civil rights era and even thicker into the current period of Native American history, generally labeled the age of Indian Self-Determination. A wide discursive field emerged that has sought to draw out parallels between Jews and Native Americans for varied, and sometimes competing, purposes. There is much insight to be gained from a careful examination of this late twentieth- and early twenty-first-century material.[1] A cursory sketch, however, suggests that these contemporary interactions center on the following frequently overlapping old themes with new valences: (1) religious preservation, including foci on linguistic revival, religious poetry, cultural autonomy, and the articulation of environmentalism through a religious lens; (2) artistic expressions of communal identity; (3) social justice activism; (4) heritage of suffering including genocide, trauma, resistance, and recovery; and (5) national consciousness and sovereignty (including engagement about Israel and Zionism). There are surprising ways that Jewish history and Aboriginal history are intertwined and, at least to some extent, mutually constitutive.

Since the 1970s, mainstream Jewish institutions like federations, JCCs, Jewish youth movements, parochial day schools, and each of the Jewish religious denominations have initiated, sponsored, and facilitated many more interactions between Jews and Native Americans. Jewish interest in Native American issues began compounding in intensity and complexity in the 1990s, when synagogues, local Jewish organizations, and the major national organizations began programming with Native American partners.

Recent decades have seen the emergence of religious fusion and religious encounters designed by rabbis and Jewish educators for their congregants and youth groups that explore the parallels between Jewish and Native American spiritualties. Rabbis in the American Southwest have run programs with elders and local shamans in synagogues, community centers and sweat lodges. Jews and Native people across the continent have run programs exploring a wide range of themes, including creation stories, language revivals, and conceptions of nature, sacred lands, and landscape. Events have blended religious ceremonies, ritual objects, and religious themes, including Aboriginal-focused Passover seders that reinterpret the "ten plagues" of the traditional Passover Haggadah as the plagues of colonialism, with Indigenous additions to the seder plate.

There is now a new wellspring of cultural creativity—films, poems, novels, installations, performance art, musical creations, and visual and plastic art—that addresses overlaps in themes, characters, and histories of Jews and Natives, like Charles Heller's and Rivka Golani's chamber music, *The Two Ravens*, which blended Blackfoot musical motifs and themes with Jewish ones, explicitly intended as inspirational music for both spiritual redemption and political reconciliation. Michael Chabon's novel, *The Yiddish Policeman's Union*, one among many novels and plays written by Jewish authors since the 1980s that have dealt with Native American themes or characters, featured Jewish and Tlingit Alaskan Native characters interacting in a counterfactual world in which Jews settle a temporary national homeland in Alaska after World War II.[2] Contemporary artists who share both Jewish and Indigenous ancestry, like Howard Adler, Nathan Adler, David Treuer, Jennifer Podemsky, Winona LaDuke, and others have explored hybrid identity and emerging themes in their poetry and film. Gordon Bronitsky, a culture promoter and booster (with a PhD in anthropology) has organized dozens of Jewish-Native interactivities and performances of song, dance, and visual art that dovetail Jewish and Native creative expressions.[3] Day-trip tours, art and museum exhibitions, lecturers, and symposia have appeared. Contemporary filmmakers have explored parallels too (including one called

"CowJews and Indians" that documents a filmmaker's efforts to have Germany pay World War II reparations directly to Native American communities on whose land displaced Jews settled—"cutting out the middleman," in the filmmaker's language—and a film about the adventures of the nineteenth-century Jewish photographer and explorer with the Fremont Expedition, Solomon Nuñes Carvalho and his encounters with Cheyenne, Delaware, and Ute Indians).

There are also now websites, documentary films, and opportunities for religious exchange between Jewish and Native communities and individuals. There are a growing number of Jewish-Indigenous youth programs—programs that focus on some aspect of genocide, language loss and preservation, and traumatic recovery. There have been junkets of Native American leaders to Israel and literally hundreds of newspaper editorials and articles about Native Americans in the American Jewish press and an equally rich trove of commentary and coverage of Jews (and Israel) in the Native American press.

Recent decades have also seen the proliferation of Jewish expressions of political and social solidarity with Native American battles, like the "Idle No More" campaign or the Standing Rock Dakota Access movement, by individual Jews in social work, academic and activist circles, in the popular and Jewish presses, and by Jewish organizational bodies large and small, including Ve'ahavta, the AJC, The Union for Reform Judaism, the Central Conference of American Rabbis, and the Religious Action Center of Reform Judaism. Jewish institutions have articulated official positions on Native American justice issues and have mobilized in political action to advance their visions of Jewish, American, and humanitarian justice. There are now health impact initiatives that Jewish organizations run in rural Indigenous communities and programs to combat homelessness, poverty, addiction, and violence run by Jewish doctors, nurses, and social workers in rural and urban settings. Individual Jewish policy advisers and philanthropists, lobbyists, lawyers, and political consultants are among the many non-Indigenous activists who work for change in Native American communities throughout North America.

But the two most common threads that Jews have interwoven with and about Native Americans in the recent engagements come together around themes and issues related to genocide and sovereignty. There has been no shortage of tension and disagreement in the comparative genocide debates, in American public and scholarly discussions about the Holocaust and other mass traumas, about the word *genocide*, and in the politics of recognition and funding vis-à-vis public and privately supported museums and commemorations.[4] But there is also a growing discourse by Jews and Native people around perceptions and articulations of shared or parallel histories of persecution, resistance, and renaissance. Jews and Native Americans have gathered to discuss and invent rituals of healing the wounds of collective trauma. Educators, community activists, lawyers, elders, therapists, youth leaders, poets, rabbis, and chiefs created and participated in tribal healing circles, testimony performances, and reconciliation marches (events that might, for example, end with benedictions in a sukkah, with the sounding of a shofar, or with the ceremonial smoking of tobacco).

Finally, in respect to national sovereignty, there are literally hundreds of mentions of Native Americans in Jewish newspapers and hundreds of mentions of Jews or Israel in Native American newspapers (and hundreds more of Palestinians and Palestine). There have been dozens of missions that Jews have organized to pay for Native American leaders, youth groups, women's groups, environmental advocates, poets, and artists to Israel. One "mission" brought a Manitoba grand chief David Harper, Australian Aboriginal leaders, Inuit leaders, and Indigenous figureheads from Samoa and Greenland to Israel—to the floor of Israel's Knesset, in fact—meant to perform the idea that *we are all Indigenous Peoples.* (There has also been a parallel stream of similar junkets arranged by Palestinians for Native American leaders and groups to travel to the Palestinian territories.)

Indeed, the subtext of some of the recent American Jewish interest in Native America, whether or not Israel is explicitly evoked, seems to be inextricably related to American Jews' passionate and fierce disagreements about the nature and virtue of Jewish settlement and sovereignty in the Middle East and the extent to which the State of Israel was, is, or ought to be conceived of as a colonial state, an anticolonial state, or a postcolonial state. This book began with a claim that exile and aboriginality were flipsides of the same conceptual coin in the late nineteenth century. The idea of *exile* had lost its popular purchase by the turn of the twenty-first century. The conceptual coin of today's discussion puts *colonist* on one side and *Indigenous* on the obverse. These twin concepts (and related keywords like *pioneering*, *settler*, *original*, and *aboriginal*) were and remain central concepts in Zionism, in American expansion, and in many other movements of migrants that involved vexing conundrums of displacement. Hotly contested, morally freighted, and explosive terms remain central to historiographical and political conceptualizations of histories of both Israel and the United States.[5] In the unresolved debates about the extent to which Zionism is/was a form of colonialism, of European expansionism, of pioneering, and/or of sovereignty reclamation by an oppressed nation, American Jews have made strategic uses the rhetoric of *aboriginality* or *indigeneity*.

I have no interest or capacity to resolve these debates, and I believe that adding these analogies to the discussion may just obscure more than it clarifies. There is little doubt, however, that these terms are battlegrounds because they resonate. What is more, the contemporary nexus of interests—still waiting to be fully unpacked—and the subtext of the recent interactions between Jews and Native Americans, in the institutions and in the pages of both Jewish and Native Americans magazines and journals, scholarly articles and editorials, are part of a global grappling with the *legacies of colonialism* and postcolonial realities. The United States is no exception; it too is among the nations, and its minorities are among the minorities struggling with the long history of empire. Similar debates are afoot in Canada, Australia, New Zealand, South Africa, Argentina, and elsewhere. Both Zionism and American Jewish settlement are part of a much larger—and genuinely complex moral and political—story of Jewish *colonial modernity*.

The discomfiting questions about how Jews fit into the broad story of global modernity—a story in which colonialism was and remains as central as capitalism—animates all discussion about Jewish and Native encounters. The American past, including the Jewish American past, is burdened by colonialism because the history of mass migration, of the relocation of Jews from Europe, Asia, North Africa, and the Middle East to the edges of western empires, *is* the history of colonialism. Mass migration, with all of its politics of inhabitation, is the sine qua non of modernity writ large.

Jews' interactions with Indians, both real and imagined, wavered between kinship and exoticism, cooperation and competition, fascination and exploitation. American Jews of the late twentieth and early twenty-first centuries expended effort to maintain Indian difference in the spirit of pluralism and liberalism; they promoted Indian cultural autonomy, Indian arts, and even to some extent political autonomy. Yet fascinatingly, American Jews seldom recognized or even hinted that Jews themselves might have played a role or contributed in any way as actors in this process. They did not look for Jews as agents of settler colonialism; they did not find them.

Colonialism and immigration connote very different things but denote the same process: the mass relocation of millions of Europeans to the American continent and the changes and impacts this human encounter wrought. The immigrants are part of the Native American story just as Native Americans are a part of American immigrant history. The great transformation of modern Jewry—namely, the long nineteenth century of migration—is not just a story of mobility and motility. The metanarrative of Jewish mass-migration that scholars of American Jewry still often tell is a heroic tale of immigrant ascent. The political and social conditions of New World liberal democracies, so the story goes, provided unique opportunities for Europe's wretched refuse, "the poor, tired, huddled masses yearning to breathe free," as the Jewish poet Emma Lazarus famously described them on the Statue of Liberty. Rather, the fundamental relocation of world Jewry from Europe to its peripheries ought to be seen as a story of conflict and contest, of the politics and possibilities of colonial encounters. There is a certain disconnect between the Native American rights and recognition activism of the left-leaning Jewish social scientists of the 1930s, 1940s, 1950s, and 1960s and their critique of American imperialism, colonialism, and its impact on Native American lives, on the one hand, and the fact that ethnic immigration history, including the Jewish experience, was part of the same broad process that so deleteriously impacted Native American life.

Native Americans occupied a peripheral but revealing place in the American Jewish popular consciousness. Judging from the sheer volume of cultural artifacts Jews produced about Native Americans, and these sources' and historical actors' fundamental heterogeneity, Jews made wide use of the Native Americans they invented and encountered. This body of discussion reflected Jews' creative efforts to understand themselves in light of America's second, if unstable, other (African Americans being the country's quintessential white foil) and the large forces of colonial settlement in which they belonged. Letters, memoirs, diaries, photographs, business ledgers, government reports, petitions, organizational documents, and family scrapbooks reveal what Jewish encounters with actual Native Americans looked like. In the essays, newspaper articles, local history books, and scholarly writings Jews authored about American Indian life, Jews wrote a version of their own roles and relationships with Native Americans as part of their efforts to plot themselves at the center of conventional American history narratives and, in a sense, to "write over" the colonial narrative. In their imaginary and face-to-face encounters with Native people, Jews put their Indian entanglements to use serving the same ultimate end—namely, to ground Jews in America. Jews operationalized Indians, in effect, for the twin ends of integrating themselves into the dominant power structures of white America and of articulating a sense of kinship with America's historically persecuted minority.

Jews imagined and related to Native America similarly to the ways other whites did but also with their own particular glosses as they tapped into the rich vein of American mythologies about American Indians. They reenacted the conflict between colonial whites and the Indians, at times proudly identifying as victorious settlers. When casting themselves in the role of pioneer or cowboy in their lived experience in the West, Jews suffered little hesitation about seeing their involvement in the settling of America in a positive light, turning themselves into heroic figures of a well-worn plot. Like other settler populations, Jews have tried to exculpate unconscious guilt of their ancestors' colonial sins with various "moves to innocence," for example, by claiming kinship bonds with Native peoples or by promoting their work to lessen some of the impacts of the colonial encounter as Jewish work.[6] Jewish engagements with Native Americans contained particularly Jewish resonances and problems, caught between liberalism and tribalism, the colonized others of Europe acting as colonizers.

Just how central or marginal should historians consider Jews to be for the overarching colonial process in which they took part and from which they benefited? On the one hand, Jews filled needed roles in the expansion enterprise that furthered imperial realities. Expansion required ideology and promise as well as the commercial traffic of merchandise, food, and supplies with which settlement was physically built. Jews played an important role in supplying the materials and commercial connections required for the development of colonies as peddlers, post traders, clothiers, and suppliers to miners, fur traders, homesteaders, gold rushers, and U.S. Army camps in Arizona, New Mexico, Colorado, Nebraska, Alaska, and elsewhere throughout the West. Jews very much participated in the long colonial saga of American Indian dispossession.[7]

On the other hand, Jews did not form part of the elite that shaped either the broad politics of expansion or the intellectual justification for it from its origins in the sixteenth century (or even earlier) through the turn of the twentieth. American Jews helped shape state power over Native Americans during the New Deal era; the policies they shaped were more progressive and liberal than any to date but were ultimately statist and, from a contemporary Indigenous perspective, therefore "recolonizing" as well. Jews did not drive the colonial process as its engines in any grossly overrepresented way. "Jewish interests" did not provide any particular motivation for American expansion or, for that matter, in Native American dislocation. Rather, Jewish actors played a part in it—a creative, meaningful part—on the practical, commercial, and ideational fronts. Jews strenuously participated in American expansionism, aiming to prove their fitness as settlers and history-making actors, even as non-Jews often excluded them or simply ignored them in the writing of the national myth of heroic but unspecified "immigrant" frontiersmen who shed their European and immigrant pasts to win the West for America.[8]

Different forces shaped interactions between Jews and Native Americans at different times and in different places. The heterogeneity of these engagements, of which this book represents the first effort at synthesis, signals not only a history with change and diversity over time and across space but also a space of encounter that allowed for Jews to advance their changing concerns and needs *through* Native Americans in remarkably plastic ways.

To what extent did Jews embrace or enable the power structures that determined and implemented policy? Did they resist it or speak against it? While moral judgment certainly lies beyond the scope of the professional historian, a significant historiographic issue underlies this question. Historians of Jewish America featured Jewish participation in the settlement process in order to underscore the idea of the West's religious latitude, its democratic flexibility, and its social landscape as one that promoted the production of a new national white type despite Jews' best efforts to retain simultaneous allegiance to other Jews and Jewish community, culture, and religion. Attention to Jewish-Indian encounters suggests that Jewish historians have quietly written Jews out of the colonial story, avoiding explicit discussions about ways that Jewish migration, life, and the conditions under which Jewish persecution and privilege fit into the larger dynamic from which no group is exempt.

I hope this study offered some aid in recasting Jewish immigration history into the broad context into which parochial immigration properly fits but within which it is rarely cast—namely, capitalist and colonial expansion. This reframing contests the celebratory narrative that is generally inherited as Jewish received memory and cuts against the grain of much of modern Jewish historiography more generally. Though Jews fled Europe and Russia as relatively powerless victims of continental imperialism, they arrived in the Americas as relatively powerful agents of French, Dutch, and British colonialism. Seen from the West and with Native Americans in mind, the Jewish experience of mass relocation across continents that so fundamentally shaped Jewish modernity was, ipso facto, an experience of forging a frontier.

This book aimed, foremost, to unsettle the generally triumphant consensus history of American Jewish life by focusing on the ways that Jewish class mobility and civic belonging were wrapped up in the dynamics of power, commerce, historical narrative, and myth making that so severely impacted Native Americans. It also aimed to historicize Jewish liberal work on behalf of Native Americans by showing how intimately Jewish lawyers, philanthropists, and scholars interwove their commitments to Native empowerment and uplift with Jewish interests; their advocacy work was an outgrowth of their efforts to laud a version of pluralism and minority rights that advanced their own Jewish interests but ironically recapitulated some of the fundamental structures of colonialism.

Ultimately this book is about Jewish participation in, and Jews' grappling with, the legacies of the colonial project upon which America rests. American Jews both participated in the ongoing colonial enterprise and resisted it—at different times, in different places, and for different reasons. They also grappled with their roles in it, at times celebrating it, at other times evading their culpability in its impacts, and at still other times expending enormous amounts of energy to alleviate its deleterious effects (in ways that both undermined and reinforced structures of dominance over Native people). They did so both as Jews and as Americans, even as their respective commitments to both Judaism and America shifted. The grappling is ongoing.

ACKNOWLEDGMENTS

I have accumulated immeasurable intellectual and personal debts to a wonderful web of supporters over the course of working on this book, and I am pleased, at long last, to be able to offer some necessarily underwritten words of gratitude about them here.

This project benefited from generous fellowships, awards, and bursaries from the Wexner Foundation, the Foundation for Jewish Culture, the Center for Jewish History, the American Jewish Archives, the Myer and Rosaline Feinstein Center for American Jewish History at Temple University, the American Academy of Jewish Research, the Goldstein-Goren Center for American Jewish History at New York University, the Western Canadian Jewish Historical Centre, and the Faculty of Liberal Arts & Professional Studies of York University.

When I began researching Jewish-Native American encounters, I had my doubts that I would be able to find enough of a paper trail to make any sort of historical argument. It started as somewhat of a fishing expedition. Dozens of archivists, librarians, and fellow scholars—really far too many to list here—crisscrossing the entire continent helped me identify primary source materials. I'm afraid I lost some of my e-mail archives that include the names of some who have helped, but I appreciate everyone who sent nuggets my way. Thanks to the particularly supportive archivists Kevin Proffitt and the team at the American Jewish Archives in Cincinnati, George Miles at Yale's Beinecke, and Jennifer Anna at the American Jewish Historical Society. Joel Weiss, Daniel Rosenthal, and Jordana de Bloeme helped me find or work through a portion of primary sources in German and Yiddish. I'm also grateful for the single-archive source-gathering help provided by Rafi Stern and Amanda Franey, among others. Josh Falek provided some clutch last-minute support with image permissions.

The Departments of History and Hebrew & Judaic Studies at NYU provided a supportive and engaged environment for the rigorous training I gained as a graduate student when this project began. I am grateful to the entire faculty and staff. Bob Chazan guided me through three degrees, two fellowships, and two stimulating public history enterprises. Barbara Kirshenblatt-Gimblett has been particularly inspiring, and I'm grateful for the ways she blurs the boundaries between scholarship, mentorship, and friendship. Shayne Figeroa was my NYU administrative angel. My dissertation committee, including BGK, Thomas Bender, Marion Kaplan, Andrew Needham, and my primary supervisor, Hasia Diner, focused their formidable intellectual powers on thinking well about my work. Sitting in the dissertation defense room with these wonderful scholars discussing my work and debating further directions it might next go provided me with encouragement that cannot be overstated. To Hasia I owe my deepest debt of gratitude. She has been my true mentor, an ally, and a steadfast champion of my work and growth since I began graduate work, and she has stuck with me since. She manages to balance precision and nurturance, encouragement and challenge, responsiveness and latitude.

I am likewise grateful for the opportunities offered to me to present parts of the research contained in this book as I worked to pull the material together into a coherent whole: Jonathan Boyarin at the American Indian and Indigenous Studies Program and the Jewish Studies Program at Cornell University, Gary Zola at the Jacob Rader Marcus Center at the American Jewish Archives, Laura Levitt at the Race & Judaism Symposium at Temple University's Center for Afro-Jewish Studies, Jessica Fechtor at the Home, Nation & Landedness in Modern Jewish Life Conference at Harvard University, Jonathan Schorsch at the Jews, Native Americans, and the Western World Order Conference at Columbia University, Rebecca Kobrin at the Jews and American Capitalism Conference at Columbia and NYU, Ira Robinson and the Concordia University Institute for Canadian Jewish Studies, and Boyd Cothran and Carolyn Podruchny at the History of Indigenous Peoples' (HIP) Network at York University. I received engaged and useful feedback from these special small gatherings, just as I have at the meetings of the American Historical Association, the Association for Jewish Studies, and the Association for Canadian Jewish Studies meetings I've managed to attend.

My colleagues at York University, for whom I'm entirely grateful for making a nest for me, have supported me over the last few years on the tenure track as I've taken on new roles and tried to find time to complete this work. They are as sharp and warm a bunch as any professional scholar could wish for. Particular thanks to Boyd Cothran, Marcel Martel, Marlene Shore, Molly Ladd Taylor, Bill Wicken, Jennifer Bonnell, Margaret Schotte, Sakis Gekas, Jonathan Edmondson, Deb Neill, and Thabit Abdullah in History, and to Carl Ehrlich, Sara Horowitz, Laura Wiseman, Yedida Eisenstat, and Kalman Weiser at the Israel and Golda Koschitzky Centre for Jewish Studies.

Elisabeth Maselli, my editor at Rutgers University Press, has been a pleasure to work with and has helped guide me, a neophyte, over the waters of book publishing. I also would like to express my gratitude to the anonymous readers of manuscript versions of this book as well as to Jeffrey Shandler, Matti Bunzel, and Marlie Wasserman, each of whom lent an editorial hand along the RUP way.

For their encouragement and critical dialogue with the key ideas in this book, I would also like to thank my colleagues and friends Rachel Rubinstein, Nancy Sinkoff, Jeanne Abrams, Ava Kahn, Rebecca Kobrin, Riv-Ellen Prell, Ellen Eisenberg, Hesh Troper, Richard Menkis, Daniel Septimus, Micah Kelber, Yona Shemtov, Evan Wolkenstein, Luke Whitmore, David Moscovitch, Caleb Yong, Dara Solomon, Miriam Margles, Tamara Edwards, and Melissa Weintraub. Extra appreciations are deserved for Jenna Weissman Joselit, Jonathan Sarna, Kalman Weiser, Rachel Kranson, Josh Lambert, Stephanie Schwartz, and Derek Penslar, under whose supervision I enjoyed a wonderful Social Science and Humanities Research Council of Canada postdoctoral fellowship at the Department of History at the University of Toronto. All seven read manuscript drafts and provided ample, careful, and valuable notes and suggestions. Their feedback and encouragement improved this work tremendously. Of course, the flaws that remain in this version rest entirely on my shoulders.

Finally, my always-supportive family, Donna and Gerry, Jordy and Evelyn, Michael and Melyssa, Ron and Sandy: you make it possible to leave for work with an open mind, and you make leaving work a pleasure. Stevie, Oriolle, and Gideon, your exuberance and curiosity have been truly inspirational. And Samantha! You read this manuscript more diligently and attentively than anyone, and you helped me through the frustrations and doubts that such a large project inevitably entails. Without you, your keen readership and patience, your support and love, not only have I no manuscript; I have no home.

NOTES

INTRODUCTION — EXILE AND ABORIGINALITY, KINSHIP AND DISTANCE

1. Mordecai Manuel Noah, *Discourse on the Evidences of the American Indians Being the Descendants of the Lost Tribes of Israel* (New York: James Van Norde, 1837), reprinted in Frederick Marryat's *Diary in America* (London, 1839) and translated into German in 1838. See also "The American Indian and the Lost Tribes of Israel," the introduction to a reprint of Mordecai Manuel Noah's *Discourse* in *Midstream* 17, no. 5 (1971): 49–64. The proclamation itself was widely reprinted in non-Jewish journals and newspapers contemporaneously.

2. See Robert Wauchope, *Lost Tribes and Sunken Continents: Myth and Method in the Study of American Indians* (Chicago: University of Chicago Press, 1962); Ronald Sanders, *Lost Tribes and Promised Lands: The Origins of American Racism* (Boston: Little, Brown, 1978); Zvi Ben-Dor Benite, *The Ten Lost Tribes: A World History* (New York: Oxford University Press, 2009).

3. The earliest Jewish reference to Indian-Israelite theory can be found in David Gans's *Nehmad we-Na'im*, written in 1613, though its central concern was with cosmography and astronomy. Manachem Mann ben Salomon Halevi in *Sheerit Yisrael*, Amsterdam, 1771, maintained that a prophecy of Isaiah had reference to America and that already in Isaiah's time many Jews lived in the western world. Most famously was Menasseh Ben Israel's *The Hope of Israel*, printed in London by R. I. for Hannah Allen at the Crown in Popes-head Alley, 1650. The Jewish popular press also enthusiastically reprinted Indian-Israelite claims. See, for example, *Die Deborah*, March 16, 1866, 147; *Sabbath Blatt*, no. 35/36 (August 30 and September 6, 1845); "Are the American Indians the Descendants of the Jews?," *Sabbath-Blatt*, no. 34 (August 23, 1845); *Allgemeine Zeitung des Judentums* 2, no. 132 (November 3, 1838): 533; *Allgemeine Zeitung des Judentums* 54, no. 13 (April 11, 1890): 5. In America, the claim had been championed in works such as Israel Worsley, *View of the American Indians: Shewing Them to Be Descendants of the Ten Tribes of Israel; The Language of Prophecy concerning Them and the Course by Which They Traveled from Media to America* (London, 1828); Harriette Livermore, *The Harp of Israel, to Meet the Loud Echo in the Wilds of America. By a Mourning Pilgrim Bound to the Promised Land* (Philadelphia, 1835); Ethan Smith, *View of the Hebrews; or The Tribes of Israel in America* (Poultney, Vt.: Smith & Shute, 1825), 217–225; and dozens of others.

4. Walter Hart Blumenthal, the bibliophile, Lincolniana collector, and Jewish literary critic, compiled perhaps the finest work of scholarship chronicling the claims and claimants. His unpublished manuscript, compiled though the 1920s as *In Old America: The Lost Ten Tribes of Israel. Prehistoric Peopling of America: A Bibliographic Survey of the Early Theory*

of Israelitish Derivation, and the Origin of the American Indians, annotated one-thousand-plus pages of bibliographic citations, arranged by theories of the origins of American Indians into themes and competing claims. American Jewish Archives (AJA), Cincinnati, Ohio, manuscript collection (MC) 229, box 1 of 1. A seventy-nine-page précis of the manuscript was published as Walter Hart Blumenthal, *In Old America: Random Chapters on the Early Aborigines* (New York: Walton Book Company, 1931).

5. Jonathan Sarna, *Jacksonian Jew: The Two Worlds of Mordecai Noah* (New York: Holmes and Meier, 1981).

6. Lewis F. Allen, "Founding of the City of Ararat on Grand Island—by Mordecai M. Noah," *Publications of the American Jewish Historical Society* 26 (1918): 173–200; "Stories of Major Noah," *Jewish Progress* 30, no. 45 (July 9, 1894): whole no. 1050; see also Thomas E. Connolly and Selig Adler, *From Ararat to Suburbia: The History of the Jewish Community of Buffalo* (Philadelphia: Jewish Publication Society of America, 1960); Sarna, *Jacksonian Jew*; and Michael Schuldiner and Daniel J. Kleinfeld, eds., *Selected Writings of Mordecai Noah* (Westport, Conn.: Greenwood, 1999).

7. Isaac Leeser, "What Can Be Done?," *Occident and American Jewish Advocate* 10, no. 9 (December 1852): 418–419.

8. Leeser, "What Can Be Done?"

9. He published similarly excited articles for nearly a decade. See the *Occident and American Jewish Advocate* 18 (1860): 153, 219–220; "Sacred Stones of the Vicinity of Newark, Licking County, Ohio," *Occident and American Jewish Advocate* 24 (1867): 65–77, 107–115; "The Alphabet on the Decalogue-Stone Found near Newark, Ohio," *Occident and American Jewish Advocate* 25 (1868): 526–529.

10. "Stories of Major Noah," whole no. 1050.

11. Wise took the claims seriously enough to grapple with them in print, even if he ultimately distanced Jews from Indians. *Israelite* 7, no. 2 (Cincinnati, July 13, 1860): 10; *Israelite* 7, no. 13 (September 28, 1860): 102; *Israelite* 7, no. 19 (November 9, 1860): 146; *Israelite* 7, no. 20 (November 16, 1860): 157.

12. Robert Berkhofer Jr., *The White Man's Indian: Images of the American Indian from Columbus to the Present* (New York: Knopf, 1978).

13. U.S. Commissioner of Indian Affairs, statistical supplement to *Annual Report of the Commissioner of Indian Affairs* (1940), 30.

14. This literature is now quite robust. See, for example, Hasia Diner, *In the Almost Promised Land: American Jews and Blacks, 1915–1935* (Baltimore: Johns Hopkins University Press, 1977); Lenwood Davis, *Black-Jewish Relations in the United States 1752–1984: A Selected Bibliography* (Westport, Conn.: Greenwood, 1984); Gretchen Sullivan Sorin, Adina Back, and Jack Salzman, *Bridges and Boundaries: African Americans and American Jews* (New York: George Braziller, 1992); Murray Friedman, *What Went Wrong? The Creation and Collapse of the Black-Jewish Alliance* (New York: Free Press, 1995); Vincent P. Franklin, *African Americans and Jews in the Twentieth Century: Studies of Convergence and Conflict* (Columbia: University of Missouri Press, 1998); Maurianne Adams and John H. Bracey, *Strangers and Neighbors: Relations between Blacks and Jews in the United States* (Amherst: University of Massachusetts Press, 1999); Cheryl Lynn Greenberg, *Troubling the Waters: Black-Jewish Relations in the American Century* (Princeton: Princeton University Press, 2006).

15. See Leora Auslander, "The Boundaries of Jewishness, or When Is a Cultural Practice Jewish?," *Journal of Modern Jewish Studies* 8, no. 1 (March 2009): 47–64; Jonathan Freedman, *Klezmer America: Jewishness, Ethnicity, Modernity* (Chicago: University of Chicago Press, 2009).

16. See, for example, Barbara Krauthamer, *Black Slaves, Indian Masters: Slavery, Emancipation, and Citizenship in the Native American South* (Chapel Hill: University of North Carolina Press, 2013); Edward E. Andrews, *Native Apostles: Black and Indian Missionaries in the British Atlantic World* (Cambridge, Mass.: Harvard University Press, 2013); Claudio Saunt, *Black, White, and Indian: Race and the Unmaking of an American Family* (New York:

Oxford University Press, 2005); James F. Brooks, ed., *Confounding the Color Line: The Indian-Black Experience in North America* (Lincoln: University of Nebraska Press, 2002); and Stephen Cornell, "Land, Labor and Group Formation: Blacks and Indians in the United States," *Ethnic and Racial Studies* 13, no. 3 (1990): 368–388.

17. Richard White, "Race Relations in the American West," *American Quarterly* 38, no. 3 (1986): 396–415; Richard White, *"It's Your Misfortune and None of It My Own": A History of the American West* (Norman: University of Oklahoma Press, 1991); Susan Lee Johnson, *Roaring Camp: The Social World of the California Gold Rush* (New York: W. W. Norton, 2000); Gary Clayton Anderson, *The Conquest of Texas: Ethnic Cleansing in the Promised Land, 1820–1875* (Norman: University of Oklahoma Press, 2005); Ned Blackhawk, *Violence over the Land: Indians and Empires in the Early American West* (Cambridge, Mass.: Harvard University Press, 2006); Karl Jacoby, *Shadows at Dawn: A Borderlands Massacre and the Violence of History* (New York: Penguin, 2008).

18. For a summary of the debate about what constitutes the West—a region, a transnational place, part of a process of frontier development—see William E. Riebsame and James Robb, eds., *Atlas of the New West: Portrait of a Changing Region* (Boulder: University of Colorado Center of the American West, 1997); Patricia Limerick, *Something in the Soil: Legacies and Reckonings in the New West* (New York: W. W. Norton, 2000).

19. Gerald Sorin, *The Jewish People in America. Time for Building: The Third Migration, 1880–1920* (Baltimore: Johns Hopkins University Press, 1992), 165.

20. Harriet Rochlin and Fred Rochlin, *Pioneer Jews: A New Life in the Far West* (Boston: Mariner Books, 2000 [1984]); Kenneth Libo and Irving Howe, *We Lived There Too: In Their Own Words and Pictures—Pioneer Jews and the Westward Movement of America, 1630–1930* (New York: St. Martin's, 1984); Moses Rischlin and John Livingston, eds., *Jews of the American West* (Detroit: Wayne State University Press, 1991); Cyril Edel Leonoff, *Pioneers, Pedlars, and Prayer Shawls: The Jewish Communities in British Columbia and the Yukon* (Victoria: Sono Nis Press, 1978); William Toll, *The Making of an Ethnic Middle Class: Portland Jewry over Four Generations* (Albany: State University of New York Press, 1982); Ava Fran Kahn, *Jewish Life in the American West: Perspectives on Migration, Settlement, and Community* (Los Angeles: Autry Museum of Western Heritage, 2002); Jeanne E. Abrams, *Jewish Women Pioneering the Frontier Trail: A History in the American West* (New York: New York University Press, 2006); Juanita Brooks, *History of the Jews in Utah and Idaho* (Salt Lake City: Western Epics, 1973); Jack Benjamin Goldmann, *A History of Pioneer Jews in California, 1849–1870* (San Francisco: R & E Research Associates, 1971); Hynda Rudd, "The Mountain West as a Jewish Frontier," *Western States Jewish Historical Quarterly* 13, no. 3 (1981): 241–256; Ida Libert Uchill, *Pioneers, Peddlers, & Tsadikim: The Story of Jews in Colorado*, 3rd ed. (Boulder: University Press of Colorado, 2000); and Leon Laizer Watters, *The Pioneer Jews of Utah*, vols. 1–2 (New York: American Jewish Historical Society, 1952); Natalie Ornish, *Pioneer Jewish Texans: Their Impact on Texas and American History for Four Hundred Years, 1590–1990* (Dallas: Texas Heritage Press, 1989).

21. The critique of "writing over" Indigenous narratives of colonialism is developed in Bonita Lawrence and Enakshi Dua, "Decolonizing Antiracism," *Social Justice* 32, no. 4 (2005): 120–134.

22. Sander Gilman, "Introduction: The Frontier as a Model for Jewish History," in *Jewries at the Frontier: Accommodation, Identity and Conflict*, ed. Sander Gilman and Milton Shain (Urbana: University of Illinois Press, 1999), 15; Sander Gilman, *Jewish Frontiers: Essays on Bodies, Histories, and Identities* (New York: Palgrave, 2003).

23. This process has been described with regards to other European engagements with Native Americans. Richard White, *The Middle Ground: Indians, Empires, and Republics in the Great Lakes Region, 1650–1815* (Cambridge: Cambridge University Press, 1991).

24. Steven Conn, *History's Shadow: Native Americans and Historical Consciousness in the Nineteenth Century* (Chicago: University of Chicago Press, 2004); Angela Aleiss, *Making the White Man's Indian: Native Americans and Hollywood Movies* (New York: Praeger, 2005);

Leah Dilworth, *Imagining Indians in the Southwest: Persistent Visions of a Primitive Past* (Washington, D.C.: Smithsonian Institution Press, 1996); Eliza McFeely, *Zuni and the American Imagination* (New York: Hill and Wang, 2001); and William Lyon, "The Navajos in the American Historical Imagination, 1868–1900," *Ethnohistory* 45, no. 2 (Spring 1998): 237–275.

25. Berkhofer, *White Man's Indian.*

26. Berkhofer, xv.

27. Alan Trachtenberg, *Shades of Hiawatha: Staging Indians, Making Americans, 1880–1930* (New York: Hill and Wang, 2004).

28. Shari M. Huhndorf, *Going Native: Indians in the American Cultural Imagination* (Ithaca: Cornell University Press, 2001); Philip J. Deloria, *Playing Indian* (New Haven: Yale University Press, 1998).

29. On Germans and Indians, see Penny H. Glenn, *Kindred by Choice: Germans and American Indians since 1800* (Chapel Hill: University of North Carolina Press, 2013); and Collin G. Calloway, Gerd Gemünden, and Susanne Zanto, eds., *Germans and Indians: Fantasies, Encounters, Projections* (Lincoln: University of Nebraska Press, 2002). On Mormonism and Indians, see Jared Farmer, *On Zion's Mount: Mormons, Indians, and the American Landscape* (Cambridge, Mass.: Harvard University Press, 2008). On Black-Indian relations, crossings, and more, see Saunt, *Black, White, and Indian*; Brooks, *Confounding the Color Line*; Tiya Miles and Sharon Patricia Holland, *Crossing Waters, Crossing World: The African Diaspora in Indian Country* (Durham: Duke University Press, 2004). In her brief study of Italians and Indians, Linda Pacini Pitelka claimed that when Italians first arrived in Mendocino County, California, the immigrants "had more in common with the local Pomo Indians than with Anglo-Americans," a process that would reverse as the Italians became settled. Linda Pacini Pitelka, "Indians and Italians: The Boundary of Race and Ethnicity in Rural Northern California, 1890–1920," in *Italian Immigrants Go West: The Impact of Locale on Ethnicity*, ed. Janet Albright Worrall, Carol Bonomo, and Elvira G. DiFabio (Cambridge: American Italian Historical Society, 2003), 55–65.

30. Isaac Leeser's metaphors of "penetrating" the wilds and "planting civilization's standard," which opened this introduction, are marked exceptions.

31. Richard Godbeer, "Eroticizing the Middle Ground: Anglo-Indian Sexual Relations along the Eighteenth Century Frontier," in *Sex, Love, Race: Crossing Boundaries in North American History*, ed. Martha Elizabeth Hodes (New York: New York University Press, 1999), 91–111; Teresa Toulouse, *The Captive's Position: Female Narrative, Male Identity, and Royal Authority in Colonial New England* (Philadelphia: University of Pennsylvania Press, 2007); Kristina Downs, "Mirrored Archetypes: The Contrasting Cultural Roles of La Malinche and Pocahontas," *Western Folklore* 67, no. 4 (Fall 2008): 397–414.

32. Patrick Wolfe, "Land, Labor, and Difference: Elementary Structures of Race," *American Historical Review* 106, no. 3 (June 2001): 866–926. See also Albert L. Hurtado, *Intimate Frontiers: Sex, Gender, and Culture in Old California* (Albuquerque: University of New Mexico Press, 1999); and Kevin Noble Maillard, "The Pocahontas Exception: The Exception of American Indian Ancestry from Racial Purity Law," *Michigan Journal of Race & Law* 12, no. 2 (Spring 2007): 351–386.

33. It is worth noting, however, that Walter Hart Blumenthal wrote a manuscript that was never published on *Pocahontas and Her Descendants*, clearly interested in both the Pocahontas myth and the historical realities thereafter. American Jewish Historical Society, Walter Hart Blumenthal Papers, P 83, subseries 3, box 4, folder 10.

34. Allan Greer, *The Jesuit Relations: Natives and Missionaries in Seventeenth-Century North America* (Boston: Bedford / St. Martin's, 2000); C. L. Higham, *Noble, Wretched, and Redeemable: Protestant Missionaries to the Indians in Canada and the United States, 1820–1900* (Albuquerque: University of New Mexico Press, 2000); Laura M. Stevens, *The Poor Indians: British Missionaries, Native Americans, and the Colonial Sensibility* (Philadelphia: University of Pennsylvania Press, 2004); Kent G. Lightfoot, *Indians, Missionaries, and Merchants: The Legacy of Colonial Encounters on the California Frontiers* (Berkeley: University of California

Press, 2005); Joel Martin and Mark A. Nicholas, eds., *Native Americans, Christianity, and the Reshaping of the American Religious Landscape* (Chapel Hill: University of North Carolina Press, 2010).

35. Francis Paul Prucha, *American Indian Policy in Crisis: Christian Reformers and the Indian, 1865–1900* (Norman: University of Oklahoma Press, 1976).

36. Eric Goldstein, *The Price of Whiteness: Jews, Race, and American Identity* (Princeton: Princeton University Press, 2006).

37. Michael Rogin, *Black Face, White Noise: Jewish Immigrants in the Hollywood Melting Pot* (Berkeley: University of California Press, 1996); Maria Damon, "Jazz-Jews, Jive, and Gender: The Ethnic Politics of Jazz Argot," in *Jews and Other Differences: The New Jewish Cultural Studies*, ed. Jonathan Boyarin and Daniel Boyarin (Minnesota: University of Minnesota Press, 1997), 150–175. See also Jeffery Melnick, *A Right to Sing the Blues: African Americans, Jews, and American Popular Song* (Cambridge, Mass.: Harvard University Press, 1999); and Stephen J. Whitfield, *In Search of American Jewish Culture* (Hanover: Brandeis University Press, 1999).

38. Diner, *In the Almost Promised Land*; Michael Alexander, *Jazz Age Jews* (Princeton: Princeton University Press, 2001).

39. Mel Marks, *Jews among the Indians: Tales of Adventure and Conflict in the Old West* (Chicago: Benison Books, 1992); Mark Slobin, "From Vilna to Vaudeville: Minikes and among the Indians (1895)," *Drama Review* 24, no. 3 (1980): 17–26; Andrea Most, "'Big Chief Izzy Horowitz': Theatricality and Jewish Identity in the Wild West," *American Jewish History* 87, no. 4 (1999): 313–341; Laikin Judith Elkin, *Imagining Idolatry: Missionaries, Indians, and Jews* (Providence, R.I.: John Carter Brown Library [Lecture Pamphlet], 1992); Michael Weingrad, "Lost Tribes: The Indian in American Hebrew Poetry," *Prooftexts* 24 (2004): 291–319.

40. "Jews, Native Americans and the Western World Order," organized by Jonathan Schorsch at Columbia University on April 25, 2010. Jonathan Boyarin, *The Unconverted Self: Jews, Indians, and the Identities of Christian Europe* (Chicago: University of Chicago Press, 2009), analyzed the ways that Medieval Christian Europe's ideas about Jews and Arabs shaped European, and hence American, views of Indians. Rachel Rubinstein, *Members of the Tribe: Native Americans in the Jewish Imagination* (Detroit: Wayne State University Press, 2010), set Jewish literary texts that engaged American Indians within the literary landscape of American modernism, arguing that Jews struggled to resolve an irresolvable tension between Jewish tribal particularism and universalist, humanitarian liberalism. Stephen Katz's *Red, Black, and Jew: New Frontiers in Hebrew Literature* (Austin: University of Texas Press, 2009) offered a close reading of a small set of American Hebrew writers' literary engagements with both African Americans and Indians.

41. Amy Greenberg, *Manifest Manhood and the Antebellum American Empire* (Cambridge: Cambridge University Press, 2005).

42. David S. Koffman, "Suffering & Sovereignty: Recent Canadian Jewish Interest in Indigenous Peoples and Issues," *Canadian Jewish Studies / Études juives canadiennes* 25 (2017): 28–59.

CHAPTER 1 — INVENTING PIONEER JEWS IN THE NEW NATION'S NEW WEST

1. Sam Aaron, "Excerpts of Autobiography: A Colorful Story of His Life on the Frontier, and in Salt Lake City, Utah, Stockton Cal, 1866–1914" (unpublished manuscript), American Jewish Archives Small Collection (AJA SC), no. 4; and Rabbi Samuel A. Halperin, "What Sam Says Is So," interview, n.d., AJA SC 4, box 1, folder 1, 1a–12.

2. Halperin, "What Sam Says Is So," 1a–12.

3. Halperin, 9.

4. William Toll has described the ways that merchants like Aaron transformed themselves "from medieval artisan to modern merchant." William Toll, "The Jewish Merchant and Civic

Order in the Urban West," in *Jewish Life in the American West: Perspectives on Migration, Settlement, and Community*, ed. Ava F. Kahn (Seattle: University of Washington Press, 2002), 83–112.

5. I use the terms *the West* and *frontier* interchangeably, though I am fully aware of the great debates among scholars of western America about the conceptual assumptions that lay at the root of each term. In general, *the West* focuses attention on place, the actual land and environment with its own continuous history. In this "West," specific locations are somewhat flexible, potentially referring to a large swath of geographies from the Great Lakes to the Rocky Mountains, beyond to the Pacific, northward to Alaska, south to Arizona, and as far east as Georgia or even Florida. Western historians like Patricia Limerick, Richard White, Donald Worster, and William Cronon have emphasized *the West* as a place rather than *the frontier* as a process in an effort to distance their assumptions from the Turnerian view of the frontier as an unstoppable, inevitable, one-way flow of civilization from the East that dominated historical thinking about the West from Turner's own "frontier thesis" of 1893 until at least the early 1960s. The West was not the site of "success" alone, and it was not home only to white European and American settlers looking to build a democracy, a nation, a civilization, and capital-rich cities and counties. Rather, it was inhabited by numerous peoples who viewed it in vastly different ways and competed, often violently to the death, for its ownership. Yet there were patterned processes of white–Indian encounters, as well as an overarching process of expansion settlement, and the transformation of the land and its resources into capital connected to a larger, country-wide economy. Though the places in this manuscript are spread across various subregions and ecologies, I have considered them all a part of "the West," the place, because I am aiming to conceptualize Jewish–Indian encounters as part of a single, albeit dynamic and changing, process. See Patricia Limerick, Andrew Cowell, and Sharon K. Collinge, eds., *Remedies for a New West: Healing Landscapes, Histories, and Cultures* (Tucson: University of Arizona Press, 2009); Patricia Limerick, *Something in the Soil: Legacies and Reckonings of the New West* (New York: W. W. Norton, 2000); Patricia Limerick, *Legacy of Conquest: The Unbroken Part of the American West* (New York: W. W. Norton, 1987); Susan Lee Johnson, *Roaring Camp: The Social World of the California Gold Rush* (New York: W. W. Norton, 2000); William G. Robbins, *Colony and Empire: The Capitalist Transformation of the American West* (Lawrence: University Press of Kansas, 1994); Donald Worster, *Under Western Skies: Nature and History in the American West* (New York: Oxford University Press, 1992).

6. For statistics on Jewish adult males' places of birth in the West circa 1880, see Toll, "Jewish Merchant and Civic Order," 94.

7. Jews were, of course, part of a much larger migration of European laborers to the West. See Gunther Peck, *Reinventing Free Labor: Padrones and Immigrant Workers in the North American West, 1880–1930* (New York: Cambridge University Press, 2000). On Italian immigrants in the West, by point of comparison, see Janet Albright Worrall, Carol Bonomo, and Elvira G. DiFabio, *Italian Immigrants Go West: The Impact of Locale on Ethnicity* (Cambridge: American Italian Historical Association, 2003).

8. Ava F. Kahn, "Introduction: Looking at America from the West to the East, 1850–1920s," in *Jewish Life in the American West: Perspectives on Migration, Settlement, and Community*, ed. Ava F. Kahn (Seattle: University of Washington Press, 2002), 213–232; Jacob Rader Marcus, *To Count a People: American Jewish Population Data, 1585–1984* (Lanham, Md.: University Press of America, 1990).

9. William M. Kramer and Norton B. Stern, "Early California Associations of Michel Goldwater and His Family," *Western States Jewish Historical Quarterly* 4, no. 2 (July 1972): 173–196; Hynda Rudd, "The Mountain West as a Jewish Frontier," *Western States Jewish Historical Quarterly* 13, no. 3 (1981): 241.

10. Kenneth Libo and Irving Howe, *We Lived There Too: In Their Own Words and Pictures. Pioneer Jews and the Westward Movement of America, 1630–1930* (New York: St. Martin's, 1984), 111.

11. Jeanne E. Abrams, *Jewish Women Pioneering the Frontier Trail: A History in the American West* (New York: New York University Press, 2006), 6.

12. John Higham, *Send These to Me: Jews and Other Immigrants in Urban America* (Baltimore: Johns Hopkins University Press, 1984).

13. Moses Rischlin, "Introduction," in *Jews of the American West*, ed. Moses Rischlin and John Livingston (Detroit: Wayne State University Press, 1991).

14. Two generations of western historians have been "overthrowing" Turner's 1893 frontier thesis. See, for example, Limerick, *Legacy of Conquest*; Robbins, *Colony and Empire*; and Richard White and Patricia Limerick, *The Frontier in American Culture* (Berkeley: University of California Press, 1994).

15. In the West, whiteness was not constructed in binary opposition with blackness. Rather, whiteness was forged in dynamic relation to Mexicans, Blacks, Indians, and poor whites. As immigrant whites jostled for position as whites in a racial borderland, Jews, as upwardly mobile and not of color, saw themselves and were seen as whites. For a broader discussion, see Neil Foley, *White Scourge* (Berkeley: University of California Press, 1998).

16. Recent scholarship has called into question the stability of tribes' "ancestral lands," given that political control over territory underwent changes before and during European contact. See, for example, Pekka Hämäläien, *The Comanche Empire* (New Haven: Yale University Press, 2008).

17. Brian DeLay, *War of a Thousand Deserts: Indian Raids and the U.S.–Mexican War* (New Haven: Yale University Press, 2008).

18. E. Hoxie Frederick, *A Final Promise: The Campaign to Assimilate the Indians, 1880–1920* (Lincoln: University of Nebraska Press, 1984); William G. Robbins and James Carl Foster, *Land in the American West: Private Claims and the Common Good* (Seattle: University of Washington Press, 2000).

19. See, for example, Israel Kreimer, "Memories of Wyoming Jewry" (unpublished memoir), AJA SC 13264; Ben Burguner, "Recollections of the Inland Empire, Describing His Early Experiences in the Pacific Northwest, Colfax, Washington," unpublished memoir, n.d., AJA SC 1419; Henry Castro, "Biographical Material Pertaining to His Views about Conditions in Texas in 1845," AJA SC 1660; Isaac A. Meyer, "My Life, Travels and Adventures by Land and Sea, 1825–1900, California and Kansas," unpublished memoir, n.d., AJA SC 8112; Joseph Sondheimer, "Muskogee Oklahoma / Indian Territory Papers. 1881–1900," AJA SC 11767; Saul Harberg, "Transcripts of Series of Interviews with Harberg by His Nephew Jim Reynolds Regarding Harberg's Life in Mora and Taos, New Mexico. Conducted 1976–1982," AJA SC 13603; and Emma Vorenberg Wertheim, unpublished memoir, n.d., AJA SC 12907.

20. On the dimensions and impacts of frontier ideology and mythology, see White and Limerick, *Frontier in American Culture*; Richard Slotkin, *The Fatal Environment: The Myth of the Frontier in the Age of Industrialization, 1800–1890* (New York: Atheneum, 1985).

21. Frederick Jackson Turner, "The Significance of the Frontier in American History," American Historical Association, Chicago World's Fair, Chicago, Ill., July 12, 1893; William Cronon, "Revisiting the Vanishing Frontier: The Legacy of Frederick Jackson Turner," *Western Quarterly* 18, no. 2 (April 1987): 157–176; John Mack Faragher, "The Frontier Trail: Rethinking Turner and Reimagining the American West," *American Historical Review* 98, no. 1 (February 1993): 106–117.

22. More recently, historians have revised the scholarly valuation of this process and have tried to disentangle efforts to forge national myths from sober history, implicating both the settlers and the historians who reproduced their subjects' values in a more complex and morally ambiguous process. Historians of the Jewish experience in the American West have been slow to take up this mantle. The Jewish immigrant story, however, ought to be taken out of its traditionally celebratory mode and placed in the larger, more morally ambiguous context to which it rightfully belongs.

23. Walter Hart Blumenthal, *In Old America: The Lost Ten Tribes of Israel. Prehistoric Peopling of America: A Bibliographic Survey of the Early Theory of Israelitish Derivation, and the*

Origin of the American Indians, American Jewish Archives, Cincinnati, Ohio, MC 229, box 1 of 1. A seventy-nine-page version of the one-thousand-plus-page manuscript was published as Walter Hart Blumenthal, *In Old America: Random Chapters on the Early Aborigines* (New York: Walton Book Company, 1931). The original manuscript contains hundreds of citations from across Europe and throughout America as per the spurious claim. Nancy Sinkoff, "Benjamin Franklin in Jewish Eastern Europe: Cultural Appropriation in the Age of the Enlightenment," *Journal of the History of Ideas* 61, no. 1 (January 2000): 133–152. See also Jonathan Boyarin, *The Unconverted Self: Jews, Indians, and the Identity of Christian Europe* (Chicago: University of Chicago Press, 2009).

24. See David Hecht, "Longfellow in Russia," *New England Quarterly* 19, no. 4 (December 1946): 531–534; Ernest B. Gilman, *Yiddish Poetry and the Tuberculosis Sanatorium, 1900–1970* (Syracuse, N.Y.: Syracuse University Press, 2015), 40–82; Alan Trachtenberg, *Shades of Hiawatha: Staging Indians, Making Americans, 1880–1930* (New York: Hill and Wang, 2004), in particular chapter 3, on Hiawatha in Yiddish. Solomon Bloomgarden Yehoyesh, *Longfellow, dos lied fun Hiyavatha* (1910); B. Shimin, *Der letsṭer Mohiḳaner* (1921); *James Fennimore Cooper Works in Russian translation: Soch.*, vols. 1–25 (St. Petersburg, 1865–1880); *Izbr. soch.*, vols. 1–6, foreword by A. A. Elistratova (Moscow, 1961–63); B. Raskin, *Dos Gezong fun Hiavata* (New York: Der Ax, 1918); I. A. Rontch, *Indianer Zummer Geklibene Lider* (New York: Biderman Farlag, 1929); S. Tannenbaum, *Der Letzter Indianer* (Warsaw: Literarishe Bleter) 14, no. 34 (August 20, 1937): 544–545; H. Shaskes, "Bi Di Oiseshtorbenen Indianer," *Heint* (Warsaw) 30, no. 195 (1937).

25. These included articles from *Hazefirah* (Warsaw), no. 18 (May 7, 1873); no. 68 (March 9, 1888); vol. 18 (1891): 146; no. 7 (1891); no. 282 (1890); no. 283 (1890); no. 284 (1890); no. 268 (1890); no. 288 (1890); *Hazefirah* (Berlin), no. 6 (August 12, 1874); no. 8 (1879); *HaMagid* (Lyck, East Prussia), no. 37 (September 16, 1868); no. 37 (March 3, 1874); *Shulamit* (Berlin) 72 (n.d.); *Die Deborah* (Cincinnati; June 6, 1856): 341; (March 10, 1865); (March 16, 1866): 147; (January 2, 1890): 4, first column; (April 2, 1896): 4; *Allgemeine Zeitung des Judentums* (Leipzig, Berlin) 2, no. 132 (November 3, 1838); vol. 45, no. 48 (November 1881); (April 11, 1890); vol. 54, no. 13 (November 1881); *Sabbath-Blatt* (Leipzig), no. 34 (August 23, 1845); no. 34 (August 30 and September 6, 1845); no. 35/36; *Die Yiddishe Velt* 1, no. 4 (August 1, 1913); 2, no. 21 (October 2, 1913); *Der Yiddisher Rekorder* (New York; June 22, 1893); vol. 1, no. 12 (May 18, 1898); no. 7:6.

26. Constance Rowell Mastores, "During My Grandfather's Time" (unpublished manuscript memoir), Western Jewish History Center, Archives of the Judah L. Magnes Museum, 2007, 5.

27. Eveline Brooks Auerbach, *Frontier Reminiscences of Eveline Brooks Auerbach* (Berkeley California: University of California Press, Friends of the Bancroft Library, 1994), 22.

28. Auerbach, *Frontier Reminiscences*, 22. Brook's choices harmonize with historian Albert L. Hurtado's findings that white men tended to choose white women for marriage rather than wed Indian or Mexican women, even though these women generally lived far from gold rush locations. Albert L. Hurtado, *Intimate Frontiers: Sex, Gender, and Culture in Old California* (Albuquerque: University of New Mexico Press, 1999).

29. Auerbach, *Frontier Reminiscences*, 24, 33–34.

30. Martha Thal, "Early Days. The Story of Sarah Thal, Wife of a Pioneer Farmer in Nelson County, N.D.," in *Pioneer Stories Written by People of Nelson County, North Dakota* (State Historical Society of North Dakota), 11–14, no. 27395, duplicate from the AJA SC 9208.

31. See also "Pioneer Tells Indian Stories. Letter by I.E. Solomon Gives Account of Escape from Death by Son, Charles," *Safford Guardian* (Tucson, Ariz.), July 15, 1930; "Pioneer Businessman Dies in Los Angeles; Founded Solomonville," Los Angeles paper clipping, December 4, 1930, in AJA MC 649, box 16, no. 11.

32. Isaac Goldberg, "An Old Timer's Experiences in Arizona," *Arizona Historical Review* 2 (October 1929 [1894, San Bernadino, Calif.]): 90–91, AJA SC 4010. Emphasis in original.

33. G. W. Harris, "Our Jewish Pioneers," *New York Times*, April 3, 1932. For further analysis on this kind of pioneering rhetoric, see Karl Jacoby, *Shadows at Dawn: A Borderland Massacre and the Violence of History* (New York: Penguin, 2008), particularly the chapter on "Subduing the Apache."

34. See, for example, Elma Ehrlich Levinger, *The New Land: Stories of Jews Who Had a Part in the Making of Our Country* (New York: Bloch, 1920); *They Fought for Freedom and Other Stories* (New York: Riverdale Press, 1953); and *Jewish Adventures in America: The Story of 300 Years of Jewish Life in the United States* (New York: Bloch, 1958).

35. Levinger, *New Land.*

36. Donald Lutz, "From Covenant to Constitution in American Political Thought," *Publius* 10 (1980): 101–122; Arthur Hertzberg, "The New England Puritans and the Jews," in *Hebrew and the Bible in America: The First Two Centuries*, ed. Shalom Goldman (Hanover, N.H.: University Press of New England, 1993); Michael Novak, *On Two Wings: Humble Faith and Common Sense at the American Founding* (New York: Encounter Books, 2003); and William Pencak, *Jews & Gentiles in Early America, 1654–1800* (Ann Arbor: University of Michigan Press, 2005).

37. Tobias Schanfarber, "Alabama," in *Jewish Encyclopedia*, vol. 1, ed. Isidore Singer (New York: Funk & Wagnalls, 1906).

38. Cyrus Adler and William S. Friedman, "Colorado," in *Jewish Encyclopedia*, vol. 4, ed. Isidore Singer (New York: Funk & Wagnalls, 1906).

39. Cyrus Adler, "Texas," in *Jewish Encyclopedia*, vol. 12, ed. Isidore Singer (New York: Funk & Wagnalls, 1906).

40. Anita Libman Lebeson, *Jewish Pioneers in America, 1492–1848* (New York: Brentano's, 1931).

41. James H. Merrell, *Into the American Woods: Negotiators on the Pennsylvania Frontier* (New York: Norton, 1999); Albert T. Volwiler, *George Croghan and the Westward Movement, 1741–1782* (Cleveland: Arthur H. Clark Company, 1926).

42. Ruth Arnfeld, "Jews in America Tradition. Some of Pittsburgh's Own Founding Fathers," *Jewish Criterion*, September 11, 1942, 30–31.

43. David de Sola Pool, *Portraits Etched in Stone: Early Jewish Settlers, 1682–1831* (New York: Columbia University Press, 1952).

44. Cyrus Adler and J. H. Hollander, "Lumbrozo, Jacob," in *Jewish Encyclopedia*, ed. Isidore Singer (New York: Funk & Wagnalls, 1906); Cyrus Adler and S. N. Deinard, "Minnesota," in *Jewish Encyclopedia*, ed. Isidore Singer (New York: Funk & Wagnalls, 1906); Cyrus Adler and A. S. W. Rosenbach, "Levy, Aaron," in *Jewish Encyclopedia*, ed. Isidore Singer (New York: Funk & Wagnalls, 1906).

45. As the director of the American Jewish Archives, Jacob Rader Marcus regularly sent out questionnaires to Jewish families who hoped to donate materials to the archives. One of the questions read, "Was anybody [in your family] a pioneer, Indian trader or first settler?," suggesting something of the synonymy of these terms. For an example of this survey, see SC 9891 Elmer Ephraim Present, 1871–1956. Harold I. Sharfman, *Jews on the Frontier: An Account of Jewish Pioneers and Settlers in Early America* (Malibu, Calif.: J. Simon, Pangloss Press, 1977), 70, 80, 86, 172.

46. Rosalie Levenson, "California's Gold Country Jewish-Named Towns Live On," *Western States Jewish History* 26, no. 4 (July 1994): 317–340. For more of these place names, see also Bernard Postal and Lionel Koppman, *A Jewish Tourist's Guide to the United States* (New York: Jewish Publication Society of America, 1954).

47. See the Solomon Speigelberg file, American Jewish Archives, S C no. 11855, box 1, folder 1. Quoted in Oliver La Farge, *Santa Fe: Autobiography of a Southwestern Town* (Norman, Oklahoma: University of Oklahoma Press, 1959), 334.

48. "Jewish Old-Timers in Sheridan Grant Abe Abrahams Honor as Oldest of Race in the County," *Wyoming Jewish Press*, September 22, 1930, 14; "Myer Friendly, Indian Trader and

Carriage Builder, Dead," *Jewish Criterion*, March 12, 1937, 23; see also Ezra Davidson, "The Jews of 1776," *Jewish Criterion*, June 27, 1941, 8.

49. Stuart Scrapbook, Historical Society of Montana, no. 2, clipping from the *Lewistown Democrat*, n.d., in Benjamin Kelsen, "The Jews of Montana," *Western States Jewish Historical Quarterly*, 183.

50. The eulogy was given by E. H. Campell (*Kendal Miner*, August 31, 1903, 2), quoted in Kelsen, "Jews of Montana," 184.

51. Jean M. O'Brian, *Firsting and Lasting: Writing Indians Out of Existence in New England* (Minneapolis: University of Minnesota Press, 2010).

52. Oklahoma Exhibition Hall, Jewish Museum of the American West, http://www.jmaw.org/oklahoma-exhibition-hall/.

53. Joseph Stocker, "Arizona's Century of Jewish Life," *Arizona Days and Ways*, no. 14 (1954): 14–15. Excerpt from "Jewish Roots in Arizona" of the Phoenix Jewish Community Council. The newspaper editor also characterized Solomon Barth in the language of glorified adventure, typified by his capture by and escape from the notorious Apache chief, Cochise, "a man whose life had been a bridge between the wild frontier and the modern epoch."

54. "Notes on Sol Ripinsky of Alaska in 1905," *Western States Jewish History* 8, no. 4.

55. Mathew Bentey, "Kill the Indian, Save the Man: Manhood at the Carlisle Indian School, 1879–1918" (PhD diss., School of American Studies, University of East Anglia, 2012).

56. Chapman, *Portrait and Biographical Records of Arizona: Commemorating the Achievements of Citizens Who Have Contributed to the Progress of Arizona and the Development of its Resources* (Chicago: Chapman, 1901), 868.

57. Gunther Plaut, *The Jews in Minnesota: The First Seventy Five Years* (New York: American Jewish Historical Society, 1959).

58. "Talmud Yelodim School, Cincinnati, Ohio," *Occident* 11 (1854): 59–61.

59. On Jewish masculinity in the West, see Sarah Imhoff, *Masculinity and the Making of American Judaism* (Bloomington: Indiana University Press, 2017), chapters 3 and 4.

60. Ken Wells, "Lest We Forget" (unpublished manuscript, Corrales, New Mexico, 1959), AJA SC 8860.

61. David A. D'Ancona, *A California-Nevada Travel Diary of 1976: The Delightful Account of a Ben B'rith*, ed. William M. Kramer (Santa Monica, Calif.: Norton B. Stern, 1975), 41.

62. Emil Teichmann, *A Journey to Alaska in the Year 1868: Being the Diary of the Late Emil Teichmann* (New York: Argosy-Antiquarian, 1963 [privately printed in 1925]), 72–73.

63. Teichmann, *Journey to Alaska*, 157–161.

64. *Jewish Chronicle* (Pittsburgh, Pa.), August 13, 1880, 7.

65. George L. Mosse, "Max Nordau, Liberalism and the New Jew," *Journal of Contemporary History* 27, no. 4 (October 1992): 565–581; David Biale, *Power and Powerlessness in Jewish History* (New York: Schochen, 1986).

66. For a similar argument about the invention of Jewish immigrant pioneers in Argentina, see Alberto Gerchunoff, *The Jewish Gauchos of the Pampas* (Albuquerque: University of New Mexico Press, 1998).

67. "Early El Paso History Recalled on Leo Schuster's Anniversary," *El Paso Times*, December 13, 1935, 5c2; and Martin O'Neill, "Pioneer Sees E.P. Growth," *El Paso Times*, June 10, 1939, 1c2; both in AJA MC 694, box 16, folder 1, "Pioneers—Schuster, Leo and Bernard." See also Hannah Shwayder Berry, "A Family History" (unpublished manuscript, April 1962), 1–12, AJA SC 11424; "Gustav Zork Dies" (no publication detail); and "Death Claims G. Zork, Pioneer Business Man of El Paso and North Mexico," *El Paso Herald Post*, January 14, 1924; both in AJA MC 694, box 16, folder 1.

68. S. H. Drachman, "Arizona Pioneers and Apaches" (handwritten reminiscences, Tucson, May 4, 1855), AJA MC 649, box 13, folder 8.

69. Auerbach, *Frontier Reminiscences*, 34.

70. Goldberg, "An Old Timer's Experiences."

71. Drachman, "Arizona Pioneers."

72. Drachman.

73. Quoted in Rudd, "Mountain West," 248; and Ray Bril, "The Jew Whom the Indians Called 'Fire Cracker,'" *Jewish Criterion* 58, no. 13 (June 21, 1922).

74. Edward Herzberg, "Lukin Family, Pioneers of Tempe, Arizona," *Western States Jewish History* 31, no. 1.

75. "'Uncle Sol' of Wisconsin Again Made Indian Chief," *Jewish Transcript* 5, no. 24 (Seattle, August 17, 1928): 1.

76. *Jewish Transcript* (Seattle), July 5, 1948, 3.

77. Harold Sharfman, *Pioneer Jews* (Chicago: H. Regnery, 1977), 61–63.

78. Sharfman, 111.

79. For a discussion of Jewish literary and theatrical "red face," see Peter Antelyes, "'Haim Afen Range': The Jewish Indian and the Redface Western," *MELUS: Multi-Ethnic Literature of the US* 34, no. 3 (Fall 2009): 15–42.

80. S. R. Lewis, interview, University of Oklahoma Libraries Western History Collections, vol. 53, interview 12064, November 5, 1937.

81. *Frontier Times*, February 1925, quoted in "Lehmann, the Indian: Oklahoma, 1870s," *Western States Jewish History* 46, no. 3.

82. "Child Stolen by Indians: Return of a White Man after Thirty Years Captivity among the Indians," *The Israelite*, March 9, 1869.

83. Captivity narratives, tales of the temptations of an alternative life and fascination with barbarism and ultimately redemption, popular from the late seventeenth century through the end of the nineteenth century in the United States, formed a highly conventional literary genre. Their factuality, as historian Pauline Turner Strong has argued, was far less important than the impact they were designed to have on their white readership. Pauline Turner Strong, "Transforming Outsiders: Captivity, Adoption, and Slavery Reconsidered," in *A Companion to American Indian History*, ed. Philip J. Deloria and Neal Salisbury (Malden, Mass.: Blackwell, 2002), 339–356; Gary L. Ebersole, *Captured by Texts: Puritan to Postmodern Images of Indian Captivity* (Charlottesville, Va.: University Press of Virginia, 1995); Kathryn Derounian, James Derounian, and Arthur Levernier, *Indian Captivity Narrative, 1550–1900* (New York: Twayne, 1993).

84. "Child Stolen by Indians: Return of a White Man after Thirty Years Captivity among the Indians," *The Israelite*, March 9, 1869.

85. "A White Apache," *Boston Hebrew Observer* 1, no. 25 (June 22, 1883).

86. Matthew J. Eisenberg, "The Last Frontier: Jewish Pioneers in Alaska, Part II," *Western States Jewish History* 24, no. 2 (January 1992), 121.

87. See also "Pioneer Tells Indian Stories"; "Pioneer Businessman Dies in Los Angeles"; Auerbach, *Frontier Reminiscences*, 73; and Albert Cahn's recalling of the near kidnapping of Caroline Cahn around 1856, Albert Cahn, Chicago, questionnaire quoted in Carol Gendler, "The Jews of Omaha: The First Sixty Years," *Western States Jewish Historical Quarterly* 5, no. 3 (April 1973): 210–211.

88. Roy Harvey Pearce, "The Significances of the Captivity Narrative," *American Literature* 19, no. 1 (March 1947): 1–20.

89. Scott Zesch, *The Captured: A True Story of Abduction by Indians on the Texas Frontier* (New York: St. Martin's, 2004).

90. Gregory Michno, *A Fate Worse than Death: Indian Captivities in the West, 1830–1885* (Caldwell, Idaho: Caxton Press, 2007), 279. Census data and information culled about Goldbaum from local newspapers found in the Special Collections, University of Arizona, MS401, Research Files, Arizona, box 12, folder 21, Goldbaum family.

91. See also Ella Fleishman Auerbach, "Romantic Story of an Indian Trader," *American Hebrew*, September 10, 1926, 501, 587.

92. Mary V. Dearborn, *Pocahontas's Daughters: Gender and Ethnicity in American Culture* (New York: Oxford University Press, 1986).

93. Sources differ on how many terms (between one and six) Bibo served as Acoma Pueblo governor. Dozens of short articles in local newspapers celebrate Bibo as an Indian chief. See, for example, Dan L. Trapp, "Jew Became New Mexico Indian Chief," *Los Angeles Times*, September 14, 1969, sec. F, AJA Bibo Family Microfilm no. 1693; LeRoy Bibo and Max Weiss (children of Solomon Bibo), interview by Dr. N.B. Stern, at Charter Oak, California, February 21, 1969, manuscript in possession of the AJA, box 2802; AJA Bibo Family Microfilm no. 1693; Sandra Lea Rollins, "Jewish Indian Chief" (unpublished article), for the University of New Mexico, January 31, 1968, in AJA Bibo Family Microfilm no. 1693, "Family Genealogies, Documents and Printed Material," Albuquerque, New Mexico, 1820–1969; Nathan Bibo, "Reminiscences of Early New Mexico," *Albuquerque* (N.M.) *Sunday Herald*, June 4, 1922, ch. 1, p. 4.

94. Some evidence of Jewish-Native marriages and sexual encounters remains. The sons of Ezekiel Solomon, an early nineteenth-century Indian trader near Mackinac in Quebec, both married Indian women. According to historian Harold Sharfman, "many Jews married Indians. Near the falls of the Ohio, one, surnamed Levi, reared three children in their Indian mother's faith." A London publication in 1844 reported on the "son of an Indian squaw and his father, a Dutch Jew": The young man, identifying himself as "Grey Bear," told the British paper, "My father was a Jewish cheat, and I don't know *his* name, but I know who my grandfather was, the fine old *Indine*, and that's more than some of these white robbers do . . . [My blood] is the blood of the Gray Bears, and was in it before that old Jew blackguard, my father, came to this country and entered into our family." Quoted in Sharfman, *Pioneer Jews*, 164–165.

95. Jacob Rader Marcus, *United States Jewry, 1776–1985* (Detroit: Wayne State University Press, 1989), 182.

96. *American Jewish Yearbook* 2 (1900–1901): 253.

97. For a detailed discussion of race, gender, and sexual boundaries in one frontier zone, see Hurtado, *Intimate Frontiers*.

98. N. B. Stern, "Herman Bendell: Superintendent of Indian Affairs, Arizona Territory, 1871–1873," *Western States Jewish Historical Quarterly* 8 (April 1976): 265–282.

CHAPTER 2 — LAND AND THE VIOLENT EXPANSION OF THE IMMIGRANTS' EMPIRE

1. See Brian DeLay, *War of a Thousand Desserts: Indian Raids and the U.S.-Mexican War* (New Haven: Yale University Press, 2008), for a discussion of the impact of the war on the Apache, Comanche, Kiowa-Apache, Kiowa, and southern Kickapoo.

2. Introduction to the Records of the Bureau of Indian Affairs, #163, #1, p. 1 RG 75, National Archives.

3. According to historian William G. Robbins, property lay at the root of animosity between classes, races, and various levels of government in the American West. William G. Robbins, "Introduction," in *Land in the American West: Private Claims and the Common Good*, ed. William G. Robbins and James Carl Foster (Seattle: University of Washington Press, 2000).

4. Some scholars see whites' violence against Indians as ethnic cleansing and as part of a race war rather than as a by-product of competition for land and resources. See, for example, Gary Clayton Anderson, *The Conquest of Texas: Ethnic Cleansing in the Promised Land, 1820–1875* (Norman: University of Oklahoma Press, 2005); and Ned Blackhawk, *Violence over the Land: Indians and Empires in the Early American West* (Cambridge, Mass.: Harvard University Press, 2006).

5. Major works of the field of western American Jewish history avoid this historiographic turn. William Toll, *The Making of an Ethnic Middle Class: Portland Jewry over Four Generations* (Albany: State University of New York Press, 1982); Ava Fran Kahn,

Jewish Life in the American West: Perspectives on Migration, Settlement, and Community (Los Angeles: Autry Museum of Western Heritage, 2002); Jeanne E. Abrams, *Jewish Women Pioneering the Frontier Trail: A History in the American West* (New York: New York University Press, 2006). Likewise, not a single mention is made of Jewish encounters with Indigenous People in Daniel J. Elazar, "Jewish Frontier Experiences in the Southern Hemisphere: The Cases of Argentina, Australia, and South Africa," *Modern Judaism* 3, no. 2 (1983): 129–146.

6. The newest and most broad, synthetic history of the Jewish "contribution" to American Pacific Coast life elaborates on the impressive role Jews took in the civic, commercial, and philanthropic growth of western American life, presenting these contributions in the conventionally celebratory tone of American Jewish history. Ellen Eisenberg, Ava F. Kahn, and William Toll, *Jews of the Pacific Coast: Reinventing Community on America's Edge* (Portland: University of Washington Press, 2010).

7. On natural resources as tools of empire, see Donald Worster, *Rivers of Empire: Water, Aridity, and the Growth of the American West* (New York: Pantheon, 1985).

8. Todd Presner, *Muscular Judaism: The Jewish Body and the Politics of Regeneration* (New York: Routledge, 2007).

9. Ellen Eisenberg, "From Cooperative Farming to Urban Leadership," in *Jewish Life in the American West: Perspectives on Migration, Settlement, and Community*, ed. Ava F. Kahn (Seattle: University of Washington Press, 2002), 113–132.

10. For a well-theorized articulation of the making of racialized national subjects, albeit in a different national context, see Sunera Thobani, *Exalted Subjects: Studies in the Making of Race and Nation in Canada* (Toronto: University of Toronto Press, 2007).

11. Julius Stern, "On the Establishment of a Jewish Colony in the United States," *Occident* 1, no. 1 (April 1843). See also "Trail Blazers of the Trans-Mississippi West," *American Jewish Archives*, October 1956, 59.

12. For more on Noah's Ararat plan, see "Stories of Major Noah," *Jewish Progress* 30, no. 45 (July 9, 1894), whole no. 1050; Jonathan Sarna, *Jacksonian Jew: The Two Worlds of Mordecai Noah* (New York: Holmes and Meier, 1981); Mordecai Manuel Noah, "Discourse on the Evidences of the American Indians Being the Descendants of the Lost Tribes of Israel," in *Midstream* 17, no. 5 (1971): 49–64; Mordecai Manuel Noah, "Proclamation to the Jews," reprinted in Max J. Köhler, "Some Early American Zionist Projects," *Publications of the American Jewish Historical Society* 8 (1900), appendix 2, 106–113, and in Michael Schuldiner and Daniel J. Kleinfeld, eds., *Selected Writings of Mordecai Noah* (Westport, Conn.: Greenwood, 1999), 105–124. See also the *Wayne Sentinel* of Palmyra, N.Y.: M. M. Noah, "Proclamation to the Jews," September 27, 1825; M. M. Noah, "Proclamation to the Jews," Sept. 15th Speech—1st half, October 4, 1825; and M. M. Noah, "Proclamation to the Jews," Sept. 15th Speech—2nd half, October 11, 1825. Lewis F. Allen, "Founding of the City of Ararat on Grand Island—by Mordecai M. Noah," *Publications of the American Jewish Historical Society* 26 (1918): 173–200, quoted in Thomas E. Connolly and Selig Adler, *From Ararat to Suburbia: The History of the Jewish Community of Buffalo* (Philadelphia: Jewish Publication Society of America, 1960), 5–12; "American Zionist Number One," *Jewish Criterion*, July 19, 1935, 5.

13. Joseph Norman Heard, "Cuming, Alexander," *Handbook of the American Frontier: Four Centuries of Indian-White Relationships*, vol. 1, *The Southwestern Woodlands* (Metuchen, N.J.: Scarecrow Press, 1987), 122–123.

14. "Georgia's Great Swamp," *Hebrew Observer* 23 (December 6, 1889): 7.

15. Taylor Spence, "Jeffersonian Jews: The Jewish Agrarian Diaspora and the Assimilative Power of the Western Land, 1882–1930," *Western Historical Quarterly* 41, no. 3 (Autumn 2010): 327.

16. Spence, 327.

17. Spence, 340.

18. Spence, 341.

19. Sarah Imhoff, "Wild Tribes and Ancient Semites: Israelite-Indian Identification and the American West," *Culture and Religion: An Interdisciplinary Journal* 15, no. 2 (2014): 227–249.

20. Bernard Marinbach, *Galveston: Ellis Island of the West* (Albany, N.Y.: SUNY Press, 1983); Jack Glazier, *Dispersing the Ghetto: The Relocation of Jewish Immigrants Across America* (Ithaca: Cornell University Press, 1999); and Gur Alroey, "Galveston and Palestine: Immigration and Ideology in the Early Twentieth Century," *American Jewish Archives* 56 (2004): 129–150.

21. Henry Cohen Papers, Dolph Briscoe Center for American History, University of Texas at Austin, 3M325, "Personal Writings: Essays and Themes, Undated," 20. Quoted in Imhoff, "Wild Tribes and Ancient Semites," 13.

22. David Bressler, *The Removal Work, Including Galveston*, presented before the National Conference of Jewish Charities, May 17, 1910 (Waltham, Mass: American Jewish Historical Society, 1910), 16.

23. "The Galveston Movement," *Jewish Herald*, January 6, 1910; and Oscar Leonard, "Come to Texas," *Jewish Herald*, January 6, 1910, quoted in Bryan Edward Stone, *The Chosen Folks: Jews on the Frontiers of Texas* (Austin: University of Texas Press, 2010), 90. For analysis of the gendered aspects of Zionism, see Mikhal Dekel, *The Universal Jew: Masculinity, Modernity, and the Zionist Movement* (Evanston, Ill.: Northwestern University Press, 2010); and Michael Stanislawski, *Zionism and Fin-de-Siecle: Cosmopolitanism and Nationalism from Nordau to Jabotinsky* (Los Angeles: University of California Press, 2001).

24. Interview with Moses Weinberger, University of Oklahoma Libraries Western History Collections, vol. 96, interview 8176, August 5, 1937, pp. 8–9.

25. Interview with Moses Weinberger, 13.

26. John R. Lovett, "Leo Meyer: Oklahoma Settler and Politician," *Western States Jewish History* 26, no. 1 (1993): 55–64.

27. Annual Report of the Department of the Interior for the Fiscal Year Ended June 30, 1902, Indian Affairs Part 1, Report of the Commissioner and Appendixes (Washington, D.C., Government Printing Office, 1903), No. 57-5, at 79.

28. Eric Voegelin and Ermine Wheeler, *Pitt River Indians of California, California Indians*, vol. 3, Garland American Ethnohistory Series (New York: Garland, 1974), 36; Garth Sanders, "Bieber's Aubrey Biber: He Knows His Town Well," *Redding Record-Searchlight*, November 30, 1977, both quoted in Rosalie Levenson, "California's Gold Country Jewish-Named Towns Live On," *Western States Jewish History* 26, no. 4 (July 1994): 326–328.

29. *San Diego Sun*, September 14, 1887, 3.

30. C. A. Sumner, "Early Days in California," *Los Angeles Times*, February 24, 1918; Norton B. Stern, "The King of Temecula, Louis Wolf," *Western States Jewish History* 22, no. 2 (1990): 99–111.

31. Carlyle Channing Davis and William Alderson, *The True Story of "Ramona": Its Facts and Fictions, Inspiration and Purpose* (New York: Dodge, 1914).

32. Harold Sharfman, *Jews on the Frontier* (Chicago: H. Regnery, 1977), 80, 81.

33. Sharfman.

34. *Prescott Weekly Courier*, June 10, 1882, 3:1. In AJA MC 649, box 13, no. 2; "Solomon Barth," *San Diego Union*, December 9, 1928, 25:4; "Barth, Solomon," *Arizona Republican* (Phoenix, Ariz.), December 22, 1928, 1:2,3.

35. Thomas Edwin Farish, *History of Arizona* (University of Arizona, Digital Books of the Southwest 1918), 5:319, http://southwest.library.arizona.edu/hav1/.

36. "Report on the Jury in the Case of the Territory of Arizona v. Solomon Barth Forgery," April 19, 1887, Court Records, Apache County Court House, St. Johns, Arizona, indictment no. 18, file no. 2. Cited in N. H. Greenwood, "Sol Barth: A Jewish Settler on the Arizona Frontier," *Jewish Arizona History* 14 (Winter 1973): 374.

37. Greenwood, "Sol Barth," 363–378.

38. "Solomon Barth," *San Diego Union*. December 9, 1928, 25:4.

39. "Cites Evidence That Jew Was Responsible for United States Purchase of Alaska," *Jewish Criterion*, December 20, 1935, 13.

40. "Samuel D. Solomon to General William Clark, St. Louis February 8th, 1813," in *The Jews of the United States, 1790–1840: A Documentary History*, vol. 1, ed. Joseph L. Blau and Salo W. Baron (New York: Columbia University Press and the Jewish Publication Society of America, 1963), 845.

41. Removal of Cherokees, Papers and Correspondences, 1835–1837, S. Doc. No. 25-120 at 1047, Indian Office Library 161.1 c74.

42. On Jews in the military in the modern period more broadly, see Derek Penslar, *Jews and the Military: A History* (Princeton: Princeton University Press, 2014).

43. Seymour Brody, *Jewish Heroes and Heroines of America* (New York: Lifetime Books, 1996).

44. Myer M. Cohen, *Notices of Florida and the Campaign*, facsimile reproduction of the 1836 edition with introduction by O. Z. Tyler Jr., Quadricentennial Edition of the Floridiana Facsimile and Reprint Series (Gainesville: University of Florida Press, 1964).

45. Cohen, 34.

46. Cohen, 66.

47. Cohen, 49.

48. Cohen, 78. See also O. Z. Tyler, "Introduction," in Cohen, *Notices of Florida.*

49. Natalie Ornish, *Pioneer Jewish Texans* (Dallas: Texas Heritage Press, 1989); "David Sprangler Kaufman," *Handbook of Texas Online*, Texas State Historical Association, http://www.tshaonline.org/handbook/online/articles/fka12.

50. Testimony in Relation to Ute Outbreak taken by Indian Affairs of the House of Representatives, May 1, 1880, H. Misc. Doc. 46-10:38 at 100.

51. Jerry Keenan, "Max Littmann: Immigrant Soldier in the Wagon Box Fight," *Western States Jewish Historical Quarterly* 6, no. 2 (January 1974): 107–111; see also Sam Gibson, quoted in Grace Hebard and E. A. Brinistool, *The Bozeman Trail* (Cleveland: Arthur H. Clark Company, 1922).

52. Keenan, "Max Littmann." See also Norton Stern, "Littmann, Max and Sigmund Shlesinger; Jewish Heros of the Indian Wars," *Western States Jewish History* 41, no. 4.

53. See Derek Penslar, "An Unlikely Internationalism: The Jewish Experience of War in Modern Europe," *Journal of Modern Jewish Studies* 7, no. 3 (2008): 309–323; Derek Penslar, "The Jewish Soldier in Jewish Memory," to be published in Hebrew in *History and Memory: Essays in Honour of Anita Shapira*, ed. Meir Chazan and Uri Cohen (Jerusalem: Zalman Shazar Center, forthcoming).

54. Simon Wolf, "Fought for the Union: Jewish Citizens Who Rendered Gallant Service during the War," *Washington Post*, December 10, 1891, 10.

55. Isaac Goldberg, "An Old Timer's Experiences in Arizona," *Arizona Historical Review* 2 (October 1929 [1894, San Bernardino, California]): 90–91, AJA SC 4010.

56. Goldberg, "An Old Timer's Experiences." See also Wolfgang Mieder, "'The Only Good Indian Is a Dead Indian': History and Meaning of a Proverbial Stereotype," *Journal of American Folklore* 106, no. 419 (1993): 38–60.

57. "Frontier Days Recalled by Death of Pioneer Who Built First Copper Smelter and Railroad in Arizona," *Arizona Daily Star*, April 26, 1924, p. 3, cols. 1, 2, AJA MC 649, box 13, folder 11. See also Jacob Rader Marcus, *United States Jewry, 1776–1985* (Detroit: Wayne State University Press, 1989), 130.

58. Harriett Rochlin and Fred Rochlin, *Pioneer Jews: A New American Life in the Far West* (Boston: Houghton Mifflin: 1984).

59. Henry Lesinsky, "Letters Written by Henry Lesinsky to His Son." This one was written in October or November 1891, published in New York, 1924, 48–50, AJA MC 649, box 15, folder 6.

60. Lesinsky.

61. Mark Simmons, *Massacre on the Lordsburg Road: A Tragedy of the Apache Wars* (College Station: Texas A&M University Press, 1997).

62. "The Finest Fighters in the World," *Boston Hebrew Observer* 1, no. 25 (June 22, 1883).

63. "Indian Scalps," *Boston Hebrew Observer* 1, no. 27 (July 1883).

64. "Canadian Indians on the Warpath," *Boston Hebrew Observer* 1, no. 26 (June 29, 1883).

65. "Massacre of Cawnpore," *Jewish Review* 11, no. 22 (August 28, 1898): 8.

66. "A Long Night Ride," *Jewish Review* 4, no. 16 (January 17, 1890): 8.

67. Michael Feldberg, ed., *Blessings of Freedom: Chapters in American Jewish History*, American Jewish Historical Society (Hoboken, N.J.: Ktav, 2002), 34–36; Solomon Breibart, *Explorations in Charleston's Jewish History*, vol. 1 (Charleston: History Press, 2005), 35–39.

68. Cyrus Adler, "Salvador, Francis," in *Jewish Encyclopedia* (New York: Funk & Wagnalls, 1901–1906).

69. See, for example, "Neighborliness Rules: Jews of Dixieland," *Jewish Criterion*, January 22, 1937; Harold Sharfman, *Pioneer Jews* (Chicago: H. Regnery, 1977).

70. Simon Wolf, *The American Jew as Patriot, Soldier and Citizen* (Philadelphia: Levytype, 1895).

71. "Synopsis of Operations in the Department of New Mexico, May 16–Dec. 28, 1863," the War of the Rebellion, compilation of the Official Records of the Union and Confederate Armies, Prepared under the Direction of the Secretary of war by the late Lieut. Col. Robert N. Scott, Third U.S. Artillery, Pursuant to Acts of Congress (Washington, D.C.: Government Printing Office, 1889), series I, vol. 26, part 1, chapter 38, no. 3.

72. "Hall of Heroes: American Jewish Recipients of the Medal of Honor," National Museum of American Jewish Military History, https://nmajmh.org/exhibitions/permanent-exhibitions/hall-of-heroes/, accessed February 11, 2012.

73. Seymour Brody, *Jewish Heroes and Heroines of America: 151 True Stories of Jewish American Heroism* (Hollywood, Fla.: Frederick Fell, 2004), 75.

74. Marcus, *United States Jewry*.

75. Quoted in Ludwig David Kahn, *The Loevinger Family of Laupeim, Pioneers in South Dakota, Its History and Genealogy*, compiled by Ludwig D. Kahn (self-pub., 1967).

76. Indian Office Report, National Archives, Bureau of Indian Affairs (1854), 159. On the murder of the Weisman children in the Dakota Territory, see George Kingsbury, *History of Dakota Territory* (Chicago: J. S. Clarke, 1915 [1953]), 306.

77. Farish, *History of Arizona*.

78. R. Michael Wilson, *Massacre at Wickenburg: Arizona's Great Mystery* (Guilford, Conn.: TwoDot, 2008).

79. Carol Gendler, "The Jews of Omaha," *Western States Jewish Historical Quarterly* 5, no. 3 (April 1973): 218.

80. Rosa K. Drachman, "From New York to Tucson in 1868," *Western States Jewish History* 22, no. 1 (October 1989).

81. Burl Taylor, interview by H. L. Rumge, field worker, Indian-Pioneer Collection, University of Oklahoma Libraries Western History Collections, vol. 89, March 18, 1937, 163.

82. Marcus, *Unites States Jewry*, 108; see also "Fire Endangers Landmark Used as Shelter against Indians," n.d., newspaper article from unknown paper, AJA Nearprint, Colorado, box P, folder 1; see also Dorothy Roberts, "The Jewish Colony at Cotopaxi," *Colorado Magazine*, 1941, published by the State Historical Society of Colorado; Flora Jane Satt, "The Cotopaxi Colony" (thesis, University of Colorado, 1950). The original, unpublished manuscript is held at the Denver Public Library Genealogy Department.

83. "A Joke by Renegade Apaches," *Jewish Review* 4, no. 38 (June 19, 1896): 8.

84. William Cronin, George Miles, and Jay Gitlin, eds., "Becoming West: Toward a New Meaning for Western History," in *Under an Open Sky: Rethinking America's Western Past* (New York: W. W. Norton, 1992), 15.

85. Donald H. Harrison, *Louis Rose: San Diego's First Jewish Settler and Entrepreneur* (San Diego: Sunbelt Publications, 2005).

86. Cyril Leonoff, "Pioneer Jews of British Columbia," *Western States Jewish History* 37, no. 3/4; "Morris Moss, Pioneer Jewish Fur Trader," Jewish Museum of the American West, http://www.jmaw.org/moss-jewish-british-columbia, accessed March 3, 2009.

87. "The Lariat Thrower," *Current Literature* 13, no. 2 (June 1893), 226.

88. *Los Angeles Star* 4, no. 26 (November 9, 1854): 2, c. 1, reprinted as "Indians and Caspar Berhrendt Perils of Los Angeles Business—1854" in *Western States Historical Quarterly* 2, no. 1 (January 1970): 64.

89. See also Juanita Brooks, *History of the Jews in Utah and Idaho* (Salt Lake City: Western Epics, 1973), 31. Her primary sources for the account were published in Thomas D. Brown, *Journal of the Southern Indian Mission*, ed. Juanita Brooks (Logan: Utah State University Press, 1972), 62; see also "A Narrow Escape: The Hostilities in the Owl's Head Mountains," *Arizona Daily Star*, June 15, 1886, which told the story of Enique Goldbaum's retributive violence. Special Collections, University of Arizona, AJA MS 401, Research Files, box 12, folder 20.

90. Abraham S. Chanin, "Zechendorf, William in Arizona and New Mexico History," in *Western States Jewish History* 32, nos. 2 and 3; 22, no. 1; and 11, no. 4.

91. Abraham S. Chanin, "How Could a Nice Jewish Man Scalp an Apache? William Zeckendorf I in the Arizona and New Mexico Territories, 1856–1878," *Western Jewish States Jewish History* 32, no. 2 and 3 (Winter/Spring 2000): 119–129.

92. *Weekly Arizonan*, April 5, 1871, quoted in Chanin, "Zackendorf, William," 123–124.

93. Chanin.

94. Goldberg, "An Old Timer's Experiences."

95. Goldberg.

96. Goldberg.

97. Historian Karl Jacoby has shown that the Camp Grant massacre outraged non-Arizonan whites. National press brandished President Grant as a murderer and turned against local whites. Karl Jacoby, *Shadows at Dawn: A Borderland Massacre and the Violence of History* (New York: Penguin, 2008).

98. Quoted in "The Marcus Goldbaum Family of Tucson," Jewish Museum of the American West, http://www.jmaw.org/goldbaum-tucson-jewish/, accessed April 11, 2010.

99. AJA MC 649, box 13, no. 4.

100. Special Collections, University of Arizona, MS401, Research Files, Arizona, box 16, folder 21, Levi Herman Company; MS401, Research Files, Arizona, box 12, folder 21, Goldbaum Family; and AJA SC 6836, "Herman Levi"

101. Isadore Straussburger, "Early Days in Montana" (manuscript at the Historical Society of Montana); and Nellie Strassburger, letter to Edgar Strassburger, December 29, 1949, both quoted in Benjamin Kelson, "The Jews of Montana—Part II," *Western States Jewish Historical Quarterly* 3, no. 3 (April 1971): 173.

102. For an account of the disastrous effects of violence and dislocation on Great Basin tribes—the Ute, Shoshone, and Paiute—see Blackhawk, *Violence over the Land.*

103. "Morris Lasker," *Jewish Criterion* 46, no. 28 (March 10, 1916).

104. Unknown author. The poem was originally printed in James B. Fry, *Army Sacrifices; or, Briefs from Official Pigeon-Holes. Sketches Based on Official Reports, Grouped Together for the Purpose of Illustrating the Services and Experiences of the Regular Army of the United States on the Indian Frontier* (New York: D. Van Nostrand, 1879). It was reprinted many times. See, for example, "Jews Proved Their Worth," *Jewish Criterion* 60, no. 24 (February 23, 1923).

105. Eleanore Stearns Venter, "In Memory of 'Nell' (A Horse Killed by the Indians in the Battle of Beecher Island)," Seattle, July 1917, AJA MC 130, box 1, folder 1, 52.

106. Morris Epstein and Anthony Tallarico, "Frontier Scout," *Highlights of History*, n.d., AJA MC 130, box 1, folder 9.

107. Wilbur Fiske Stone, ed., *History of Colorado*, vol. 4 (Chicago: S. J. Clarke, 1919), 640.

108. Inez Hunt and Wanetta W. Draper, *To Colorado's Restless Ghosts* (Denver: Sage Books, 1960), 292.

109. The details of the Mears story are compiled from duplications of materials of the State Historical Society of Colorado at the American Jewish Historical Society, P-781. These include "Otto Mears—the Pathfinder of the San Juan," *Illustrated Weekly*, October 24, 1900,

1, col. 1–2, State Historical Society of Colorado, Dawson Scrap Book 62 articles; *Denver Post*, November 23, 1902, and July 5, 1903, 357; *Denver Republican*, April 12, 1907, 359; and *Denver News*, April 23, 1909, 369; Sidney Jocknick, *Early Days on the Western Slope of Colorado and Campfire Chats with Otto Mears* (Denver: Carson Parker Co., 1913); Interview with Mears's daughter, Mrs. J. R. Pitcher, Pasadena, California, in LeRoy R. Hafen, "Otto Mears, 'Pathfinder of the San Juan,'" *Colorado Magazine* 9, no. 2 (March 1932): 71–74.

110. Hunt and Draper, *To Colorado's Restless Ghosts.*

111. The article appeared in *Saguache Chronicle* in 1875 and was reprinted in the *Colorado Springs Gazette* and *El Paso County News*, quoted in Hunt and Draper, *To Colorado's Restless Ghosts*, 298–299.

112. Hunt and Draper.

113. "Otto Mears, Russian Jew Who Built Southwest Empire and Fought Indians, Dead at 91," *Jewish Archives* (Boston), July 21, 1931, reprinted in *Western States Jewish History* 25, no. 4 (July 1993): 311.

114. "Otto Mears, Pioneer, Dead at 91," *Jewish Criterion* 78, no. 8 (July 3, 1931).

115. Joseph Emerson Smith, "Jewish Builders of Colorado," *Intermountain Jewish News* (Denver) 25, no. 37 (September 15, 1939), sec. C, 1–4. Similar celebrations would actually continue beyond the scope of my study into the 1960s. See, for example, Hunt and Draper, *To Colorado's Restless Ghosts*. James G. Schneider of Kankakee, Illinois, wrote a twenty-nine-verse ballad about Mears as a form of public education protesting the Colorado highway department's failure to replace the granite marker crediting and honoring Mears for building a highway. The marker read, "In Honor of Otto Mears—Pathfinder of the San Juan—Pioneer Road Builder—Built this Road in 1881—Erected by a Grateful People" in 1924. James G. Schneider, "The Ballad of Otto Mears, The Pathfinder of the San Juan Mountains," Kankakee, Ill., 1969, with cover art, sheet music, lyrics, and explanatory text, AJA P-781, box 1, folder 3.

116. Richard Slotkin, *Regeneration through Violence: The Mythology of the American Frontier, 1600–1860* (Middletown, Conn.: Wesleyan University Press, 1973).

117. A notable exception was Walter Hart Blumenthal, *Scalping Bounties and White Scalping*, a scathing indictment of settler violence. The manuscript, however, was never published. Walter Hart Blumenthal Papers, P 83, subseries 2, box 3, folder 6. American Jewish Historical Society.

118. "3 Indianer Gelintched," *Forverts* 1, no. 178 (November 15, 1897).

119. "Indianer In Kampf," *Forverts* 4, no. 56 (March 2, 1900).

120. "A Milchama Mit Indianer," *Forverts* 1, no. 163 (October 30, 1897).

121. "Der Indianer Oifshtand," *Forverts* 3, no. 1899 (August 4, 1899).

122. "Indianer Untzufriren" *Forverts* 4, no. 1135 (February 22, 1901).

123. No Title Item, *Forverts* 5, no. 1433 (December 12, 1901).

124. In her analysis of the Yiddish press's treatment of African Americans from 1915 to 1935, historian Hasia Diner showed that American Jews, for the most part, identified with the plight of African Americans. The press's treatment of Native Americans differed considerably. The *Forverts*' tendency to identify with whites instead of Native Americans resulted, I would suggest, from the crude fact of white-Indian competition for land and a smaller national pro-Indian voice in the broader American culture before the 1920s. Hasia Diner, *In the Almost Promised Land: American Blacks and Jews, 1915–1935* (Baltimore: Johns Hopkins University Press, 1977).

125. Native Americans received citizenship only in 1924.

126. "Mlchemos Fun Apache Indianer un Mormonen," *Forverts* 4, no. 1039 (November 18, 1900).

127. "Mora Fun An Indianer Oifshtand," *Forverts* 4, no. 1034 (November 13, 1900).

128. "Die Indianer In Oifshtand," *Forverts* 4, no. 1110 (January 28, 1901).

129. Jonathan Boyarin, *The Unconverted Self: Jews, Indians, and the Identity of Christian Europe* (Chicago: University of Chicago Press, 2009).

CHAPTER 3 — JEWISH MIDDLEMEN MERCHANTS, INDIAN CURIOS, AND THE EXTENSIONS OF AMERICAN CAPITALISM

1. The term "exalted subject" comes from the critical Canadian scholar Sunera Thobani in her broad discussion of Canada's deployment of race thinking and policy in North American colonialism. Sunera Thobani, *Exalted Subjects: Studies in the Making of Race and Nation in Canada* (Toronto: University of Toronto Press, 2007).

2. William Toll, "The Jewish Merchant and Civic Order in the Urban West," in *Jewish Life in the American West: Perspectives on Migration, Settlement and Community*, ed. Ava F. Kahn (Seattle: University of Washington Press, 2002), 83.

3. Leah Dilworth, *Imagining Indians in the Southwest: Persistent Visions of a Primitive Past* (Washington, D.C.: Smithsonian Institution Press, 1996).

4. A similar "heritage move" effect has been well noted in the commodification of Jewish objects and sites of Jewish memory/history in Poland and elsewhere in Eastern Europe after World War II. Barbara Kirschenblatt-Gimblett, *Destination Culture: Tourism, Museums, and Heritage* (Berkeley: University of California Press, 1998).

5. Yuri Slezkine, *The Jewish Century* (Princeton: Princeton University Press, 2004); Hasia Diner, *Roads Taken: The Great Jewish Migrations to the New World and the Peddlers Who Forged the Way* (New Haven: Yale University Press, 2015).

6. See Ruth B. Phillips, "The Turn of the Primitive: Modernism, the Stranger, and the Indigenous Artist," in *Exiles, Diasporas, and Strangers*, ed. Kobena Mercer (Cambridge, Mass.: MIT Press, 2008), 46–71; Gwynne Schrire, "The German Jewish Immigrant Contribution to South African Art," *Jewish Affairs* 65, no. 2 (2010): 8–14; Richard I. Cohen, *Jewish Icons: Art and Society in Modern Europe* (Berkeley: University of California Press, 1998); Sven Beller, *Vienna and the Jews, 1867–1938: A Cultural History* (Cambridge: Cambridge University Press, 1989); Michael Brenner, *The Renaissance of Jewish Culture in Weimar Germany* (New Haven: Yale University Press, 1996).

7. William G. Robbins, *Colony and Empire: The Capitalist Transformation of the American West* (Lawrence: University Press of Kansas, 1994); and William Cronon, *Nature's Metropolis: Chicago and the Great West* (New York: W.W. Norton, 1991); William Cronin, George Miles, and Jay Gitlin, eds., "Becoming West: Toward a New Meaning for Western History," in *Under an Open Sky: Rethinking America's Western Past* (New York: W. W. Norton, 1992).

8. Kenneth Libo and Irving Howe, *We Lived There, Too: In Their Own Words and Pictures—Pioneer Jews and the Westward Movement of America, 1630–1930*, 1st ed. (New York: St. Martin's/Marek, 1984).

9. Diner, *Roads Taken.*

10. Jonathan Sarna, *American Judaism: A History* (New Haven: Yale University Press, 2004).

11. Diner, *Roads Taken.*

12. Interview with Barney Zimmerman, Works Progress Administration, Indian-Pioneer History Project for Oklahoma, University of Oklahoma Libraries Western History Collections, vol. 101, Interview 12548, December 30, 1937.

13. Interview with Barney Zimmerman.

14. Interview with Barney Zimmerman.

15. Biographic details about Lumbrozo and his business dealings were compiled by George Ely Russell, a "certified genealogist" in the 1970s. His file on Lumbrozo can be found at the AJA GF 639, folder 1. See also Cyrus Adler and J. H. Hollander, "Lumbrozo, Jacob," in *Jewish Encyclopedia*, ed. Isidore Singer (New York: Funk & Wagnalls, 1906), http://www.jewishencyclopedia.com/.

16. Joseph Jacobs and Clarence I. de Sola, "Solomons, Levy," in *Jewish Encyclopedia*, ed. Isidore Singer (New York: Funk & Wagnalls, 1906).

17. Cyrus Adler and A. S. W. Rosenbach, "Levy, Aaron," in *Jewish Encyclopedia*, ed. Isidore Singer (New York: Funk & Wagnalls, 1906).

18. Cyrus Adler and S. N. Deinard, "Minnesota," in *Jewish Encyclopedia*, ed. Isidore Singer (New York: Funk & Wagnalls, 1906).

19. Matthew J. Eisenberg, "The Last Frontier: Jewish Pioneers in Alaska, Part II," *Western States Jewish History* 24, no. 2 (January 1992): 120–121.

20. See also another Jewish sealer, the German-born Joseph Boscowitz, who operated several ships and shunners on the Pacific Northwest and opened a chain of stores, leading the coastal sealing industry as a partner in the British Columbia Merchants Line, the Boscowitz Steamship Co., from the 1880s to the turn of the century; his suppliers were all Natives. Cyril Leonoff, "Pioneer Jews of British Columbia," *Western States Jewish History* 37, no. 3/4 (2005), http://www.jmaw.org/boscowitz-jewish-victoria/.

21. Gustav Kahn and the Kahn family, Memoirs of Gustav Kahn of Santa Fe, New Mexico, Recollections of a New Mexico Merchants, 1964, AJA SC 6017, box 1, folder 1.

22. Esther Leiser, interview by Benjamin Kelsen, Missoula, Mo., quoted in Benjamin Kelson, "The Jews of Montana—Part II," *Western States Jewish Historical Quarterly* 3, no. 3 (April 1971): 188.

23. "Indians Trading," *Boston Hebrew Observer* 1, no. 21 (May 25, 1883).

24. "Decay Hits Oldest Town," *Los Angeles Times*, September 24, 1924.

25. This argument was often made implicitly rather than explicitly. It is significant, however, given that the "missionary spirit" was at the heart of much of Indian relations. Though Jews were excluded from harnessing this missionizing spirit, they nonetheless adopted an adapted version of it that removed religion from the equation.

26. Hyman O. Danoff, "Indian Traders of the Southwest: The Danoffs of New Mexico," *Western States Jewish Historical Quarterly* 12, no. 4 (July 1980): 291–303.

27. Danoff, "Indian Traders."

28. Juneau, Alaska's Russian-born Reuben Goldstein exchanged furs for "tickets" only redeemable at the Goldstein Store. See Eisenberg, "The Last Frontier," 119–135.

29. Eisenberg, "The Last Frontier."

30. Richard L. Carrico, "Simon Goldbaum of San Luis Rey," *Western States Jewish History* 13, no. 2 (July 1991); and Richard L. Carrico, "Wolf Kalisher: Pioneer Merchant and Indian Advocate," *Western States Jewish History* 15, no. 2, and 38, nos. 3 and 4.

31. Melvin J. Glatt, "A Torah, a Cannon, a Jewish Chaplain," *Jewish Times* (Boston), September 11, 1958, 37.

32. Lewis Meyer, *Preposterous Papa: A Hilarious and Affectionate Portrait by His Son* (New York: Hawthorn Books, 1959), 21–22.

33. Victoria K. Haskins, *Matrons and Maids: Regulating Indian Domestic Service in Tucson, 1914–1934* (Tucson: University of Arizona Press, 2012).

34. Interview with Nat Dickerson, University of Oklahoma Libraries Western History Collections, 6227, June 1, 1937, 24:4–5.

35. MS, RG 75, Records of the Bureau of Indian Affairs, Office of Indian Trade, Letters Sent, volume B., National Archives, reprinted as "John Mason to Jacob Marks, 1811," and "John Mason to Ben Sheftall, 1813," in Joseph L. Blau and Salo W. Baron, eds., *The Jews of the United States, 1790–1840: A Documentary History*, vol. 1 (New York: Columbia University Press and the Jewish Publication Society of America, 1963), 112–115. The political reality of this history is that the process was by no means a straightforward or simple matter of the state paving the way for commerce at the expense of Native agency or interests. See David Andrew Nichols, *Red Gentlemen and White Savages: Indians, Federalists, and the Search for Order on the American Frontier* (Charlottesville: University of Virginia Press, 2008).

36. William J. Parish, "The German Jew and the Commercial Revolution in Territorial New Mexico, 1850–1900," *The University of New Mexico Sixth Annual Research Lecture*, May 1, 1959. Parish made no mention of these Jews' business with Native Americans nor of profiting from the broad transformation in Native American economics, politics, geography, and culture that their business affected.

37. Hal K. Rothman, *Devil's Bargains: Tourism in the Twentieth-Century American West* (Kansas City: University Press of Kansas, 1998), 82.

38. Rothman.

39. See in Blau and Baron, *Jews of the United States*, 847, 852; on Elhart, see *Letters of Benjamin Hawkins, 1796–1806, Collections of the Georgia Historical Society*, ix, 169, 258, 476, in Blau and Baron, 986.

40. Jews supplied Indian reservations with foodstuffs, flour, beef, corn, and general merchandise through state-backed contracts. See letters in the Microfilm Records of the New Mexico Superintendent of Indian Affairs, roll #24, cabinet 59, drawer 10, T1, 1875–1880, with letters from Louis Rosenbaum dated June 30, 1876, from Las Cruces, N.Mex., the Spiegelberg brothers in Santa Fe, throughout the summer and fall of 1875, D. Bernard Koch of Santa Fe in March 1897, and Z. Staab in January 1875.

41. From 1795 to 1822, the U.S. government operated trading houses, the so-called factory system run by the Office of Indian Trade, to control Indian trade throughout its Indian Territories. After 1822, it provided licenses to traders and prescriptions of conditions for private trade.

42. Cronon, *Nature's Metropolis*, part 3, "The Geography of Capital."

43. Lewis Levy, W. Cohn, Joseph Boscowitz, Morris Dobrin, Abraham Martin, Abraham Israel of the firm "Martin and Israel—Indian Traders," Abraham Frankel, Hyman Copperman, Julius Seitz, Nathan Solomon, owner of "The Indian Store," Aaron Oldenburg, Leopold Blum, Lewis Goldstone, Samuel Myers, Henry Nathan, and Jules Friedman. Archives of Sarah H. Tobe, Cyril E. Leonoff, Christopher Hanna, and David Rome, "More Early Pioneers of British Columbia, 1858–1880s," Jewish Museum of the American West, http://www.jmaw.org/jewish-pioneers-british-columbia/, accessed December 11, 2001.

44. See, for example, Eileen Hallett Stone, *A Homeland in the West: Utah Jews Remember* (Salt Lake City: University of Utah Press, 2001); Benjamin Kelsen, "The Jews of Montana, Parts II–V," *Western States Jewish Historical Quarterly* 3, no. 4 (1971): 227–242; Benjamin Kelson, "The Jews of Montana, Part I," *Western States Jewish Historical Quarterly* 3, no. 2 (1971): 113–120.

45. George Colpitts, "Jewish Merchants and First Nation Trappers in Northern Canada's Industrializing Fur Trade, 1916–1939" (unpublished conference paper, Canadian Historical Association, June 3, 2013, Victoria, BC).

46. George Colpitts, "Itinerant Jewish and Arabic Trading in the Dene's North, 1916–1930," *Journal of the Canadian Historical Association / Revue de la Société historique du Canada* 24, no. 1 (2013): 163–213.

47. Ava Fran Kahn, *Jewish Life in the American West: Perspectives on Migration, Settlement, and Community* (Los Angeles: Autry Museum of Western Heritage, 2002); Jeanne E. Abrams, *Jewish Women Pioneering the Frontier Trail: A History in the American West* (New York: New York University Press, 2006); Ellen Eisenberg, Ava F. Kahn, and William Toll, *Jews of the Pacific Coast: Reinventing Community on America's Edge* (Portland: University of Washington Press, 2010).

48. See, for example, Floyd S. Fierman, *Guts and Ruts: The Jewish Pioneer on the Trail in the American Southwest* (New York: Ktav, 1985).

49. Hasia Diner, *Hungering for America: Italian, Irish, and Jewish Foodways in the Age of Migration* (Cambridge, Mass.: Harvard University Press, 2001); Hasia Diner, *The Jews of the United States, 1654–2000* (Berkeley: University of California Press, 2004).

50. Rothman, *Devil's Bargains*, 97.

51. Roland W. Hawker, "The Johnson Street Gang: British Columbia's Early Indian Art Dealers," *B.C. Historical News* 22, no. 1 (Winter 1989): 10–14.

52. Along with the market for Southwest and Pacific Northwest Native American goods, the third center of the curio trade was in the Plains. Omaha, Nebraska's Julius Meyer was a significant player there. Earlier markets in upstate New York, Upper Canada, and the Great Lakes Region emerged with an earlier wave of colonizing settlement. Those markets included few or no Jews, though Jewish firms ran several important Indian fur trading operations.

53. See Floyd S. Fierman, *The Speigelbergs of New Mexico, Merchants and Bankers, 1844–1893*, vol. 1:4 (El Paso: Texas Western College Press, 1964). Astonishingly, Flora Speigelberg left a

confession that Willi, her husband, purchased an Indian orphan in 1905, whom the family named Joseph, educated, and raised. Speigelberg Family Papers, AJA SC 11853, Cincinnati, Ohio.

54. Jonathan Batkin, "Some Early Curio Dealers of New Mexico," *American Indian Art Magazine* 23, no. 3 (1998): 69.

55. Though these are different markets with different distribution networks, different final consumer destinations, and are ultimately made up of objects with meanings that differ on account of the various discursive worlds to which they belong, for my broader purposes in this argument I am treating them as one bundled market, irrespective of market segmentation. For a similar use of these objects bundled together, see Kate C. Duncan, *1001 Curious Things: Ye Olde Curiosity Shop and Native American Art* (Seattle: University of Washington Press, 2000).

56. Carter Jones Meyer and Diana Royer, eds., "Introduction," in *Selling the Indian: Commercializing and Appropriating American Indian Cultures* (Tucson: University of Arizona Press, 2001), xi.

57. Robert Fay Schrader, *The Indian Arts & Crafts Board: An Aspect of New Deal Indian Policy* (Albuquerque: University of New Mexico Press, 1983). See also Kathleen Howard, "Creating an Enchanted Land: Curio Entrepreneurs Promote and Sell the Indian Southwest, 1880–1940" (PhD diss., Arizona State University, 2002).

58. Art historians, anthropologists, and historians of Native America have understood the production and sale of Indian cultural commodities in various ways. Critics of capitalism have bemoaned the commodification of everyday goods and ceremonial artifacts, with particular emphasis on the loss of cultural meaning during this transformation. The curio trade has been examined from the perspective of the collectors, focusing in some cases on the accumulation of wealth by Americans, increased leisure time, and Victorian sensibilities—that is, on the cultural changes brought about by advancing industrial capitalism. Others have focused on the colonial aspects of the trade in which curios or "grotesques" contributed to the discourses of power and control between the strange and the familiar and the systems of belief that "projected the American anti-self onto Indian tribes." See Patricia Fogelman Lange, "Nineteenth Century Cochiti Figurines: Commodity Fetishes," *Museum Anthropology* 19, no. 1 (1995): 39–44. Still other scholars have attended to the economic processes that transformed Indian culture. Some of this work emphasizes the experiences and consequences of exploitation, and some emphasizes Native people's agency in the operations. See Ruth Phillips in her introduction to B. Phillips and Christopher B. Steiner, eds., *Unpacking Culture: Art and Commodity in Colonial and Postcolonial Worlds* (Berkeley: University of California Press, 1999), 4. Finally, scholars have also considered the curio from the perspective of the invention of the tourist "Indian" and the invention of place-bound tourism. See, for example, Eliza McFeely, *Zuni and the American Imagination* (New York: Hill and Wang, 2001); Rothman, *Devil's Bargains*.

59. Henry Russell Wray, "A Gem in Art," *Weekly New Mexico Review*, p. 4, col. 6, 1894.

60. Victoria Directory and *Victoria Times* advertisement, in *Scribe: The Journal of the Jewish Historical Society of B.C.* 19, no. 1 (1999): 9n28.

61. Helen Akrigg and G. P. V. Akrigg, *British Columbia Chronicle: Gold & Colonists* (Vancouver: Discovery Press, 1977).

62. Cyril Edel Leonoff, *Pioneers, Pedlars, and Prayer Shawls: The Jewish Communities in British Columbia and the Yukon* (Victoria, BC: Sono Nis Press, 1978).

63. Christopher J. P. Hanna, "The Early Jewish Coastal Fur Traders," *Scribe: The Journal of the Jewish Historical Society of B.C.* 19, no. 1 (1999): 9–14.

64. *Victoria Evening Express*, September 9, 1864, 3.

65. Christopher J. P. Hanna, "Mike Cohen: 'King John of the Red House,'" *Scribe: The Journal of the Jewish Historical Society of B.C.* 19, no. 1 (1999): 29–34.

66. Boas's Jewishness is subject to a growing scholarly discussion. See Douglass Cole, *Franz Boas: The Early Years, 1858–1906* (Seattle: University of Washington Press, 1999); Regna

Darnell, *And along Came Boas: Continuity and Revolution in Americanist Anthropology* (Amsterdam: John Benjamins, 1998); Jeffrey David Feldman, "The Jewish Roots and Routes of Anthropology," *Anthropological Quarterly* 77, no. 1 (2004): 107–125; Gelya Frank, "Jews, Multiculturalism and Boasian Anthropology," *American Anthropologist* 99, no. 4 (1997): 731–745; Leonard Glick, "Types Distinct from Our Own: Franz Boas on Jewish Identity and Assimilation," *American Anthropologist* 84 (1982): 545–565.

67. Douglas Cole, *Captured Heritage: The Scramble for Northwest Coast Artifacts* (Seattle: University of Washington Press, 1985).

68. Sarah H. Tobe, "Victoria's Curio Dealers," *Scribe: The Journal of the Jewish Historical Society of B.C.* 19, no. 2 (1999): 15–18.

69. Hawker, "Johnson Street Gang."

70. Dun & Bradstreet Corporation Records, Baker Library Historical Collections, Harvard Business School.

71. R. G. Dun & Co. Credit Report Volumes, Baker Library Historical Collections, Harvard Business School, California, vol. 14, San Francisco, n.d., 171.

72. New Mexico, vol. 1, July 31, 1858, 355; Las Vegas, April 18, 1870, and August 15, 1873, 384.

73. Western Territories, vol. 2, Indian Territories (Oklahoma), 1846–1876; Western Territories, vol. 3, Indian Territories, 1871–1876; Silver City, April 1870 and March 5, 1874, 210.

74. Santa Fe, October 31, 1871, and August 1873, 396.

75. Western Territories, vol. 1, Nevada, 1850–1881, order no. 85–1509, reel 8, October 7, 1859, 145.

76. Howard, "Creating an Enchanted Land," iii.

77. Philip J. Deloria, *Playing Indian* (New Haven: Yale University Press, 1998); Rayna Green, "The Tribe Called Wannabee: Playing Indian in America and Europe," *Folklore* 99, no. 1 (1988): 30–55; and Jay Mechling, "'Playing Indian' and the Search for Authenticity in Modern White America," *Prospects* 5 (1980): 17–33.

78. Here I am using the language of Robert F. Berkhofer Jr., *The White Man's Indian: Images of the American Indian from Columbus to the Present* (New York: Knopf, 1978).

79. Jonathan Batkin, "Tourism Is Overrated: Pueblo Pottery and the Early Curio Trade, 1880–1910," in *Unpacking Culture: Art and Commodity in Colonial and Postcolonial Worlds*, ed. Ruth B. Phillips and Christopher B. Steiner (Berkeley: University of California Press, 1999), 282–297.

80. Batkin, "Some Early Curio Dealers of New Mexico," 68–81.

81. *Omaha Morning Bee*, May 11, 1909, cited in Carol Gendler, "The Jews of Omaha," *Western States Jewish Historical Quarterly* 5, no. 3 (April 1973): 217; Mel L. Marks, *Jews among the Indians: Tales of Adventure and Conflict in the Old West* (Chicago: Benison Books, 1992).

82. R. G. Dun & Co. Credit Report Volumes, Baker Library Historical Collections, Harvard Business School, Nebraska, vol. 4, Nebraska Territory, 1872–1877, Omaha, March 15, 1873, and December 20, 1875, 491.

83. Susan Ludmer-Gilebe, "Box-Ka-Re-Sha-Hash-Ta-Ka from Nebraska," *Toledo Jewish News*, July 1929, 18.

84. Marks, *Jews among the Indians*, 50.

85. Picture Collection 2980: Julius Meyer—store in Omaha, c-2284, posed with Indians N-2535, Indian wigwam store n-2538, d-403, Julius Meyer with Red Cloud, Sitting Bull, Swift Bear, and Spotted Tail n. 2536, photo with chief standing bear, 29752, n2534, AJA, Cincinnati, Ohio.

86. Picture Collection 2980.

87. For a broader discussion, see Gerald R. McMaster, "Tenuous Lines of Decent: Indian Arts and Crafts of the Reservation Period," *Indian Arts and Crafts*, publication of the Canadian Museum of Civilization, 205–236.

88. Cole, *Captured Heritage*.

89. Jonathan Batkin, "Mail-Order Catalogs as Artifacts," *American Indian Art Magazine* 29, no. 2 (2004): 40–49.

90. Batkin, "Some Early Curio Dealers of New Mexico."

91. Batkin, "Mail-Order Catalogs."

92. The Indian curio boom ought also to be seen within the context of booming markets for other exotica—Japanese and Chinese antiques and curios, African heritage objects, and relics from ancient defunct empires. See, for example, David Lowenthal, *Possessed by the Past: The Heritage Crusade and the Spoils of History* (New York: Free Press, 1996).

93. Batkin, "Mail-Order Catalogs," 40–49.

94. Catalog of Gold's Free Museum, 1889, Beinecke Rare Book and Manuscript Library, Yale University, ZC54 889go.

95. For example, Black Hills Retail Catalog #12. Est. 1884 (1911): *Indian Relic and Curio Establishment.* L. W. Stilwell Wholesale and Retail. Deadwood, S.Dak., ZC35 911LW, Beinecke Rare Book and Manuscript Library, Yale University.

96. Catalog of Collection of Curios, ZC56 893dy, Beinecke Rare Book and Manuscript Library, Yale University.

97. An October 1881 article about a topical remedy called St. Jacob's Oil in which Tammen was quoted described him as "a well known and reliable collector of Colorado curiosities." *Rocky Mountain News* 8 (1881): 43; Martin Padget, "Claiming, Corrupting, Contesting: Reconsidering 'The West' in Western American Literature," *American Literary History* 10, no. 2 (Summer 1998): 378–392.

98. Quoted in Batkin, "Some Early Curio Dealers."

99. Hartmut Lutz, "German Indianthusiasm: A Socially Constructed German National (ist) Myth," in *Germans and Indians: Fantasies, Encounters, Projections*, ed. Colin G. Calloway, Gerd Gemunden, and Susanne Zantop (Lincoln: University of Nebraska Press, 2002), 167–184.

100. Catherine Albanese, *Nature Religion in America: From the Algonkian Indians to the New Age* (Chicago: University of Chicago Press, 1990); and Roderick Nash, *Wilderness and the American Mind* (New Haven: Yale University Press, 2001).

101. Sarah H. Tobe, "New Frontiers," *Scribe: The Journal of the Jewish Historical Society of B.C.* 19, no. 2 (1999): 10.

102. Sarah H. Tobe, "J.J. Hart on the Map," *Scribe: The Journal of the Jewish Historical Society of B.C.* 19, no. 2 (1999): 3–9.

103. *British Colonist*, August, 10, 1866, 3, quoted in Hawker, "Johnson Street Gang," 11.

104. *British Colonist*, December 14, 1904, 5, quoted in Tobe, "J.J. Hart on the Map," 3–9.

105. *British Colonist*, December 14, 1904, 5, quoted in Tobe, "J.J. Hart on the Map." Countless discussions of Indian life throughout the nineteenth century had linked their ancient ancestors with those of the biblical Israelites as well as discussions (and sales) that linked Indians with ancient Egyptians. Claims that American Indians descended from the "Lost Tribes" of ancient Israel, popular from the sixteenth century through the early twentieth, comprise a significant amount of literature. There is surprisingly little scholarship on Jews' response to the claim, though it did engage many of the most significant Jewish leaders of the mid-nineteenth century, among them Mordecai Manuel Noah, Isaac Meyer Wise, Isaac Leeser, David Philipson, and even Abraham Gieger in Germany. On Lost Tribes claims, see Robert Wauchope, *Lost Tribes and Sunken Continents: Myth and Method in the Study of American Indians* (Chicago: University of Chicago Press, 1962); Walter Hart Blumenthal, *In Old America: Random Chapters on the Early Aborigines* (New York: Walton Book Company, 1931); and Zvi Ben-Dor Benite, *The Ten Lost Tribes: A World History* (New York: Oxford University Press, 2009).

106. Museum of New Mexico, Neg. no. 7890, reprinted in Tomas Jaehn, ed., *Jewish Pioneers of New Mexico* (Albuquerque: University of New Mexico Press, 2003); Harriett Rochlin and Fred Rochlin, *Pioneer Jews: A New American Life in the Far West* (Boston: Houghton Mifflin: 1984), 62.

107. John R. Lovett, "The Levites of Apache, Oklahoma," *Western States Jewish History* 24, no. 4 (July 1992): 299–307. Levite was among the estimated thousand Jews arriving in

Oklahoma Territory after the state opened it to whites in 1889. His customers included Kiowa, Comanche, Apache, Wichitas, Kiowa Apache, Caddo, and other smaller tribes, many of whom had fought and lost in the recently ended wars for the southern plains (Apache Indians were technically still prisoners of war at Fort Sill).

108. George Levite, *By George! For Lilly*, pamphlet published by George Levite (1974), reprinted by Georgann Levite Vinyard and Molly Sue Levite Griffis, 1986, 10–16.

109. D. H. Lawrence, as well as the Taos group that included Mabel Dodge Lujan, Martha Graham, Alfred Steiglitz, Georgia O'Keefe, and many others, saw the Indians of the Southwest as key symbolic forces of authentic American aboriginality out of which could grow an American sensibility and expression finally detached from Europe. See, for example, Phyllis Deery Stanton, "Processing the Native American through Western Consciousness: D. H. Lawrence and the Red Indians of the Americas," *Wicazo Sa Review* 12, no. 2 (Autumn 1997): 59–84; and Lois Palken Rudnick, *Utopian Vistas: The Mabel Dodge Luhan House and the American Counterculture* (Albuquerque: University of New Mexico Press, 1996).

110. On John Collier's place in Luhan's circle, see Flannery Burke, *From Greenwich Village to Taos: Primitivism and Place at Mabel Dodge Luhan's* (Lawrence: University Press of Kansas, 2008).

111. Marta Weigle and Barbara A. Babcock, *The Great Southwest of the Fred Harvey Company and the Santa Fe Railway* (Phoenix, Ariz.: Heard Museum, distributed by the University of Arizona Press, 1996); Kathleen Howard and Diana Pardue, *Inventing the Southwest: The Fred Harvey Company and Native American Art* (Flagstaff, Ariz.: Northland, 1996); and Dilworth, *Imagining Indians*; Howard, "Creating an Enchanted Land," 37.

112. Howard and Pardue, *Inventing the Southwest*; and Dilworth, *Imagining Indians*.

CHAPTER 4 — JEWISH RHETORICAL USES OF INDIANS IN AN ERA OF NATIVIST ANXIETIES

1. Historian Richard White has described a "middle ground" between mostly French Europeans and Great Lakes region Native Americans from 1650 to 1810. In these middle spaces, both whites and Natives exercised cooperative power in order to meet mutual needs. New cultural forms emerged from the amalgamation of accommodations, adjustments, misunderstandings, and erroneous assumptions. I have avoided the phrase "middle ground" in order to avoid evoking this broader phenomenon. Richard White, *The Middle Ground: Indians, Empires, and Republics in the Great Lakes Region, 1650–1810* (Cambridge: University of Cambridge Press, 1991).

2. Walter Benn Michaels, *Our America: Nativism, Modernism, and Pluralism* (Durham: Duke University Press, 1995); John Higham, *Strangers in the Land: Patterns of American Nativism, 1860–1925* (New Brunswick, N.J.: Rutgers University Press, 2002).

3. Barbara Chiarello, "(Un)Veiling American Imperialism: The Co-contextualization of Early Twentieth Century Jewish American and Native American Literature" (PhD diss., University of Texas at Arlington, 2000); Carol J. Batker, *Reforming Fictions: Native, African, and Jewish American Women's Literature and Journalism in the Progressive Era* (New York: Columbia University Press, 2000). Likewise, Steven Katz examined American Hebrew writers' preoccupations with African and Native Americans. In discussing a handful of epic poems and novels, Katz extrapolated on American Jews' "curiosity about other groups, out of sympathy with how other marginalized fared . . . in America." Stephen Katz, *Red, Black, and Jew: New Frontiers in Hebrew Literature* (Austin: University of Texas Press, 2009), 1.

4. William H. Tucker, *The Funding of Scientific Racism: Wickliffe Draper and the Pioneer Fund* (Urbana: University of Illinois Press, 2002).

5. William H. Tucker, *The Science and Politics of Racial Research* (Urbana: University of Illinois Press, 1994).

6. Race-based legislation in the United States on matters of immigration, miscegenation, and citizenship were carefully studied by Nazi legislators from 1933 to 1935 and even influenced the shape of the Nazi Nuremberg Laws. Nazi legal scholars looked at American legislation about Blacks, Indians, and Jews (among others). James Q. Whitman, *Hitler's American Model: The United States and the Making of Nazi Race Law* (Princeton: Princeton University Press, 2017).

7. On Jewish racial status in the nineteenth century, see Eric L. Goldstein, "Different Blood Flows in Our Veins: Jews and Racial Self-Definition in Late Nineteenth Century America," *American Jewish History* 85 (March 1997): 29–55.

8. Goldstein, 388.

9. Svingen J. Orlan, "The Case of Spotted Hawk and Little Whirlwind: An American Indian Dreyfus Affair," *Western Historical Quarterly* 15, no. 3 (July 1984): 281–297.

10. Samuel George Morton, *Crania Americana; Or, A Comparative View of the Skulls of Various Aboriginal Nations of North and South America. To Which is Prefixed an Essay on the Varieties of the Human Species* (Philadelphia: J. Dobson, 1838).

11. Louis Menand, "Morton, Agassiz, and the Origins of Scientific Racism in the United States," *Journal of Blacks in Higher Education*, no. 34 (Winter 2001–2002): 110–113.

12. Menand, 189.

13. Menand, 21.

14. Goldstein, "Different Blood Flows," 395.

15. Jane E. Simonsen, *Making Home Work: Domesticity and Native American Assimilation in the American West, 1860–1919* (Chapel Hill: University of North Carolina Press, 2006).

16. Theodore Lothrop Stoddard, *The Rising Tide of Color against White World-Supremacy* (New York: Charles Scribner's Sons, 1921); and Theodore Lothrop Stoddard, *Revolt against Civilization: The Menace of the Under Man* (London: Chapman and Hall, 1922).

17. Alfred P. Schultz, *Race or Mongrel: A Brief History of the Rise and Fall of the Ancient Races of Earth: A Theory That the Fall of Nations Is Due to Intermarriage with Alien Stocks: A Demonstration That a Nation's Strength Is Due to Racial Purity: A Prophecy That America Will Sink to Early Decay Unless Immigration Is Rigorously Restricted* (Boston: L. C. Page, 1908), 42.

18. Schultz, 43–44.

19. Nathaniel Shaler, *The Neighbor: The Natural History of Human Contacts* (Boston: Houghton Mifflin, 1904), 59–60.

20. Shaler, 63.

21. Shaler, 63.

22. Shaler, 320.

23. Shaler, 199.

24. Shaler, 202.

25. Madison Grant, *The Passing of the Great Race: Or, The Racial Basis of European History* (New York: Scribner, 1916), 46–47, 90.

26. Grant, *Passing of the Great Race.*

27. Restriction of Immigration, Hearings before the Committee on Immigration and Naturalization House of Representatives, No. HR6540-68, at 570, 571 (January 5, 1924).

28. William Z. Ripley, *Races of Europe: A Sociological Study* (New York: D. Appleton, 1899), 395, 396.

29. Ripley, *Races of Europe.*

30. William Christie Macleod, *The American Indian Frontier* (New York: Knopf, 1928), 383.

31. H. J. D. Astley, *Biblical Anthropology: Compared with and Illustrated by the Folklore of Europe and the Customs of Primitive Peoples* (London: Oxford University Press, 1929).

32. Astley, *Biblical Anthropology*, 35–42.

33. Astley, 67.

34. W. J. Tinkle, "Heredity of Habitual Wandering," *Journal of Heredity* 18 (1927): 548–551.

35. Edward M. East, *Heredity and Human Affairs* (New York: Charles Scribner's Sons, 1929), 179, 188–189.

36. East, *Heredity and Human Affairs.*
37. Goldstein, "Different Blood Flows," 389–390.
38. John R. Commons, *Races and Immigrants in America* (New York: Macmillan, 1907), 213.
39. Commons.
40. Commons, 175.
41. Commons, 94.
42. Commons, 133.
43. Prescott Farnsworth Hall, *Immigration and Its Effects upon the United States* (New York: Henry Holt, 1908), 8.
44. Hall, *Immigration and Its Effects*, 23–24.
45. Hall, 61.
46. Hall, 117–118.
47. Hall, 348.
48. Hall, 352.
49. Hall, 363.
50. Frank Julian Warne, *The Immigrant Invasion* (New York: Mead, 1913).
51. Warne, *Immigrant Invasion*, 87–88.
52. These included Senators Bruce (p. 5955) and Jones (p. 6614) and Representatives Bacon (p. 5902), Byrnes (p. 5653), Johnson (p. 5648), McLoed (p. 5675–6), McReynolds (p. 5855), Michener (p. 5909), Miller (p. 5883), Newton (p. 6240); Rosenbloom (p. 5851), Vaile (p. 5922), Vincent (p. 6266), White (p. 5898), and Wilson (p. 5671; all references to *Cong. Rec.*, April 1924). Restriction of Immigration, Hearings before the Committee on Immigration and Naturalization House of Representatives, No. HR6540-68, at 580–581 (January 5, 1924).
53. Kevin Bruyneel, "Challenging American Boundaries: Indigenous People and the 'Gift' of US Citizenship," *Studies in American Political Development* 18, no. 1 (2004): 30–43.
54. Mae M. Ngai, "The Architecture of Race in American Immigration Law: A Reexamination of the Immigration Act of 1924," *Journal of American History* 86, no. 1 (June 1999): 67–92.
55. Gary C. Stein, "The Indian Citizenship Act of 1924," *New Mexico Historical Review* 47, no. 3 (1972): 257–247.
56. Indian Rights Association, Collection 1523, Abstract, Historical Society of Pennsylvania.
57. Jonathan Spiro, *Defending the Master Race: Conservation, Eugenics, and the Legacy of Madison Grant* (Burlington, Vt.: University of Vermont Press, 2009), 209.
58. Approved June 2, 1924. H.R. Doc. No. 6355-69, at 233 (June 2, 1924), Public, No. 175. See Certificates of Citizenship to Indians, H.R. Rep. No. 222-68 (February 22, 1924).
59. Restriction of Immigration, Hearings before the Committee on Immigration and Naturalization, House of Representatives, 68th Cong., first session, on H.R. Doc. No. 5-68, 101-68, 561-68, 6540-68 (1924), Washington, Government Printing Office.
60. Batker, *Reforming Fictions.*
61. Kevin MacDonald, *The Culture of Critique: An Evolutionary Analysis of Jewish Involvement in Twentieth-Century Intellectual and Political Movements* (Santa Barbara, Calif.: Praeger Books, 1998), 309.
62. MacDonald.
63. Chin Jou, "Contesting Nativism: The New York Congressional Delegation's Case against the Immigration Act of 1924," *Federal History Online* 3 (2001): 66–79.
64. These organizations included the American Defense Society, the American Eugenics Society, the Citizens Committee on Immigration Legislation, the Eugenics Research Association, the American Prison Society, the American Bison Society, the American Association of Mammalogists, the National Parks Association, and the National Parks Committee. Spiro, *Defending the Master Race.*
65. Spiro, 231.
66. See, for example, Advertisement, *Jewish Criterion* 67, no. 11 (January 22, 1926); "Review of Jewish Books and Authors. Winning of the West. Review of Sidney Herschel Small's

Sword and Candle. Bobbs-Merrill Co.," *Jewish Criterion* 71, no. 17 (March 2, 1928); "[Rabbi] Dr. Freehof Sees Carl Carmer Revealing the True Soul of America," *Jewish Criterion* 89, no. 4 (December 4, 1936): 9.

67. Rudolph I. Coffee, "'The Land Is Mine,'" *Jewish Criterion* 38, no. 16 (May 22, 1914): 3–4.

68. Leo Wiener, *The History of Yiddish Literature in the Nineteenth Century* (London: John C. Nimmo, 1899), 10–11.

69. American Jewish Hebraists feared this process as did Yiddishists. See Katz, *Red, Black, and Jew*. So too was this fear shared by a range of Reform, Conservative, and Orthodox rabbinic custodians of the tradition.

70. Warburg lauded the turn to Jewish agriculture in America, Argentina, Palestine, and Russia, claiming that "Jews today are more and more turning to the land for their livelihood is one of the most encouraging signs that point to the survival of the Jewish race and the Jewish spirit in the future." "Warburg Touches Vital Spot in American-Jewish Life," *Jewish Criterion* 75, no. 12 (January 31, 1930): 39.

71. "Warburg Touches Vital Spot."

72. "Congressman William Sulzer, of New York, on the Immigration Question," *Jewish Immigrant* 1, no. 1 (August 1908): 7.

73. "Congressman William." Emphasis in original.

74. "Mr. Stead, We Object," *Jewish Criterion* (Pittsburgh, Pa.) 34, no. 1 (February 9, 1912): 8.

75. "Mr. Stead, We Object." See also "The Cry of the Defeated," *Jewish Criterion* (Pittsburgh, Pa.) 30, no. 4 (March 4, 1910): 8 for a similar argument advanced by Joseph two years prior.

76. B. M. Goldsmith, "The Crucible. Assimilation,—Not Absorption," *Jewish Criterion* (Pittsburg, Pa.) 46, no. 6 (October 8, 1915): 3.

77. Beryl D. Cohon, "Two American Superstitions," *Jewish Criterion* (Pittsburgh, Pa.) 73, no. 11 (January 18, 1929): 36.

78. Cohon, "Two American Superstitions." A virtually identical argument was put forward by Gifford Ernest, "The Jew in Our Midst," *Jewish Criterion* (Pittsburgh, Pa.) 66, no. 15 (August 8, 1925): 31.

79. 222–224.

80. Israel Zangwill, *The Melting Pot: A Drama in Four Acts* (New York: Macmillan, 1909).

81. Henry Pratt Fairchild, *The Melting Pot Mistake* (Boston: Little, Brown, 1926), 10.

82. Fairchild, 13.

83. Fairchild.

84. Fairchild, 24, 41. Emphasis in original.

85. Fairchild, 44.

86. Fairchild, 111–112.

87. Fairchild, 154–155.

88. Fairchild, 141.

89. Fairchild, 199–201.

90. 224–225.

91. Mary Clark Barnes and Lemuel Call Barnes, *The New America: A Study in Immigration* (New York: Fleming H. Revell, 1913).

92. Barnes and Barnes, 65.

93. Barnes and Barnes, 103.

94. Barnes and Barnes, 104–105.

CHAPTER 5 — JEWISH ADVOCACY FOR NATIVE AMERICANS ON AND OFF CAPITOL HILL

1. Felix Cohen, "City College Speech Draft," March 9, 1953, Beinecke Rare Book and Manuscript Library, Yale University, WA MSS S-1325, box 71, folder 1127.

2. My argument builds on the work of Hasia Diner, *In the Almost Promised Land: American Blacks and Jews, 1915–1935* (Baltimore: Johns Hopkins University Press, 1977), and Marc Dollinger, *Quest for Inclusion: Jews and Liberalism in Modern America* (Princeton: Princeton University Press, 2000).

3. Alice Beck Kehoe, *A Passion for the True and Just: Felix and Lucy Kramer Cohen and the Indian New Deal* (Tucson: University of Arizona Press, 2014), 164.

4. For more on midcentury Jewish liberalism, see Michael Staub, *Torn at the Roots: The Crisis of Jewish Liberalism in Postwar America* (New York: Columbia University Press, 2002), and Stuart Svonkin, *Jews against Prejudice: American Jews and the Fight for Civil Liberties* (New York: Columbia University Press, 1997).

5. Sykes to Geary, November 16, 1860, in United States, Office of Indian Affairs, *Letters Received by the Office of Indian Affairs, 1824–1880*, National Archives Microcopy 234, roll 612, NADP Document D65.

6. Edward Rosewater, AJA MS 503, box 7, folder 10 contains copies of letters sent from Rosewater to W. H. Jones, the commissioner of Indian Affairs, the Secretary of the Interior James R. Garfield, and President Roosevelt, along with dozens of pages of affidavits, letters, and documents.

7. In David W. Daily, *Battle for the BIA: G. E. E. Lindquist and the Missionary Crusade against John Collier* (Tucson: University of Arizona Press, 2004), 171n50. See also Association on American Indian Affairs (AAIA) 133 / 3, 8, 10, 16, 21, and 22.

8. Fred Stein and Kate Vosberg were among its early national directors; Edward F. Glaser served as chairman of the California Committee on Indian Relief's from 1931 to 1933. AAIA 59 / 10.

9. Morris Leopold Ernst, MLE Papers, Manuscript Collection MS-1331, Harry Ransom Center, University of Texas at Austin; see also AAIA 36 / 1, 106 / 2, 115 / 3, 140 / 1.

10. Samuel Walker, *In Defense of American Liberties: A History of the ACLU* (New York: Oxford University Press, 1990), 88, 97.

11. Leonard Dinnerstein, "Jews and the New Deal," *American Jewish History* 72, no. 4 (June 1983): 461–476, especially 465–466.

12. In Henry Feingold's assessment, Jews who worked in the Department of the Interior "did little to promote civil rights for Jews, [but] were instrumental in contributing to reforms in Indian affairs." Henry L. Feingold, *Jewish Power in America: Myth and Reality* (New Brunswick, N.J.: Transaction, 2008), 25–33.

13. Beth S. Wenger, *New York Jews and the Great Depression: Uncertain Promise* (New Haven: Yale University Press, 1996).

14. Quoted in Stephen L. Pevar, *The Rights of Indians and Tribes* (New York: Oxford University Press, 2012), 10.

15. Morton J. Horwitz, *The Transformation of American Law, 1870–1960: The Crisis in Legal Orthodoxy* (New York: Oxford University Press, 1994).

16. Morton J. Horowitz, "Jews and Legal Realism," in *Jews and the Law*, ed. Ari Mermelstein, Victoria Saker Woeste, Ethan Zadoff, and Marc Galanter (New Orleans: Quid Pro Books, 2014), 309–319.

17. See David A. Hollinger, "Communalists and Dispersionist Approaches to Jewish History in an Increasingly Post-Jewish Era," in his *After Cloven Tongues of Fire: Protestant Liberalism in Modern American History* (Princeton: Princeton University Press, 2013), 138–162.

18. Nathan Margold, "The Plight of the Pueblos," *The Nation*, February 4, 1931, 121–123.

19. Elmer R. Rusco, *A Fateful Time: A Background and Legislative History of the Indian Reorganization Act* (Reno: University of Nevada Press, 2000), 182.

20. See Felix S. Cohen Papers Addition, WA MSS S-2602, boxes 18, 19, folders 378–411.

21. Morris helped establish the Conference on Jewish Relations and the scholarly journal *Jewish Social Studies* and was the president of the Jewish Occupational Council. Morris was "a child of the old piety of his ancestors [and] had his first deeply-rooted interests in

Hebraic culture," wrote one of his students shortly after his death. She described Cohen's "Talmudic, biblical and general Hebraic erudition," his "constructive and tireless activities in furthering the interests of his fellow Jews," and his "application of philosophic vision and technique to the problems of American Jewry." Leonora Cohen Rosenfeld, "Morris R. Cohen, the Teacher," *Journal of the History of Ideas* 18, no. 4 (October 1957): 568; see also Milton R. Konvitz, "Morris Raphael Cohen," *Antioch Review* 7, no. 2 (Winter 1947): 487–501; and "Cohen, Morris Raphael," in *Encyclopedia Judaica*, ed. Michael Berenbaum and Fred Skolnik, vol. 5, 2nd ed. (Detroit: Macmillan Reference, 2007).

22. Beinecke LKC Papers, box 3, folder "Membership Cards," box 1, folder 2, "Correspondence, courses, conferences, causes, jobs, personal 1937–1939."

23. Kehoe, *Passion for the True and Just*, 70.

24. Kehoe, 91.

25. Kenneth R. Philp, "Termination: A Legacy of the Indian New Deal," *Western Historical Quarterly* 14, no. 2 (April 1983): 165; Charles F. Wilkinson and Eric R. Biggs, "The Evolution of the Termination Policy," *American Indian Law Review* 5, no. 1 (1977): 170.

26. Alison R. Bernstein, "Walking in Two Worlds: American Indians and World War Two" (PhD diss., Columbia University, 1986), 10, 11.

27. Vine Deloria Jr. and Clifford M. Lytle, *American Indians, American Justice* (Austin: University of Texas Press, 1983 [2004]), 14.

28. Deloria and Lytle, 97.

29. Vine Deloria Jr., "Laws Founded in Justice and Humanity: Reflections on the Content and Character of Federal Indian Law," *Arizona Law Review* 3, no. 1 (1989): 203–223; Russel Lawrence Barsh and James Youngblood Henderson, *The Road: Indian Tribes and Political Liberty* (Berkeley: University of California Press, 1980), 112; Richard Grounds, George E. Tinker, and David E. Wilkins, *Native Voices: American Indian Identity and Resistance* (Lawrence: University Press of Kansas, 2003).

30. Kehoe, *Passion for the True and Just*, ix–x.

31. Some of these highlights of Cohen's achievements were summarized in D'Arcy McNickle's toast to Felix Cohen upon his leave-taking from the Department of Indian Affairs. "I am supposed to speak for the Indians," he said, "Indians will feel the loss of your going." Toast pamphlet, Beinecke WA MSS S-1325, box 92, folder 1490, 13–14.

32. Felix S. Cohen to Larry M. Ellanak, president, Council of Karluk Native Village, October 7, 1948, Beinecke WA MSS S-1325, box 86, folder 1364.

33. Felix S. Cohen, "Indian Wardship: The Twilight of a Myth," March 24, 1953, Beinecke WA MSS S-2602, box 10, folder 243.

34. Felix S. Cohen, *The Legal Conscience: Selected Papers*, ed. Lucy Kramer Cohen (Hamden, Conn: Archon Books, 1970), 264.

35. D'Arcy McNickle, *Indian Man: A Life of Oliver La Farge* (Bloomington: Indiana University Press, 1971), 167.

36. Kehoe, *Passion for the True and Just*, 140.

37. Felix S. Cohen, "Socialism and the Myth of Legality," *American Socialist Quarterly* 4 (1935): 8.

38. Cohen, "Indians Are Citizens," in *Legal Conscience*, originally published in *American Indian* 1 (1944); Dalia Tsuk Mitchell, "Jews and American Legal Pluralism," in *Jews and the Law*, ed. Ari Mermelstein, Victoria Saker Woeste, Ethan Zadoff, and Marc Galanter (New Orleans: Quid Pro Books, 2014), 2–22.

39. Felix S. Cohen, "Colonialism, US Style," *The Progressive*, February 1951, 15–18.

40. Cohen, 18.

41. Cohen.

42. "Letter to John Slawson, American Jewish Committee from Felix S. Cohen," February 25, 1948, Beinecke WA MSS S-1325, box 50, folder 751.

43. Felix S. Cohen, "The Erosion of Indian Rights—1950–1953: A Case Study in Bureaucracy," *Yale Law Journal* 62, no. 3 (February 1953): 348–390.

44. Cohen, and issues around American Indians in general, has been all but ignored in American Jewish history. Cohen and Indians are notably absent from Svonkin's otherwise excellent *Jews against Prejudice*. Neither Cohen nor Indians are mentioned in Jerold Auerbach, *Rabbis and Lawyers: The Journey from Torah to Constitution* (Bloomington: Indiana University Press, 1990); Steven M. Cohen, *The Dimensions of American Jewish Liberalism* (New York: American Jewish Committee, 1989); Jack Greenberg, *Crusaders in the Courts: How a Dedicated Band of Lawyers Fought for the Civil Rights Revolution* (New York: Basic, 1994); Peter Irons, *The New Deal Lawyers* (Princeton: Princeton University Press, 1982); or Carole S. Kessner, ed., *The "Other" New York Jewish Intellectuals* (New York: New York University Press, 1994).

45. See Beinecke WA MSS S-1325, box 50, folders 763, 764, and 765 for Cohen's correspondence with the Consultative Council of Jewish Organizations along with his drafts of the statement. See also "International Protection of the Human Rights of Minorities," Beinecke WA MSS S-1325, box 51, folder 767.

46. Index to the Felix S. Cohen Papers, by Susie R. Bock, Lucy M. Kramer, and George Miles, Yale University, Beinecke Rare Book and Manuscript Library, Yale Collection of Americana, WA MSS S-1325.

47. Simon Segal, American Jewish Committee, to Felix Cohen, August 6, 1948, Beinecke WA MSS S-1325, box 50, folder 752.

48. Felix S. Cohen to Harry Rosenfield, July 7, 1950, Beinecke WA MSS S-1325, box 50, folder 755.

49. Felix S. Cohen to Harry Rosenfield.

50. Quoted in Kehoe, *Passion for the True and Just*, 88.

51. Felix Cohen is barely mentioned in the annals of American Jewish history. One exception is the Golden Book Foundation of America, which included Cohen's biography as part of their efforts to record the "history, achievements and accomplishments of American Jewry and their contribution to Democracy, Humanity and Judaism" in their publication "American Jews, Their Lives and Achievements." See letter from Abraham W. Scheinberg to Felix Cohen, Beinecke, WA MSS S-1325, box 92, folder 1472.

52. Kehoe, *Passion for the True and Just*, 88.

53. AAIA, folder 13: Cohen's "Alaska's Nuremberg Laws" in *Commentary* 6, no. 2 (August 1948).

54. Southeastern Alaska Conservation Council, "Tongass History," http://www.seacc.org/successes/tongass-history, accessed January 25, 2010.

55. Felix S. Cohen, "Alaska's Nuremburg Laws: Congress Sanctions Racial Discrimination," *Commentary Magazine*, August 1948.

56. Cohen.

57. Felix S. Cohen, "Exclusionary Immigration Laws," *Contemporary Jewish Record*, American Jewish Committee, April 1940, 141–155; "Exclusionary Immigration Laws: Their Social and Economic Consequences," condensed from *National Lawyers Guild Quarterly*, October 1939, and reprinted in *Contemporary Jewish Record*, 141–155.

58. Felix Cohen Papers, box 90 / folder 1451, Beinecke. Quoted in Mitchell, "Jews and American Legal Pluralism," 339–340.

59. Mitchell, "Jews and American Legal Pluralism," 321–345.

60. Deloria and Lytle, *American Indians, American Justice*, 17.

61. Deloria and Lytle, 16.

62. Philp, "Termination," 165; Wilkinson and Biggs, "Evolution of the Termination Policy," 139–184.

63. Wilkinson and Biggs, "Evolution of the Termination Policy," 139–184.

64. Wilkinson and Biggs, 152–156.

65. Philp, "Termination," 161, 180.

66. William Zimmerman Jr., "The Role of the Bureau of Indian Affairs since 1933," *Annals of the American Academy of Political and Social Science* 311 (May 1957): 31–40.

67. AAIA 36 / 5, Felix Cohen to Amos Lamson, Chairman Omaha Tribal Council, May 12, 1950.

68. Imre Sutton, ed., *Irredeemable America: The Indians' Estate and Land Claims* (New Mexico: University of New Mexico Press); Harvey D. Rosenthal, *Their Day in Court: A History of the Indian Claims Commission* (Albuquerque: University of New Mexico Press, 1985); Pevar, *Rights of Indians and Tribes*; Harvey D. Rosenthal, "Indian Claims and the American Conscience: A Brief History of the Indian Claims Commission," in *Irredeemable America*, ed. Imre Sutton (Albuquerque: University of New Mexico Press, 1985), 35–70.

69. R. Warren Metcalf, *Termination's Legacy: The Discarded Indians of Utah* (Lincoln: University of Nebraska Press, 2002), 60–61, 110.

70. Metcalf, 62.

71. Michael Lieder and Jake Page, *Wild Justice: The People of Geronimo vs. the United States* (New York: Random House, 1998), 64. The commission would be expanded five times, in 1957, 1962, 1967, 1972, and 1977.

72. Edward Lazarus, *Black Hills, White Justice: The Sioux Nation Versus the United States, 1775 to the Present* (New York: HarperCollins, 1991), 185.

73. Lazarus, 66.

74. Lazarus, 185–186.

75. Rosenthal, *Their Day in Court*, 3.

76. Mitchell, "Jews and American Legal Pluralism," 341.

77. Mitchell, 109.

78. Felix Cohen, "Indian Claims," in *Legal Conscience*, originally published in *American Indian* 2 (1945): 3–11. Quoted in Mitchell, "Jews and American Legal Pluralism," 340.

79. Cohen, *Legal Conscience*, 265.

80. Signing Statement, August 13, 1946, in Lieder and Page, *Wild Justice*, 67.

81. Rosenthal, *Their Day in Court*, 118.

82. Rosenthal.

83. Kehoe, *Passion for the True and Just*.

84. Deloria and Lytle, *American Indians, American Justice*, 144.

85. Deloria and Lytle.

86. Lieder and Page, *Wild Justice*, 262–263.

87. Lieder and Page, 248.

88. These included J. M. Schiltz, Norman Littell, Walter Rochow, J. Gruber, Edwin Rothchild, Louis Rochmes, David Rein and Joseph Forer, Leonard Strahan, Abraham Ziedman, Howard Shenkin, Jack Joseph, Frank Miskovsky, and Abe Barber; #81, Coeur D'Alere, 1957; #136, Pueblo De Cochiti, 1959; #58, 18E. Red Lake Band and Ottawa and Chippewa of Michigan, 1959; #67, 124, 314, 337, Miami Tribe of Oklahoma, 1954; #67, 124, 314, 323, 337, Miami Tribe of Oklahoma, 1954, 1958; #191, Little Shell Band of Chippewa, 1954; #81, Coeur D'Alene Tribe, 1955; Lieder and Page, *Wild Justice*, 99; See also Christian W. McMillian, *Making Indian Law: The Hualapai Land Case and the Birth of Ethnohistory* (New Haven: Yale University Press, 2007), 167–168, 258; "Examiners Report on Tribal Claims to the Released Railroad Lands in Northwestern Arizona," Haulapai Tribe of the Haulapai Reservation, Arizona v. USA, ICC Docket 90, box 1055, RG 279, Records of the ICC, 230n31. See also Jeffrey P. Shepherd, *We Are an Indian Nation: A History of Hualapai People* (Tucson: University of Arizona Press, 2010), 112.

89. Deloria and Lytle, *American Indians, American Justice*, 141.

90. Deloria and Lytle, 142.

91. Edward Charles Valandra, *Not without Our Consent: Lakota Resistance to Termination, 1950–59* (Urbana: University of Illinois Press, 2006).

92. Wolfgang Saxon, "Marvin J. Sonosky, 88, Lawyer Who Championed Indian Cause," *International New York Times*, July 21, 1997.

93. Lazarus, *Black Hills, White Justice*, 212–215.

94. Lazarus, xi.

95. Lazarus, 194.
96. Lazarus, 148.
97. Indian Claims Commission Decisions, http://www.digital.library.okstate.edu/icc/index/html, accessed May 16, 2015.
98. Deloria and Lytle, *American Indians, American Justice*, 147.
99. Lazarus, *Black Hills, White Justice*, 192, 197.
100. Walter Hart Blumenthal, *American Indians Dispossessed: Fraud in Land Cessions Forced Upon the Tribes* (Philadelphia: George S. MacManus, 1955).
101. Blumenthal, 147.
102. Lazarus, *Black Hills, White Justice*, 218.
103. AAIA 36 / 5.
104. Association on American Indian Affairs Papers, Princeton Mudd Library, MC 147, 1851–1995, Princeton University.
105. AAIA 1 / 1–23, folder 1.
106. Folder 7.
107. McNickle, *Indian Man*, 120–121.
108. AAIA 158 / 11.
109. These included Arthur J. Cohen, Howard Gans, Rose Goldman, Mrs. E. A. Grossman, Mrs. Harry Ittleson, Joseph Keppler, Mrs. C. O. V. Kienbusch, Anita Kushner, Sam A. Lewinson, Charles Rosenthal, Edgar Rossin, Mr. and Mrs. Eustace Seligman, Robert Ulman, Elinor Zipkin, Mrs. Harry Ittleson, Joseph Keppler, Mrs. Herbert Feis, Robert Gessner, Sam A. Lewinson, Charles Rosenthal, Edgar Rossin, Robert Ulman, Elinor Zipkin, Mrs. Herbert Feis, Robert Gessner, Mrs. S. W. Schaefer, and Florence Swartz. Folder 12, AAIA 30 / 17, and AAIA 30 / 17, membership lists.
110. AAIA 85 / 5.
111. AAIA 56 / 1, Fundraising.
112. AAIA 56 / 1–6, folder 1.
113. AAIA 54 / 7–8, Contributors.
114. AAIA 36 / 5.
115. AAIA 36 / 5.
116. Alexander Lesser to Felix Cohen, October 9, 1950, AAIA 36 / 5.
117. The case resolved all outstanding Aboriginal claims in Alaska. The act permitted the state's Native peoples to organize into corporations and awarded Native Americans more than forty million acres of land and $962 million. Lazarus, *Black Hills, White Justice*, 313–314.
118. AAIA 162 / 6.
119. AAIA 10; 140 / 11.
120. In Dorothy R. Baker, *Singing an Indian Song: A Biography of D'Arcy McNickle* (Lincoln: University of Nebraska Press, 1992), 214; and Victor Rabinowitz, *Unrepentant Leftist: A Lawyer's Memoir* (Urbana: University of Illinois Press, 1996), 164. See also AAIA 159 / 23, 76 / 5.
121. AAIA, folder 2.
122. Emil Schwarzhaupt Foundation, Papers, Special Collections Research Center, University of Chicago Library.
123. Funders for the AAIA included Lucy Kramer Cohen, Herbert H. Lehman, Mrs. Robert L. Rosenthal, Mrs. Edgar L. Rossin, Harry L. Shapiro, and Iphigene Bertha Ochs, who married the publisher of the *New York Times*, Arthur Hays Sulzberger.
124. Lawrence C. Kelly, *The Assault on Assimilation: John Collier and the Origins of Indian Policy Reform* (Albuquerque: University of New Mexico Press, 1983), xvii.
125. Kelly.
126. Robert Marshall Papers, MC 204, AJA, Cincinnati, Ohio.
127. Robert Marshall Papers, MC 204, box 5, folders 11, 12; box 6, folders 1–7; box 8, folder 2; box 9, folder 9–11; and box 10, folders 1–6.
128. Robert Marshall Papers, MC 204, box 6, folder 1.

129. Philp, "Termination," 177.

130. Thomas Biolsi and Larry W. Zimmerman, eds., *Indians and Anthropologists: Vine Deloria, Jr. and the Critique of Anthropology* (Tucson: University of Arizona Press, 1997), 141.

131. Felix S. Cohen, *On the Drafting of Tribal Constitutions*, ed. David E. Wilkins (Norman: University of Oklahoma Press, 2007), xxii.

132. Deloria and Lytle, *American Indians, American Justice*, 15.

133. Jean Dennison, *Colonial Entanglement: Constituting a Twenty-First Century Osage Nation* (Chapel Hill: University of North Carolina Press, 2012).

134. Stephen M. Feldman, "Felix Cohen and His Jurisprudence: Reflections on Federal Indian Law," *Buffalo Law Review* 35 (Spring 1986); Cohen, *On the Drafting of Tribal Constitutions*, 483.

135. Quoted in Vine Deloria Jr., "Reserving to Themselves: Treaties and the Powers of Indian Tribes," *Arizona Law Review* 31 (1989): xvii.

136. Kehoe, *Passion for the True and Just*, 117.

137. Quoted in Vine Deloria Jr., *Behind the Trail of Broken Treaties: An Indian Declaration of Independence* (New York: Delacorte, 1974), 225–226.

138. John Echohawk, "Termination, Indian Lawyers, and the Evolution of the Native American Rights Fund," in *Native Americans and the Legacy of Harry S. Truman*, ed. Brian Hosmer, vol. 4 (Kirksville, Miss.: Truman State University Press, 2010), 82–86.

139. Dillon S. Myer, "Oral History Interview with Dillon S. Myer," interview by Helen S. Pryor, Berkeley, California, July 7, 1970, by the University of California Bancroft Library/Berkeley Regional Oral History Office, quoted in Bernstein, "Walking in Two Worlds," 279.

140. Bernstein, "Walking in Two Worlds," 279–281.

141. Bernstein.

142. Lieder and Page, *Wild Justice*, 267.

143. Lieder and Page, 68.

144. Lieder and Page, 389–391.

145. Laurence M. Hauptman, "The American Indian Federation and the Indian New Deal: A Reinterpretation," *Pacific Historical Review* 52, no. 4 (November 1983): 378–402.

146. Hauptman, 395.

147. AAIA 60 / 5.

148. AAIA 60 / 5.

149. AAIA 60 / 5.

150. In response, the BIA infiltrated AIF, sent spies to surveil it, and reported to Ickes and Collier. AAIA 60 / 5.

151. Quoted in Kehoe, *Passion for the True and Just*, 86.

152. Quoted in Wilkins's "Introduction" to Cohen, *On the Drafting of Tribal Constitutions*, xi.

153. Cohen, xvi.

154. Cohen, xvii.

155. Kehoe, *Passion for the True and Just*, 3.

156. Deloria and Lytle, *American Indians, American Justice*, 14–15.

157. Bernstein, "Walking in Two Worlds," 10, 11.

158. Kehoe, *Passion for the True and Just*, 141; See too Stephen Haycox, "Felix Cohen and the Legacy of the Indian New Deal," *Yale University Library Gazette* 54 (April 1994): 138.

159. Dalia Tsuk Mitchell, "The New Deal Origins of American Legal Realism," *Florida State University Law Review* 29, no. 1 (Fall 2001): 194.

160. Quoted in Theodore Haas, ed., *Felix S. Cohen, a Fighter for Justice* (Washington, D.C.: Chapter of the Alumni of the City College of New York, 1956), 7.

161. Bernstein, "Walking in Two Worlds," 330.

162. Thomas W. Cowger, *The National Congress of American Indians: The Founding Years* (Lincoln: University of Nebraska Press, 1999), 31.

163. Cowger, 53, 86–87.

164. Cowger, 35.

165. By the 1980s, the AAIA was mostly staffed by Native Americans, though two Jews served as its executive directors throughout the entire decade: Steven Unger from 1980 to 1985 and Idrian Resnick from 1985 to 1989.

166. Cowger, *National Congress of American Indians*, 3.

167. Cowger, 6.

168. Cowger, 8.

169. Report from James E. Curry, general counsel of the NCAI, to the Convention at the Congress at Denver on December 12, 1948, NCAI Records, box 55. James E. Curry, Attorney Correspondence, 1947–1950, page 1 quoted in Cowger, *National Congress of American Indians*, 62.

170. Cowger, *National Congress of American Indians*, 86–87.

171. Kehoe, *Passion for the True and Just*, 163, 196.

CHAPTER 6 — ANTHROPOLOGICAL VENTRILOQUISM AND DOVETAILING INTELLECTUAL AND POLITICAL ADVANCEMENTS

1. For an engaging philosophical discussion about the distinctions between speaking "for" and "about" others, see Linda Alcoff, "The Problem of Speaking for Others," *Cultural Critique* 20 (Winter 1991/1992): 5–32.

2. Jennifer Glaser, *Borrowed Voices: Writing and Racial Ventriloquism in the Jewish American Imagination* (New Brunswick, N.J.: Rutgers University Press, 2016), 8.

3. See David A. Hollinger, "Rich, Powerful, and Smart: Jewish Overrepresentation Should Be Explained Instead of Avoided or Mystified," *Jewish Quarterly Review* 94, no. 4, The Jewish Experience in America (Autumn 2004): 595–602.

4. Paul Ritterband and Harold S. Wechsler, *Jewish Learning in American Universities: The First Century* (Bloomington: Indiana University Press, 1994), 124.

5. Susanne Klingenstein, *Jews in the American Academy, 1900–1940: The Dynamics of Intellectual Assimilation* (New Haven: Yale University Press, 1991); Peter Novick, *That Noble Dream: The "Objectivity Question" and the American Historical Profession* (Cambridge: Cambridge University Press, 1988).

6. Klingenstein, *Jews in the American Academy.*

7. Jay H. Bernstein, "First Recipients of Anthropological Doctorates in the United States, 1891–1930," *American Anthropologist* 104, no. 2 (2002): 551–564.

8. Bernstein, 554.

9. George Stocking Jr., "The Basic Assumptions of Boasian Anthropology," in *A Franz Boas Reader: The Shaping of American Anthropology, 1885–1911*, ed. George Stocking (Chicago: University of Chicago Press, 1974), 20, 331–332.

10. David L. Lewis, "Parallels and Divergences: Assimilationist Strategies of Afro-American and Jewish Elites from 1910 to the Early 1930s," *Journal of American History* 71, no. 3 (December 1984): 543–564.

11. Quoted in Marshall Hyatt, *Franz Boas, Social Activist: The Dynamics of Ethnicity* (New York: Greenwood, 1990), 85.

12. Franz Boas, "Race and Race Prejudice," *Jewish Social Service Quarterly*, Jewish Communal Service Association of North America, National Conference of Jewish Social Service (December 1937): 227–232. Interestingly, Ernst Boas, Franz's son, became a physician, noted for his work in cardiology, and like his father, he was very much involved with liberal social causes as well as Jewish ones. He served as a medical consultant and lecturer to numerous organizations and health care institutions, including Beth Israel Hospital of Passaic, New Jersey; the New York Guild for the Jewish Blind; and the Workmen's Circle, the Central Bureau for Jewish Aged, Inc., the Association for Jewish Charities of Baltimore, the American Jewish Congress, the Council of Jewish Federations and Welfare Funds, and the Federation of

Jewish Philanthropies of New York. He did some medical research on Jewish health issues for the Independent Order Brith Abraham, the Jewish Sanatorium and Hospital for Chronic Diseases, the Jewish Welfare Federation of Detroit, and the Orthodox Jewish Home for the Aged—that is, he worked with Jews from the 1920s through the 1950s. Ernst P. Boas Papers, American Philosophical Society, 1907–1955. Mss. Ms. Coll. 10.

13. Sapir was born in Lauenburg, Germany, to an orthodox Jewish family. Regna Darnell, *Edward Sapir: Linguist, Anthropologist, Humanist* (Berkeley: University of California Press, 1989). Radin was born in Lodz, Poland, and his father was a rabbi. Stanley Diamond, ed., *Culture in History: Essays in Honor of Paul Radin* (New York: Columbia University Press, 1960). Lowie was born in Vienna, Austria. Robert F. Murphy, *Robert H. Lowie* (New York: Columbia University Press, 1972).

14. The question of the Jewishness of Jewish anthropologists was largely effaced from the discipline's history until Virginia Dominguez broached the question, Does anthropology have a "Jewish problem"?, in 1993. Virginia Dominguez, "Questioning Jews," *American Ethnologist* 20 (1993): 618–624. Since then, a lively discussion has taken place. See Barbara Kirshenblatt-Gimblett, "Coming of Age in the Thirties: Max Weinreich, Edward Sapir, and Jewish Social Science," *YIVO Annual of Jewish Social Science* 23 (1996): 1–103; Jeffrey D. Feldman, "The Jewish Roots and Routes of Anthropology," *Anthropological Quarterly* 77, no. 1 (Winter 2004): 107–125.

15. Karen Ann Russell King, "Surviving Modernity: Jewishness, Fieldwork, and the Roots of American Anthropology in the Twentieth Century (Franz Boas)" (PhD diss., University of Texas at Austin, 2000); see also Diner, *In the Almost Promised Land*; Gelya Frank, "Jews, Multiculturalism and Boasian Anthropology," *American Anthropologist* 99, no. 4 (1997): 731–745.

16. George Herzog sought to preserve Native American heritage through studying and writing on Indian musicology, and Leonard Bloomfield studied and published on Algonquian linguistics. Leslie Spier, who built anthropology programs at the Universities of Washington and New Mexico, studied Northwest and Southwest tribes and trained dozens of students. Born in Vienna in 1883, Robert Lowie helped establish anthropology as a discipline at the University of California, Berkeley, and conducted significant ethnographic fieldwork among the Arikara, Shoshone, Mandan, Hidatsa, and Crow peoples on the plains. Edward Sapir, among the most influential linguistic anthropologists and a student of several West Coast Indian languages, was born in Lauenburg, Germany, in 1884 to an observant Jewish family. Alexander Goldenweiser, born in Kiev in 1880, immigrated to the United States in 1900, earned a doctorate under Boas, and eventually taught on Native American life, particularly totemism and cultural diffusion, at several major universities across the United States. Paul Radin, born in Lodz, Poland, to Rabbi Dr. Adolf M. Radin, wrote key works on the Winnebago.

17. Melville Jacobs Papers, 1926–1971, 1693-001, University of Washington, Special Collections.

18. Melville Jacobs Papers, box 7, folder 16.

19. Melville Jacobs Papers, box 2, folder 16.

20. Melville Jacobs, "Anthropology and Social Work," box 14, folder 3, n.d.

21. Jacobs, "Anthropology and Social Work."

22. Jacobs.

23. Melville Jacobs Papers, box 2, folder 19.

24. Melville Jacobs Papers, box 3, folder 5.

25. Melville Jacobs Papers, box 5, folder 25.

26. Stanley Diamond, "Paul Radin," in *Totems and Teachers: Key Figures in the History of Anthropology*, 2nd ed., ed. Sydel Silverman (Walnut Creek, Calif.: Altmira Press, 2004), 52.

27. Diamond, 53–54.

28. Louis Ginsberg, *Legends of the Jews*, 7 vols. (Philadelphia: Jewish Publication Society of America, 1959–1969).

29. Jonathan Boyarin, "Tricksters' Children: Paul Radin, Stanley Diamond and Filiation in Anthropology" (lecture, London School of Economics, May 15, 2009). See, for example, Paul Radin, *Monotheism among Primitive Peoples* (London: Allen & Unwin, 1924).

30. Irving Hallowell, "Frank Gauldsmith Speck," *American Anthropologist* 53 (1951): 67–87.

31. Edward Sapir to Stanley Newman, August 12, 1935, 1; Ruth Benedict, "Edward Sapir," *American Anthropologist* 41 (1939): 465–468, according to Philip Sapir, personal correspondence with Regna Darnell, 205.

32. Edgar E. Siskin, "The Life and Times of Edward Sapir," *Jewish Social Studies* 48, no. 3/4 (Summer 1986): 283–292.

33. Edward Sapir, *Time Perspective in Aboriginal American Culture: A Study in Method* (Ottawa: Government Printing Bureau, 1916).

34. Darnell, *Edward Sapir*.

35. David Mandelbaum, "Edward Sapir," *Jewish Social Studies* 3 (1941): 131–140.

36. Darnell, *Edward Sapir*, 109.

37. Darnell.

38. Edward Sapir, "Notes on Judeo-German Phonology," *Jewish Quarterly Review* 6 (1915): 231–266.

39. Sapir, "Notes," 203.

40. Sapir, 291.

41. Sapir, 405–406.

42. Sapir.

43. Sapir, 406.

44. Morris Swadesh, "Edward Sapir," *Language* 15 (1939): 132–135; Morris Swadesh, "Lewinsohn's View of the Jewish Problem," *Menorah Journal* xii (1926): 217.

45. Jacob David Sapir's personal correspondence with Regna Darnell.

46. Gene Weltfish, for example, born to German Jewish immigrants, wrote on Pawnee Indian cultural survival, art, theory, race, and prejudice as well as Cochiti, Hopi, San Carlos Apache, Jicarilla, and Mescalero basket weaving, pottery, and pipe making. All were topics, she claimed, that had consequences for "other of our ethnic groups." Gene Weltfish, *The Lost Universe: Pawnee Life and Culture* (New York: Basic Books, 1965); Douglas R. Parks and Ruth E. Pathé, "Gene Weltfish 1902–1980," *Plains Anthropologist* 30, no. 107 (1985): 59–64, quote from page 59; Ruth E. Pathé, "Gene Weltfish," in *Women Anthropologists: A Biographical Dictionary* (New York: Greenwood, 1988), 372–381; Ruth Benedict, *Race: Sciences and Politics* (New York: Viking Press, 1945); and Ruth Benedict and Gene Weltfish, *The Races of Mankind* (New York: Viking Press, 1959).

47. David M. Fawcett and Teri McLuhan, "Ruth Leah Bunzel," *Women Anthropologists: A Biographical Dictionary* (New York: Greenwood, 1988), 29; Regna Darnell, "Bunzel, Ruth Leah," in *Biographical Dictionary of Social and Cultural Anthropology*, ed. Amit Vered (London: Routledge, 2004), 80. Esther Schiff Goldfrank, raised "in a Jewish household that was largely acculturated to American ways," according to one of her biographers, was also one of Boas's assistants; she contributed substantially to the field of Pueblo and Zuni culture, pottery, mythology, and ritual poetry. On Esther Schiff Goldfrank, see Barbara A. Babcock and Nancy J. Parezo, "Esther Goldfrank, 1896–," in *Daughters of the Desert: Women Anthropologists and the Native American Southwest, 1880–1980: An Illustrated Catalogue* (Albuquerque: University of New Mexico Press, 1988); Margaret M. Caffrey, *Ruth Benedict: Stranger in This Land* (Austin: University of Texas Press, 1989); Esther Goldfrank, taped interviews, Wenner-Gren Foundation, New York; Melville J. Herskovits, ed., and Barbara Ames, "Goldfrank, Esther S.," *International Directory of Anthropologists*, 3rd ed. (Washington, DC: National Research Council, 1950); Charles H. Lange, "The Contributions of Esther S. Goldfrank," in Nancy J. Parezo, ed., *Hidden Scholars: Women Anthropologists and the Native American Southwest* (Albuquerque: University of New Mexico Press, 1993); Gloria Levitas, "Esther Schiff Goldfrank," in *Women Anthropologists: Selected Biographies*, ed. Ute Gacs et al. (Chicago: University of Chicago Press, 1988); Babcock and Parezo, *Daughters of the Desert*, 38–39; Margaret Ann Hardin, "Zuni Potters and the Pueblo Potter: The Contributions of Ruth Bunzel," in Perezo, *Hidden Scholars*, 259–269.

48. Darnell, "Bunzel, Ruth Leah," 80; Pamela T. Amoss, "Erna Gunther," in *Women Anthropologists: A Biographical Dictionary* (New York: Greenwood, 1988), 133–139; Viola E. Garfield and Pamela T. Amoss, "Erna Gunther (1896–1982)," *American Anthropologist* 86, no. 2 (1984): 394–399.

49. From the biographical note to the Guide to the Erna Gunther Papers, University of Washington Library Special Collections, Record Group 19.26.0614.

50. Erna Gunther Papers, University of Washington Library Special Collections, Seattle, Washington, folder 13; Activist writes to Zimmerman 1/7, and Bureau of Indian Affairs (BIA) box 1, folder 4, and box 8, folder 16, AAIA 8 / 12–13.

51. For a similar argument about ways that American Jewish historians managed the tension between the filial/cultural demands of their Jewish communities and their professional academic responsibilities, see Hasia R. Diner's discussion of Oscar Handlin. Hasia R. Diner, "The Study of American Jewish History: In the Academy, in the Community," *Polish American Studies* 65, no. 1 (Spring 2008): 41–55.

52. Gertrude Toffelmier, "Edwin Meyer Loeb, 1894–1966," *American Anthropologist* 69, no. 2 (1967), 200–203.

53. Robert A. Hall Jr., *A Life for Language: A Biographical Memoir of Leonard Bloomfield* (Philadelphia: John Benjamins, 1990).

54. Swadesh taught at seventeen different institutions in the United States, Canada, and Mexico and published an extraordinary amount, some 130 articles and 21 books. "Morris Swadesh, 1909–1967," *American Anthropologist* 70, no. 4 (1968): 755–756.

55. The same can be said about Bernard J. Siegel (Pueblo studies) and Morris Wolf (Iroquois studies).

56. Papers #14-25-3238, Division of Rare and Manuscript Collections, Cornell University Library.

57. Indian Claims Commission Docket no. 22-C List in box 86, Legislation and Planning after 1934, box 86, folders 1, 2.

58. "Morris Edward Opler," *American Anthropologist* 102, no. 2 (June 2000): 328–329.

59. Box 125, folder 9.

60. Box 125, folders 13 and 18.

61. Marvin K. Opler, "Northern Arapoho," in *Acculturation in Seven American Indian Tribes*, ed. Ralph Linton (New York: Appleton-Century-Crofts, 1940); Marvin K. Opler, "The Integration of the Sun Dance in Ute Religion," *American Anthropologist* 43, no. 4 (October–December 1941): 551–572.

62. Marvin Kauffman Opler Papers, 1914–1981, Columbia University Health Sciences Library Archives and Special Collections.

63. Pierre Birnbaum, "The Absence of Encounter: Sociology and Jewish Studies," in *Modern Judaism and Historical Consciousness: Identities, Encounters, Perspectives*, ed. Andreas Gotzmann and Christian Wiese (Leiden: Brill, 2007), 228. See Peirre Birnbaum's ambitious assessment of Jewish intellectuals in the social sciences, history, and philosophy throughout the twentieth century not only in the United States but in France, Germany, and other parts of Europe as well. Virginia R. Dominguez, "Questioning Jews." *American Ethnologist* 20, no. 3 (1993): 618–624; Seymour Martin Lipset, "Jewish Sociologists and Sociologists of the Jews," *Jewish Social Studies* 17 (1955): 177–182; Lewis A. Coser, *Refugee Scholars in America: Their Impact and Their Experiences* (New Haven: Yale University Press, 1984), 85; see also Amos Morris-Reich, *The Quest for Jewish Assimilation in Modern Social Science*, Routledge Studies in Social and Political Thought, vol. 54 (London: Routledge, 2008); Kevin MacDonald, *The Culture of Critique: An Evolutionary Analysis of Jewish Involvement in Twentieth-Century Intellectual and Political Movements* (Santa Barbara, Calif.: Praeger Books, 1998).

64. David Morrison, "Paul Lazarsfeld: The Biography of an Institutional Innovator" (PhD diss., Leicester University, 1976), 127, quoted in Coser, *Refugee Scholars in America*, 107.

65. Karl Popper, *Unended Quest: An Intellectual Biography* (La Salle, Ill.: Open Court, 1976), 25, 67, 305. Rutledge and Kagan David, 1993, 119–120.

66. Quoted in James Burns MacGregor, "Introduction," in Harold J. Laski, *The American Presidency: An Interpretation* (New Brunswick, N.J.: Transaction, 1980 [1940]), vi.

67. Marshall Sklare, "The Jewish American in Sociological Thought," in *Observing America's Jews*, ed. Jonathan Sarna (Hanover: Brandeis University Press, 1993), 159–180.

68. David Mandelbaum worked on the Plains Cree in Saskatchewan. Walter Goldschmidt published on the Tlingit of Alaska, among many others. Alexander Lesser studied the language, religion, and culture of Plains Indians. Bernard Aginsky, born of Russian Jewish immigrants, changed his name from Benjamin before he married Ethel Aginsky, and both worked and published on the Pomo Indians of California.

69. Horace P. Beck, "Frank G. Speck, 1881–1950," *Journal of American Folklore* 64, no. 256 (1951): 415–418.

70. Frank G. Speck Papers, American Philosophical Society, 1903–1950, Mss. Ms. Coll. 126; 10/4; see also Felix and Morris Cohen's *Readings in Jurisprudence and Legal Philosophy*, vol. 2 (Washington: Little, Brown, 1951), 814. "The Indian as a Factor in American History, 1500–1900," n.d., box 20.

71. Beck, "Frank G. Speck."

72. May Mandelbaum Edel Papers TAM.345, 1930–1939, Special Collections, University of Washington Libraries.

73. R. A. Pathe, "Gene Weltfish," in *Women Anthropologists: A Biographical Dictionary*, ed. C. Gacs, A. Khan, J. McIntyre, and R. Weinberg (New York: Greenwood, 1988), 372–381.

74. Paul Hockings, "Foreword," in *Dimensions of Social Life: Essays in Honor of David G. Mandelbaum*, ed. Paul Hockings (Berlin: Mouton de Gruyter, 1987), vii–viii.

75. "Anthropology and the Indian Service Program," from the Office of Indian Affairs, report of completed or underway activities, professor at Indiana, 1927–1936.

76. Box 25, folder 1; box 80, folder 2.

77. Anita Brenner Papers, Harry Ransom Humanities Research Center at the University of Texas at Austin, series 1, box 4, folder 3; series 2 research files, box 10, folder 7; box 11, folder 16; box 17, folders 2, 12.

78. Anita Brenner Papers, box 32, folder 9; and box 29, folder 7.

79. Anita Brenner Papers, box 26, folder 1.

80. Ruth Landes Papers, National Anthropological Archives, Smithsonian.

81. The work was not published until 1967 as Ruth Landes, "Negro Jews in Harlem," *Jewish Journal of Sociology* 9, no. 2 (1967): 175–189.

82. The other researchers were Conrad Arensberg, Sula Benet, Natalie Joffe, Irene Rozeney, and Mark Zbrowski. Ruth Landes and Mark Zborowski, *Life Is with People: The Jewish Little-Town of Eastern Europe* (New York: International Universities Press, 1952); and Ruth Landes and Mark Zborowski, "Hypothesis Concerning the Eastern European Jewish Family," *Psychiatry* 13 (1950): 447–464.

83. Ruth Landes Papers, National Anthropological Archives, Smithsonian Institution, box 25, subseries "Judaism and Other Religions"; and box 26, Research Materials.

84. Melville J. Herskovits Papers, 1906–1960, Northwestern University Archives, Eavanston L., "Indian Bureau: 34–35" 10/4.

85. Jerry Gershenhorn, *Melville J. Herskovits and the Racial Politics of Knowledge* (Lincoln: University of Nebraska Press, 2004), 13, 21.

86. Melville J. Herskovits, "When Is a Jew a Jew," *Modern Quarterly* 4 (June–September 1927): 114. See too Melville J. Herskovits, "Who Are the Jews?," in *The Jews: Their History, Culture and Religion*, vol. 4, ed. Louis Finkelstein (Philadelphia: JPS, 1949), 1151–1171.

87. Herskovits, "Who Are the Jews?"

88. "Native Self-Government," *Foreign Affairs* 22 (April 1944): 413–423; "Brains and the Immigrant," *Nation* 120 (February 11, 1925): 139–141; "Letter to Rabbi Wolf," *American Jewish Review*, March 27, 1920.

89. Joseph C. Greenberg, *Melville Jean Herskovits, 1896–1963: A Bibliographic Memoir* (Washington: National Academy of Sciences, 1971), 65–93. Fails to mention Jewish; and see

Papers 1906–1963, Africana Manuscripts 6, series 35/6, Northwestern University, Folders on American Jewish Committee, 1934–1941 (2/10). B'nai Brith of Cincinnati (3/31), Hillel Foundation, 1929 (3/32), its magazine, its orphanage (3/34), Conference on Jewish Relations 1936 (6/6), National Conference of Jews and Christians (38–39)(14/8), Jewish Bibliographic Bureau, 1927–1929 (10/19), Chicago's Jewish People's Institute, 1929, 34, 38 (10/21), Jewish Charities of Chicago, 1936–1937 (10/20), Council of Jewish Federations, and the Welfare Funds, 1937, of the Bureau of Jewish Social Research (6/15). Papers 1906–1963, Africana Manuscripts 6, series 35/6, Northwestern University. Folders on American Jewish Committee, 1934–1941 (2/10).

90. "The American Race Problem" and "Forces That Divide Us" addresses to Great Lakes Naval Training Center, "The Myths of Prejudice" lecture, 13, 14, 17.

91. Box/Folder: 24/2, 27/22, 36/15, 38/11, 43/26, 43/35, 140/18. On Korn, see *American Jewry and the Civil War*, 1951. Korn also wrote *The Jews of Mobile, Alabama, 1763–1841* (1971); *Benjamin Levy: New Orleans Printer and Publisher* (1961); and *Jews and Negro Slavery in the Old South, 1789–1865* (1961).

92. Quoted in Gershenhorn, *Melville J. Herskovits*, 129; "Applied Anthropology and the American Anthropologists," *Science* 83 (March 6, 1936): 215–222.

93. Melville Herskovits, "Native Self-Government," *Foreign Affairs* 22 (1943–1944): 413–423.

94. Gershenhorn, *Melville J. Herskovits*, 129–130.

95. Bernard Stern, *The Lummi Indians of Northwest Washington* (New York: Columbia University Press, 1934).

96. Box 6, folder 7: Memorandum to Samuel H. Flowerman, American Jewish Committee; and see David H. Price, "Bernhard Stern: A Sense of Atrophy among Those Who Fear," in *Threatening Anthropology: McCarthyism and the FBI's Surveillance of Activist Anthropologists* (Durham: Duke University Press, 2004), 136–153, Bernhard J. Stern papers, coll. 026, University of Oregon Libraries—SPC, 1299, University of Oregon.

97. Bernhard J. Stern papers, box 6, folder 7, coll. 026, University of Oregon Libraries, Special Collections and University Archives; and Interview with Bernard Stern, Philadelphia, July 1982, in Murray Friedman, *Philadelphia Jewish Life* (Philadelphia: Temple University Press, 2003), 247n58.

98. Melford E. Spiro, *Kibbutz: Venture in Utopia* (Cambridge, Mass.: Harvard University Press, 1956).

99. Rabbi Maurice L. Zigmond (1904–1998), Papers; P-112; American Jewish Historical Society, New York, N.Y. See also MS-133, Maurice L. Zigmond Papers, American Jewish Archives, Cincinnati, Ohio.

100. Maurice Zigmond, *Kawaiisu Ethnobotany* (Salt Lake City: University of Utah Press, 1981); see also Maurice Zigmond, "Kawaiisu Mythology—an Oral Tradition of South Central California," Ballena Press Anthropological Papers, no. 18, 1980; and Maurice Zigmond, "Death Comes to an American Indian Tribe," in *Dimensions of Social Life: Essays in Honor of David G. Mandelbaum*, ed. Paul Hockings (Berlin: Mouton de Gruyter, 1987), 167–176.

101. Albert Isaac Gordon, *Jews in Transition* (Minneapolis: University of Minnesota Press, 1949); Albert Isaac Gordon, *Jews in Suburbia* (Boston: Beacon Press, 1959); and Albert Isaac Gordon, *Intermarriage: Interfaith, Interracial, Interethnic* (Boston: Beacon Press, 1964).

102. Papers of Rabbi Albert I. Gordon, P-86, American Jewish Historical Society, New England Archives.

103. David Goodman Mandelbaum Papers, 1899–1991, BANC MSS 89/129 cz. Bancroft Library, University of California, Berkeley.

104. David Mandelbaum, "All American All-Americans: Geronimo," BANC MSS 89/129, cnt. 2, folder 31, 1940, 1, 5.

105. Carton 2, folder 31, n.d.

106. Cnt. 3, folder 38, "Friendship in North America," 1936.

107. David Mandelbaum, "A Study of the Jews of Urbana," *Jewish Social Service Quarterly* 13 (1936): 223–232; David Mandelbaum fonds, Saskatchewan Archives Board, F15.

108. Mandelbaum, "A Study of the Jews of Urbana," 231.

109. Mandelbaum, "A Study of the Jews of Urbana."

110. David G. Mandelbaum, "The Jewish Way of Life in Cochin," *Jewish Social Studies* 1, no. 4 (1939): 459.

111. Mandelbaum.

112. David Mandelbaum, "Prolegomena to Jewish Social Studies," BANC MSS 89/129 cz. cnt. 4, n.d, 1.

113. Mandelbaum, 2.

114. Mandelbaum, 15.

115. David Mandelbaum, "Change and Continuity in Jewish Life," Oscar Hillel Plotkin Library, North Shore Congregational Israel, Glencoe, Ill., 1955, published lecture from 1954 (crt 3, folder 11).

116. Mandelbaum, 3.

117. Mandelbaum, 43.

118. Edgar Siskin Papers, AJA MSS No. 64. See too Human Studies Film Archives, Smithsonian Museum Support Center, Suitland, Md., HSFA 89.10.2., Video Dialogues in Anthropology: Edgar Siskin and Norman Markel, 1984. Edgar Siskin @ University of Nebraska Oral History Program, Ethnographers Among the Washoe, *The Chroniclers*. Tape 2: "while student preaching in Tucson, Az, first experience with Indians, Pima and Papago." Tape 5: "president of the Yale Anthropology club, experience of anti-Semitism of some faculty members." Tape 6: "discussion of Jews among early settlers of Nevada, Dangbergs in Carson Valley." Tape 7: "Central Conference of American Rabbis"; Tape 8: "Mandelbaum, anti-Semitism a part of American culture."

119. Edgar Siskin, "The Impact of the Peyote Cult upon Shamanism among the Washo Indians" (PhD diss., Department of Anthropology, Yale University, 1941); Edgar Siskin, et al., "Tribal Distribution in the Great Basin," *American Anthropologist* 40, no. 4, n.s., part 1 (October–December 1938): 622–638; and Edgar Siskin, "The Impact of American Culture upon the Jew" (lecture to the Central Conference of American Rabbis, Buffalo, N.Y., Central Conference of American Rabbis Records, Manuscript Collection 34, Box 41, Jacob Rader Marcus Center of the American Jewish Archives, 1952). He published *Washo Shamans and Peyotists: Religious Conflict in an American Indian Tribe* (Salt Lake City: University of Utah Press, 1983), based on his dissertation research conducted in the late 1930s. Nehemia Stern, "Edgar E. Siskin: Assimilation, Resistance, and the Locus of Culture in Early American Anthropology" (unpublished paper, Annual Meeting of the American Anthropological Association, New Orleans, November 2010).

120. Edgar Siskin, "A Rabbi-Anthropologist in Israel," *Journal of Reform Judaism* 34, no. 2 (Spring 1987): 3.

121. Siskin, "Rabbi-Anthropologist in Israel."

122. Siskin, 4.

123. Edgar Siskin, "The Impact of American Culture upon the Jew," CCAR Yearbook, vol. 26, 1953, 360–378; For more detail, see "Transcendental and Folk Aspects of Judaism," in Hockings, *Dimensions of Social Life*, 201–214.

124. Siskin, "Impact of American Culture," 369.

125. Siskin, 378.

126. Siskin, 376.

127. Edgar Siskin, *American Jews: What Next?* (Jerusalem: Jerusalem Publishing House, 1988).

128. AAIA, folder 18: Field Research—Frank Speck, Otto Klineberg, 1943, Meetings: Mrs. Edgar L. Rossin, Gov., Relations: Mrs. Rosin, Mrs. Robert Ullman, Nominating Eustance Seligman; folder 19: Gene Weltfish joins in 1945, as does Albert Hirst, Mrs. Richard Loeb, Rose Goldman, Mary Lasker, and Michael Lerner.

129. AAIA 172 / 14.

130. AAIA 407 / 5.

131. Will Herberg, *Protestant—Catholic—Jew: A Study in American Religious Sociology* (Chicago: University of Chicago Press, 1955).

132. Walter Zenner, born in Nuremberg, trained in anthropology at Columbia University and at the Jewish Theological Seminary of America and researched Syrian Sephardic Jews in Israel, Canada, and Mexico. He did not study Indians. American Sephardi Federation (ASF), Walter P. Zenner Papers (1933–2003), ASF AR-4.

133. Irene Rozeny, "Negro Jews in Harlem," *Jewish Journal of Sociology* 9, no. 2 (1967).

134. Natalie Joffe, "The Dynamics of Benefice among Eastern European Jews," *Social Forces* 27 (1949): 238–247; and Natalie Joffe, "Non-reciprocity among Eastern European Jews," in *The Study of Culture at a Distance*, ed. Margaret Mead and Rhoda Metreau (Chicago: University of Chicago Press, 1953), 386–387.

135. H. D. Rosenthal, *Their Day in Court: A History of the ICC* (New York: Garland, 1990), 124.

136. Morton H. Fried, "The Myth of Tribe," *Natural History* 84, no. 4 (April 1975): 12–20, quoted in Rosenthal, *Their Day in Court*, 125.

137. Lieder and Page, *Wild Justice*, 164.

138. Lieder and Page, 170.

139. Sol Tax Papers 1923–1989, Special Collections Research Center, University of Chicago Library; "Sol Tax," in Amit, *Biographical Dictionary*, 707.

140. George Stocking Jr., "'Do Good, Young Man': Sol Tax and the World Mission of Liberal Democratic Anthropology," in *Excluded Ancestors, Inevitable Traditions: Essays toward a More Inclusive History of Anthropology*, ed. Richard Handler, History of Anthropology, vol. 9 (Madison: University of Wisconsin Press, 2002): 171–254, especially 202.

141. National Congress of American Indians, AJA MS 204, box 5, folder 11. On the Jewishness of Sol Tax, see Stocking, "Do Good, Young Man," 171–264; Feldman, "Jewish Roots," 107–125; and Judith Daubenmier, *The Meskwaki and Sol Tax: Reconsidering the Actors in Action Anthropology* (Ann Arbor: University of Michigan Press, 2003); see, too, "Indians Achieve Two Milestones," *New York Times*, March 8, 1953; "Full Citizenship for Indians," *National Catholic Weekly Review*, March 21, 1953. Tax also published Indian advocacy and antirace articles for newspapers in Detroit; Bemidji, Minnesota; Phoenix; Des Moines; Albuquerque; Billings, Montana; Scotts Bluff, Nebraska; and Malone, New York papers, AJA MS 204, box 6, folder 1.

142. AAIA 163 / 23; paper delivered at symposium on "Termination" at Central States Anthropological Society in Madison, Wisconsin, May 1957; "Can Social Science Help to Set Values or Offer a Choice between Alternative Value Systems?" from Social Science Research Council report delivered at Princeton, 1949, box 264, folder 3.

143. Frederick Osmond Gearing, et al., eds., *Documentary History of the Fox Project, 1948–1959: A Program in Action Anthropology* (Chicago: University of Chicago Press, 1960); Sol Tax, "Action Anthropology," *Journal of Social Research* 11, no. 1–9 (March–September 1959).

144. Robert A. Rubinstein, "A Conversation with Sol Tax," *Current Anthropology* 32, no. 2 (April 1991): 175–183.

145. "Federal Indian Policy and the National Congress of American Indians," speech given at Annual Convention in Claremore, Okla., October 1957, Records of the National Congress of American Indians, 1933–1990, box 265, folder 7.

146. Laurence M. Hauptman and Jack Campisi, "The Voice of Eastern Indians: The American Indian Chicago Conference of 1961 and the Movement for Federal Recognition," *Proceedings of the American Philosophical Society* 132, no. 4 (1988): 316.

147. Nancy Lurie, "The Voice of the American Indian: A Report on the American Indian Chicago Conference," *Current Anthropology* 2 (1961): 478–500.

148. "Declaration of Indian Purpose: The Voice of the American Indian," proceedings of American Indian Chicago Conference (University of Chicago, June 13–20, 1961).

149. American Indian Chicago Conference Records, 1960–1966, National Anthropological Archives, Smithsonian NAA MS 4806; Nancy Oestreich Lurie, "Sol Tax and Tribal Sovereignty," *Human Organization* 58, no. 1 (1999): 108.

150. Thomas A. Niermann, "The American Indian Chicago Conference, 1961: A Native response to Government Policy and the Birth of Indian Self-Determination" (PhD diss., Department of History, University of Kansas, 2006).

151. Jewish-ness file 5/1; 6/10 trad sermon.

152. Stocking, "Do Good, Young Man," 171–254, especially 223.

153. Stocking, 225.

154. Stocking, 173.

155. Series 1, subseries 2, Community and Political Activities, includes material box 276, folder 1; box 211, folder 5; and others.

156. Stocking, "Do Good, Young Man," 228, 298.

157. Sol Tax, "Jewish Life in the United States: An Anthropological Perspective," paper prepared for invitational colloquium at YIVO, N.Y., May 1978.

158. Native American Educational Services, Robert Rietz, Papers, 1961–2000, Special Collections Research Center, University of Chicago Library.

159. Biographical note in Native American Educational Services, Robert Rietz, Papers, Special Collections Research Center, University of Chicago Library.

160. Albert L. Wahrhaftig, "The Carnegie Project: Action Anthropology among the Oklahoma Cherokees," and "Vignette: Jews Are Indians from the Other Side of the Water," in *Action Anthropology and Sol Tax in 2012: The Final Word? Journal of Northwest Anthropology*, Memoir Series Book 8, ed. Darby C. Stapp (Richland, Wash.: Journal of Northwest Anthropology, 2012).

161. Wahrhaftig, "Vignette."

CONCLUSION — PATHS OF PERSECUTION, STAKES OF COLONIAL MODERNITY

1. For a fuller analysis of this recent Jewish interest in Indigenous communities and affairs in Canada, see David S. Koffman, "Suffering & Sovereignty: Recent Canadian Jewish Interest in Indigenous Peoples and Issues," *Canadian Jewish Studies / Études juives canadiennes* 25 (2017): 28–59.

2. See Sarah Phillips Casteel, "Jews among the Indians: The Fantasy of Indigenization in Mordecai Richler's and Michael Chabon's Northern Narratives," *Contemporary Literature* 50, no. 4 (Winter 2009): 775–810.

3. These creative engagements have been subject to an unpublished analysis by Eugenia Sojka (University of Silesia), "Exploring the Idea of 'Indigenous Shtetl' in Canada: Aboriginal-Jewish Writers and Artists Embracing Their Complex Histories, Identities and Cultures in the 21st Century," paper presented at the Polish Association for American Studies, *Polish Association for American Studies Newsletter*, no. 35, 2014.

4. Ward Churchill, *A Little Matter of Genocide: Holocaust Denial in the Americas, 1492 to the Present* (San Francisco: City Lights, 1997); Ward Churchill, *Indians Are Us? Culture and Genocide in Native North America* (Toronto: Between the Lines, 1994); *Struggle for the Land: Indigenous Resistance to Genocide, Ecocide, and Expropriation in Contemporary North America* (Monroe: Common Courage Press, 1993); Richard Drinnon, *Keeper of Concentration Camps: Dillon S. Myer and American Racism* (Berkeley: University of California Press, 1987); Russell Thornton, *American Indian Holocaust and Survival: A Population History since 1492* (Norman: University of Oklahoma Press, 1987); Elizabeth Cook-Lynn, "Part V: Genocide," in *Anti-Indianism in Modern America: A Voice from Tatekeya's Earth* (Urbana: University of Illinois Press, 2001), 182–260.

5. Ilan S. Troen, "Frontier Myths and Their Applications in America and Israel: A Transnational Perspective," *Journal of American History* 86, no. 3, The Nation and Beyond:

Transnational Perspectives on United States History: A Special Issue (December 1999): 1209–1230.

6. Shari Huhndorf, *Going Native: Indians in the American Cultural Imagination* (Ithaca: Cornell University Press, 2001); Rayna Green, "The Tribe Called Wannabee: Playing Indian in America and Europe," *Folklore* 99, no. 1 (1988): 30–55.

7. David E. Stannard, *American Holocaust: The Conquest of the New World* (New York: Oxford University Press, 1992).

8. Richard Slotkin, *The Fatal Environment: The Myth of the Frontier in the Age of Industrialization, 1800–1890* (New York: Atheneum, 1985).

INDEX